IT'S BEEN AN EDUCATION

Ted and Doris

with love

Tony

"A teacher affects eternity; he can never tell where his influence stops."
Henry Brooks Adams

"One man in his time plays many parts."
**As You Like It, Act II, scene vii,
Shakespeare**

IT'S BEEN AN EDUCATION

An Autobiography

TONY ELDER

BROWN
DOG
BOOKS

Published under licence by Brown Dog Books and
The Self Publishing Partnership
7 Green Park Station, Bath BA1 1JB

www.selfpublishingpartnership.co.uk

ISBN printed book: 978-1-78545-010-5
ISBN e-book: 978-1-78545-011-2

Cover design by Andrew Easton

Printed and bound by CPI Group (UK) Ltd, Croydon CR0 4YY

CONTENTS

Acknowledgements

I am indebted to a number of people who have given me a lot of assistance in the preparation and writing of this book. My good friend Dennis Johnson, having turned out his loft to find the necessary papers, made sure my details were accurate, as far as his records went, regarding Bedfordshire Schools Athletics. Having contacted Pat Marchant, a friend of his in Woodford Green AC, Tony Maxwell, organiser of "Athletes Reunited", helped me go through many back copies of Athletics Weekly, borrowed from Pat, and was as keen as I was to ensure that I recorded athletes' details, both accurately and thoroughly. I am very grateful to him and to Pat. Before her untimely death, Rita kindly went through some of the highlights of her athletics career with me. How I wish she were here now. My old friend from Essex days, Derek Hayward, was able to fill in a number of gaps to do with PE teachers in Essex schools a long time ago. Useful information was also provided by then Essex Schools Secretary, Rob Edwards, and by statisticians, Peter Matthews and Melvyn Watman. My thanks also to two former colleagues, Nick Sorensen and Mark Sheridan, whose help I much appreciated. Some of the former athletes I coached have helped to fill in gaps in my knowledge and memory and I am most grateful to them. Thanks also to you, Steve, with your knowledge of publishing for your advice and information.

I am particularly grateful to my wife, Donna, for her patience and support while my book was being written, as it has taken longer than either of us originally envisaged. I thank Donna also for reading through the first draft and pointing out all my mistakes, for her helpful suggestions, many of which I agreed with and for regularly bringing her computer expertise to my assistance.

And to all of you, friends and family, who have given me support and encouragement – many thanks.

Introduction

Doris Lessing said that writing an autobiography is a small piece of history, so as a historian, I am pleased to have added a tiny morsel to the great collection. For much of my life I have been involved in teaching and learning, the management of schools and coaching athletes, so my autobiography concentrates largely, but not exclusively, on these aspects. I write about my parents and grandparents who preceded me, and my children and grandchildren who have come after me, therefore family also makes a big contribution to my story.

Naturally, nostalgia plays a larger part in one's life when you have a lot to look back on and remember, and even though I often forget what happened a few days ago, my memory is surprisingly good when it comes to years long gone by and the people and the places that filled those years.

I decided to write this book so that all those memories would be committed to paper in the hope that my children and grandchildren would find the details of my life informative and of some interest. I also hope that the book has a wider audience and that it may appeal in particular to many teachers, parents, athletes, coaches and indeed others.

I have tried my best to be accurate and almost everything that you read here is true to the best of my recollection. My apologies to anyone who finds mistakes; any errors and omissions are down to me and for those I am sorry. Occasionally, when memory does not provide the complete picture, I have filled in the gaps to the best of my ability, though I am pleased to say that this wasn't often necessary. Obviously I don't remember actual conversations which took place 50 or more years ago, so what you read is as close as I can get to what I think was actually said. In some places I have changed the names of particular individuals for obvious reasons.

I have enjoyed writing this book; I hope you have as much pleasure reading it.

Part One

Preparing to Become a Teacher

"And gladly wolde he lerne and gladly teche."
Prologue, *Canterbury Tales*, Geoffrey Chaucer

1

To teach or not to teach...

It was a dull, damp September morning in Finchley, North London.

"You'd better be going, or you'll be late," Mother said from the kitchen.

I didn't really know what I needed to take with me. Today was to be the start of a journey into the unknown.

I had graduated from Oxford in the summer. Three years of university life had been very good, but I had no real idea what to do next. With school and university over, the future looked quite daunting. As Tom Lehrer sang, in *Bright College Days*, "soon we'll be sliding down the razor blade of life". I wasn't too sure about that! Earning some money seemed to be an immediate priority, so maybe a career in business, commerce or industry would be good, but what? And where? I applied for several jobs in different companies. *Management Trainee sounded interesting*, I thought, *Junior Sales Executive, possibly not*. I had several interviews. I was to find out that having B.A. Oxon on my CV wasn't the passport to riches it was thought to be by some people. At every interview, in Bristol (cardboard boxes), in London (very junior in the City), in St Helens (glass – Pilkington's no less) where at least the train journey from Liverpool was an education, they didn't seem to like me very much and, I have to say, the feeling was mutual.

This late summer experience was frustrating and disappointing, but it taught me that I wasn't cut out to be a captain of industry. I doubt whether I ever thought I was. After all, my political leanings were to the left of centre, and I would have made a reluctant capitalist, maybe even a subversive one. Which is why, on this September morning, I was about to begin an experiment as a teacher: an apprenticeship, you might say.

Would I be any good as a teacher? Would I like being a teacher? And how would I cope with children? Did I really want to go back to school? I had no idea. In those days, mid 1950s, my degree gave me the status of a qualified teacher, which I thought was odd, but I could use this to my advantage. In the local paper I saw that two local schools were looking for supply teachers for the start of the new school year. I took the plunge: I applied, and was interviewed and asked to start at a school on September 4th. I was given a contract for half a term. At another school I was told I could work there for the second half of the term. At each school I was impressed by what I saw, what I was told and the people I met. The lady deputy head at Hillview Secondary Modern was charming, though quite thorough in her questions. At my second interview at William Grimshaw School, the head teacher saw me, though it was more of a chat than an interview. We talked about Chelsea FC and the cricket I had played in the summer. I guess he wanted to find out what kind of guy I was, reasonably enough, although, ominously, he asked me what I would do if I came across a fight in the corridor.

I had put on some light brown trousers and a sports jacket. A white shirt and "quiet" tie completed what I thought was smart but not overdressed. It was difficult to know what was expected. I closed the front door and put my briefcase in the pannier of my light blue, much loved Lambretta. I gave it a kick-start and, with a loud splutter, always a friendly noise, I was off. It was a very grey day, promising to rain, so I buttoned up my parka and set off for Hillview, less than ten minutes away.

As I parked my scooter, teachers' cars were arriving in the car park; children were making their way to their entrance at the side of the building. The three-storey school building looked quite new, freshly painted and smart. I found Reception and was about to glance at some brochures on the table when a female voice said, "Can I help you?"

The smiling receptionist seemed to be expecting me, a good sign, I thought, and I was directed to a room along the main corridor, labelled "Deputy Head". I knocked and was greeted by "Come in" and, as I opened the door, the lady who had earlier interviewed me stepped forward, smiled and shook my hand.

"Hello, I'm Jane Thomas. Come in, take a seat."

I walked in and she closed the door. Her desk was against the far wall close to the window. It wasn't a large room: shelves of files and papers took up much of the space on one wall.

"Thank you," I said, feeling somewhat nervous and unsure about what was to happen next.

I took a bit more notice of Jane Thomas than I had when she had interviewed me several weeks ago. She shuffled through some papers. She was, I would guess, in her 40s, but her manner and appearance made her seem younger. She had a pleasant habit of smiling when she spoke. Jane said, "As you are here as a temporary supply teacher, you will have different classes to take, depending on which of our teachers are absent. You do appreciate that, don't you?"

"Yes," I replied, not really understanding the significance of this.

"Although we do know that Mrs Bliss is going to be away for at least three weeks, so you can take her classes during that time," Jane Thomas said with a smile. "For some of her classes, she has left work, so you won't have to make anything up!"

"That's good," I said, not quite sure what "make anything up" implied.

"What subjects does Mrs Bliss teach?" I asked.

"Business Studies, some Needlework and some Art," Jane Thomas told me.

"But..."

"Oh! Don't worry, work will have been set," as Jane attempted to put me at ease.

I wasn't reassured but I thought, *No turning back now. I'm doing this for the experience.*

"I'll give you your timetable for today. The Staff Room is just along at the end of this corridor and at break time you can meet some of your colleagues. First we have Assembly. You can probably hear classes coming down from the first floor. I'll take you there myself."

With that, Jane Thomas got up and walked to the door. I followed her into the corridor, which was full of chattering boys and girls walking and pushing their way towards the Hall.

"Don't push. Walk quietly," she said, with a voice of authority, and some of them obeyed.

I sat at the back during Assembly. I didn't take much notice of what was going on as I had glanced at the timetable I had been given, and saw that my first lesson was Shorthand in Room 26 with 4th Year Commercial Girls. I had to read that a second time.

What had I let myself in for?

2

Teaching at Hillview

I walked up the staircase at the end of the corridor and found Room 26. I didn't know what to expect. Presumably with their teacher away for three weeks – as the headmistress had told the school in assembly – the 4th Year Commercial Girls didn't know what to expect either. I opened the door and walked in. The class was already there and most were in their seats.

"Good morning," I said, as I made my way to the teacher's desk at the front of the class.

The rest of the class sat down, but I didn't receive a reply to my greeting. They were probably used to supply teachers. There were 16 girls in the class in four rows of four. On the desk I found some instructions from Mrs Bliss, so I was able to get them started on some work.

"Your teacher has set some work for you to do," I said. "My name is Tony Elder." I wrote my name on the blackboard. Then I read out the work that Mrs Bliss had left for them to do. It involved using their shorthand books and they all seemed to understand the instructions, which was a relief. This was my first day as a teacher – my first class – my first lesson.

With the class at work, I had the chance to have a look at the girls. They were all 14 years old, I learned later, but some looked nearer 16; they wore their school uniform: a dark blue skirt with a light blue top, quite smart, though some were wearing a white top. They settled down well to work and I had little or nothing to do. This was obviously a good class, I thought, learning a skill, shorthand, which they could see would be of use to them in their future lives. One of the girls leaned across and asked her friend something. It was clearly relevant to their work so I said nothing. I walked around the class, which didn't seem to faze the girls at all. They finished the work set a few minutes before the end of the lesson.

Then one girl at the front said, "Are you going to set us homework, sir?"

Panic! Homework? Thinking rapidly and "on my feet", something I came to realise was very useful as a teacher, I said, "Yes; I'd like you to take your notebooks into assembly tomorrow morning and take down in shorthand everything the headmistress says."

The girls seemed to like this; there was some giggling; they had never been told to do that before, I gathered. The bell went and, with a few smiles, the girls trooped off to their next lesson. I was amazed that I had dreamed up a homework task for them "out of the blue", but thought no more about it.

I was looking forward to meeting the 4th Year Commercial Girls next day. During the evening I suddenly realised that I would need to know what the headmistress said in assembly! So the following morning saw me sneak in to the back of the hall, with an exercise book, ready to write down everything Miss Bloor said – in longhand! I don't think she noticed, but several members of staff gave me odd looks. *Weird supply teacher.* After assembly I had the opportunity to spend some time in the Staff Room, where I tried to make sense of my assembly scribbles.

The lesson after break, I arrived again at Room 26. This time I was there before the girls. Later I was to learn that this is good practice, to arrive at the classroom before the class when possible. Other classes were going past on their way to their rooms, some quietly, others noisily. Then I saw a face I recognised from the day before.

"Sorry, we're late," she said. This was to be the lesson when I tried to learn all their names and later I found out this was Sophie. "We got held up in PE."

It was amazing how many things occurred in those first few days which, I was later to learn, are all too common in the life of pupils and teachers. Classes arriving late for their next lesson because they'd come from PE being one of them!

Sophie waited by the door of the classroom. "The others are just coming."

For some reason, I don't know why as I hadn't been told to do this, I waited until all the class had arrived and were waiting in line before I opened the door and said, "In you go." I guess on reflection I was demonstrating that I was in control. Or was I remembering, subconsciously, what some, certainly not all, of the masters had done when I had been a pupil?

The girls went into the classroom when I was ready, when I said so. It emphasised that they were a class, not a collection of random individuals. When everyone was present, then they could go into the classroom. It may not have been how Mrs Bliss did it, but the girls were learning that it was my way. Actually, I was also learning that this was my way! I felt quite pleased with myself! After all, they didn't know what a novice I was. The girls sat down at their desks.

"Good morning," I said. "Today I'm going to try to find out all your names, and while I do that, I'll give you a little task. Take out your notebooks, where I hope you will find the notes you made in assembly this morning. I want you to transcribe your shorthand notes into longhand and write them out neatly on the piece of paper I'm going to give you."

They took their notebooks from their bags, looking quite pleased with themselves. I gave each of them a sheet of lined A4.

"Please write your name clearly at the top of the paper," I said, "and as you are working, I can come round and find out all your names."

I felt quite proud of this strategy, but as I was to learn later, this was a cooperative class, so my task was comparatively easy.

As they worked, I walked round the class noting their names on their sheets of paper. Jane, Susan, yes here was Sophie, Shazia and

Mary. I wrote down the names according to where they were sitting, so I would be able to identify them from the front of the class. When they had finished I collected their work in, thanking each one individually by name. I told them I would mark it and give it back next lesson, in two days' time. When I saw the class again I handed back their work having noted their marks. Then I made my big disclosure. I told the girls that their new, temporary, shorthand teacher knew no shorthand at all. They were surprised, amused and cross. It had been a useful experience for me. Being a teacher isn't just teaching what you know, it's also being an actor, playing a part, in fact a whole series of parts. This is what I had, subconsciously, been doing. I hadn't had much choice. For the next two weeks, 4th Year Commercial Girls and I got on well, and I was somewhat disappointed when Mrs Bliss returned.

Another class I took at Hillview was a 5th Year Art class. Again it consisted only of girls. There were about 25 of them. However, unlike the shorthand, only chosen by girls, I later learned that this gender divide was the result of the vagaries of the timetable. While the girls did Art, the boys had Games and vice versa. These girls were 15 or 16, in their final year, and my first impression on entering the large Art Room was how attractive many of them were. One girl at the back looked about 18 and was gorgeous. *I could definitely become a teacher if these were to be my pupils,* I thought. I told them my name. At first they took little notice of their new teacher. Working on their art portfolio for the exam, they talked to each other constantly, and I judged it was probably what they were used to and not something I should attempt to stop, though their chatter probably had more to do with what happened with the boyfriend last night than their Art. They also wandered about the Art Room when they felt like it, collecting a new drawing instrument or another sheet of paper. I was realising that the kind of order and control a teacher needs to have in a classroom depends to an extent on the subject. This amount of movement by senior pupils doing Art seemed quite acceptable. The Art Rooms were on the top floor with large glass windows on two sides of this one. It was very bright and airy. Fortunately they were drawing, not using paint. I sat and observed, then had a walk round the class.

"Have you come to see my etchings?" one girl asked, to giggles all round.

"Well, I'd like you to show me what you are drawing," I replied diplomatically.

As I bent down to look at her drawing of what looked like a large building in a storm, I said, "Tell me about your picture."

"It's Miss Haversham's house in *Great Expectations*. We have to draw something from our reading in English," she explained.

"Oh! I see; it's very good," I said. She looked up at me and smiled. Either she was pleased at my comment or she realised I was no expert in Art.

Suddenly and without warning, as if a starter's gun had been fired, pencils and crayons went flying, they leapt out of their seats and excitedly rushed over to the window. *What on earth is going on?*

"Hey, what are you doing?" I called out, unheard. I went over to the window to see what had caused this sudden surge of activity. In the playground below, the 5th Year boys were returning from Games. In their football shirts and shorts they looked up at the Art Room windows and waved at the girls, who of course waved back and called out. *Wonderful! School kids today*, I thought. It wasn't like that at my school, but then it was only a boys' school. I had been powerless to prevent the girls doing what they did, but I did now say, "Come on, back to your seats please."

The boys had all gone in to get changed, so the girls complied. It was a strange interlude. Did the girls do this when Mrs Bliss was there? I never found out.

When I returned home at the end of each day, I tried to answer my two questions: *Am I any good as a teacher? Do I like being a teacher?* In practice this became *What sort of a day have I had?* At Hillview most of my experiences were positive but I felt that I couldn't really do a good job or enjoy the experience until I knew the children better and they knew me. This was not going to happen while on supply for a few weeks. My learning curve was about to get steeper.

3

William Grimshaw School

After half term, I started at William Grimshaw School, another Secondary Modern, in Hornsey, slightly nearer the middle of London. It was an older building and a bit run down. When I arrived, I had the feeling this wasn't going to be so smooth a ride.

"Hello! I'm Alan," said one teacher as he got out of his car in the car park. "I wouldn't leave your scooter there; it's better round the back, out of sight," he said.

"Thanks," I replied as I walked my Lambretta to where he indicated. I went in with Alan, introduced myself to him, and found the secretary's office, where I had been told to report.

"Mr Elder, welcome," she said. "I'll take you to meet Molly Brown. She looks after our supply teachers. There are two of you starting today."

We walked along a corridor and up some stairs to a room on the first floor where the secretary knocked on the door.

"Come in," said a voice. I entered a small office. There were two women inside. One stood up and introduced herself as Molly Brown. She had grey hair in a kind of bun and wore a long skirt of what looked like carpet material. Around her shoulders was a kind of shawl. Her glasses were perched on her head.

"You must be Tony Elder. Come in, sit down." Already seated was a young woman, with longish blond hair, dressed very smartly in a dark green skirt and a light green blouse. She certainly had my attention, as she was very attractive.

"This is Patricia Robinson," said Molly Brown. "You are both starting today."

With all three of us sitting down, the room seemed full. I said hello to Patricia Robinson and she smiled, which was the best part of the morning so far.

"I'll give you your timetables for today," said Molly Brown. On her desk she found some papers, which she decided were for us.

"Oh yes, and a map to show you where the rooms are. Mr Elder, you will be starting in Room 8A, a Maths room, and Miss Robinson, you are on the first floor in Room 16 teaching English. But first there is assembly. First lesson begins at 9.15. Do you have any questions?"

Molly Brown had clearly done this many times before and her brusque manner made me think she hoped there wouldn't be any questions.

"Will work have been set for each class?" asked Patricia, somewhat anxiously.

"Oh, yes. It will be on the desk in the room," she was told.

Looking at my timetable, I asked, "What time is morning break, Ms Brown?"

"10.35, Mr Elder. You'll find the Staff Room at the far end of the main corridor. I will come and introduce you to the other teachers."

Assembly followed the usual pattern, as at Hillview: some attempt at singing, a reading, not from the Bible but from Laurie Lee, plus some notices and advice from the head teacher. I made my way out of the hall towards my teaching room.

"Good luck," I said to Patricia as she went off to find the stairs, trying to dodge the mass of pupils. There was a fair amount of pushing and shoving.

"Thanks. I think I'm going to need it."

The first lessons went off without too many problems. Work had indeed been set for my 3rd Year class. Maths isn't my strongest subject but the level of work wasn't too demanding, even for me, though I was asked some tricky questions which I managed to fend off.

There were about 25 teachers in the Staff Room at break, and they looked a very mixed bunch. Some had obviously been at it for many years, others looked no different from my friends at university. Not much interest was shown in the two new supply teachers. One or two looked up from their newspapers, others carried on with their conversations. I was later to learn that break time was precious to teachers, an oasis of calm away from the unruly hordes.

Patricia seemed to attract more attention in the Staff Room than I did. Her natural timidity had an endearing quality and several of the younger male members of staff obviously wanted to put her at ease. One of the Games teachers showed a particular interest.

"Let me get you a coffee. Patricia, wasn't it?"

"Oh! Thanks. Black. No sugar."

I moved across the room towards Patricia. "How was your morning, so far?" I asked.

"Not too bad. The 5th Year class are doing "Macbeth", which, fortunately, I know quite well, so I managed to engage a few of them," she said. "But they don't have a lot of interest, even though they have their exams this year."

The tracksuit arrived with a black coffee. "I'm Joe," he said, optimistically.

"Thanks, Joe."

My attention was then taken by a disturbance outside the window. There was a fight going on and a crowd had gathered.

"Who's on duty?" bellowed a large guy with a moustache. Before anyone could answer, several blokes went out to stop the fight.

"Is it often like this?" I asked another member of staff, who was standing next to me.

"We do have fights quite often," he said. "It's the estates and the gangs. They bring their arguments into school. Then we have to deal with them."

The fight was broken up and, soon after, the bell went to signal the end of break. I realised I'd missed my coffee!

This half term was a tougher experience for me than the first had been. It was often a struggle to get quiet in the classroom. My status as a teacher wasn't recognised or accepted by many of the pupils, especially the older ones. They had probably had quite a few supply teachers anyway. I realised that even as a teacher you had to earn their respect, and as I was only there for six weeks, this was not likely to happen. On several occasions I went home and said to my parents, "I don't think I can do this." Many times I felt defeated. I knew that the lessons had not gone well. I wasn't achieving anything. The pupils hadn't behaved and they hadn't learned. The school was in a fairly deprived area and many pupils saw school as a waste of time, especially the older ones who would sooner have been at work. Attendance was poor and it seemed to me that some of the teachers had given up and were merely doing a holding job as best they could. The corridors at break time were a cross between rush hour at Euston Station and the terraces at Stamford Bridge at final whistle.

In one lesson with a low-stream 1st Year English class, (it was actually 1G), as I walked into the classroom a lad at the back stood up and started "machine-gunning" me, repeating "rat-atat-atat" several times, "the gun" pointed at me. At first I ignored this, but he continued "shooting" and I realised that he was carrying on because he thought he hadn't hit me, so I pretended to be hit, and staggered about, in a kind of induced role-play. He seemed satisfied at this as he smiled, stopped shooting and sat down in his seat. I then began the lesson. When I mentioned this in the Staff Room, they said, "Oh! That's Max. He often does that."

I learned that as a teacher you have to be prepared for the unexpected, it helps to have a sense of humour and that a bit of acting comes in handy too.

Apart from that incident, two lessons stand out in my memory but for different reasons. In about my third week I was taking a 2nd Year Maths class. They were getting on with the exercise their Maths teacher had left them to do, when a lad put up his hand, and said, "Please, sir, how do we do number 6?"

I looked in the Maths textbook. I realised I had no idea how to do number 6.

"Listen a moment," I said to the class, raising my voice to get their attention, "who knows how to do number 6?"

Immediately several hands went up, eager 12-year-olds keen to show off their superior skills.

"All right, David, come out and show the class how to do number 6."

I handed David some chalk and stood at the side so that I could see the blackboard. David put some numbers on the board.

"David, explain to the class what you are doing," I said. I didn't say, "Explain so I can understand."

David arrived at an answer: "55 square yards," he said. "That's the answer, and that's how you do it," David said, throwing both arms in the air, as if he had scored a goal. I thought that was a bit cocky, but he was only 12, and it had been a convincing explanation. As David sat down, another boy on the far side of the room, said, "That ain't right, sir. The answer's 70 square yards."

Cries of support and denial followed. Well I certainly had no idea, so I decided to apply democracy to Mathematics.

"Hands up all those who think 55 square yards is the right answer." Lots of hands went up. "And who thinks 70 square yards is right?" Not as many hands went up.

"There you are, David. You were right. 55 it is." Just then the bell went, so further debate was thwarted. There was some arguing and pushing as they left the classroom.

The scariest incident took place a few weeks later in a 4th Year English class. They were meant to be reading *Animal Farm*, but some of the class, boys mainly, had no intention of reading or trying to enjoy the novel. One lad got up and went over to talk to a girl sitting in the corner. I told Gary to get back to his seat. He sauntered back but stood talking to someone else. Several at the front turned round to see what was going on. Gary now had the attention of the class, which he seemed to enjoy.

"Gary, sit down, stop talking and read your book," I said firmly.

"Nah; waste of time, read it yourself," Gary said defiantly, gazing around at the class.

"Do as I say, Gary, or..."

"Or what?" said Gary, with a sneer, now looking directly at me.

This was the first direct confrontation I had had, so I said, quite slowly and deliberately, "Gary, do as I say, or get out!" and when he did neither, I said, "Go on, leave." And I pointed towards the door.

Gary stood by his desk in the middle of the room. He was wearing a black leather jacket with studs and tassels. He was quite tall with black greasy hair. He looked at his mates and smiled.

"Make me," he said boldly.

I had never been in a situation such as this before. I could feel my pulse racing. I knew I mustn't lose face, and that the situation mustn't become physical. So I walked slowly over to my right to the door of the classroom and opened it wide. The whole class were watching. Then I slowly walked to the other side of the classroom, still at the front, by the windows. I did this so that there was a clear path for Gary to take, from the middle of the room to the door. He would not have to pass me.

"Get... Out!" I repeated, each word said slowly and with emphasis, though I didn't shout. I didn't want to lose my temper or raise my voice. The class had been looking at me, but now their eyes were back on Gary. He shifted from side to side and again smiled at his mates, but he said nothing. I took this as a good sign, though I had no idea what I was going to do next.

Once more I said, with even more authority, I hoped, "Gary... Out... Now!" And I pointed again towards the now open door. The class waited. I waited. Then to my amazement and relief, Gary shuffled slowly over to the door. He didn't look in my direction, just walked out. I swiftly went and closed the door and said to the class, "Now we can get on." I had no idea where Gary went.

I learned recently that Rod Stewart attended William Grimshaw School and, given his age at the time, he would have been a young pupil at the school while I was teaching there. Maybe he was in one of my classes. Come to think of it – I did have a lesson all about sailing ships and the change to steam. Do you think...? No, I doubt it!

It was during this half term that the Suez Crisis erupted. On the first Sunday in November I went up to London to join thousands of others who were protesting at the aggressive policy of Britain's Prime Minister, Anthony Eden, towards Egypt's Colonel Nasser, who had nationalised the Suez Canal. The police were struggling to control the crowd. Police horses were deployed to prevent demonstrators from entering Whitehall, and it was in Parliament Square that I was barged into by a police horse and nearly sent flying. Although the police had a difficult task, I felt they were over-zealous and failed to recognise the right of people to peaceful demonstration. Fortunately, after an initial intervention in Egypt, British forces were withdrawn. The shameful episode had damaging consequences, both economic and diplomatic, and for Eden, personal ones, as he had to resign. As a historian I found all this fascinating, but it would be some while before it was realised just how damaging Suez had been to Britain's position in Africa.

4
Jenny

Thankfully it was a Friday, so I had the weekend to get over the trauma of Gary, my less than cooperative William Grimshaw pupil. Being Friday it also meant I could see Jenny, my girlfriend at the time. It was a cold December evening and we spent a quiet time in a couple of pubs and in our favourite coffee house on Heath Street in Hampstead.

"You did well; you came out on top," Jenny said reassuringly, as she squeezed my hand and smiled. Jenny worked in a bank in London. "Not all schools and not all students will be like that." Her attempts to make me feel better did have some effect, as I realised I could be teaching in another school next term.

Jenny and I liked each other, and she wanted me to be happy and successful. She was a pretty girl, medium height, with short, fair hair and a nice figure. We had met at the athletics club. A few weeks later, at one of Highgate Harriers' dances, we got to know each other better. She often reminded me of what happened that evening.

"You said to me, 'Can I take you home, Jenny? My sports car is parked outside.' And, yes, I was impressed, so I agreed." I always had to smile at this. "And then when we got outside, what did I find? A Lotus? No! An old Standard 10! But I forgave you!"

The story was basically true, and my excuse was that it showed just how much I wanted to see her. We went out a lot after that, walks over the Heath, to the cinema, the theatre, for curry at the Shahbag in Hampstead, to the Hampstead coffee house, and once or twice to the "Lord Nelson" pub. We enjoyed each other's company and we were fond of each other.

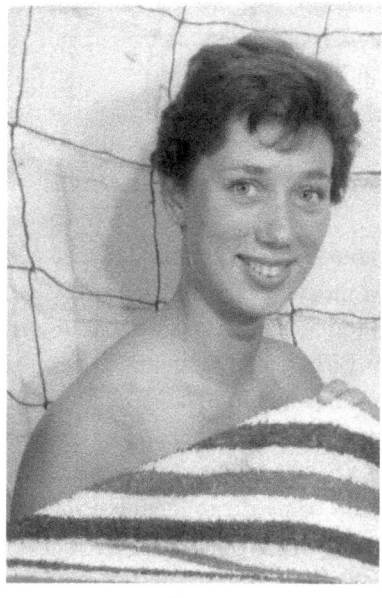

Jenny

The following morning I had arranged to go round to Jenny's house. On my way there I called in at our local newsagent and happened to see a copy of the paper in which teaching jobs are advertised. When I arrived, Jenny helped me look through the *Times Educational Supplement*.

"Here, look, what's this?" Something had caught her eye. "There's a school here advertising for a teacher for the Spring Term. Oh! Wait, that's no good, it's in Oxfordshire."

I had a look: "Teacher required for one term only. Mainly History and Games, but willing to help in other subjects if needed. Newly qualified teachers are welcome to apply."

"That would suit me, wouldn't it?" I said, looking pleased.

Jenny said she didn't want me to spend three months in Oxfordshire. "We'd never see each other."

I pointed out that Oxfordshire isn't that far from Finchley and, in any case, I hadn't got the job yet. Then I looked at the date that applications had to be in.

"Next Monday!" I exclaimed. "I haven't got time to write for a form and send it in."

"Oh! What a shame," Jenny said, with more than a trace of sarcasm.

"I know. I'll ring them up and see if they will accept a late application."

I tried, but of course there was nobody at the school on a Saturday.

"I'll ring on Monday," I said. But Jenny had gone upstairs.

On Monday I didn't have to go into school until ten o'clock, so I was able to ring St Birinus, the school in Oxfordshire, and say that I would like to apply, but was I too late?

I was put through to the headmaster who asked about my qualifications and what I was doing currently. He seemed satisfied, as he told me I could come the following Thursday for an interview when two other candidates would also be there. I could complete a form then, I was told. He gave me the address of the school, in Didcot, a place I had to admit I had never heard of. "We'll expect you at 10.30 on Thursday then. Goodbye."

Wow! An interview! All I had to do now was persuade Jenny that it was a good idea. And find Didcot on the map and work out how I was going to get there. And tell Molly Brown that I wouldn't be in on Thursday.

Mum and Dad were excited for me. "That sounds good, but where would you live?" said Mum, ever practical.

"I'll cross that bridge later, Mum. I haven't got the job yet!"

Now I might be returning to Oxfordshire, and not far from Oxford.

Luckily, Thursday morning was dry, but it had recently snowed and on some roads I had to take great care and slow down. It took just over two hours on my scooter to reach Didcot and I found the school with 15 minutes to spare. It was near the end of a long straight road out from the centre of Didcot, just as the local library had told me when I had phoned. The school was an unimpressive two-storey building in need of paint and some TLC; there was a playground and some playing fields. I parked my scooter and found the main entrance. At the school office I was handed the official application form to complete. The young receptionist took me to the school library, and brought me a coffee.

There were three of us to be interviewed and I was to go in last. It was the first time I had been in a competitive interview situation, and I was aware of the adrenaline rush. I quite enjoyed the challenge. First to go in to the adjacent interview room was a middle-aged guy who, I learned, had been working abroad. *More experience than I have,* I thought. I sat outside next to a lady best described as the archetypal vicar's wife, very prim and proper, hair in a bun and no legs showing. We didn't have a lot to say to each other. This was a semi-rural or small town boys' Secondary Modern, and I decided the job was between me and the fellow now being interviewed. He came out after about 35 minutes.

"They don't know what they want," he said enigmatically, and went off for a smoke.

I had finished my coffee, and after the vicar's wife, it was my turn. I had just finished filling in the form, which I took in with me.

There were three interviewers sitting behind a long table. I couldn't help wondering why it needed three people to conduct an interview for a one-term temporary post. They took it in turns to look at my form. I was asked about my degree, what I had done since and what my interests were. They were very courteous but not very probing. The head asked most of the questions. He seemed to like the fact that I had decided to spend a year finding out whether I would like to be a teacher. The lady chairman asked a couple of questions; the Local Education Authority (LEA) chap didn't.

Then they asked if I had any questions. I hadn't thought about this, but I asked where I might live locally, and was told that there were two or three landladies in the town who "took in" teachers. In reply to my question about what I would be teaching, I was told that hadn't been finalised yet, but would involve History, Games and English and could be any years in the school. I returned to the waiting area and joined my competitors, as I increasingly saw them.

After about 20 minutes the LEA chap came out and said, "Mr Elder, would you come back in, please." This was my first experience of a proper, formal interview and I thought perhaps that they wanted to ask me some more questions. Instead, the lady chairman offered me the post. The other two shook my hand. The education officer went out, presumably to inform the other candidates of the decision.

I had a brief chat with the head, who said he would send me my timetable and other details about the start of the new term in January. After a snack lunch and a quick tour of the school, and after I had been given the details of potential landladies, I set off for home. I hadn't been overly impressed with the school, but I felt pleased with myself. *At the very least,* I thought, *I'll be getting paid up to Easter.*

That was my introduction to St Birinus. I had only seen the advertisement on the previous Saturday, and now, five days later, I had been appointed a teacher at the school. I had a job for the Spring term, when I could continue my apprenticeship as a teacher. I knew my parents would be pleased, but how was Jenny going to take the news?

5

Didcot

I left William Grimshaw School just before Christmas. Fortunately, I didn't have to teach the 4th Year class again, though I passed Gary in the corridor a couple of times: we eyeballed, but there was no confrontation. I was still uncertain about a career in teaching, but now I had another term to test myself.

Jenny was very good about the Didcot situation. She was pleased for me but said, "Will we ever see each other?"

"At weekends, like now."

"But you'll be so far away."

"Absence makes the heart…"

"Yes, yes! I know!" Jenny gave me a hug and a kiss. I felt we were going to be all right.

I started in the first week of January: a new year, a new term, a new school.

My term at St Birinus was interesting and in many ways rewarding. The History teaching wasn't wonderful as the school had only one set of history text books, closely guarded by a lady whose main role seemed to be holding hymn-singing practice. The books, which had seen better days, were kept in a cupboard next to the piano in the hall. Both the cupboard and the piano were also past their best! I had only been there a couple of weeks when I realised there were boys who would be leaving school at the end of the year, in July, barely able to read or do simple Maths, so at a staff meeting I decided to speak up and voice my concerns. It was Wednesday in week three. This was my first ever staff meeting and I was of course the very new boy, and several teachers looked at me with a mixture of surprise, annoyance and what I suppose was condescension.

"Yes, we do know that, Mr Elder; what do you suggest we should do?" was the response from the head, with a shrug and raised eyebrows, which reinforced the question.

"Well, perhaps someone should teach them the basics, with a lesson each day," I said, feeling out of my depth, but still quite angry that such a situation should be allowed to exist. One teacher sitting opposite me smiled and shook his head, presumably at my naivety.

The head looked round the room at his staff. Some had clearly been at the school a long time. One guy in the corner looked like a retired major general. Another, who was barely awake was, I felt sure from his appearance, a shepherd or farmhand. Changes to routine and established practice were not to be welcomed. A sense of irritation was growing.

"Are you volunteering, Mr Elder?" came a voice from the corner of the room.

The head was well aware of the entrenched position taken by most of his staff, but he also recognised that here was a young teacher with the desire to make a difference. *Why not let him try; he'll soon see how impossible it is.* Was that what he was thinking?

Or perhaps, *The school has nothing to lose; you never know, he might be successful with one or two.* And maybe some of the diehards were thinking, *If this new teacher is going to take the most illiterate and innumerate boys every day, we won't have to teach them.*

"I would be willing to give it a go," I said, "but there must be others with much more experience who would do a better job."

The head looked round the room at his troops, several of whom were now smiling and chatting about my offer.

No chance!

"I think we ought to let Mr Elder see what he can do."

This produced murmurs of approval.

"Arthur, have a look at the timetable and find a room for Mr Elder first thing each morning up to break with our most underperforming boys in the top year." Turning to me, he said, "You can start next week."

I was pleased that now something would be done to address the problems these boys had, but I was aware that I had walked into a potential minefield. I had had no training in teaching 15-year-old boys with long-term learning difficulties, so I would have to do things by instinct. It was clear that I wasn't going to receive any advice or practical help.

Leave him to his own devices.

I had a few days before next Monday. For the Maths, after school one day, I visited the large local grocery store in the town and asked if they could help. To my amazement they found a load of empty display boxes of things like corn flakes, soap powder, soups etc. and some price tags and labels. With these I thought I would be able to have some sessions on adding and subtracting, money sums, maybe percentages, and that this would be more fun than working from a textbook. The local library let me borrow some sets of simple readers for young children, which would be a start, I thought. A newsagent agreed to keep back some of the papers that would normally be returned and, although they would be a day or more out of date, I felt sure they would come in useful.

Monday morning I arrived in good time and walked into the room I had been given: it was on the top floor, with a sloping ceiling and quite small, not a normal classroom, and I thought it would be fine if I only had a small number to cope with. I carried my various teaching aids into the room and waited for the pupils. I had a plan of sorts in my head, but I had no idea how this was going to work out. I didn't even know who was going to arrive or how many: I hadn't been told. I was there early so I could prepare a few easy tasks for them. There were no desks, but several old tables, which I actually thought might be better, as the boys wouldn't be sitting on their own at individual desks. They might be able to help each other. I had visited the school stationery store and obtained paper and exercise books for them to work in. There was a blackboard in the room, but no chalk, so I quickly went downstairs and raided a nearby room and returned armed with several sticks of chalk.

At 9.15 a.m. four boys arrived at the door, closely followed by two more. The door was open.

"Come in," I said.

The six lads trooped in. Although there were boys lower down in the school with learning difficulties, I had been given six "leavers", whose needs were more immediate.

"Sit down, boys. My name is Tony Elder," I said.

They looked and smiled at each other. I don't think they were used to teachers introducing themselves with a Christian name. They told me their names and I explained what we were going to do. They didn't look at all hostile, nor eager either. Just another day, another teacher...

We met for an hour every morning for almost the remainder of the term. In that time, we struck up a really good relationship. The boys appreciated what I was trying to do, and they all did their best. Probably for the very first time, they had someone who was treating them as individuals and addressing their particular needs. Although I knew their chronological age, I had no idea what their IQs were or their actual level of attainment; all I was told was that their numeracy and literacy skills were virtually non-existent.

The boys enjoyed some of the activities I devised for them to do. At least it was different from "normal" school lessons. In particular they enjoyed "playing shops". Although that sounds very basic and childlike, it served my purpose of getting them to become able and more confident about using figures. And role-playing was a bit of fun and gave them some confidence. Andy liked being the shopkeeper, while the others came shopping. But we rotated roles and their skill levels quickly increased as their confidence grew. They didn't much enjoy writing reports to "Head Office" about the daily transactions, but it got them writing and reading, as every report had to be checked!

We also acquired a darts board, which proved immensely

popular, especially with Bob, the best player. Their mental arithmetic improved very quickly indeed. Not far from the school was a big area of open grassland where racehorses exercised, often first thing in the morning, so I took the lads there to observe, and we had some experience with stopwatches. When we heard that one of the horses was going to race next week, we opened up a bookmaker's business in our classroom, and after getting permission, teachers and the lads' mates were able to come and place bets on the racehorses. Only pennies and shillings were allowed, up to a one-pound maximum. One thing the lads learned was that the bookmaker almost always wins. It wasn't long before their numeracy skills had shot through the roof. I did tell them that "countless people are innumerate," but I had to explain that to them.

We found that the best medium for developing reading skills was the newspaper. Four of the boys were unable to read at all when they first came but, by the end of term, they could all read the fairly simple language of the sports columns and the local paper. There was no exam at the end of our work that would give them a qualification, but we did produce an in-house certificate to take away as a record of their work and achievement. The boys were very appreciative of what I had done with them, as were some of their parents. A couple of the parents wrote and thanked me and one dad came up to the school and said he wanted to thank me personally, but as he shook my hand I did wonder whether he had come to thank me because, like his son, he hadn't been able to write a letter.

I think one reason our little experiment worked so well was because I didn't treat the boys as a class. They didn't sit at desks waiting to be told what to do. I said to them at the beginning that any success they might achieve would be the result of their own efforts. They were aware of how limited their futures were going to be if they didn't acquire better basic skills. In the second week I asked each boy to tell me – out of ten – how much he felt he had improved, and also out of ten, how hard he had been working. They had never been asked anything like this before. It seemed to motivate them. When I asked them again, later, everyone's score had gone up. When

I left at the end of the term, they all said that what we had done was only the start; each one said he would go on to read more and become more proficient with numbers. I think I had pointed them in the right direction.

One event I organised while I was at St Birinus was a trip in April to London by train. Some of the boys had never been to London. On the journey, Tom and Andy, two of my special class, borrowed my stopwatch and tried to calculate the speed of the train from the time it took to pass from one mile marker at the side of the track to the next. I was quite proud of them. The whole party had an unplanned boost to their learning when we discovered we were in the centre of London at the same time as the supporters of the Scottish football team who had been playing England at Wembley. I told the boys that Piccadilly Circus isn't always like this.

"What are they singing?" Brian asked me.

"I don't think you'd want to know," I replied unhelpfully.

The captain of the school cross country team, having found out that I liked running, took me on a run around the school cross-country course, which seemed to me to go straight across the main London to Bristol railway line, "With marshals to stop the runners if a train was coming," he said. I have a feeling he was pulling my leg, as there was a road tunnel under the railway line close to where we were when he said it.

Two or three times a week I went out for a run in the evening. Occasionally I went into Oxford to run on the roads, usually up Headington Hill, with Phil Porter from Oxford City Athletics Club. Mostly I ran on the roads around Didcot and as it was January and February, usually in the dark. I kept to the middle of the road, following the white line where there was one, and I could always see well in advance if a car was coming. One bright moonlit evening, I was striding along on the tarmac in the dark, with fields and hedges and trees silhouetted in the evening darkness, all relaxed without a care in the world when, suddenly, I ran into a large obstacle in the middle of the road. I shuddered to a halt. There was a loud noise. I don't know who was more shaken, me or the cow I had run into! The cow thundered away into a nearby field. I was shaken and bruised, but as there was no one else there to laugh at my predicament, I had to do so! I limped home.

The head teacher at the school held some memorable morning assemblies, but he wasn't great on communication. There had been some trouble in and around the school's bicycle sheds, so the head felt he had to say something.

"The bicycle sheds don't have any gates; you should all know that they are sacrosanct." From then on, all the boys believed that sacrosanct was a bicycle shed without gates.

Occasionally the head organised what were called "initiative tests". This involved a number of boys being taken out in a large van or lorry and then dropped off, one by one, in the local countryside. The test was to see who could make it back to the school quickest on their own initiative. I was not aware of any problems during these expeditions, but I doubt if such activities would be allowed in today's world of "health and safety".

In Didcot I stayed with Mrs Wilkins. She lived in an old-style terraced house just off the main street. She had some shrubs and flowerbeds in her small front garden. She had recently lost her husband, so she welcomed the company and the rent. Flo Wilkins was lovely and I couldn't have been happier there. She was a short, dumpy woman, with rosy cheeks, always smiling and almost always wearing her apron. She had a jolly laugh, which matched her personality. I had never had such large breakfasts. Cereal and toast, yes, but there was always something cooked and often with one or two vegetables. It was here that I first tasted pigeon pie, and at breakfast! She couldn't do enough for me and I stayed from January to Easter. She became a kind of surrogate Granny and, at the end of term, around Easter, she came and stayed with us in Finchley for a few days. My parents loved her, as I did.

One very rainy Friday afternoon, disaster struck. I was cycling home from school to my digs, with a set of boys' History exam answers in my saddlebag. They had to be marked over the weekend. It was absolutely pouring, and it was windy, and I wanted to make it up the hill and back to Mrs Wilkins as quickly as possible. I don't know why, but I suddenly looked round, and there behind me, strewn all over the road, were the exam scripts, fallen out from my saddlebag: some lying soaked in the puddles, others blowing in the wind. Panic! I did the only thing I could. I put the bike down, secured the saddlebag so no more papers fell out, and then went back to retrieve the now sodden scripts. Some were a hundred yards down the road. I didn't know if I had them all, but I made my way, totally drenched, to my digs. Mrs Wilkins was a gem.

She insisted I have a bath, "You don't want to catch your death."

While I did that, she sorted my papers and began to dry them. Some of the writing couldn't be read but I had managed to collect up all the answers, and with some creativity, they all received a mark, ready for Monday.

With Mr Weekes, another teacher, I took a group of boys on a cycling expedition one weekend. It was late in the term when the weather was better and the days longer. We planned the weekend, gained parents' consent, had all the boys' bikes checked for roadworthiness and safety, booked up the Youth Hostel where we'd be staying, checked out the rules and regulations including insurance, and set off early one Saturday morning. Two teachers meant that one could be at the front, with the other bringing up the rear to discourage stragglers. We took eight 12- and 13-year-olds. Luckily the weather stayed dry and we made good progress. We avoided main roads except those we had to cross, and we insisted on the boys cycling singly or in pairs and on keeping up. Much of our ride took us along the old Roman Icknield Way. Our destination was Ivinghoe in Bedfordshire, about 45 miles away. Everything went remarkably well: around midday we collectively collapsed on to a grassy bank for our lunch, comprising sandwiches, sausage rolls and pork pie. Occasionally we paused to admire a particular view or to study the map to see where we were, and we arrived at our YHA hostel in Ivinghoe just before 5 p.m. Rooms and beds were allocated and we met up with some Dutch teenagers who were also cycling in the area. Evening meal was fish and chips; "free time" meant a stroll into the village. The boys had lots of fun and, to my relief, were very well behaved.

The bicycle expedition

After a good night's rest the boys helped to prepare breakfast. We took a slightly different route home. The one puncture was soon repaired. The roads were almost deserted on this sunny Sunday, though Mr Weekes and I stressed the safety aspects several times and the boys all did as they were told. Towards the end of our ride, quite a few were getting pretty tired and saddle sore, but a certain team spirit seemed to develop. Back in Didcot, once we were sure everyone was safely home, Mr Weekes and I wearily found our way home too. It had been a worthwhile enterprise. The boys had had an adventure, seen some of the countryside and learned self-discipline, developed some individual self-confidence and learned to work as members of a team. Back in school on Monday they talked of nothing else. Some parents took the trouble to write and thank Mr Weekes and myself for our enterprise, which we much appreciated.

At St Birinus I learned a lot about becoming a teacher. I had gained in confidence; I had done my best to address the needs of a small group of pupils, by taking the initiative and thinking on my feet; I had also found that I got a lot of satisfaction from helping pupils. I had also managed to get home on several weekends to see

Jenny and my parents. Jenny popped round for coffee one Saturday morning and I told her and my parents that I wanted to apply to do a one year postgraduate diploma and become a properly qualified teacher. My parents were delighted. Jenny was again torn, as she knew it was what I wanted to do and needed to do, but it would also take me away again, this time for a year.

I took Jenny to our favourite Indian restaurant in Hampstead where we planned to have a heart to heart. We soon realised that the Indian restaurant wasn't the best place for such a conversation, so instead we concentrated on our biryani and dansak. My parents had let me borrow their car for the evening, so I took Jenny to her home, where we were better able to talk over our problems. Jenny's mother had left a note saying she would be in late. We talked for what seemed like hours. We didn't make love, as Jenny would never go quite that far, though she enjoyed the intimate times we had.

We both knew that we wanted to be together. At one stage, Jenny suggested that she come with me when I do my teaching diploma, but we realised that wasn't practical: Jenny had a good job in the bank in London; she would be away from all her other friends; and in the middle term next year I would be doing teaching practice, which could be anywhere in England. Reluctantly we came to the conclusion we would have to be apart for a year.

As her little carriage clock struck midnight, we kissed, and as I heard her mother park her car in the garage, I prepared to leave.

Her mother came in, just as I was opening the door. "Hello, Tony, you're late."

"I was just about to say that to you," I replied with a smile.

She laughed and I said my goodbyes to her and to Jenny.

On the drive home I couldn't help wondering if things would work out for us or whether we were about to part.

6
Hitchin

Halfway through my term at St Birinus I applied for a one-term post at the boys' Grammar School in Hitchin in Hertfordshire. Hitchin is a pleasant, small market town quite close to the Garden City of Letchworth. I went for an interview a fortnight before Easter and was successful; I would be teaching some History, some Geography and Games. Two things would make this term different: this was a Grammar School, and it was the Summer term. When I had been a pupil at school, the Summer term was always the best, and it proved to be at Hitchin, too. The weather was good and we were out on the field, with cricket or athletics most afternoons. The school had a large games field, though not entirely flat, and a nice pavilion. I enjoyed my time at Hitchin. The general discipline in the school was good, and most of the teachers commanded the respect of the boys. I continued to learn more about being or becoming a teacher by observing the good practice on a daily basis. My year had begun in a mixed London Secondary Modern and was to end in a boys' Grammar School in Hertfordshire. I was lucky to have had such experience. I taught History to the Lower 6th and to some junior classes, as well as Geography to a Year 1 class, but my main recollections of the term were to do with sport, either cricket, or more often, athletics.

One beautiful sunny afternoon in my second week I was on the field with a class of 1st Year boys, about to be taught some cricket basics by Trevor, the head of PE. The 30 boys, in their white shirts and trousers, all young and eager, were standing in an arc, facing Trevor and me. Trevor began to explain what they were going to do. Suddenly he noticed one lad on the left of the bunch talking to the boy next to him and not paying attention. Trevor stopped addressing the class and fixed the lad with a stare.

"You," he said. Then, after a pause, "How old are you?"

"Twelve, sir," the boy replied.

"Do you want to be 13?" Trevor asked.

A moment's hesitation, then, "Yes, sir," the lad replied.

"Well pay attention when I'm talking then," said Trevor, in quite a severe voice.

Dealing with this kind of minor misbehaviour and dealing with it immediately, I realised, was very effective, especially with 1st Year boys, who grew up in the school knowing what was expected of them. Trevor may have put the frighteners on that particular lad and the class as a whole, but he would never have a problem with those boys again.

A similar incident occurred not long after but with an older boy. I had organised the school's senior boys' athletics team, which was taking part in the District Schools Championships, from which the team to represent the District in the County Schools would be chosen. One lad, Jeff, a shot putter, had failed to turn up, and on the following Monday morning, when I was in the main school corridor with one of the other PE teachers, I saw Jeff approaching, so I asked him why he hadn't been there.

"Couldn't make it; had to work," Jeff said offhandedly, as he went to continue his walk down the corridor.

PE teacher Tom grabbed Jeff by the front of his collar and stood him up against the wall almost lifting him off his feet, and Jeff was a big fellow, a shot putter no less.

"How dare you speak to one of my colleagues in that manner? What about an apology? You let the school down, and your fellow athletes, and Mr Elder." There was a pause. "Well?"

"Sorry, sir," he said to Tom.

Then looking at me, as Tom let him slide off the wall, "Sorry, Mr Elder."

Although Jeff was one of the senior boys in the school, Tom was showing him, and me too, that nobody gets away with disrespect to a teacher. Although somewhat shocked by what Tom did, I was suitably impressed.

I travelled with Trevor and Tom, in Trevor's small, old car, to Southampton for the English Schools Track and Field Championships. On arrival we had to park in a field and Trevor had to back the car up against a wooden fence. It was late on Thursday evening and quite dark. I was in the back of the car.

"See me back, Tony," said Trevor.

I peered out of the small back window as the car slowly reversed. "Bit more ... bit more." Then the car hit the fence.

"Stop!" I cried.

No discernible damage was done, either to the car or the fence.

"You're supposed to say 'stop' before I hit the fence!" said Trevor, laughing. This set the scene for the weekend.

It rained on Friday and Saturday, and the high hurdles races were held on grass. We were all astonished when one of the competitors slipped on the wet grass and slid under a hurdle, instead of going over it, before emerging on the other side to carry on and finish his race! One of Hitchin's 440 yards runners, representing Herts Schools did very well to reach the final of his event. This was my introduction to these Schools Athletics Championships; I was to attend many more in the years ahead.

Trevor and I also took some boys to the London v New York floodlit athletics match at the White City Stadium in July. It was the memorable evening when Derek Ibbotson ran superbly to break the world record for the mile, with 3:57.2.

My digs in Hitchin were different from my experience in Didcot, not so homely, but very adequate. I stayed with a family in their modern and quite large house on the outskirts of the town: Mum and Dad with a young son at Junior School. It was the first time I had been expected to take off my shoes as I entered a house. They grew asparagus on the dry, sunny slopes in their garden, which for me was a novelty. During the week I spent my evenings either in my room or in The Sun in Hitchin, where I acquired a taste for Makeson and lemonade! Thankfully I did grow out of that fairly quickly. I was responsible for one minor disaster when I decided to iron one of my shirts. Nobody had told me that one shouldn't iron a nylon shirt, so I managed to ruin not only the shirt but also my landlady's iron. Most weekends I went home on my scooter to spend time with Jenny and to see my parents, as it was only a short journey from Hitchin back to Finchley. Much sooner than I expected, the term was over and it was holiday time once again.

7
Primary School Experience

Having decided after these varied and valuable experiences that I did want to teach, I also made the decision not to just carry on, "qualified" as I was, but to acquire professional training and qualification. I applied to do a PGCE year at Bristol University, as I had heard many good things about the course there. As an insurance, I also sent in an application to the Oxford University Department of Education. It was just as well that I did, as Bristol couldn't or wouldn't offer me a place. I never discovered why. I was quite excited to be returning to Oxford, and to my old college, St Catherine's. It was going to be a bitter sweet kind of experience because my old flame, Jane, would no longer be there. She was now engaged and therefore "long gone", except there would be loads of places that would bring back memories of our time together: pubs, cafes, the river, the Parks and many more.

During the summer holiday I reflected on my year of teaching. My two half terms in the two London Mixed Secondary Moderns had been a steep learning curve. Several times I had wondered if I was sensible to continue, and I have to admit one reason I did carry on was because I couldn't see a viable alternative. The Spring term in a boys' semi-rural Secondary Modern had been a better experience, for several reasons. I was there for a whole term, which, although only 12 weeks, gave me a better chance to get to know at least some of the boys, and for them to get to know me. Also it wasn't London. Big city social deprivation seems to have a markedly different effect on children, schools and education than small town and rural social deprivation. At least that had been my experience. The London children I had met were louder, brasher, more confrontational and less amenable than those in the sticks. They were more difficult to discipline, no doubt partly because of my inexperience, but not entirely so, as the other teachers in those schools were also having problems of control in classrooms and corridors. The difficulties that I faced at Didcot were no less, but they were different. There was not the same built in opposition to authority. There, even the least able, often socially disadvantaged, had a wish to improve, to seize an opportunity if it was made available. Some from the farming community questioned the value of education, but their children, on the whole, respected authority. Although my observation was that many teachers, though not all, seemed resigned to accepting mediocrity and underperformance, both the children's and theirs.

Hitchin Boys' Grammar School was different again: here the issues were more to do with the process of education than with discipline or control. Intellectually able children present their own challenges to teachers and I found this both stimulating and at times difficult to deal with. As a teacher you need to know that the tasks you are giving the most able pupils are going to challenge them; if not, then you may well have disaffected pupils and probably disaffected parents too. Remembering my own experiences as a pupil in a London Grammar School helped me to relate to the Hitchin youngsters, and I was allowed to teach some 6th Form History. Now as a teacher I could make comparisons with my former teachers, making use of what I thought were the best pedagogic examples and ignoring the rest.

The Oxford Department of Education sent me a book list, of course, and despite the fact that I had signed up for the Secondary Education PGCE, also said I should have two or three weeks' experience in a Primary School before starting their course. They selected a school in Hampstead Garden Suburb, only a few miles from my home in Finchley. I had never taught or been for long in the company of 5- to 11-year-olds, so this was to be another fresh learning experience. I was assigned to a class of 10-year-old children, about to begin their final year before moving on to a secondary school. Their teacher was a Mrs Elton and at her invitation I went to meet her on the Friday before the new term began. She was young and lived in a large house a few roads away from where I lived.

"Mr Elder, do come in," she said when I arrived in mid-afternoon.

"Tony, please," I said.

"Oh good, I'm Emmy, short for Emmeline," she giggled. "Do go through, into the garden. It's such a beautiful day. Can I get you some tea? Or a cold drink?"

I said tea would be fine. Emmy went back into the kitchen. It was a lovely garden, and I couldn't help thinking that Emmy must have a husband with a good job to be able to afford such a nice house in this area. *He's probably "something in the city",* I thought. It also struck me as ironic that for a three-week post observing, here I was in a garden about to have tea, a welcome I had not received elsewhere.

Emmy returned with a pot of tea and some cakes. She was wearing a short, pleated white skirt and a loose, pink T-shirt. Emmy began asking me about my wish to become a teacher. She was intrigued by the fact that I had already done a year's teaching.

"I wish I had done that," she said. "I went straight from school to Training College, and then to Greenways."

She said she had been at the school for three years, about to start her fourth, and had gone up through the school with the same pupils.

"Tell me about the pupils," I asked, "what are they like and what will you want me to do?"

It suddenly occurred to me that I would be spending three weeks in a classroom with Emmy and the children, something I had certainly not experienced before. Emmy had to be about the same age as I was. She was an attractive young woman, obviously self-confident and with, I noticed, very warm, smiling blue eyes. Her long fair hair was tied back in a ponytail.

"What would you like to do?" Emmy said, as she poured out the tea and passed me my cup.

"I've really got no idea," I said, unhelpfully. "As you know, I have to spend three weeks observing, before starting my course. I shall enjoy observing the children. And I'm sure I shall enjoy observing you, as you teach the pupils."

This wasn't meant to be cheeky, but as I said it, I realised Emmy might not approve of such boldness.

"What I mean is...."

"I understand," Emmy said. "I shall enjoy having you with me in the classroom." She laughed. "I'm sure we'll get on well together. And you can help. Another pair of hands is always welcome in a classroom of 10-year-olds."

We didn't get any further discussing what I would be doing, nor did she tell me much about her pupils, apart from, "They're lovely!" This was because Emmy wanted to hear about my teaching experiences in the different schools I had been in, also because we got on to the subject of Hampstead and the Garden City, and lastly because after about an hour, Emmy's husband arrived home from, yes, the city! Michael Elton was a banker in the City. *Good for Emmy*, I thought. And good for Mike, as I got to know him, for marrying Emmy.

I arrived at Greenways on Monday morning and was shown to the small staffroom. Emmy was already there and came over to greet me.

"This is Tony, everyone. He will be with us for three weeks and he'll be with me in Class 6."

Several voices said, "Hello", but everyone was naturally busy doing final preparations for the start of term. I accompanied Emmy to her classroom, which was large and very light with windows on two sides, cupboards and pinboard down the right hand side and at the back, more small cupboards with three animal cages on a shelf, containing what I later discovered were rabbits and guinea pigs. Next to the blackboard at the front were posters and maps. Soon children started arriving,

"Good morning, Mrs Elton," each one said.

Soon all 26 were sitting at their desks. They all knew where to sit as they had had a rehearsal at the end of the previous term, but to remind them, Emmy had stuck a label on each desk with a child's name on it. I was introduced.

"What do you say to Mr Elder?" asked Emmy.

"Good morning, Mr Elder," chorused Class 6.

Assembly was to be later that morning, so Emmy began by asking several of her class what they had done in the summer holidays. Soon she had them all writing an account of their favourite day in the holiday. I was given a class seating plan, so I quickly found out who was Dennis and who was Annie.

Each class was taken to the main hall for assembly by their class teacher, but I noticed some exceptions. Some children stayed in their classroom or were taken to another room. This was later explained to me. Greenways was an LEA school in mainly affluent Hampstead Garden Suburb, which has a large Jewish population. Parents of Jewish children had the right to withdraw their child from main school assembly, in order to have smaller, Jewish assemblies of their own. The architects and planners had not taken this into account when designing the school, and since more than 50% of the children were from Jewish families, the main hall had lots of empty spaces at assembly time. It would actually have made more sense to let the Jewish children have the main hall for their assembly, but that of course was not possible.

I enjoyed working and observing in Emmy's class. They were a well behaved and friendly bunch and I soon got to know their names and they got used to having me around. One or two incidents stand out. One morning as I was pushing my scooter up the school drive, a large Daimler drew up and out jumped Marcus, from Class 6.

"Hello, Marcus," I said. "Is that Daddy's car?"

"No, that's Mummy's," Marcus replied without a trace of irony.

Another part of Greenways that I really enjoyed was football practice. One of the few male teachers, Stuart, had asked me if I'd like to help each Wednesday with 1st XI football training. My task was to side-foot the ball in from outside the penalty area to an advancing forward who would attempt to score a goal past the school goalkeeper.

Stuart gave the forwards instructions, "Use your right foot," or "left foot this time."

They got surprisingly good at this, and it was also excellent practice for the goalkeeper. Thankfully the goal had a net and behind the goal was a high fence, so we didn't have long to wait before the ball was returned, and the school did have several good quality footballs. While I was there I didn't see any practices for the full backs. Obviously the philosophy was "attack!"

In the first week a new boy came into Class 6. His name was Janek. Emmy found out that he had a Czech father who had met and married an English girl while in England during the war. Janek had spent almost all his life living just outside Prague. He was now in England with his mother, as the marriage had broken down, and mother was returning to her roots. Janek seemed quite bright and he did the work asked of him, but he said absolutely nothing to anyone. He was silent all day for several days, despite joining in with the rest of the class in painting and drawing, working in the school garden and doing sums and writing. Emmy had the rest of the class to deal with, so she asked me if I could spend some time with Janek, and try to get him to open up and communicate. He understood English, as he and his mother had always spoken English together, while father had apparently conversed with Janek in Czech. He seemed to enjoy reading and looking at books with me. He even joined in football practice, when I explained the problem to Stuart. But I could not persuade him to speak.

Then I had an idea. His mother had told us that Janek played the recorder in Prague and loved music. So I took in to school a couple of records I had at home: some extracts from Smetana's "The Bartered Bride", and Dvorak's "Slavonic Dances". It was the Dances that did the trick. As soon as he heard them, Janek's face lit up and he said, "Good, good." They were the first words he had spoken to us in five days. I asked him if he recognised the music, which he obviously did, and he said, "Yes, Czech dances." He went into the classroom and told Emmy and the class, with his face lit up, "I hear my music. Good, good." His mother who had become very worried at Janek's silence at school was overjoyed. From then on Janek settled down and joined in, and talked, with the rest of the class. We thought part of the problem was missing his Dad, and probably missing his friends and all the places where he had grown up. His instinctive and subconscious reaction had been to shut out speech. Perhaps by talking again, Janek was tacitly accepting his changed circumstances. Whatever the explanation, he became a normal, talkative little boy. It was pure luck that I had found the key. Emmy was impressed!

It was early in my second week that Emmy told me she would in late the next day, and would I look after them until after Break. I was delighted and they all got on with the work they had been set to do. After about 15 minutes, two girls got up from their seats and went into a cupboard at the back of the classroom. Puzzled, I walked over to ask them what they were doing.

"We're going to feed the guinea pigs," one said, and pointed to a box on a shelf at the back of the room, where there was, indeed, a pair of guinea pigs, which I must have previously missed.

"Do you have to do it now?" I asked.

"Oh! Yes. They have to be fed every day at the same time," said Dulcie, as she collected the required feed and walked over to the box, which she carefully opened and put in the food for the guinea pig. I had obviously not noticed this happening in my first week. Dulcie and her friend closed the box, then went to wash their hands. Having done this, their task for today, they returned to their seats. *Strange are the ways of the Primary School,* I thought. They were about to become even more strange.

The children were all busy working at their desks, when suddenly, Maggie, a tall, striking girl with jet black hair, came up to the front of the class and handed me a brown paper parcel. I had no idea why or what was in it, but she was clearly intent on giving me this gift.

So I said, "Thank you, Maggie," and put the parcel on Emmy's desk at the front. Maggie returned to her seat. At Break, when they all went outside to play, I took the parcel into the Staff Room, where

I would have my cup of coffee.

"I've been given a present," I announced to the half dozen or so teachers who were there. Some teachers stayed in their classrooms at Break, while others would be on Break duty.

"Did Maggie give you that?" asked a lady who I later learned was Jo, in charge of first aid.

"Yes, she did," I said, wondering how she knew and handing the parcel to her.

Jo opened the parcel and revealed a clean pair of knickers.

"Maggie had an accident yesterday. These are the school knickers she was loaned and which her mother has washed and returned," Jo explained with a smile.

"All in a day's work, I suppose," I said, returning Jo's smile, as I made my way to the coffee machine.

I was sad to leave Greenways when my three weeks was up. Emmy and Class 6 bade me a fond farewell, and I said I would try to visit them during one of my vacations.

"We ought to keep in touch," said Emmy.

"Yes, I'll let you know how I'm getting on," I replied.

Was Emmy showing more interest in me than she should, or more than I had any reason to expect? She was a very attractive young woman and I had been excited every day at the prospect of spending time with her, albeit in the company of twenty-five or so 10-year-olds. Moreover Emmy was married, apparently happily so. *No,* I decided, *one shouldn't have such thoughts.* Emmy was just being friendly because I was leaving.

"Pop round some time before you go up to Oxford. You know where I live."

These were her parting words, which left me even more confused. "You know where I live," she had said. Not, "You know where we live."

Should I have gone? As it was I didn't, as I didn't really have the time. Term started the following week. At least that's what I told myself.

I did take Jenny out for a drive in the country the weekend before

I left. Borrowing Dad's car again! Somehow some of the warmth had gone out of our relationship. Was that the Emmy effect? Or was it Jenny's response to me going away again? We parted in the evening on friendly enough terms, but there was no passion. During the first term at Oxford I invited Jenny to come up for a weekend, but she always found an excuse not to come. *Would Emmy have come had I invited her,* I wondered? I didn't, so I never found out.

8
PGCE

I was looking forward to returning to the lovely city of Oxford where I had so many memories, so many connections, though most if not all of my St Catherine's mates would be long gone. I still have those memories today, reinforced of course by the Morse and Lewis programmes on TV. I arrived in Oxford in late September. I had arranged digs in North Oxford, just off the Woodstock Road, convenient for Norham Gardens where the Oxford Department of Education was situated.

The first term was spent attending lectures on the theory and practice of education, together with the occasional essay to write, plus seminars. Almost all the other students were starting this course not having previously taught. I was the exception. Sometimes this was an asset, as I could contribute my experiences in seminars, for example. At other times the tutors found my experiences annoying, as I sometimes pointed out, "It doesn't work like that." I was very conscious that I didn't want to sound like, "I know it all," as I patently didn't, so I tried to contribute sparingly.

"Strategies for Classroom Control" was a very necessary topic, but I found that their recommendations were somewhat at variance with reality. It was often said, unkindly, that the tutors and lecturers, in the main, were former teachers who had not made the grade. There were exceptions, such as Petersen's lectures, which were relevant and helpful, and Fiske's tutorials, which were always useful.

I was studying for a Post Graduate Certificate in Education in Secondary teaching with main subject History. We all had to select a subsidiary subject, which would also be examined, and I chose Physical Education. I did this because I had begun to take an interest in athletics coaching, and also because I knew this would take me out of the classroom on to the games field. During this first term I spent some time in a local school working with their PE staff, in the gym and on the field. I thoroughly enjoyed this. My minor dissertation was entitled "Circuit Training in Schools".

As a post graduate student at Oxford I had to have a college affiliation and it made sense to be once again a member of St Catherine's. It was great to return to old college haunts, but I found the antics of the current undergraduates very juvenile. I had to remind myself that that had been me only a year ago. I must have matured more than I had realised. Behaviour that no doubt I had indulged in, I now found embarrassing. Most of my contemporaries had left Oxford, but one or two who had been one year behind me, such as my good friend, Barri Bishop, I now found were also doing a PGCE.

The most useful part of the year was the middle term, when all the PGCE students went on Teaching Practice. Oxford's system was for their students to spend the whole term at one school, which I thought was brilliant. I have long believed that teachers should do their training, or the bulk of it anyway, in schools, so I was looking forward to the term after Christmas. I was assigned to Hemel Hempstead Co-educational Grammar School in Hertfordshire. Once I had negotiated their extraordinary "Magic" roundabout without mishap, I found my way to where I was to stay.

My accommodation had been arranged for me, and in the week before term started I found the address I had been given, which turned out to be a small, modern, semi-detached house: this was to be my base for the next 12 weeks.

These digs were a trifle unusual. My landlady, Meg, had six different kinds of wallpaper in her lounge, a large Buddha on the television and her aged father asleep in bed in the corner, and she spent our first meeting telling me how her third husband had left her while on a yacht in China.

My 12 weeks at the mixed Grammar School gave me some valuable experiences, some directly related to teaching History, many others not. One of the first things I noticed that was different was the 6-day timetable. This meant that instead of the timetable having five "days" from Monday to Friday, this one had six "days", so Monday's timetable in week one was repeated on Tuesday in week two. In every corridor and in the main school entrance there were large notices reminding everyone what day it was, Day 1, Day 4 etc. I quickly got used to this, but it had one unintended outcome, which I found hilarious. I was not the only one on teaching practice at the school. Two young ladies from the London Institute of Education were also doing their training at Hemel Hempstead. They came, as was the custom at the Institute, on two days each week, on Tuesdays and Thursdays. Week one was fine, but when they arrived the following week, they found their classes of the previous week weren't there. Alarm! Confusion! Each of the girls had prepared lessons for classes that didn't exist! Tuesday and Thursday in week two was now Day 1 and Day 3, with completely different timetables. The girls took some time to work this out, as did the school. It seemed that no one had informed the London Institute that the school operated a 6-day timetable.

I was given an excellent timetable, consisting of a Lower School class, 2C; a Middle School class, 4A; and, best of all, a 6th Form class of A level students. In addition I had two double lessons of Games. This gave me two double lessons each day for planning, review, keeping my own records and observing other teachers. I was looking forward to this. 4A were very bright, top stream pupils who had just begun their examination syllabus, so it was important I did a good job with them. They were doing a 19th-century British and European period, which was fine for me. 2C was the most difficult class, though "a piece of cake" compared with the London Secondary Modern oiks. They were middle stream, ages only 12 or 13, but quite cocky as they had lost any initial wariness they might have had a year ago. With them I had to remember what I knew about the Romans! Best of all were the 6th Form group, consisting of four boys and eight girls. Their topic was European Revolutions, which again suited me. I soon got my teeth into this.

At first I had one of the school History teachers in my lessons with me, not always the same one. I remember thinking that this is what it must be like in a London hospital. A senior surgeon would have to be there, at least initially, when the trainee doctors were making a diagnosis and surgeons began operating on a patient! However, I was quite glad when they stopped coming in, after a fortnight, and let me get on by myself. Any teacher will tell you that having someone else in the room while you are teaching, however good you are, changes the overall ambience and can affect your relationship with the class. I had to make and keep lesson plans and record my observations about the lessons afterwards. My tutor from Oxford would visit during the 12 weeks and would want to see these.

I also enjoyed the Games lessons, when I was able to be out on the field with footballers and was able to help prepare the cross-country teams. This is how I met Cliff Redman, a very promising 15-year-old runner, who had just joined Watford Harriers. I had started to do some coaching back home, at the Parliament Hill track, and was able to give Cliff advice on what training he should do. He amazed me with his dedication and ability. One of the standard sessions that middle-distance runners did then, and still do, is a series of 400 metres' runs (440 yards in those days), say eight or ten, in a certain time, with a set period of recovery between them. I set Cliff to do eight of these and told him to progress to 12, then 16, gradually over the next few weeks. He told me, after just five weeks, that he had done 24 x 440 yards at a rate of 70–75 seconds, and he had managed to reduce the recovery times! "Rather too many at your age," I said. I continued to coach Cliff after I left Hemel Hempstead and, two years later, he ran 9 minutes 11 seconds for 2 miles, and 14 minutes 14 seconds for 3 miles, both being British Junior Bests at that time. He ran for his club, Watford Harriers, on many occasions and always did well in road and cross-country relays. Recurring injuries prevented

Cliff from achieving success as a senior athlete.

One afternoon I had been on the field and came back into school to teach my 4th year class. I was wearing my tracksuit and didn't have any time to change, so went straight into the classroom. Halfway through the lesson I was explaining via the blackboard the causes of the Crimean War when Brian, the Head of History, came into the room. He took one look at me, stayed for perhaps five minutes and left. At the end of the day he told me my attire was not appropriate for the classroom. I noted his comments, even though I didn't agree with him. The pupils quite liked the idea that their History teacher was also active on the Games field.

On another occasion, in 2C, one of the boys asked if he could sit next to his friend, and I said he could. I gave the class some work to do, and as they sat in double desks, it was not unusual for the boys and girls to talk to each other about the task in front of them. I welcomed this. Once again, Brian came in to see how I was doing and, as the class was working, he took me to one side and said, "Why are Alan and Frank sitting together? I separated them last term, as they always talk to each other."

"They are friends," I said, "and they help each other."

"Help each other? They should be getting on with their own work, not helping each other."

"Can we talk about this, at the end of the day?" I said.

"Huh! I suppose so." And out he went.

Brian and I clearly didn't agree. I pointed out that this was only a 2nd Year class. It might be different if they were in the 5th year preparing for an exam. I think the pupils in the class were aware of this issue, and I was amused when, a day or so later, I saw Brian walking down a corridor having just come out of another class, with a large letter L attached to the back of the gown that all teachers wore. I said nothing.

The students at Hemel Hempstead were a lively and, at times, inventive lot. One morning, the 6th Formers played a practical joke. With the whole school in assembly, a 6th Former went into every classroom where the first lesson was to be taught by a female teacher.

50

They removed the chalk from the cardboard chalk box, put the chalk in a drawer in the teacher's desk, and placed a live white mouse in the upturned chalk box. They calculated that, after assembly when classes and teachers went to the first lesson, at almost the exact same moment, lady teachers would reach for the chalk box and turn it over, and mayhem would ensue. Their scheme worked brilliantly. Suddenly, synchronised screams could be heard throughout the school, as dozens of lady teachers could be seen running out of their classrooms, chased by real or imagined white mice. It had required planning and artistry, it was both funny and clever, and it was relatively harmless, though not everyone enjoyed the joke. I don't know if the 6th Formers had arranged to catch all the escapee mice. I rather doubt it.

This was the first time I had taught 17- and 18-year-old girls and I enjoyed the experience. Some were extremely attractive, so much so that I always looked forward to my A level lessons, but in addition, the girls could discuss and argue so much better than the boys who, although the same age, always seemed to have less maturity. Sarah and Sally were especially mature; we regarded each other as equals, which helped when discussing the intricacies of the French or the Russian Revolution, though I had to remind myself that, while they and I were students, I was considered to be a teacher. I tried not to do all the work, and we had some excellent role play sessions, involving, for example, Lenin and Trotsky, Kamenev and Zinoviev, and I tried to pose questions to them, rather than always providing answers. I asked each student to write his or her own definition of a revolution. "How are social revolutions different from political revolutions?" I asked. And, "Are revolutions a good thing?" Quite rightly they said the answer depended on who you were. So I asked them to describe what they would have done if they had been living at the time, as, say, a land-owner, a soldier or a peasant. We spent some time comparing the French and American Revolutions, partly because they were almost contemporary and had both similarities and differences, and the students found it interesting to analyse the background of each revolution: the ideas, the leaders and the outcomes. The students enjoyed being "stretched" and made to think.

The 4th Year class was quite challenging, not because of any misbehaviour, but because they always wanted to argue and put forward their point of view. Whether we were studying the government's domestic policy in the early nineteenth century or Britain's role in Europe, there were always those in the class with a view they wanted to air. "Of course the Tory Party didn't want a reformed House of Commons..." Or, "Why was Britain getting involved in Europe anyway?" The boys were more argumentative then the girls; some became quite violent, or perhaps I should say passionate, as no actual blows were struck. At that age, in mid adolescence, boys find it very hard to see another's point of view: all they can see is their own, which, of course, is why many parents of teenage boys have a hard time.

After I had been teaching them for a few weeks and we had got to know each other and developed a rapport, I had another kind of challenge to deal with. At the end of one of our lessons, at the end of the afternoon, two of the girls in 4A, Deb and Alice, waited behind until the others had all gone. They sat on two of the desks.

"Will you meet us tonight, sir, by the canal, about eight?" Alice said.

"Yes, please do," added Deb. "We'll give you a good time, won't we, Alice?"

These girls were probably just 15, and although the 1960s was still in the future, they had already discovered how to shorten their skirts to show off their legs, and they knew that I would notice. They were both pretty, both had fair hair, and I was at first at a loss as to how to react. As I hadn't immediately responded, the girls upped their demands.

"Will you take us for a drink, sir?" Alice asked. "If you think we're too young we can sit in the garden in the pub by the canal and you can bring us our drinks."

"And after a few drinks, you don't know what might happen, do you, sir?" Deb smiled.

"Absolutely not," I said. "I am a teacher and I can't be seen meeting girls from the 4th Year and going for a drink. It's out of the question. But thanks for the offer, anyway."

"So you'd come with us for a good time, if you weren't going to be seen, is that right, sir?"

"No, Alice, I didn't mean it like that at all."

"Oh well, we'll ask you again, you know." At which, the two girls got off the desks and walked slowly out of the room.

"If you change your mind, we'll be at the canal around eight," Deb said as she left.

I must admit I did wonder if I should go to the canal to see if they were there, out of curiosity you understand, but I thought better of it.

In the lessons that followed the girls seemed to be more flirtatious and I did my best to ignore them. I realised that this was one of the dangers a young teacher would have to face when teaching mixed classes. Coping with girls who have a crush on you is one thing, but having two girls together offering their teacher "a good time" was quite another. I did wonder if I should report them but I decided not to, as no harm had actually been done and, had I agreed to meet them, it would have been me who was in trouble.

Usually I went home at weekends, on my Lambretta, but occasionally I stayed in Hemel, either with work to do or because one of the teachers had invited me over for a meal. It was some way through the term when my landlady, Meg, said to me one Friday evening, when I hadn't gone home, "Why don't you come with me tomorrow morning? I'm going to meet up with my friends in St Albans. You'd be very welcome."

As it happened I couldn't go, but at the time I didn't know quite what the invitation entailed.

"I'm sorry, Meg," I said. "I can't make that. I'm meeting Andy at 11."

Andy was another young athlete that I had said I would advise on his training.

"Oh! That's a shame. Perhaps another time," said Meg.

I discovered later that Meg went most Saturday mornings to a garage in St Albans to drink Meths with a group of Irish workers. I have had many landladies, but Meg certainly was the most unusual. It was another invitation that I was glad to have turned down.

All in all, I learned a lot at Hemel Hempstead, and not only about teaching History!

I kept in touch with Cliff Redman for many years and he went on to be a very successful junior athlete. He had a friend at Watford Harriers, Frank North, also an athlete, though not in the same class as Cliff. I had been coaching some runners in my athletics club, Highgate Harriers, at home, and occasionally we got together, either for training weekends on the sand dunes at Camber, in Sussex, or sometimes based at Frank North's mother's house where sumptuous teas were provided. It was here that Frank earned the sobriquet of "Eating North", as no matter how many sandwiches or cakes or jam rolls were left when we had all had our fill, Frank would polish off the lot. And he remained slim and healthy!

I had one very unusual experience in my last term at Oxford. A number of us on the PGCE course were asked if we would agree to take part in some research at the Warneford Hospital in Oxford, where they specialised in treating patients with mental health or psychiatric problems. A few of us agreed. At the hospital, we were given a series of tests to carry out, mainly of the ink blob variety: which is the odd one out? What comes next? What is missing? What does this suggest to you? It lasted well over an hour and, after being thanked, we made our way back to our digs and thought no more about it. The tests were not for our benefit, so we wouldn't hear any more except for a formal thank-you letter for taking part. The purpose of the tests, we were told, was to see how "normal" people dealt with the tasks that were routinely given to their "disturbed" patients. Some while later, I happened to bump into a young man from the Warneford who had been involved in our testing and I asked if they had learned anything useful. He told me that they had been surprised by the results, which seemed to indicate that their patients were more normal than we, the graduates, were. I said I hoped that said more about their tests than about us!

This final term of the PGCE was something of a formality, involving reflection on our teaching practice and a small amount of additional work. We had been continuously assessed. I was awarded a distinction for my teaching practice and commended on my dissertation on Circuit Training in Schools. We had been advised to apply in April or May if we wanted to begin teaching in a school in the following September. I regularly read the *Times Educational Supplement* and saw plenty of possible posts, but many were too far away. One post I applied for in the spring was in Chelmsford in Essex; I was interviewed and offered a permanent post, starting in September, at King Edward VI Grammar School. Wahay!

Part Two

Early Years

""Young blood must have its course, lad,
And every dog his day."
Charles Kingsley

9

War and Boarding School

My own school days had been quite varied. I suppose I had taken them all in my stride, without much thought. My first school had been a little private school in The Grove in Isleworth in Middlesex. This was the road Mum and I lived in so I didn't have far to go to school. Two things I remember: firstly, being bullied by a rather large boy with ginger hair named Ian. He chased me down the road and made me cry, though I soon got over that. Secondly, one morning at school, as our hymn for the day, we sang, "Eternal Father, strong to save", which includes "for those in peril on the sea". This was 1940 and I was 6 years old. Even at that age I knew that some of our ships had been sunk by German U-boats, and that lives of British seamen had been lost, and I knew that my Dad, in the Royal Engineers, was soon to go by boat to India as part of his Army service. I can remember crying as I stood and tried to sing, but I don't think anybody noticed.

My grandpa and grandma, my mother's parents, lived at the other end of The Grove, so I saw them a lot. Grandpa (as I called him), William Trenance Kenwood, my mother's father, was born and bred in Devon. His father had been a mould maker in a local pottery. Grandpa began teaching at Bovey Tracey Grammar School in 1882, at the age of 16! Moving on to Edlington Grammar School, he passed his Oxford Senior Local Exams in 1884 and came 4th in the country in the exam he took when applying to London University in 1887. He was awarded a 1st in his final BA in 1890. He taught at Highbury Park School and Carpenter's School, both in London, before moving on to the Wyggeston School in Leicester. It was from there that, in 1903, WTK was appointed Headmaster at Isleworth Grammar School, a post he held until he retired in 1931. I have the grandfather clock he was presented with on his retirement. He became a JP in 1935. He was a lovely man, tall and straight and very distinguished-looking. Grandma was Eveline, shortened to Eva; she and my grandfather had married in 1904. She was a little, gentle woman, who often wore her hair in a bun, very much the junior partner in the marriage, as was expected in those days.

Before the war my grandparents lived in Thornbury Road, Isleworth, just up the road from the school where Grandpa had been Headmaster. In Ronald Hyam's *History of Isleworth Grammar School*, Grandpa is described as "a man of such tremendous personality ... a fine headmaster of the old Victorian type, he inspired fear in many small boys, but among Old Boys his memory is revered". His son, Tommy, was a pupil at the school and, from 1925, my mother, his daughter, was School Secretary. What hit Grandpa very hard was the loss of so many Old Boys in the 1914–18 war. Eighty-one Old Boys died, youngsters who Grandpa had seen develop into fine young men. One Old Boy was awarded the Victoria Cross, which Grandpa called, "the greatest honour of all".

While my grandfather was Headmaster at Isleworth Grammar School, he got to know the Principal of Borough Road College, virtually adjacent to the Grammar School. This was Frederick Attenborough, later Principal of University College, Leicester, and father of Richard and David. I remember my mother telling me that she knew both the boys as they were growing up: she would have been 19 when David was born. And I know that Grandpa, after he retired, kept in contact with Frederick when he moved to Leicester.

Grandpa

Grandpa retired three years before I was born. When I was quite little, he used to take me on my tricycle to the traffic lights at Great West Road to watch the cars roar past. Fast cars, lots of noise, changing traffic lights – wonderful! One day there was a dreadful accident. A car was travelling very fast from the Staines direction and the driver either thought he could beat the lights or he didn't see the red light. A cyclist was coming down the hill and across the dual carriageway, where the light had changed to green, and the car hit him broadside on. The cyclist was flung up into the air, landing in the road much further on. There was a lot of blood. He was killed outright. Not the sort of sight for a 4-year-old to witness. It shook me up quite badly and for weeks I could taste blood when I went to bed at night.

When the war started in September 1939, I was taken by my grandmother to a farm near Looe in Cornwall, where we stayed with the farmer and his family. Immediate evacuation of children from London was the order of the day, as German bombing was thought to be imminent. My one recollection of our brief stay was my grandmother sitting on the farm gate and being pushed violently to and fro by the farmer's wife to great cries of amusement, but not from my Gran, who was highly embarrassed by the whole episode.

"Stop it! Stop it at once, do you hear?"

My Gran was quite meek and quietly spoken, so this outburst was very uncharacteristic. I don't think she ever forgave the farmer's wife for her boorish behaviour. When there had been no bombs, my Gran and I returned to London, whereupon my mother, who was living on her own as my Dad was doing his Army service, decided I should go away to boarding school.

From late 1940 to 1945, from the age of 6 to nearly 11, I attended Seaford House School in Malvern Link, Worcestershire. It was a Preparatory School, meant to prepare young boys for entry to one of the Public Schools. My mother and I were both crying our eyes out as she put me on the train at Paddington. I'm sure she felt that what she was doing was for the best, but sending her 6-year-old boy away was very painful for her. I remember feeling really upset when the train started to move and my mother disappeared out of sight. I had my label and gas mask, and a large, black tin trunk containing all my possessions. These included my new school uniform, which Mum and I had gone to Kinch & Lack in Victoria to buy some days before. There was a blazer, a cap, regulation short, grey trousers and white shirts as well as games kit, including some new football boots. It must have cost a fair amount of money. The dozen or so boys on the train were accompanied by one of the teachers, Mr. Venables. He was not tall, probably late forties, neatly dressed in a dark suit, looking almost dapper, as though he would be more at home in the Ritz than in a railway carriage with a load of small boys. He turned out to be a teacher of French, who we later discovered had an irritating habit, when waiting for trains, of marching briskly up and down the platform, Poirot-like, no matter who was with him. The journey to Worcestershire passed surprisingly quickly. At Malvern Link Station we were escorted to the school, only a short walk away. The school had taken over a large house with extensive grounds and a small farm. We walked through the main gates and up the drive to the house. Our luggage came from the station in a large van and was dumped on the stone floor of the large entrance hall. We were given some orange juice, a jam sandwich and a bun.

Off the main entrance hall was a large, wide staircase, leading to the two floors above. There were 12 of us 6-year-olds in one dormitory on the top floor, with older boys in other rooms nearby. Matron told us the rules: no talking after "lights out"; no getting out of bed, except to go to the toilet; no turning lights on; no interfering with the curtains. From the very first night, we didn't like Matron. She didn't seem to like us very much either. She was very bossy and rarely smiled. At first, I was very unhappy and homesick. The first few nights, we all cried ourselves to sleep. If one of us was caught talking after "lights out", we had to stand outside the dormitory, until Matron allowed us to go back to bed. Matron's room was on the same floor, just at the top of the stairs. If someone persisted in talking or if they had done something really naughty, such as move the curtains to look out of the window, Matron would take us down stairs to the Headmaster. In the bathroom one evening, as usual, we were playing about. Flannels flew all round the room, and mine ended up on a pipe quite high up along one wall, opposite the big bath. I had to retrieve it before Matron came in. I climbed up on to a washbasin and when I stood on tip-toe I could just reach it with the aid of a loofah brush handed to me by Alan. All the boys stood watching my agile feat of bathroom mountaineering. At this moment Matron chose to return.

"Get down! At once!" And then, angrily, "Downstairs to the Headmaster. Yes. Now!"

The Headmaster, Mr Milton, could have been mistaken for a farmer or a country publican. He was not a young man. He usually wore breeches and boots and had a more or less permanent drip on the end of his large, pink, scabby nose. Standing outside his room in the evening, having been sent down by Matron, waiting on the stone floor, could be quite frightening. In the winter the floor was especially cold on our bare feet. When he emerged, we either got a stern telling off, or we were caned. If it were to be a caning, Mr Milton would return to his room leaving the door ajar, so we could see in, and he would select a cane from under the cloth on top of the billiard table in the middle of the room. Then he would come back out into the hall, order us to bend over and cane us in our pyjamas, two strokes or maybe three, though one boy got four. Thin pyjamas gave no protection to our tender, young backsides. We would yell and then cry and have sore buttocks for days. I was caned several times during my four years at the school. I don't think Mr Milton did any teaching; the only things I remember him doing were mucking out in the little farm and caning.

We 6 and 7 year olds soon became friends; I remember Alan and Maurice in particular. We began to think up ways of getting back at Matron. Each evening she put a saucer of milk outside her room for her cat. We decided to grind up some glass really small and mix it in with the milk. If Matron's cat died from eating powdered glass, this would be justice, we felt. The cat consumed the entire contents of the saucer on two consecutive nights and was none the worse for the experience. We felt thwarted, but thought of another plan. Matron had a bike with a small motor attachment, what we called a "pop-pop". We thought we would put some sugar in the engine, which somebody said would have a disastrous effect when Matron got on and started up the engine. We never carried out this plan, because some of us felt that, while it was all right to kill a cat, which of course we hadn't, we drew the line at doing the same to Matron.

In the dormitory we had contests between the Roundheads and the Cavaliers, and we played I-spy and alphabet games, where you had to say a name beginning one letter on from the last person's word, e.g. Alan ... Brian ... Charlie ... or we had to begin the next word with the last letter of the previous word e.g. Worcester ... Reading ... Guildford, and we played this with boys' names, girls' names, places in England, capitals, things to eat and any others we could think of. Looking back, I'm amazed at how much we knew. After "lights out" of course, we were in trouble if Matron heard us talking.

For our meals we sat on long, hard forms at long, wooden tables in the dining hall. Breakfast was always lumpy porridge, which many of us disliked, so when porridge eating was over and the not very empty bowls were sent down from one end of the table to the other in a giant pile, all the uneaten porridge oozed out, creating an awful mess, to the daily annoyance of teachers there to supervise. Happy days! At least the toast was usually edible. The parcels of food, usually a cake or biscuits, which our mums sent, often with a little book or a new card game, were a real godsend. It can't have been easy, with rationing and bombing and the cost of postage, for our mothers to send these things but we were grateful and wrote letters of thanks, which I know my mother loved to receive.

I was also beginning my stamp collection, which was to grow when I returned home after the war. Some of the boys had parents who lived abroad, so their letters provided a ready supply of foreign stamps. I'm sure that spawned my interest in geography. Our other interest, quite naturally, was in aircraft and warships, ours and those of the enemy. We learned their names and markings from posters and pictures. Occasionally the whine of a fighter or the drone of a bomber could be heard beyond the school walls, and we would look out of a window and try to identify it. Where we were in rural Worcestershire, we didn't see or hear Flying Fortresses or Lancaster bombers but, on rare visits to London, I did.

We were taken out on walks, crocodile fashion, around the roads next to the school, always in uniform, including caps. On Sundays we were marched to church in Great Malvern. Going to church meant a temporary escape from the confines of school and I liked the music and often the words of the hymns. I didn't understand the prayers, and the sermons, often long and boring, made us want to get back to school. We were always the subject of much curiosity among the local churchgoers.

When a mother came to visit at a weekend (it was always the mother, never the father, who was probably fighting somewhere, and it was always on a Saturday or a Sunday), the lucky boy was allowed to take a friend with him to tea in the Winter Gardens, in Great Malvern, which was the usual venue for such visits. I went with several of my friends for such treats, and on the rare occasions that my mother could get away from London and the Blitz, I invited a friend to come with me. A string quartet played in the Winter Gardens and it was good to get away from school and out into the real world for a brief afternoon, even if it was only the Winter Gardens. The scones and jam were delicious. I was not the only one whose mother could rarely visit, but every day we would all look, eagerly, for letters from home.

One teacher at the school was an Austrian, Mr Fischer (I don't know why he hadn't been interned), who used to take us for football. He was tall, young and fit. All the boys liked him. In games, he used to barge us over but catch us before we fell down! He organised matches with nearby schools, and there was great excitement when we went in a coach to one match and by train, through a tunnel, to another. In the winter, he took us some Saturdays for long walks on the Malvern Hills, where we had massive snowball fights, which were tremendous fun. He taught us geography and I still remember his lessons on clouds and how impressed I was by the word cumulonimbus. Memories eh!

Out on the field we also played a game which I later discovered was a version of Danish Longball. It was a variant of Rounders and Baseball except that, after hitting the ball, instead of running to bases placed in a circle, you ran away at right angles to a predetermined "base" where you could rest until you decided to try to make a return run. We had lots of fun playing this game.

Mr Healey, who taught us Latin, was very old, certainly in his 70s. He was a large man with white whiskers and he usually wore a light brown, tweed suit and occasionally, plus fours. We were fascinated by the watch chain he always wore in his waistcoat. He was a very good teacher. He sat us in a line facing him, eight or ten of us, and fired questions at us. If we got the question right we moved up a place, to our right. If we gave a wrong answer we moved down a place to the left. At the end of each lesson he made a note of our position, being on the right scoring higher than being on the left. Next lesson we began in the places we had finished the previous lesson. Looking back, I can see how this motivated us, kept our attention and it explains how we learned so much Latin. Years later when I went to Grammar school in London, aged 12, I was told my Latin was GCE

(O level) standard.

My mother was in London during the war, driving ambulances in the Blitz. I went home in some school holidays but usually only for a few days. This was partly because Mum couldn't look after me if she was working, plus the perceived danger from air raids. I saw sandbags in front of important buildings, blackout to every window and strips of black across car headlights. Iron railings had all been removed as demanded by the war effort. Everyone was saturated with slogans, which were meant to keep up our spirits. I only went home for longer periods towards the end of the war when it was considered safe. Some school holidays were spent at school. This was actually quite good fun, as I helped out on the school farm, learning about Sussex Whites and Rhode Island Reds, looking after pigs and guinea pigs, and making friends with Marion, the Land Army girl who helped on the farm and became a special pal to us boys. Even Mr Milton was friendly then.

Some other holidays, I stayed with some folk that my grandparents knew in Leicester, the Kirkwood family. They lived in a large house on the main road just outside Birstall. At the rear of the house was a huge garden, with a paved terrace and steps down to a large expanse of lawn, which led to a shrubbery and a garage at the far end. On one side was a tennis court, so I had lots of exercise but not many friends.

Staying with the Kirkwoods was enjoyable as I rode my tricycle endlessly and, I'm told, furiously. Some days I was joined by Jack, who lived nearby. He and I had tricycle races around the extensive garden paths: it was the start of Formula 1 Tricycle Racing! I was taken to Bradgate Park to see the deer, where I played in the little streams and climbed up to Old John and saw the house where Lady Jane Grey had lived. Most of the time I was with Molly Kirkwood, the pretty, dark-haired, young 20-year-old Kirkwood daughter, who tried, unsuccessfully, to teach me to play tennis.

She was a real heroine one day. The Kirkwoods had three black Labradors, a mother and puppies. I loved being with them. One afternoon, I was playing on the floor in the main living room of the house with Mitzi, the older dog. It was a very hot summer's day and

Mrs Kirkwood was hoovering upstairs. Suddenly, Mitzi must have had enough of the heat, the noise of the hoover and my playing or teasing and she attacked me, biting my face badly. Molly heard my screams and she and her mother came running into the lounge where I was lying, crying and bleeding profusely. I remember being carried and put into the back of the Morris 10, and Molly driving very fast, through several red lights, to Leicester Royal Infirmary, where I had my bleeding face repaired with loads of stitches. I had part of my nose hanging loose and one bite had been very close to my eye, so I was fortunate the outcome wasn't worse. I was in hospital for several days and was very upset when I was told that the dog had been put down. Fortunately, I was not put off dogs by this experience.

My grandparents' house had been destroyed by a German bomb in the autumn of 1940. Fortunately, they were away at the time, but they returned home to Isleworth and turned the corner by the fire station at the end of The Grove, only to see their house in ruins, totally demolished. It is hard to imagine how they must have felt, as they were both pensioners and had lost practically everything. This prompted a move to Evington, an outer suburb of Leicester, and in some respects my grandfather was making a return, having taught at the Wyggeston Boys' School there. When I didn't stay with the Kirkwoods, I went to live with them there.

Grandma enjoyed taking me by bus to the Johnscliffe Tea Rooms in Newtown Linford, near Bradgate Park, where we had tea and cakes. On Saturday mornings she took me to Simpkins & James, the large department store in Leicester, where I had to endure having coffee with her elderly female friends, including her sister, Auntie May, who lived at Burley House in Birstall, just across from the Kirkwoods. Grandma's other sister, Mabel, lived in South Africa. The sisters were all members of the Hickling family, their brother being Percy Bell Hickling, a successful and well-known artist and illustrator of Ladybird books, such as *The Inquisitive Harvest Mouse* (1949) and many more.

Grandpa used to let me come into the bathroom in the morning to watch him shaving. I sat on the floor with a couple of cars, and it was here that I learned how to spell "Wednesday" and "Leicester", while watching Grandpa shave! I used to play with my toy cars on the arm of his leather chair, which now sits in my study. One summer

Grandpa took me to Grace Road to watch County cricket. I loved Grandpa very much.

When I got to do "my thing", if I wasn't adding to my stamp collection, playing with my cars or throwing a tennis ball up, endlessly, against the back wall of the house, I cycled round the roads near their house in Evington, occasionally as far as Victoria Park. I enjoyed this but it could be hazardous. I was nearly run down by a huge American army lorry, only escaping by taking to the pavement as it roared past. On another day, I got my bicycle wheels stuck in a tramline. It was an easy thing to do, but I had great difficulty lifting my bike out of the way as the bellringing, clanking, Leicester tram bore down on me. Luckily, I just made it to safety. Another interest I cultivated while staying with my grandparents was a study of the Leicester buses. There were many different, competing, bus companies and, in addition to collecting and listing the numbers of all the buses, I was fascinated by their colouring. My favourite was Bowyers, because I liked their shape, and they were yellow.

Grandpa had a great sense of humour. A tale was often told that centred on one of the dinner parties my grandparents gave for some friends. Their dining room had portraits and pictures on the walls. During the meal, one of the guests asked,

"Who are the ladies in the portraits and photos on the walls?"

Grandpa replied, "Oh! They are some of my mistresses."

There were some gasps; then a few of the guests remembered he was a headmaster, so it was all right to have mistresses, mistresses who teach!

One of Grandpa's best friends was a guy called Jimmy Went, who had something of a reputation for overeating. At a meal one day, so the story goes, when everyone else was looking at their empty plates and Jimmy was still eating, Grandpa said,

"The difference between you and me, Jimmy, is that I know when I've had enough; you know when you can't eat any more!"

Before the war my grandparents employed a maid called Eliza. She did some of the cooking and most of the cleaning and was well liked and respected. Grandma liked to cook from time to time, and there was a story that was frequently retold. Grandma had returned to the sitting room after doing some cooking, when a head appeared in the doorway. It was Eliza, who said,

"Your cake's rose lovely in the oven, ma'am."

My grandparents often had friends round in the evening to play bridge. One couple who came were Harold and Alice, both good players. Harold had been a magistrate like Grandpa. Sometimes I would watch and try to follow the bids and the way they played their hands. One thing that regularly annoyed Grandpa was the chat that went on between Grandma and Alice that had nothing to do with the game.

"Are we here to play bridge or discuss knitting?" he would say.

After the war, as a teenager, I often went up to Leicester to visit my grandparents. In the Spring of 1949, Grandpa was 81 and was now very frail and close to dying, but Leicester City had reached the FA Cup Final and he really wanted them to win. He lay in his bed on 30 April and we listened to the match commentary on the radio together. Unfortunately, Leicester lost to Wolves. Grandpa passed away next day.

Although I didn't realise it at the time, Grandpa had made a big impact on me between the ages of about 6 and 11 while I was growing up and later when I was a young teenager. With my dad in India, Grandpa was an important male influence. We seldom saw Tommy, my mother's brother. I really missed Grandpa, and Mum was heartbroken when he died, as was Grandma, now alone after 45 years of marriage. A few years later, she came to live with us in Finchley.

As soon as I had started at boarding school, the bombing of London began. I was unaware of how serious it was or how much danger my mother was in. Much later she told me some of her experiences, though I'm sure she didn't tell me everything.

It was a short journey from her home in The Grove to the main ambulance station in Bulstrode Road, Hounslow or to the other ambulance headquarters near Busch Corner. Her job involved responding to call-outs when there had been casualties from air raids.

48 The Grove, Isleworth, where Mum and I lived before and (me occasionally) during the war

She told me that once, late at night, all the ambulances were directed to go to a dance hall, which had received a direct hit. Tragedy greeted them. On hearing the air raid siren, everyone in the dance hall had taken shelter in the basement, but the water main had been hit, the basement flooded and everyone had drowned. That night her only task was to recover bodies. Driving through the London streets while an air raid was taking place was a hazardous undertaking. Speed was of the essence, yet there was often almost total blackness apart from flares and fires, which came and went in an instant as the ambulance sped on. Usually there was the noise of the bombers and the bombs, the crash of falling buildings and dogs howling, mixed in with the shouts and cries of injured Londoners. I was reminded recently of what my mother must have gone through when reading Sarah Waters' *The Night Watch*.

They had a different task to perform on another night, my mother told me. A platoon of soldiers had been marching along the High Street into Hounslow when they received a direct hit from falling bombs. They were all killed, but worse, they were blown apart into pieces. Mother said that the task she and her colleagues were given was to collect the body parts and assemble them in order to find out just how many soldiers had lost their lives.

"Here's part of a leg."

"Isn't that another head over there?"

It must have been horrendous. Every body part had to be accounted for. I found it hard to imagine my lovely mother having to carry out such gruesome tasks. I still do. The women ambulance drivers were some of the real heroes of the bombing on London and I'm sure the same could be said in other cities too, such as Plymouth and Coventry.

Mother at the back on the right

At boarding school I followed some of the events in the war: the sinking of the Bismarck, the battles in the Atlantic, with the U-boats and allied convoys. I had charted on a map the bombing raids on Germany and I knew the names of all the German towns and cities visited by the super Flying Fortresses and the Lancaster bombers. Dusseldorf was one of my favourites! I was vaguely aware that the conflict had not gone well at first for Britain but that the war was gradually being won. We were shown maps of North Africa and then of Italy. The real turning point came with D-Day in June 1944 and we followed on maps the progress of the allied armies as they moved across France and into Germany. The teachers tried to be sensitive when doing this, as many of the boys had fathers who were fighting, and one lad had an older brother in the Royal Navy.

The only time I experienced any of the bombing of London was in 1944. I had been allowed to come home one school holiday as it was now considered safe. Then came the V1s, the "doodle bugs". They made a slow droning noise, which was fine so long as you could still hear it. If the noise cut out, then the V1 was on its way down, so you quickly took cover and hoped it wouldn't land where you were. I was in bed one morning when I heard them coming. I was excited and scared at the same time. I listened intently. The drone got louder until it seemed to be overhead. Then it stopped. I hid under the sheets, not that they would have given much protection, but when the bang came it didn't sound very near. Later I learned that some buildings had been hit about two miles away. Having been hidden in distant Worcestershire during the bombing, I was shocked at the extent of rubble in the streets and the number of damaged and destroyed buildings in and around Isleworth.

I was still at boarding school on VE Day, May 8th 1945, when victory in Europe was celebrated. We were allowed to listen to Winston Churchill's broadcast to the nation in the afternoon. We were all overjoyed and, aged nearly 11, I could understand much of the significance. War against Germany was over; we had won; now I could go home. Soon after, we all left the school, as term was over, and I never went back. I was in London when VJ Day was celebrated on August 14th. I went up to London with Mum and joined in the celebrations with crowds of happy, excited people in Piccadilly Circus. I didn't know and she couldn't tell me what she had gone through. I wasn't told anything about my dad and I don't remember asking.

Right at the end of the war I was given a new sports bike, and Mum and I went on several cycle rides, one as far as Coldharbour in Surrey. I liked trying to keep up with the cyclists who raced along the Great West Road cycle track every Sunday morning. One weekend, when I must have been 10 or 11, I went to stay near Staines with Bruce and his family, friends of my mum, cycling there of course. It was summer, and on Sunday morning we rode our bikes out to Virginia Water and lay in the sun by the Thames. It was during that weekend that I had a real scare on my bike. Bruce and I were not far from Runnymede, where King John had met the barons and signed Magna Carta in 1215. We were cycling down a really steep, country lane that led to the Thames. When I tried to slow down, my brakes wouldn't work. Bruce slowed but I kept going faster and faster. I was really frightened because I knew that at the bottom of the hill was a road and on the other side of the road was the river. I thought about cycling into one of the hedges at the side of the lane, which would probably have brought me to a very painful stop. Instead I kept going. As I got nearer to the bottom of the hill, pedals whirling round, my feet in the air, my instinct told me I should try to steer to the left and hope no car was coming. I was really scared that I would be hit, but I was lucky. I raced across the road, ending up in a tangled heap on a grassy bank very near the river, where Bruce found me several minutes later. It took me a while to recover from the shock, knowing what could have happened. Bruce's dad fixed my brakes. Neither I, nor my bike, was too badly damaged. I didn't tell my mother for about a week.

When I was about 10 I remember a particular grocer's shop in Isleworth, where, if I was lucky, the owner would give me a chocolate finger biscuit. We were in the shop one day and I happened to mention to Mum that she owed me sixpence.

"What do you owe your mother?" said the shop owner.

The question required no answer and anyway I couldn't think of one. I can recall having a ration book with coupons that the shopkeeper would cut out in exchange for rationed items. And it was in Isleworth High Street, probably in a school holiday when there wasn't any bombing, that I first saw my mother wearing trousers. The war led to many changes.

10

After the War – I meet my new dad

Once war was over I was back in London with my mother. I wasn't told anything about my Dad and I don't remember asking. I was quite unaware of my mother's financial position or indeed her emotional or personal life: such details are not usually known by 11-year-old sons, especially if they haven't lived with their mother for the previous five years. Mother had been unable to keep our large flat in the house in Isleworth. She had had to give this up along with quite a lot else including her beloved grand piano. Long before the war and prior to her marriage, my mother had studied at the Royal Academy of Music and gained her LRAM. She loved playing the piano and accompanied singers such as Heddle Nash in recitals and concerts. She had worked with the composer, Edmund Rubbra. Music had been a big part of her life ever since St Paul's Girls' School, where Celia Johnson, later to become a famous actress, was one of her friends and where Gustav Holst had been her music teacher. The war had ended all that.

In September I would have to go to school somewhere. My mother entered me for an exam to gain entry to Christ's Hospital School in Horsham, which makes places available to "needy" parents;

this would have meant boarding school again. I remember sitting the exam in a hall not far from Marble Arch. My English was OK, my Latin wasn't tested but the Maths questions I found far too difficult: I didn't get a place at the school. Mum and I lived for a few months in a flat in Hyde Park Mansions, just off the Edgware Road. Actually it was one large room with two screens at one end of the room where we slept, and a wash-basin and small cooker at the other end. On the other side of the Edgware Road, my mother's brother, Tommy, lived in a top floor flat with his wife, Dee, and their Alsatian dog, Jai. I went to play chess with my uncle a few times, but mother never came, as she had fallen out with her brother a while ago over something I knew nothing about. Tommy had been an engineer: he was involved in the design of the bridge over the Thames at Richmond. He hadn't always been so successful, I was told, as he had once decided to build a caravan in his garage, only to find when it was completed that he couldn't get it out of the garage! *C'est la vie.* Whenever I visit Richmond these days, I am reminded that it was at the cinema opposite the end of Richmond Bridge that I saw my first film, Walt Disney's *Bambi*.

One evening, in our little flat, my mother sat me on her knee, and said, "Tony, I have something I need to tell you. Your father has left us. He's still in India, and he won't be coming back."

Naturally, I was shocked but I cannot remember any more reaction or how I responded to this news. I had not seen my father since I was 5, and I hadn't heard from him while at boarding school. I had very few memories of him. I did have a photo, and I could recall a journey when I must have been about 4 or 5, when I sat in the dicky seat at the back of his Triumph car as we drove along Kingston bypass one late, warm, spring evening. Before Isleworth, we had lived in Sutton in Surrey, in Egmont Road, and the only two things I remember there were being very upset when my tortoise escaped through a hole in the garden fence, and being bitten on the ankle by our little terrier dog.

With my horse and with Mum and Dad in the garden of our house in Egmont Road Sutton

To my mother's news I think I said something like, "What are we going to do then?"

Mum didn't answer, maybe because she didn't know, but we had a big hug and quite a few tears. It was not until nearly 50 years later that I learned more about my father.

The next day, Mum and I went to a café nearby and walked over to one of the tables. "There's someone I want you to meet," she said "This is Bob," pointing to a man sitting on the opposite side of the table. He had dark hair, a small moustache and glasses.

"Hello, Tony. Very pleased to meet you," Bob said, as he got up from his seat.

He was tall and well-built and looked strong. The three of us sat down and Bob ordered cups of tea and some sandwiches. I don't remember what we talked about, but I do remember that he made me laugh. It was a favourable first impression.

I later learned that, during the war, Bob had worked in Heavy Rescue, trying to find and rescue people trapped under debris and rubble in bombed buildings in London. It was dangerous and hard work, but he rarely spoke about it after the war ended. While doing this he had met my mother, who was driving ambulances taking rescued and injured people to hospital. With my father away in

India, they had become close friends. Bob Hayland was to become an important part of my life, not only as my mother's partner, but also as my substitute dad. I never saw or had any contact with my biological father again.

It must have been a difficult time for my mother. She had developed a relationship with Bob, and her son's father was not going to return to play any part in her son's life. Having failed to pack me off to another boarding school, she probably realised that I would have to know about Bob, and that the three of us were going to have to get on together, hence the meeting in the café.

Very early in our relationship and while we were still in that part of London, Bob took me just up the road to the Metropolitan Theatre, Edgware Road, to see a show starring Max Miller. I was too young to understand many of his jokes, which was probably just as well, but I loved his colourful, outrageous garments, especially the long, flowery overcoats, and he was obviously very popular with the audience, especially the ladies.

"They call me the cheeky chappy,
The jokes I tell are snappy,
All the pretty girls they smile at me."

The carnival atmosphere in the theatre was something new to me and I have fond memories of that occasion. I am very glad I saw Max Miller in person on stage.

Both my mother and Bob had to find jobs and I had to go to school. We spent the winter of 1946–47 in Lowestoft, in Suffolk. Mum and I moved there because Bob had a job to go to. My memories of Lowestoft are the smell of fish, the cold, the bitter wind and the swing bridge. It was one of the coldest winters on record and we nearly froze in our flat in The Avenue, at Pakefield, in the south of Lowestoft. The sea froze when it was not battering the sea wall defences. At weekends we sometimes went to the most northern part of town and watched the enormous waves crashing against the sea wall with so much force and noise. I had never seen anything like it: the majestic violence of the sea – awesome and terrifying. Occasionally, when it was slightly warmer, Bob liked to have a swim in the sea off Pakefield. One afternoon, Mum and I were trying to keep warm on the beach when Bob emerged from the water. Unfortunately, his woollen swimming trunks, much to his and our embarrassment, began to unravel. Mum quickly found a towel to cover his predicament, as it were, and we soon found ourselves laughing about it. It would not be the last time Bob found himself in a delicate situation, mainly of his own making.

I was sent to Bungay Grammar School as a weekly boarder. I caught the bus in the centre of Lowestoft early on Monday morning, taking with me all I would need for the week, and returned late afternoon on Friday. I quite enjoyed this; Bungay GS was a bit like being in a youth hostel, as we had to do some of the work preparing meals and cleaning.

In my first week at the school I was in the kitchen area when Emily, the lady in charge of all the cooking, turned to me and said, "Tony, would you cut some bread for tea, please." Emily was a kind-hearted, middle-aged lady of ample proportions, who I soon came to realise all the boys really liked. She always wore a large, flowery apron. She had a big smile and was like a communal auntie to us boys.

I looked round and saw several loaves of bread on the work surface. Emily handed me a large bread knife.

"Yes, Miss Rawson." We didn't call her Emily to her face.

What Emily didn't know was that I had never cut a loaf of bread into slices in my life, though she was soon to find out. I held the loaf still with my left hand, then began to use the large bread knife, but I didn't make a very good job of it. My first slice took ages and was hard work, and even then, one end was thick, while the other was thin.

"Oh! My goodness," said Emily, more astonished than cross. "You've not done this before, have you? Here, let me show you. Don't try to press down on the loaf," she said, "not with your hand or with the knife. Use the knife like a saw, and watch where it's going, so you saw straight. Like this," and of course she made it look easy.

After a few botched attempts I became quite proficient. My

second and third loaves were cut into even slices, not too thick, nor too thin. Emily said I had done well and that it must have been down to her teaching. At which she laughed long and loudly. I remember Bungay mainly as the school where I first learned to cut a loaf of bread into slices.

We returned to London when Bob's job came to an end and lived in a couple of flats in Hampstead, one in Hollycroft Avenue, where the bath water was brown when I turned on the taps, another in the next road, Ferncroft Avenue. This was a leafy and pleasant part of Hampstead, though our flats were dingy and cramped. At the weekend, Mum, Bob and I used to walk up West Heath Road to the White Stone Pond and "Jack Straw's Castle". I began to discover Hampstead Heath. On bank holidays there was always a fair on the Heath, just off the Spaniards' Road. Bob was working as a decorator and Mum worked in an office. They didn't have much money coming in. After a few weeks we moved into a top floor flat in Adelaide Road, halfway between Chalk Farm and Swiss Cottage. Now our weekend walks took us to Primrose Hill and sometimes beyond, to Regents Park. Our flat was small, three rooms, basically. My bedroom was no more than a box room. Mum and Bob's room was next door and then there was the largest room which was sitting room, kitchen and washing area combined. The toilet was downstairs.

We still used our Ration Books for some years after the war. I had grown up with rationing: it was what I was used to. Some items were even put on rationing after the war, such as bread and potatoes. When money was scarce, Mum and I used to eat at what were called British Restaurants. They had been started during the war by the Government and were run by local councils to provide cheap meals. There was one in the Finchley Road, near the station, and the meals there were wholesome and quite acceptable. I enjoyed going there. As I said, I had known nothing different.

I had nothing to compare our Adelaide Road flat with, so I was happy enough, though we were somewhat crowded. Towards the end of the war I had listened on the radio to ITMA (*It's that man again*, with Tommy Handley), and I had also enjoyed The Inkspots, an iconic music group, now very dated. In our Adelaide Road flat, in 1947, I tuned in religiously to *Dick Barton – Special Agent* on the radio: it was my favourite piece of escapism. My parents and I listened regularly to Paul Temple, with its haunting theme tune, *Coronation Scot*, and we all liked *Down Your Way*. In the school holidays I listened to *Workers' Playtime*. No television in those days of course, at least not for us, and as with most families the wireless was our main source of entertainment, supplemented by an occasional visit to the cinema. I became engrossed in the novels of John Buchan, *Greenmantle*, *Prester John*, *The 39 Steps* and many more. I enjoyed listening to *Music While You Work* and the bands of Geraldo and Mantovani. All this was as a young teenager, maybe not very exciting by today's standards, but I was quite content. Mum and Dad, as I began to call Bob, took me to a performance in London by the Crazy Gang, including Flanagan and Allen, of *Underneath the Arches* fame. It was brilliant. Above our three rooms was a flat roof where I used to sunbathe and read in the hot summer of 1947. When winter came and with it lots of snow, with a couple of friends I spent most of one day sliding down Primrose Hill and the road next to it, standing on a large piece of corrugated iron, with our chins resting on the leading edge: quite dangerous but great fun and we all survived!

Now that I was back in London, I rediscovered my love of red London buses. Before the war Grandpa and I had regularly caught the No. 37 opposite Isleworth Station on our way to Richmond. Now I decided to find out all the routes of the buses in London, starting with the No. 31, which ran along Adelaide Road. For me the red London buses, plus the underground, epitomise London. I loved living in London when I was young, and all my life I have enjoyed returning. To me it feels like home, even if in recent years there are fewer true Londoners living in London. Some of the bus routes haven't changed: the 73 still goes to Stoke Newington and the 38 to Victoria. I used to love jumping on to the rear platform of the old, red, London buses, which later became the Routemasters, and holding on to the pole and leaning back as you jumped off before it had stopped. And many of the underground lines that I learned to use in the 1950s are the same: the Northern Line is still coloured black on the tube map and still divides at Camden Town for either Edgware or Barnet. Wonderful! Today, new lines reflect the pace of change: the Jubilee Line and the Docklands Light Railway testify to London's continuing development. St Pancras Station, close to my boyhood stamping ground, has undergone a complete redesign and not only looks good, but is very much fit for purpose. I love the John Betjeman statue! Despite the changes, London for me still feels the same today as it did just after the war, although it's much cleaner now.

We lived not far from Lord's cricket ground, and when there was a test series I liked to go on the Saturday of the 2nd test match, queuing to get in, and sitting in the upper stand at the nursery end, where I tried to keep the scorecard. In the summer of 1947, South Africa were the visitors and I saw Compton and Edrich score centuries. The following year we hosted the Australians, and I have fond memories of watching Don Bradman, Keith Miller and Lindsay Hassett, as well as Edrich, Compton, and Alec Bedser, as these were the sporting stars of that era. Sometimes Bob, my new Dad, came to Lord's too. Mother occasionally went to Twickenham with some of her friends, just as she had before the war.

The big sporting event around this time in London was of course the 1948 Olympic Games. We went a couple of times and I saw some of the star athletes at Wembley. I particularly remember seeing the tall, graceful, long-striding, West Indian, Arthur Wint, win the 400 metres and come 2nd in the 800 metres. I was also amazed at Emil Zatopek, not just for winning the 10,000 metres but for making it look really hard work! I probably spent too much time collecting autographs, but I do still remember seeing some great races on the track. My interest in athletics probably began here.

Another hobby, overtaking stamp collecting, that I started around this time, was collecting "paper tops". I used to cut off the newspaper headings, the titles, and keep them, all properly documented and catalogued. There were the national dailies (e.g. *Daily Herald* and *News Chronicle*, both now dead), and Sunday papers (e.g. *The*

Observer, The People), regional papers (such as the *Western Morning News* or the *Yorkshire Post*) and local evening papers (*Leicester Mercury* and in London at that time, *Star, News & Standard*). Whenever we travelled anywhere by car, I would ask if we could stop so that I could pop into a local newspaper shop and buy the local paper, to add to my collection. I never really branched out into foreign titles, as in those days we didn't go abroad. I was quite proud of my somewhat unusual hobby, which must have fed my interest in geography. At its height, my collection of paper tops numbered over 400, but one day, probably around the time I went to university, they were all disposed of. No doubt one of Mum's clearances!

11
Owen's School – the formative years

In 1947 I became a pupil at Dame Alice Owen's School, close by the Angel, in the very heart of London. Alice had narrowly avoided being struck by an arrow and, as thanks for her good fortune, later, in 1613, she founded a school with the help of the Worshipful Company of Brewers. In 1947 it was a boys' grammar school, with the girls' school just across the road, though ne'er the twain were supposed to meet. I began in what was then called the 2nd Year, having had an interview with the Headmaster, Oliver Mitchell, who was impressed by my Latin, but not by much else. My first classroom was next to an outside corridor and adjacent, across the passageway, were the outside toilets. Not very salubrious, and the classroom was quite cold I remember. The school was in a small street sandwiched between two main London roads, St John Street and Goswell Road. The building was quite old, with an impressive facade and three substantial storeys plus a large basement.

At Owen's School I did progress, sometimes due to the teachers and quite often in spite of them. My dismal performance in Woodwork was down to my own lack of ability. All I ever made was a toast rack and a toboggan, which I did find use for on Primrose Hill and later on Parliament Hill. My interest in Science was never great, but the teachers didn't help, not me anyway. One Physics teacher had an eyesight problem so that, when he spoke to you, he was looking at the boy sitting two seats away. Definitely a communication malfunction! Our Chemistry teacher, "Butch" Baker, was aptly named. Once, when he returned from the adjoining "prep" room, he saw one of our class putting some ice down a Bunsen burner. Not recommended obviously, but "Butch" Baker's reaction was swift and severe. He marched up to the offending youth and delivered a straight right to the jaw. Knocked him clean out. There was a collective gasp. We were shocked. The lad went down onto the floor, very nearly hitting his head on the side of the bench. One learned not to cross Mr Baker. And I didn't develop any love or aptitude for science.

One of our French teachers was hard of hearing, so, being inventive as well as cruel, our class rigged up an alarm clock inside one of the desks. When it went off, several minutes before the end of the lesson of course, he was always so pleased to have heard "the bell" that he let us go. My Latin went downhill for the first two years, as we didn't start until the 4th Year. By then what knowledge or skills I had had were largely lost. I struggled to keep up. We had a rather dour Latin master, who had a small moustache that gave him the appearance of having to endure a bad smell. One day as he gave back our homework, he turned to me and said, "Elder, your nought is a little better this week." It was meant as a statement of fact, no humour or irony intended. I have always thought it a classic comment.

As we approached our School Certificate exams, I became more interested in History, English and Geography. But there were still distractions. One Geography master had a habit of throwing chalk up in the air and catching it throughout the lesson. So John Oliver, in our 5th Form class, ran a book on how many times the teacher would throw up and then catch the chalk, and how often he would drop it. John set the odds and we placed our bets. Naturally, there was far more attention paid to the chalk throwing than to the Geography, as we all watched and kept count. At break the bookie paid out, though he usually seemed to win, which is one lesson worth learning at school! My break time was usually spent kicking a tennis ball around on the concrete which served as our "play area", just across the little road at the front of the school; great fun but ruinous to our shoes.

At the start of the 5th Year we were given a Maths teacher we had not had before. He was the head of department and we were probably Set 3 or 4. We sat waiting and he walked in.

"Good morning," he said, as he pulled his gown around him. Not all teachers said that to their classes. He surveyed us. "We haven't met before, have we?" He paused and had a good look round the class. "Let's get one thing clear from the beginning." Then he said slowly and very clearly, "In the summer you are all going to pass your Maths School Certificate."

Nobody said anything, though there were some looks of disbelief. We thought he must be slightly mad, or at best, misinformed about our ability level. For many of us there was no chance we would pass Maths. We had always got low marks, and we knew we weren't very good. We had been told often enough. We looked at one another.

"The man's a fool," I heard Johnny say under his breath.

"What? Don't you believe me?" said Mr Hopkins. "We'll see. All you have to do is to work hard, always do your homework, and listen to what I tell you." He paused. We sat silent. He continued, "I really do believe you can all pass. But to do so, you have to believe it too. So start having faith in yourself and in me." Another pause. "Right, let's make a start."

As the weeks went by, we came to see his point. He made us work hard but he was a first class teacher and we began to think that for some of us his prediction might be right. I know I often spent ages over my Maths homework, trying to work out difficult problems with the help of my mother. Little by little we all began to improve. In the summer we all passed and many of us gained the important "credit" level, which some of us would need for university applications. I learned a lot from that experience, and later I applied those principles both in my teaching and my coaching of athletes. Before you can achieve success you have to believe that you can. With self-belief and a good teacher or coach who believes in you, anything is possible.

A unique feature of Owen's School was the distribution of "beer" money to every pupil at the end of each school year, courtesy of the Brewers' Company. We would take our turn to file into the school entrance hall, past Dame Alice's statue, to be given new coins of the realm, with the older boys receiving the most. At first, as a young pupil, the money was taken home and shown to parents with pride. Senior pupils often spent the money in the nearest pub, sad to say.

My journey to school from Adelaide Road to the Angel was by bus to Camden Town, then either by underground to the Angel or by trolleybus via King's Cross. The tube was always crowded and very hot in the summer, and there was more to see on the trolleybus. I had no school friends who lived near me, so I went on my own. This was one of the downsides of going to a grammar school: boys came from all parts of London, so you were lucky if you happened to have school friends who lived near you. I didn't. So meeting up with mates after school often meant going to Stoke Newington or Golders Green, and returning home somewhat late. But I enjoyed my morning experiences on the bus, tube or trolleybus. It gave me some independence and increased my self-confidence.

I enjoyed living in North West London. Dad took me to watch Chelsea when he could and I became a lifelong supporter. The first match I saw at Stamford Bridge was in November 1945. I was 11. Dad and I saw Chelsea play Moscow Dynamo, a very famous club and the first team to come to England after the war. The score was 3–3. The crowd was huge, officially nearly 75,000, though I heard that many more managed to get in. It was very crowded and difficult to see, standing on the terraces. I wish I'd kept the programme from that match. After that Dad used to take me to Chelsea whenever he could, either in his old red van or we caught the 31 bus. Dad was a keen football fan: he had been at the first ever Cup Final at Wembley in 1923, when Bolton beat West Ham. Over 120,000 spectators were there that day and Dad told me about the policeman on his white horse, "Billy", who gradually moved the crowd off the pitch to allow the game to start.

When I was about 14, I was off school unwell for a while but as

I got better the doctor said I should take some exercise, go out for a walk. With Mum and Dad at work, I decided to walk from our flat in Adelaide Road to Chelsea, following the route of the No. 31 bus. Armed with a bottle of orange squash I set off: Swiss Cottage, Maida Vale, Kilburn High Road, Notting Hill, Kensington, Earls Court and finally Chelsea. It took me most of the day, but I didn't feel at all tired. I didn't do anything when I got there. The challenge had been to follow the 31 bus route. I returned by bus and explained to my astonished mother where I had been for my walk!

I enjoyed all sport at school. Our PT teacher (it was called physical training in those days) had been on the books of a famous North London football club and he knew all the tricks. He taught us how to go into a tackle "over the ball" so as to inflict damage to an opponent's leg, not that any of us did this. I played for the school 1st XI at soccer, as a forward, and at cricket where I was wicket keeper. One of the best sportsmen at Owen's while I was there was Del Barclay, a tall, good looking lad who played centre-half for the 1st X1. He was one of those footballers, a bit like Bobby Moore in the 1960s, who could control the game. Del was also a brilliant honky-tonk pianist and one morning when our whole year group was assembled in the main school hall for a lecture and the visiting lecturer was delayed, while we waited, Del entertained us all with his fantastic playing. He was very popular. For our Games' lessons we had to travel by trolleybus to Whetstone to the school's playing fields in Chandos Avenue. A year or two later, on the day we had Games, we went there for the whole day, having lessons in huts in the morning before Games in the afternoon. It must have been a logistic nightmare to timetable. In the summer it was cricket and athletics, and some boys played tennis. A track was laid out on the grass and the houses competed to see who could amass the most points. My house was Hermitage and we usually did well. By the time I was in the 6th Form, I had joined Highgate Harriers, where I made many more friends at the Parliament Hill track.

During one 1st XI school soccer match, I went up to head the ball and was struck by the large opposing centre half and fell to the ground. His shoulder had caught my neck and I lay concussed. After several minutes I played on, as we had no substitutes, but when I began to play for the other side, the Referee and our Sports Master decided I should come off. I changed and made my way home by bus. After a journey of about an hour, eventually I got home but nobody was in. It was Saturday lunchtime and I lay down on the couch in the living room and promptly went to sleep. Mum came in some while later and was surprised to find me at home already and asleep. She wasn't sure what to do, but decided to let me carry on sleeping. I woke up just before lunchtime on Sunday! I had slept for almost 24 hours. Mum, of course, didn't know that I had been concussed. I emerged none the worse for this experience but today I think teachers would be more likely to take greater care of a schoolboy footballer injured in this way.

Brian Martin was our school 1st XI goalkeeper and also a good boxer. In one match this proved very useful. The opposing centre forward was putting his weight about, and he bundled over two or three of our players.

"Leave him to me," said Brian.

Soon after, a cross came in from the winger; Brian kept one eye on the ball and the other on the centre forward. He waited and made sure that the centre forward arrived at the same time as the ball and, as he caught the ball with one hand, with the other he delivered a short, hard punch to the solar plexus. The forward went down, clutching his stomach and complaining to the Referee, who had seen nothing. He was less aggressive after that.

Two other Chelsea games that I particularly remember were the FA Cup semi-finals against Arsenal in 1950 and 1952. In the first of these, Mum, Dad and I were standing on the terraces at White Hart Lane and Chelsea went 2–1 ahead. Standing directly in front of us was a very annoying little man, an Arsenal supporter (no segregation of supporters in those days), who threw his scarf in the air when Arsenal scored and kept shouting, "Yes, Yes, come on you Reds!"

My mother found it hard to contain her feelings and, as he became more vociferous, she became more angry and, in the general hubbub after a goalmouth incident, she deliberately brought both hands down hard on the little man's head, knocking off his hat. As he tried to pick up his hat, my mother turned away, continuing to cheer, so he couldn't possibly know who was responsible. It may not be generally known, but I can confirm that my mother's actions that day were the beginning of football hooliganism! Unfortunately, Arsenal equalised in the last minute with a Leslie Compton headed goal.

Chelsea players in those days included Roy Bentley, Peter Sillett and "Chopper" Harris. I went on my own to the semi-final replay also at Tottenham's ground. This time I was standing at the front, directly behind the goal, very close to the pitch. Late in the game, with the scores level, an Arsenal player pushed the ball slowly towards the Chelsea goal. I watched the ball coming towards both me and the goal. I knew what I had to do: leap over the little wall and on to the pitch and kick the ball away. I so wanted to, but I didn't. The ball trickled slowly into the net: Arsenal had scored. Had I stopped the goal, I guess the consequences for me would have been horrendous, so although "we" lost, it was probably just as well I stayed where I was.

We also went to the semi-final in 1952, also at White Hart Lane and again drawn, this time 1–1. Arsenal won the replay. At Chalk Farm there was a café, run by an ardent Chelsea supporter, and he had a notice outside the café for years which said, "Free meal for all my customers when Chelsea win the FA Cup."

We all said, "He's pretty safe there!"

It was another 15 years before Chelsea finally made it to the Cup Final, and their first win was not until 1970, when they beat their arch-rivals, Leeds United. The phrase "The agony and the ecstasy" well sums up what it is to be a life-long Chelsea supporter. I used to enjoy the times when Chelsea had won, and over the loudspeakers they played, "Who's sorry now?"!

In the 5th year at Owen's, we had a Welsh form master, Mr James, with whom we all got on really well. He was a lovely, quiet man with a gentle humour. Two of us wanted to go to the England v Italy match that was being played, again at Spurs' ground, one

Wednesday afternoon, so we decided to bunk off school, but to do it officially. Just before lunch Alan went to the school secretary, said he was feeling unwell and was allowed to go home. I went to Mr James having rubbed chalk into my face to make me look really pale, and said I felt unwell, and could I be excused school for the afternoon.

"Of course, son," he said.

The ground was packed and we only just managed to get a vantage point by perching on a ledge where we crouched down to watch the match. I remember the chants that day: "Oggie – Oggie – Oggie: oi oi oi;

Oggie – oy – Oggie – oy;

Oggie – Oggie – Oggie: oi oi oi!"

It was a good match and ended 1–1.

Next morning as I walked into the classroom, Mr James looked at me and said, "Did you enjoy the match, laddie?"

I didn't know what to say, so I said nothing and went to my place and sat down. He was still smiling at me. He knew. No punishment or reprimand was necessary. He knew that I knew that he knew. Sufficient. Lovely man!

In the summer before going into the 6th Form, a group of us from school went, with one of the masters in charge, on a potato picking "holiday" in Yorkshire. We stayed on a camp in some very basic huts and spent most of each day breaking our backs, digging out potatoes. In my hut, on the wall behind my bed, some girls had written their names and addresses, saying, "Contact us." We guessed they were last week's spud pickers. We had our bicycles with us, so my mate, Morgan, and I decided that at the weekend we would cycle and surprise these girls. (These days they would have left their mobile number!)

Our camp was near Bawtry and the girls' addresses were in Mexborough, not far away. On Sunday morning, Morgan and I set off. The first part of our journey was fine: beautiful countryside, not much traffic but it was very hot and we soon tired. Worse, I got a puncture in my back wheel and, although we tried, we couldn't mend it. What were we to do? We gave up thoughts of the girls, ate our sandwiches sitting on a grassy bank and tried to work out how to get back to the camp. We couldn't cycle, so we decided to try to hitch – but with two bicycles? And on Sunday? It seemed unlikely, but as we waited beside a road that was for long periods devoid of any traffic at all, a large Co-op lorry came into view and as we waved at it he pulled up.

"What's the problem, boys?" the driver enquired.

"We need to get back to where we're staying, in Bawtry," I said. "But I have a puncture. Can you help us?" We explained that we had tried to mend it without success.

"I've got a call to make, then I'm heading for Doncaster," he said. "You might be able to catch a train to Bawtry from there. I can take you. Do you want to hop in?"

"Yes, thanks a lot," we said.

Doncaster sounded better than being stuck out where we were, though we had no idea what we would do when we got to Doncaster. The lorry driver loaded our bikes inside the back of his lorry, we got in the cab and he set off. After he had delivered a package just up the road, he drove on to Doncaster and left us, with our bicycles, near the station. We thanked him profusely.

"We haven't any money," I said to Morgan. "How are we going to catch a train without any money?"

As we stood there, looking and feeling forlorn, a police car drew up. "Got a problem, lads?" the PC said, seeming more helpful than censorious.

It was the second time we had been asked that question that afternoon. We explained our dilemma, and the PC said that if he could speak to our teacher back at the camp, to confirm our identities, he would lend us the money to catch the train.

"Thanks, that's very helpful," we both said.

We gave the camp phone number to the PC and he spoke to our teacher.

"All's well," the PC said. And he gave us the money for the fare. An hour or so later we arrived back at Bawtry with our bikes, to be greeted by a surprisingly cheerful teacher.

"Trust you two to get into a fix," he said.

We hadn't visited the girls, and they had no knowledge of our mission or misfortunes. They would never know what they had missed! It is the only time I have ever been lent money by a policeman! It was back to the potatoes on Monday.

Before I joined the 6th Form we moved to Boscastle Road, off Highgate Road, not far from Parliament Hill. We had far more space, though it was only a flat on the first and second floors. Our lounge, (where I had gone to sleep after my football concussion!) was huge compared with what I had been used to. There was a large marble fireplace and in the centre of the high ceiling was a kind of candelabra. "Very grand," Dad said. I had a good-sized bedroom on the top floor. The journey to school was a similar distance but now I caught the bus in Highgate Road before passing through Kentish Town to Camden Town or Kings Cross by bus before transferring to the tube to the Angel.

It was in the 6th Form that I found my studies more rewarding and enjoyable. My interest in History was developed by "Dickie" Dare, who was a very effective teacher who ensured we were organised and knew what we needed to know. He didn't encourage us to be inventive or to take the initiative or do any research. He was always in control. From him I learned how to write a good history essay. He didn't get us to think or to face issues or discuss with each other or reach our own conclusions. But he made the history interesting. Somewhat unusually, we studied the medieval period, which, among other things, involved reading an account of the Hundred Years' War in French. When I told my mother, she said she had studied German history in German when she was at St Pauls Girls' School and that, once a week at lunch, there was a French table and a German table on which the girls could speak only that language while having lunch. Much later I was to hear of schools who chose to teach some individual subjects in a foreign language, Geography in Spanish for example, when apparently not only did Spanish exam results improve, but Geography's did too.

I enjoyed studying English at Advanced level. We read several

Shakespeare plays, including *Antony and Cleopatra* and *The Winter's Tale*, which I went to see in the West End, with John Gielgud playing Leontes. We also read the poetry of Keats, novels by a range of authors and Chaucer's *The Canterbury Tales*, which we were taught to read aloud in the original old English, which was fun. There was nothing modern as would be the case today. I enjoyed the debates that our teacher, Mr Smith, organised. I remember being quite unpopular in one of our debates when vehemently advocating the case that Communists should be allowed to take their place in the House of Commons if so elected. Communist Willie Gallacher had just lost his seat at the 1950 election. I felt I was being liberal and democratic in my views, and not in any way Communist. After all, Bolshevik Lenin had closed down Russia's elected Constitutional Assembly in 1917 when he didn't like the result!

In the Sixth Form at school

The inventiveness of young people was demonstrated one evening at a London theatre. A party of 6th Formers were watching a play. There were about twenty of us occupying seats in the back two rows of the Upper Circle. Late in the Third Act, our teacher realised that we were going to miss our coach's scheduled departure time if we waited until the play ended. He decided we would have to leave early but very quietly, so he said we should file out one by one without disturbing the rest of the audience. He said this to the lad sitting next to him and told him to pass the message on along the row.

"He wants us to exfiltrate," said Stuart, who was sitting next to me. I do like it when students invent new words, especially when they are so accurate.

With Owen's School being very close to the Angel, I often went to Sadler's Wells Theatre before school and "reserved" a seat in the gallery for the evening performance of an opera. This cost five or ten pence in old money, a ridiculously small amount. My lifelong love of opera probably began here, though I was also influenced by the concerts in London given by such stars as the Italian tenor, Beniamino Gigli, to which my parents took me. Gigli was the Pavarotti of his day and I remember being spellbound at the sound of his voice and the amazing notes he was able to produce. I also enjoyed many of the arias he sang, and it wasn't long before *La Bohème* became my favourite opera as well as Dad's. Uncle Don, Dad's brother, was also an opera buff, being a member of the English National Opera (ENO) and a regular at the London Coliseum. Being a member, he often went backstage to see sets being prepared and to meet some of the stars. My parents also took me to shows in London such as *Annie Get Your Gun*, *Oklahoma*, *Carousel* and others, all of which I enjoyed very much. My mother may have given up her piano, but not her love of music, and this she undoubtedly passed on to me. In the 6th Form and later at University, I often went to a Promenade Concert with mates, as I enjoyed not only the music but also the informality of the Prom audience.

I was roped in to play chess for the school. There were some inter-school matches and a chess tournament for those at school in London. I remember winning some of these encounters but I was certainly no budding "Grand Master"!

Some of the Owen's school prefects, of which I became one, often visited Lyons Corner House at the main Angel junction for a coffee and a natter during a free period. After school, I liked to explore Chapel Street market, an amazing collection of stalls and colourful market traders. Dad had taken me a few times to Petticoat Lane

Market in East London, which I thought was an amazing place: so many stalls, a great crowd of people and a cacophony of stallholders' shouts, though I didn't approve of the stalls selling animals. We often visited markets; in fact, when I was a teenager, Dad and I used to go each Christmas Eve to the markets in Camden Town to buy our Christmas presents. It would be his first day off work and in those days many people took the opportunity to do Christmas shopping on the Eve of Christmas. At Christmas, Owen's 6th Formers went carol singing in the roads just off City Road near the school, raising money and having a good time, though I don't suppose the singing was that great!

All these experiences made me realise that education happens out of school as well as in it. I also learned about responsibility and helping others when I was made Head Boy at Owen's. This was a considerable honour though some duties went with the position, such as representing the school when needed.

It was while I was a 6th Former that I had a very embarrassing experience in London. I had taken a girl friend, Angela, to a rather expensive restaurant near Soho. I must have been trying to impress. As we were ordering, I kept a close mental tally of the mounting cost, noting what Angela was ordering and adding that to mine, as I knew how much money (or how little!) I had with me. No credit cards in those days. By the end of the meal, I knew we were OK and that my limited funds would just cover the cost of our meals. Imagine my horror when the waiter brought me the bill and the amount was far greater than I had calculated and, worse, far more than I had with me. What was I to do? The meal had been to impress my girlfriend; I couldn't now admit that I didn't have enough cash to pay the bill. How embarrassing would that be? Should I ask her for a contribution? Out of the question. But I had to do something. *How could I have been so mistaken in my calculations?* I asked myself.

"Is something wrong?" Angela asked.

What was I to say? "I haven't got enough money to pay the bill." Surely not.

"I think they have made a mistake with the bill," I said, on an impulse.

"Let me see," said Angela, who was quite a forthright sort of girl, one of the reasons I liked her. "This is not our bill; look at what it says; we didn't have that, or that. No, this isn't ours."

I realised that I had only looked at the total. I looked at the bill again, this time with Angela.

At that point one of the waiters came close to our table and I called him over.

"I think there has been a mistake," I bravely said. And I showed him the bill.

He then took it away, only to return a minute later, "I am so sorry, sir. This isn't your bill. I do apologise. I'll be back in a moment."

When he returned he had with him our bill, but he said, "Because of the error, sir, we have reduced your bill. I can only apologise again."

"All's well that ends well," I said to Angela.

But Angela turned to the waiter and said, "So how did the mistake happen, then? Whose bill were we given?"

"I'm afraid you were given the bill for that party over there," and the waiter pointed to a group of four people who had been in the restaurant when we arrived.

I said to Angela, "They've probably been here since breakfast!"

My finances could easily stretch to the correct bill, especially as it was now reduced. I have never returned to that restaurant.

As 6th Formers we had the opportunity to attend the annual CEWC (Council for Education in World Citizenship) conference at the Central Hall in London where we listened to distinguished speakers on a variety of current topics and international issues. This complemented my growing interest in History. After lunch the 6th Form participants broke into seminar groups to discuss the morning lectures. This was great: the debates helped me formulate my own views on some of the issues of the day, and it gave me the opportunity to meet some 17- and 18-year-old girls who, like me, had come primarily to listen and learn. During the tea session, which followed the seminars, I found myself chatting to Jo and Ann.

Jo had dark hair, was petite and attractive, and was dressed smartly in skirt and blouse. She told me she lived in a flat in Hammersmith with her mother. Jo invited me to visit one afternoon soon after, but our date was a total disaster. Being with one girl, alone together in her flat and sitting on the bed, just the two of us, was clearly an opportunity, but I had no idea what Jo might be thinking, and sad to relate, I froze. It was very different from being with several girls and boys in a hall in London. Looking back now, it is embarrassing to realise that she may have wanted me to make a move, but I didn't. We talked: we spoke about our parents and our A levels, and eventually I left. She did write to me when I was at Oxford to tell me she had gained a place at Edinburgh but I never saw her again.

I had also arranged to meet up with Ann. She lived in a different part of London, in Dalston, but we arranged to meet in Trafalgar Square one Friday evening.

"Hi, Tony." Ann had seen me approaching and walked to meet me.

"Hi, Ann, good to see you," I said, and Ann then gave me a kiss on the cheek. Ann was wearing a smart green coat and her long, light brown hair fell over the collar. She was medium height with a good figure. I felt at ease with Ann; I was to find out that she was a naturally warm kind of person, someone who mixed easily, was interested in other people, was a good listener and had a lovely smile. As I held her hand, I said, "Where shall we go? I know quite a nice pub by the station," pointing in the direction of Charing Cross.

"Sounds fine," said Ann, "What have you been up to?"

In the pub we talked about all sorts, her studies and plans and mine, our families, as well as making observations on the other people in the bar. I had a couple of pints of beer and Ann drank gin and tonic. We talked easily and had plenty of laughs. As it became more crowded and noisier, we decided to leave and walked down Villiers Street to the Embankment.

It was a pleasant evening, dry, but colder by the river. We stood and watched some small boats and listened to the sounds of the Thames, and it was then that I had my first taste of gin, as we kissed and held each other tightly. I had my arms around Ann's waist and it seemed the most natural thing in the world, yet I realised I had never held and kissed a girl in this way before. We were oblivious to the noise of traffic roaring past; we didn't say much and I think we could both have spent some time there on the Thames Embankment but, as it became a lot colder, we hurried into Embankment Station.

Ann said there was no need for me to take her home, but I insisted, so I bought my ticket. When we arrived at her house in Mare Street, it was quite late. We had a goodnight kiss on her doorstep and then I set off for home. It was a walk I was to take several times in the next few weeks. Although it was a long way and usually late at night, somehow I didn't mind. The worst part was along Balls Pond Road and St Paul's Road to Highbury Corner, probably because I didn't know this part of London at all well. Then came the Holloway Road, the "Nag's Head", and the long trek up Tufnell Park Road. Meandering through the remaining back streets to Boscastle Road didn't take long, though by then I was usually very tired and cold. I don't think Ann ever realised just how far I had to walk or how long it took, but because of my feelings for her, I just got on with it.

Ann was my first real girlfriend and our relationship lasted several months. I took her to the cinema at Finsbury Park, the Astoria, which had a veritable sky of stars on the ceiling and where we saw Geraldine Chaplin in *Limelight*; we spent a lovely day on Hampstead Heath, ending up at the "Old Bull & Bush", then walking down the hill to Golders Green. On another occasion we watched some cricket on a village green when I borrowed my parents' car for the day. Always relaxed in each other's company, we never said goodbye, just drifted apart. Ann and I went off to different universities and I think we both put our relationship into the bank of experience. We kept in touch for a while, but after going up to Oxford I never saw her again. What did we have: just memories and a sense of what might have been? But that's not so unusual, is it? Maybe it's all part of a useful and necessary apprenticeship. I didn't think that at the time.

My parents and I often went to the cinema on a Saturday night, queuing for the 1s/9ds at The Forum at Kentish Town or at one of the Camden Town cinemas. Dad used to get very annoyed at the pro-American sentiments of some of the films, such as *Halls of Montezuma*, with the Marines' Hymn ending the film with the Stars and Stripes waving across the screen.

"Why do they have to do that?" he would say angrily. "It's arrogant and nationalistic. Who do they think they are anyway?"

When we got back home, hot sausages, coffee and a discussion about the film we had seen became a ritual. I loved these late night chats with Mum and Dad and, though I didn't realise it at the time, I'm sure it must have helped me to develop my ability to think for myself, express my opinions and listen to the views of others. I don't remember any arguments, only discussions and an exchange of views and opinions. I didn't realise at the time how lucky I was to have parents who spent time with me in this way.

When we could afford a summer holiday we went by car to Westgate, next to Margate in Kent. We stayed in a small bed and breakfast guesthouse close to the sea and my memories are of having lots of fun, meeting other families, playing French and proper cricket on the beach and the obligatory ice cream. In the evenings we often went to a bar nearby, where there was an amazing pianist, playing fantastic honky-tonk music.

It was at one of the seaside variety shows that Dad "disgraced" himself! During the interval Dad bought us all an ice cream. What he didn't realise was that while eating his choc ice during the second half of the show, some chocolate fell on to his trousers. It was a hot summer evening and the chocolate melted and spread, all the more so as Dad had a habit of moving his legs about when watching anything intently. Only when we got up to leave at the end of the performance did this embarrassing mess become apparent. It was very brown and very extensive. When she noticed it, my mother was appalled.

"What on earth have you done?" she said to Dad, looking with horror at his crotch area.

Dad hadn't realised that anything was amiss until he looked down. "Oh! Good Lord!" he said. "How awful. That must have been the chocolate."

That's all right then!

No visit to the Gents would have rectified the situation, so we had to make a hasty retreat to our guesthouse and hope the landlady wasn't there when we returned. What mother did with the trousers I have no idea.

There was an incident, one year, when we were driving down the A2 towards Margate in our old Hillman. Mum was in the back; Dad was driving. The roof panel was open.

Mum said, "It's getting a bit windy back here. Could we have the roof thing closed, do you think?"

"Of course," Dad said, "would you slide it back, Tony?"

"Sure," I said.

As I lent up, grabbed hold of the roof panel handle so I could pull it forward, the wind got underneath the panel and lifted it clean off the car! We watched in the mirrors as the panel flew through the air behind us, performing a kind of aerial dance, with cars doing their best to avoid the flying object. Fortunately, the panel landed harmlessly by the side of the road and no one was hurt, and afterwards we could see the funny side and laugh about it.

Another holiday destination was Lyme Regis, which we all loved, especially the tiny cob and harbour. It was here that Dad got very sunburnt one summer and lay on his own in agony all night.

"Serve you right," said my mother, very unsympathetically!

This wasn't the only time Dad did this: he lay far too long in the hot sun on Hampstead Heath one Sunday and ended up looking like a lobster.

We also had holidays at Woolacombe in North Devon, where we enjoyed the massive expanse of beach, and at Beesands in South Devon, a little village close to Start Point and not far from Kingsbridge and Salcombe. Here we stayed in a caravan, virtually on the edge of the beach. They were simple holidays but great fun. We went to Beesands just before I went up to Oxford. I was 19 and went along to watch a preliminary FA Cup game between Beesands and the 3rd XI of one of the larger Devon clubs. As the time for kick off approached, the Referee hadn't arrived. Apparently he had rung to say he would be late. The local officials were keen for the match to start on time and asked over the primitive loudspeaker if anyone was a qualified referee. I had done a course on refereeing, though I hadn't taken any exams, and when I told them this, they said,

"Do you want to referee until the official Ref arrives?"

"Yes, if you think that will be all right," I said.

I was on holiday; I was wearing shorts; I was given a whistle. This is how I came to referee an FA Cup match for all of ten minutes! There was a short pause in the game as I handed over to the proper Referee when he arrived. I told him that there had been no goals and all the players had behaved well. He thanked me and the game went on.

In the evenings, Mum, Dad and I used to go to the little pub in Beesands, where the scrumpy was lethal and where the accents of the darts players was so broad, we often couldn't understand a word they were saying. Some days we walked along the cliff path to Start Point, passing Hallsands, or drove to Slapton or Blackpool Sands, both with lovely sandy beaches. They were good days.

Caravan holidays were all Mum and Dad could afford some years, but they provided a good base for getting out into the local area, at least until it rained! Being cooped up in a caravan while it is pouring with rain is no fun at all.

One day it seemed to rain and never stop. After yet another cup of tea, Mum said, "What are we going to eat this evening? We haven't anything in." We were in a caravan park close to the Pebble Ridge at Westward Ho!

"We could get some fish and chips," said Dad. "Tony and I could go." It was still absolutely pouring, and there was a lake outside the door of the caravan.

"You'll get soaked," Mum said, but she knew there was no real alternative.

Dad and I put on all the waterproofs we had including stout shoes, though even these were soon enveloped by the lake we had to wade through to reach the car.

"What if the car won't start, Dad?" I said.

"Don't say such things, son," Dad retorted.

The car did start and we made our way, pretending we were in an amphibious vehicle, into town. The car park by the slipway was under water and, as we parked, we could see that despite the rain there was a queue at the fish and chip shop! Holiday-makers were standing in the pouring rain to queue for their fish and chips! We sat for a while, waiting for the queue and the rain to subside, which to our surprise they did. We bought skate, my Dad's favourite, and a lot of chips, as we all deserved a good meal! Next day the sun came out!

Right from the start I got on well with my new dad. He and Mum were obviously very fond of each other, and he left it to her to deal with any issues that arose when I needed to be told off for something. He was quite a funny guy, and he had some expressions that I had never heard before. "Well, I'll go to the foot of our stairs" was one of his favourites. He said this when he was surprised by something he had seen or read in the paper. I have since learned that this is a Northern expression, so how he got hold of it I have no idea. "When hell freezes over" was another, in other words, "That's never going to happen."

Mum and I were in the lounge one day and we didn't know where Dad had got too. Suddenly he appeared.

"Where have you been?" said Mum.

"I've only been up the apples," Dad said, "sorting a few things out."

He was by no means a cockney, yet he did come out with rhyming slang occasionally. Snow was on the ground when one of his workmen arrived at work one morning to inform everyone, "Cor it's 'taters out today!"

My Dad replied, picking up on the slang, "Well, would you Adam and Eve it!"

They all had a chuckle. And it was quite common to hear, "I'm on me Jack" or "Let's have a butcher's" or "He told me on the dog". I was told more than once, "Use your loaf, boy." And another favourite saying of Dad's, though not rhyming slang, was, "Never send a boy on a man's errand." He was definitely interesting to live with. On the other hand I didn't intend to follow his example when it was my turn to start shaving, as Dad always used a lethal looking cut-throat razor.

Living just off the Highgate Road in NW3, we were fortunate to have various travel options available close by. Buses from Parliament Hill Fields heading for Central London passed along Highgate Road, and not far away at Kentish Town was the Northern Line of the Underground. We also used Gospel Oak quite frequently. This was a station on a line that ran from Broad Street in East London to Richmond in the West. The stations on this line were old and somewhat neglected, and the trains weren't much better, but it was a very convenient and usually reliable route: it took us to Finchley Road, close to where my mother worked, and Willesden Junction gave us access to White City and the athletics meetings in the 1950s. I came to love Gospel Oak, with its quaint name and draughty platforms. From the station it was a short walk to Parliament Hill, the lido, the athletics track and Hampstead Heath. Today that railway line and the stations on it have been modernised and transformed, being part of the impressive London Overground. From Gospel Oak you can now access Stratford, as I did in 2012 en route to the London Olympic Park. Travelling along that line and through Gospel Oak brought back many happy memories.

Not everyone shared my liking for Gospel Oak. Just beyond the bus terminus at Parliament Hill Fields was Highgate West Hill, where I used to deliver the weighty Sunday newspapers to those who lived in the opulent blocks of flats that adjoined West Hill. It was an impressive hill, giving access on the side opposite the flats to the Highgate Ponds and the Heath and, at the top, to Highgate Village, "The Flask" public house and Highgate School. John Betjeman lived on West Hill and in his autobiographical *Summoned by Bells*, he wrote:

> *"Here from my eyrie as the sun went down,*
> *I heard the old North London puff and shunt,*
> *Glad that I did not live in Gospel Oak."*

Dad took me on several occasions to Speakers' Corner in Hyde Park. I was fascinated, listening to all these guys, and occasionally women, standing on little platforms, spouting away, telling the world their views and opinions in no uncertain terms. A lot of it was extreme, much of it was rubbish, but I loved listening to it all. Some was political, some religious and there was usually plenty of heckling. Free speech is one of the features of a democracy and this there was in abundance at Speakers' Corner on Sunday mornings.

One evening Dad was attempting to drive home from Central London in a typical London smog, a "pea souper" as it was sometimes called, and he couldn't see a thing. He decided he would follow a bus that he knew went right past the end of our road. He diligently drove in the wake of this bus, following it as closely as he could. All went well, until he realised it had stopped. When he got out to see what the problem was, he realised that he had followed the bus into the bus garage! Later, when we lived in Finchley, he used to come home from work on the Northern line to Finchley Central. One evening he fell asleep on the train, waking only when the train had reached Barnet, the end of the line. There was nothing for it, but to travel back the few stops to Finchley Central. Unfortunately he fell asleep again and woke amid the hubbub of central London! This time, on his return journey, he sensibly travelled standing!

After my A levels, I stayed at school for one term until Christmas to do my Oxbridge entrance exams and then left, as I needed to earn some money. After a brief stint with St Pancras Borough Council, I worked for a while for Dad, whose building company was decorating a couple of large houses in Belsize Park. I was shown the ropes by two of his workmen, one of whom, George Hanks, a lovely guy, probably in his forties, was lightning fast in plastering or sizing, or painting walls or ceilings. He knew I couldn't keep up with him, so I think he went even faster, but it was fun to try. Ernie, somewhat older, was a general labourer.

"Can you bring over the tarpaulin from the other house?" Dad said to him one day.

When he arrived, Ernie, never very good with words, said, "I've got the tar-po-le-on, Guv."

One fellow only worked for Dad for a short while, as he was permanently miserable.

"He made sin seem cheerful," said George, who often came out with witty comments.

It was while working for my Dad that I met his son, Eric. I knew nothing of Dad's marital background. Eric and I worked together for a few days and we got on fine.

Unfortunately, Hayland Bros., the building and decorating business Dad had started, initially with his brother, Victor, began to run into difficulties, chiefly because customers wouldn't pay what they owed for work that had been done. Then Dad couldn't pay his workmen. Sometimes Dad would put three coats of paint on walls when he had only quoted for two, because he thought it would look better. Eventually and reluctantly, Hayland Bros. died a death. Dad was loath to lay off George, his best workman, but George understood and soon got more work. Not having to find the cash to pay his workmen at the end of each week was a relief, not only for Dad, but for Mum too, who shared the weekly wages trauma.

Fortunately, Dad was able to start work for a company in London that owned lots of large properties. He was put in charge of planning and costing the renovation and decoration of older properties bought up by this company. The job took him to some interesting parts of London, such as Kensington and Pimlico. He enjoyed the work, and came to terms with being an employee rather than the employer, receiving a pay packet instead of trying to fill others' pay packets.

One Christmas, Mum and I were at home; Dad was at the firm's Christmas party. As it approached midnight, we wondered why he hadn't yet returned. Suddenly there was a knock on our front door. Mum went to see who it was.

"Mrs Hayland?" the policeman asked.

"Yes, what is it?" Mum answered.

"It's your husband, Mrs Hayland. There's been an accident. It's not too serious. But Mr Hayland has been taken to St George's Hospital at Hyde Park Corner. His car collided with a bollard in Hyde Park."

I had joined Mum at the front door and heard this.

"Is he badly hurt?" Mum asked.

"I'm told it isn't too serious," the PC said, "but you'll have to contact the hospital yourself in the morning."

"All right, we will. Thank you for coming to tell us," Mum said, and the PC left.

When we rang the hospital, they said we could visit after lunch. Mum and I drove up to London from Finchley and into Hyde Park near Lancaster Gate. Suddenly we saw a demolished bollard.

"Look, there it is," I said. We both imagined him driving into it. We continued on our way.

"Oh! My goodness. There's another," Mum said.

We saw in all four bollards that had been damaged, presumably by errant vehicles.

At the hospital we were directed to the ward he was in. Dad was sitting up in bed. Mum asked him how he was and what had happened.

"I don't really remember. I was driving home; there was a bang; the car came to a halt and I must have passed out. Next thing I knew I was here in hospital," Dad said.

We told him about the damaged bollards, which he found quite amusing. He also said that the police had come to take a statement from him, and that Matron had sent them away, saying he wasn't well enough to be interviewed. This was because he had obviously been drinking at the party, and Matron didn't want the police to pin a drink-driving charge on him. Things were a little different in those days. Dad spent the following night in hospital and we collected him the next day.

Some weeks later he had to go to court, where he was defended by an AA (Autombile Association) solicitor.

"How much had you had to drink that evening, Mr Hayland?" the prosecutor asked.

The AA solicitor jumped to his feet.

"I object," he said, "My client has not been charged with driving under the influence of alcohol. Whether he had been drinking is irrelevant."

"Agreed," said the magistrate.

Dad was found guilty of driving without due care and attention, which seemed a reasonable verdict as he had driven into and demolished a bollard. He recovered from the accident and his car was soon repaired.

This wasn't the only time Dad was involved in a road accident. On the North Circular Road, where three lanes approaching some traffic lights became two lanes beyond the junction, his red van collided with another vehicle, as he refused to give up his piece of road. I had to go to the yard, where his smashed up van had been taken, to recover his glasses, which I found in the footwell covered in blood. Dad wasn't the best of drivers. Later, when he and Mum had retired and they lived in Devon, his driving nearly gave her a heart attack on more than one occasion. But he always blamed the other drivers, of course! When he parked next to the quay in Bideford, we always insisted on getting out of the car before he drove too close to the water!

I am glad to be able to say that during my formative years, growing up in London, I managed to avoid getting into trouble with the police, except on one occasion, and then it wasn't my fault! I was in Kentish Town one evening standing outside the Post Office at the junction of Kentish Town Road and Prince of Wales Road, not far from Camden School for Girls. It was early evening and suddenly a fight broke out on the wide pavement in front of me between two groups of youths. There must have been about a dozen 16- or 17-year-olds altogether. It was a mass fistfight with some kicking, and I stood back against the wall of the post office, partly to watch and also being too scared to move. I was about 15 at the time. Suddenly a police car and a Back Maria roared up. The youths were cornered and I watched as about six of them were dumped in the back of the Black Maria, but then, so was I. My protests were ignored, and I was carted off to the nearby police station. I was very scared, even though I knew I had done nothing wrong. Once there, I think my manner and behaviour must have convinced the custody sergeant that I was nothing to do with the youths, most of whom were known to the police anyway. I had to give my details but my story was believed and after a couple of hours, Mum was rung and I was allowed to leave. It had been my first brush with the law.

I tended to avoid the pubs in Kentish Town and Camden Town, as they weren't the sort of places I wanted to be or to take a girlfriend. Dad bought me my first pint, along with a jar of cockles, which we shared, at the "Horseshoe" pub in Heath Street just up from Hampstead Tube Station when I was 17 and in the 6th Form. Later, I enjoyed some pleasant evenings in "The Spaniards" with Mum and Dad or with Jenny. At the White Stone Pond was "Jack Straw's Castle" and just down the road was "The Old Bull and Bush". Dad and I had some pleasant evenings in "The Flask" in Highgate Village, and another pub I used to visit was "The Load of Hay" nearer Golders Green. I have fond memories of these warm and friendly pubs, all with interesting histories.

We spent several days at the Festival of Britain in 1951. Two of my South African cousins came over to stay with us during the Festival. Sheila and Betty, slightly older than I was, were Mabel's, my grandmother's sister's, daughters. Both were "liberal" in their views on the politics of South Africa, being opposed to Apartheid and the way blacks were treated in their country. They later became friends with the liberal politician, Helen Suzman, but they had to be careful, as the authorities clamped down on any too obvious opposition.

I showed Sheila and Betty around London, during which I discovered places I hadn't known existed, so it was an education for me as well. One evening we all went to a show in a West End theatre. We had seats in the Stalls and, at the interval, two black men stood up a few rows in front of us, about to go for an interval drink. Sheila and Betty froze in their seats. Each one grabbed my arm tightly. At first, I didn't know why. Then I saw their gaze, directed at these two black guys, very smartly dressed, making their way to a bar. What had spooked my South African cousins was that they had never experienced anything like this before. In South Africa under the Apartheid laws, blacks and whites did not mix, did not socialise and certainly did not attend the same theatres. Even though Sheila and Betty were very liberal in their outlook and views, the experience had been unnerving. They soon got over it and were able to talk about it.

During the 1950s and the Apartheid era, Sheila in particular did all she could to assist young black South Africans, especially any who wanted to come to study in England. Such students were granted an exit permit, which entitled them to leave South Africa, but they could not return. One such lad I met in London where he was studying law at University College. Sheila wanted to write to him, but she dared not, as letters to such exiled students would be censored, so she sent her letters to him via me, and he was very grateful to receive them. Back in South Africa, Sheila's father was stopped by the police one night, when he was taking their black housekeeper back in his car to the township where she lived. Maggie was in the back of the car, but as a result of his actions, he was charged under the Immorality Law. Sheila told us many stories like this; thankfully Apartheid was eventually brought to an end.

Several of us were in the Prefects' Room at school in February 1952, when we heard on the radio the news of the King's death. It was agreed that I should go and tell the Head, Mr Garstang, who probably wouldn't have had the radio on in his office. He prepared a special Assembly for the following morning. I had been too young to know anything about the abdication crisis, so George VI was the only monarch I had had any experience of and I had seen pictures of the part he and his wife had played during the war, especially in London during the blitz. Elizabeth, his eldest daughter, was in Kenya at the time of her father's death, staying at Treetops, a game reserve that I was to visit many years later. She was now Queen and returned home the next day.

The system for Oxbridge entrance was exams at individual Cambridge and Oxford colleges. At Sidney Sussex College, Cambridge I was interviewed by historian David Thompson. I was to read more of his work later. I sat an exam at Lincoln College, Oxford and as I had expected, I met several "toffs", obviously lads from public schools, judging by their dress and accents. But I got a surprise at breakfast. We had started on the cereal and black coffee was being served, when the guy sitting next to me lent in my direction and said, in a very broad Yorkshire accent,

"Eh! Lad, is there any milk in't jug?" pointing to a white jug to my left.

We were in fact a very mixed bag.

I didn't know what to expect from these entrance exams and interviews. We had had no specific preparation at Owen's School, unlike those from Independent Schools who were usually groomed to perform well. At one college I had to write a two-hour essay on "The Noble Savage". A mate of mine from Owen's had impressed his university interviewer by telling him that his specialist interest was "Medieval sewage in the North of England."

"But you don't know anything about medieval sewage," I said.

"I know. But then neither did he!" Joe said.

And on the strength of that interview, Joe was given a place. As the weeks went by, I had almost forgotten entrance exams and interviews. Then one Saturday morning I was still in bed when my mother brought up the post.

"It's got an Oxford postmark," Mum said. "Go on, open it."

Suddenly wide awake, I sat up and tore open the letter.

"What's it say?"

"It's from St Catherine's Society. They're offering me a place! Wow!"

Big hug! "That's great. Well done! I'm so pleased for you," Mum said.

In October my life was about to take on an entirely new direction.

Overall, Owen's School had been good for me. I had managed to put together enough O and A levels to be considered for a place at university. I had even performed in public, when as a member of the chorus, I sang the Anvil Chorus in a school production of Verdi's opera *Il Trovatore* in St Pancras Town Hall! At Owen's I had made a lot of good friends, some of whom I was to meet again at Oxford. I had tried to make a contribution to the life of the school and I was proud to have been Head Boy and represent the school in different sports. The school has long since left its old site close to the Angel and is now situated at Potters Bar in Hertfordshire. I recently attended a specially arranged concert at the Royal Albert Hall to celebrate the 400th anniversary of the school and it was obvious how far it has come since my day.

Shortly before leaving Owen's but before going up to Oxford, I became involved in the Derek Bentley case. It became a "cause celèbre". Bentley, who was 19, and another lad, 16-year-old Christopher Craig, had been on a roof in South London, intent on burglary, and were confronted by the police. Unknown to Bentley, Craig had a gun, and when one of the policemen told him to hand over his gun, Bentley said, "Let him have it, Chris." Unfortunately, there was a shot and PC Miles died. At their trial, the jury found both lads guilty of murder and asked for clemency for Bentley, but because Chris was too young to be hanged, the judge decided that Bentley should pay the price, being an accessory, though not the one to fire the fatal shot. The view of those, like myself, who campaigned on behalf of Bentley, was that he had told Chris to hand over the gun, and he was of very low intellect and should not be made the scapegoat. There were meetings and protests and much press coverage. Many MPs urged the Home Secretary to show clemency. It was all to no avail and Derek Bentley was hanged in January 1953. A long campaign to clear his name succeeded in 1998, when Bentley received a posthumous pardon.

The summer of 1953 soon came and went. It was the Stanley Matthews Cup Final, Everest was climbed by Edmund Hillary, and the new Queen Elizabeth was crowned. It was also the year Stalin died and Playboy magazine had its first nude centrefold – in the shape of Marilyn Monroe! The 1950s was the decade I left school, went to university and started my first full time job, though some of that was in the future. I was classified D4 in my medical for National Service: my doctor said I must not get water in my ear because I had had a mastoid operation when a child. I had read some of the books recommended by St Catherine's for those about to take Modern History. In September, I found some digs along the Abingdon Road, just over Folly Bridge, not far from St Catz, and in October, off I went.

12
Oxford

I thoroughly enjoyed my three years at Oxford, though, on reflection, I probably enjoyed it too much and didn't get the balance right between work and play. I didn't fully appreciate how fortunate I was to have been given a place at Oxford University. I certainly didn't realise how quickly the three years of our degree course would go. Each term was only eight weeks, so we should have been capable of doing a fair amount of academic work in that time. But it was all so new. And the time went so quickly. I hadn't been prepared for so much independence and freedom. And there were so many distractions. Reasons? Or excuses? You decide!

Each week there was work to do as well as sport and social activities. My degree involved studying what was called Modern History, which began with the Romans (it was modern as opposed to ancient, not medieval). The Oxford system relies heavily upon weekly tutorials, when the student (or undergraduate, as they are known in Oxford) reads out an essay written on a title given him the week before. The tutor may not be from your own College. My first tutor was at University College in the High, and my first essay, set in my first week, was "'The Romanisation of Britain was skin-deep': Discuss". Ouch! I had virtually no knowledge of Roman Britain, so I had to visit the St Catz library and the Radcliffe Camera, the university History Library, read and ingest as much as I could, make some readable notes, think, try to make sense of it all, and write an essay which answered the question set! All in a week! I hadn't been prepared for this. At school I had been used to my teacher telling us all the main facts prior to my essay writing! We hadn't been expected to find things out for ourselves. The Oxford tutor is not looking for the right answer (there are very few of these in History), but hopes to find evidence of research, understanding, originality, evidence and conclusions. I think I may have disappointed my first tutor.

Some experiences with tutors over the three years were quite amusing. One tutor, whose house in North Oxford I had to visit once a week for a term in my second year, was known to be an inveterate homosexual. The first week was all right. In week two, I cycled from my digs just off the Iffley Road in pouring rain. I arrived absolutely soaked and, as the front door opened, I was greeted with, hands in air, "Oh! My poor boy, you're soaked through; look at you; come in; you must take off your trousers." It was just as well I had been warned! I declined to accept his kindness, preferring wetness to the alternative.

Sometimes two of us went together for a tutorial and this was the case when Geoff Connell and I had tutorials with Agatha Ramm at Somerville College on Wednesday afternoons. We were studying European History 1815–1914 as one of our special modules. In those days there were several women-only colleges, Somerville being one of them. Miss Ramm was therefore more used to having females to tutor, and it was widely acknowledged that female undergraduates worked rather harder than many of their male counterparts. There were fewer places at Oxford for girls in those days, so the standard expected of them was somewhat higher. Geoff and I were ushered into her study. Geoff was from Connah's Quay in North Wales. He and I both played football for St Catherine's, though at opposite ends of the field, as he was our goalkeeper.

Miss Ramm handed each of us a long reading list.

"Do you have French or German?" asked Miss Ramm.

"A liitle French," we both offered.

"Oh dear! Well, never mind," she said. "Have a look at the

reading list I've just given you."

Geoff and I looked at the list of some 20 books, and glanced at each other. *We're never going to be able to read all of these.* We asked which books were the most important for us to read, and when Miss Ramm picked out about ten, we asked which we should start with. Looking somewhat concerned at this, Miss Ramm identified three or four from the list. Geoff and I thanked her. We could cope with three or four books, at least to start with.

Our sessions with Agatha Ramm went quite well, though I sensed we didn't quite match up to her expectations, our essays not reaching the level she was used to. It was in about the 5th week of term that Geoff said to her, "Miss Ramm, I wonder whether we could rearrange the time of our tutorial next week, as Tony and I are going to the Rugby match on Wednesday afternoon."

"Oh dear! I don't think that will be possible," she said sternly, suddenly sitting more upright. No doubt the girls that she tutored didn't dare to make such requests. "I'll have to speak to your College tutor about this."

"That's fine," said Geoff, "he's coming with us to the match." It was the annual encounter between the University XV and Major Stanley's XV.

"Oh well, I suppose so; when can you come?" And we rearranged the time of our tutorial.

At the end of the term, Agatha Ramm was surprised and not a little embarrassed I suspect to receive a large bunch of flowers from her two male undergraduate tutees.

"Oh dear! Thank you," she said, almost blushing. And we got a rare smile.

Our St Catherine's tutor was medieval historian George Holmes who was a lovely guy. He helped us greatly by the supportive way he conducted his tutorials and by his wise advice. He was always smiling and gave the impression that he enjoyed listening to us. In one bizarre tutorial, my good friend, Colin Barham, and I were visiting Peter Dickson, another history tutor from St Catherine's. Colin began to read out his essay, while our tutor and I sat and listened. Colin had read for about three minutes, when Peter Dickson got up from his chair, went over to one of his bookcases ("Carry on reading," he said), took down one of the books, opened it to a particular page, and then read along with Colin. It was very embarrassing, and our tutor was annoyed and disappointed at such blatant plagiarism. Colin was more careful in future.

Lectures also played a part in the life of an Oxford student, though attendance was entirely voluntary. The lecture programme was organised by the different University faculties and the lectures were delivered either in the university main lecture hall or, more often, in the lecturer's own college. By far the best two series of lectures that I attended were given by Alan Taylor (Magdalen) and Hugh Trevor-Roper (Christ Church). Taylor's lectures were amazing: they began at 9.00 am, which was quite unusual, but there was always full attendance, both at the beginning and, remarkably, at the end of the 8-week series too.

A J P Taylor, later to become nationally famous for his popular television lectures, never used notes; he gave his lectures on different aspects of recent modern history "off the cuff". His undergraduate audience was spellbound. Occasionally he would delve into a pocket and retrieve a piece of paper from which he would read a quote. Apart from that it was 50 minutes of masterly originality. He was often provocative in his conclusions but that only made his lectures even more appealing. For many of us historians, listening to A J P Taylor was the highlight of the week.

Hugh Trevor-Roper lectured at Christ Church College on the Stuarts and on Cromwell and the Commonwealth. He was always entertaining and would often lace his lecture with an amusing aside; I had the impression that these were things that he found amusing rather than anything he thought might amuse us. Then he would spend a few moments giggling at what he had just heard himself say! Other than A J P, he was the best history lecturer that I attended. He had such a thorough grasp of his subject that you could not help but be impressed.

Many lecturers were dull and their lectures disappointing and unhelpful. Often it appeared they were merely regurgitating their most recent book and I found it more useful to read the book, or the parts that I needed to read. When my mother came to visit, I asked her if she would like to attend one of the university lectures. She said that would be great, but she was quite worried.

"What if he asks me a question?" she said.

I reassured her that the lecturers didn't ask questions, so, suitably gowned, as all undergraduates attending lectures had to be, we spent an interesting hour in the main lecture hall one Friday morning, listening to a history lecture.

With Mum in Oxford

Each week we did our essay preparation in a library or in our digs, usually both. In those days each essay was handwritten and the pressure to achieve the required standard in the allotted time was considerable. And the tasks were not made any easier by the many distractions available.

Unless you were a scientist or a medic, it was generally understood that each afternoon would be devoted to sport or some other non-academic pastime. I found it quite easy to occupy my time from lunch to tea with football or cross-country in the winter and track athletics with occasional cricket in the summer. St Catherine's had some good footballers, so apart from an occasional outing in the 1st XI, I found myself playing in what became an unbeaten 2nd XI along with some of my best friends, Norman Goddard our captain, Alan Wortley, Dick Beardsley and our goalkeeper Geoff Connell, of whom I wrote earlier.

Freshers' Cross Country 1953: I am just behind Tony Jaffe (187)

St Catherine's undefeated Soccer 2nd XI

Both in winter and summer, I spent many hours at the Iffley Road athletics track, where I trained for, and ran, 880 yards and one mile. I didn't perform with great distinction but trained with some very good runners, such as Ian Boyd and Alan Gordon, under the coaching of Franz Stampfl.

"It is only pain!" he would shout as we endured another 440 yards interval on the track. I enjoyed the training, and it was always good fun competing for St Catherine's in "Cuppers", but I was never good enough to earn a "blue".

Franz was Roger Bannister's friend and mentor and I was fortunate to be at the track on that famous day in May 1954 when Bannister, who had already graduated, ran the first sub-4 minute mile. There had been talk of a possible attempt on the mile record, and in any case it was the annual match between the University and the AAA (Amateur Athletics Association), so, as keen athletes, we were there. The trackside was packed with eager spectators. I was standing on the back straight and I was impressed by how organised the whole race was. From the moment Chris Brasher took the lead and ran through the first two laps, then to be overtaken by Chris Chataway who led, past the bell, up to 300 yards from the finish, Bannister seemed to be just where he wanted to be, relaxed and trailing the others and very much in control. Once at the front Bannister kept his flowing stride going almost right up to the tape.

After a wait came the announcement: "Result of the one mile ... three minutes..."

We couldn't hear any more because of the roars of the crowd. We all began jumping up and down with excitement.

"We were there!" History had been made. 3:59.4 was not only the first sub-4 minute mile, but it was also, naturally, a world record.

Franz was a lovely, cultured man, an Austrian with a warm and very likeable personality, who many of us at the track got to know well. He told some good stories, at times against himself. At the track one afternoon, we were sheltering in the pavilion as it was absolutely pouring. In his distinctive accent, and speaking quite slowly, Franz said, "I must tell you this. I was at a concert on Saturday at the

Festival Hall in London, and the orchestra was playing a very quiet piece. Faintly I heard a noise, then I heard it again, a low rumbling sound, which I didn't understand. Then I suddenly realised, to my horror, that it was my stomach!"

Franz left Oxford in August 1955 to coach in Australia, becoming a rival to Percy Cerutty. My own career as a coach owed a lot to my early experiences training under Franz Stampfl.

Being an undergraduate member of St Catherine's Society meant living in digs, as the College was at that time non-residential. I only stayed one term in my first digs along the Abingdon Road. I had the feeling early on that my stay would be temporary when I saw a list of rules pinned up on the side of the staircase. There followed several other landladies, most of them very kind and hospitable, one further along the Abingdon Road, two others, just off the Iffley Road, in Parker Street. At Mrs Pritchett's you knew what day it was according to what was served for breakfast: it was always Kippers on Thursdays! At weekends my friends and I often spent time in our digs. Listening to music was one of my favourite pastimes, as Mum and Dad had given me a record player. My tastes were varied: I bought some of the current singles, such as Lonnie Donegan, but I also had several classical records: violin concertos, symphonies, some opera, as well as my traditional jazz records. During winter months it was often difficult keeping warm. With friends gathered around the electric fire, armed with my long, three pronged fork, toasted crumpets were a regular feature. They were good days.

We ate in St Catz dining hall two or three times a week. I used to arrive just before 7 p.m. ready for the meal at 7.30 p.m. The routine was to check my pigeon hole, then take the opportunity to have a drink and a chat in the JCR (Junior Common Room) before the meal. My friend, very good runner and Blackheath Harrier, Tony Weeks-Pearson, with whom I shared digs in Parker Street one year, used to say, "Come up to the Library; do some reading."

And I would reply, "No, I want to have a drink with some of my mates; you carry on."

"You'll waste half an hour's study time," he'd reply. "That's an hour and a half each week, or twelve hours each term."

He went up to the Library; I went into the JCR and had a drink. Maybe that's why he got a better degree than I did, and why I had plenty of friends.

There were many other distractions at Oxford, quite apart from sport. My friends and I almost certainly spent too much time visiting curry houses and pubs and playing cards, not to mention punting on the river, going to the cinema and that other distraction, female undergraduates. Once, when I was playing cards with friends, we became so absorbed that we only became aware of the time when dawn broke and light shone through the windows! I hurriedly cycled back to my digs and when my landlady said, "You're up early, Mr Elder," my convincing reply was that I hadn't been able to sleep so I had gone for an early morning bike ride.

One year my friends and I went to a summer College Ball where Chris Barber and his jazz band were playing. Word got round that playing at another college was Humphrey Lyttleton and his jazz band. Someone had the bright idea of getting them to play together, and imagine the euphoria when this happened as they and the college revellers marched up the High to the Carfax at midnight! "When the saints go marching in!" never had so much significance.

St Catz' Ball. Gents (from the left): Alan Wortley, Jim Pare, Norman Goddard, me, Barri Bishop, Dick Beardsley. Cannot identify the girls!

Apart from the summer ball, I didn't spend much time with any Oxford girls until my last year. Then I made what turned out to be a fatal mistake. It was in the Radcliffe Camera, where we were both studying, that I met Jane. Our feet met under the desk and I asked her out for a coffee. Let's just say that things developed from there and we spent a lot of time together during that year. The problem was that she was in 2nd year and I was in 3rd year. I couldn't afford to be spending as much time as I did with Jane as I approached finals. At Oxford, studying History, we had "Prelims" in the first term, after which we had no further exam until "Finals", over two years later, so there was a lot to recall at the end of the 3rd Year. My "Finals" performance undoubtedly suffered from the "Jane effect".

"Prelims" for me had not been entirely straightforward. After two terms we sat six exams: on De Tocqueville, the Venerable Bede, Historical Geography (for which I studied in the lovely Rhodes House), unseen French and Latin, and the philosophy of John Locke. The exams were held over three days, two exams each day. Because I didn't do well enough, I had to retake the unseen Latin in the summer, an annoying interruption to my enjoyment of the summer term. My friend from Yorkshire, Classicist, Alan Wortley, kindly helped me with the Latin and I survived to continue with my degree.

Jane was from Lewes in East Sussex, a place I was to get to know well many years later. She was an undergrad at Lady Margaret Hall where her best friend was Judy, daughter of Labour politician, Patrick Gordon-Walker. Jane and I, plus Judy and her boyfriend, often went to a Friday or Saturday night dinner dance. Jane was petite and pretty and I liked her a lot. One vacation we spent an enjoyable ten days hitchhiking in the West Country. More than once I travelled down from London by train to see Jane, staying at her parents' house in Lewes. We walked on the racecourse, took a boat out on the river and visited local pubs. I thought our relationship had a future. It was not to be.

As Lady Margaret Hall was adjacent to the University Parks, from time to time I used Jane's room to change for my run in the Parks. The college porter must have been somewhat bemused when a male runner, in shorts and t-shirt, disappeared out through the gate. I did my best to return without being seen. Having a shower in what was an all girls' college was something of a challenge. Fortunately the bathroom with the showers was just across the corridor from Jane's room. Jane told me when the coast was clear and I would make my way, suitably towelled, into one of the shower cubicles and lock the door to have my shower. On one occasion when I was there a group of girls came into the bathroom area and spent some time there chatting and giggling, putting on make-up etc., obviously unaware that a naked man was showering close by! I managed to make it back to Jane's room undetected on each occasion.

The weekly debates in the JCR at St Catherine's were always good fun. "This house prefers bed to breakfast" for example, though we did have serious debates as well. One week a guy gave his whole speech to the assembled St Catz undergrads while riding a bicycle! Thankfully, nobody had the courage to gymnologise. A favourite pastime of mine when in the JCR was playing Shove Ha'penny. I had never played before, but I really enjoyed it and became quite good, college champion even! A pity there was no "blue" awarded for it!

I joined the Oxford Union and went to some of the debates, and in the Union building once a week a group of us clustered around the radio to listen to *The Goons*, "He's fallen in the water!" In the very crowded, smoky, Union cellar, I regularly went to enjoy the University jazz band, as traditional jazz was one of my passions. They were great evenings. What I didn't know at the time was that the jazz band pianist, while I was there, was one Dudley Moore! I had joined the Oxford Union as a Life Member, something I forgot over the years, until quite recently, on a return trip to Oxford, I discovered they still had my records and, yes, I was entitled to use the facilities of the Union.

There were some eccentric characters at Oxford. We had at least one of them at St Catherine's. With confirmed and proud links with the Plantagenet family of kings who ruled England in the middle ages, Plantagenet Somerset Fry was a determined nonconformist. With his russet beard, he could usually be seen wearing a cape and often carrying a cane, as he made his way around Oxford. I was emerging from Lady Margaret Hall one afternoon, after visiting Jane, when Somerset Fry arrived on his bicycle carrying a red rose, wrapped in newspaper, presumably for his current lady friend at the college. He was affable and harmless but seemed to operate to a different agenda from the rest of us. Later he wrote several books, some for children, and became quite a celebrated historian, though he didn't have a happy or settled personal life.

Unconventional behaviour was fairly normal. Another St Catz man gave a talk in the college one afternoon on his travels abroad in Asia and Africa, illustrated with slides. His talk was both interesting and informative. Later we were told that he had never been further south than the Isle of Wight. My only claim to even a smidgeon of eccentricity was one morning when it was absolutely pouring, I cycled from St Catz up St Aldates to Carfax with my umbrella up. At the traffic lights, wanting to turn right into the High, I waited in the outside lane for the lights to change. While I waited, a bus attempted to turn left from the High, into St Aldates, but couldn't do so because my umbrella was in the way. The driver politely stopped, allowing me to lower my umbrella, and the bus was able to proceed on its journey. Naturally, as soon as the bus passed and the lights changed in my favour, I put my umbrella up again. Practical rather than eccentric!

We had an Australian Geographer at St Catz whose claim to fame was that, in a former life, he drove the post van from Darwin to Alice Springs. He said it was virtually a straight road for much of the 900 miles, so much so that he was known to fall asleep only waking when he hit a sheep on the road.

There were many American servicemen in Oxford at that time, one of whom, Steve, an Air Force Sergeant, I got to know quite well, having met him one evening in a bar in George Street. He was from Chicago and based at Upper Heyford. Our meeting led to an invitation for a St Catz team to go to the American base for a basketball match. We were soundly beaten, as you might expect, but we had a great time. During the game one very tall Yank leapt up to catch the ball and landed on my ankle, which remained sore for weeks.

Cycling back to my digs in Parker Street, just off Iffley Road, one night, a very strange incident occurred. It was about a quarter past midnight and I had just crossed Magdalen Bridge. A policeman stepped out from a darkened shop doorway and asked me to stop.

"You have no lights, sir," he said, more in sorrow than in anger, it seemed. "That is an offence. I shall have to book you."

It was true that the battery on my front light had run out. It was a fair cop!

"You're a member of the university, aren't you, sir?" the PC said.

"Indeed I am," I replied.

"Well, it's past midnight, sir. You aren't supposed to be out after midnight, are you, sir?" He now had his notebook open and pencil poised.

"It'll look bad for you if I put down a time after midnight, will it not?" He didn't seem to expect an answer, so he went on, "I tell you what, sir; I'll book you in at ten minutes to midnight. That'll be better for you, won't it?"

"Thank you very much," I said.

He started writing. What he didn't know, and what I didn't tell him, was that I had just come from a popular nightclub in Cornmarket Street, which had been raided by the police at midnight and everyone's name had been taken.

I was duly summoned to appear in court to face the charge of riding my bicycle without lights. My defence was watertight. I could prove that I could not have been on the far side of Magdalen Bridge just before midnight: in my defence I could call a policeman in whose notebook my name was recorded as having been in the middle of Oxford at midnight. It would have made for an interesting exchange. However I decided that the PC who had stopped me had been trying to do me a favour, and that he would have been in all sorts of trouble if I had called another PC to prove he had falsified the details of the arrest. I pleaded guilty and was fined ten shillings.

In the summer before 3rd Year, I had the opportunity to spend three weeks in Poland attending the 5th World Festival of Youth and Students, a Communist initiative, but attracting students of all religious and political persuasions from all over the world. Groups went from Oxford, Cambridge, London and many other universities in UK. The journey there was an experience in itself. The ferry to Calais was fine, but the three-day train journey from Calais to Warsaw was dire. Hygiene was not the highest priority: the toilets became disgusting and the corridors were not much better. But we were young, it was an adventure and we had high expectations of what was to come. There was an excellent jazz band on board and when we stopped at a station, the band went on to the platform and played, to the initial bewilderment and subsequent delight of local train travellers on the platforms. Often they blew their trumpets and trombones out of the train windows. At the longer stops everyone was out on the platform, stretching their legs and breathing in some fresh air. Once we reached the communist east, we were subject to stringent searches, so had to stay in our seats. Soldiers with rifles marched along the tracks peering in every window.

On reaching Warsaw, we were taken on coaches to the hostels where we were billeted. I had made friends with Richard from London University who spoke fluent Russian, and Alan, a dentist from Leeds, and the three of us spent a lot of the three weeks together. We were fed on our arrival; it was the first time I had tasted cold cherry soup. Our 16-bed dormitory overlooked the River Vistula. The Festival brought young people together from all over the world to share sporting and cultural experiences, and although it was communist sponsored, there was no overt propaganda at all.

Some of us took part in various sports: I ran in a cross-country race where I found myself running alongside a young Czech guy, Jiri, and we got chatting. As soon as the race was over we had a few beers together and became good friends. After the Festival we exchanged letters and family photographs; he worked in Czech television and we corresponded for several years. Jiri was a "liberal" communist, with reformist views, and after the Prague Spring and Russian clampdown, sadly I never heard from him again. I fear he was one of the many Czech victims of that cruel episode. Each time I visit Prague these days, I wonder what happened to Jiri. We went to an athletics meeting where Emil Zatopek ran, the Lenin Symphony Orchestra gave a concert, we saw the Russian Ballet and a group of Indian dancers. There were many impromptu activities and meetings where international friendships were made. Richard and I went for a few drinks with some young Russian guys, when we discovered what an excellent sense of humour some Russians have, contrary perhaps to the popular impression. Going for a drink involved a choice, either the awful Polish beer, Piwo, or the more expensive vodka: usually we mixed the two. Lying in bed one morning with a hangover, feeling unwell and sorry for myself, I heard some traditional jazz being played in the next room and I immediately felt better. I have tried this "remedy" since when not feeling well and for me, trad jazz is definitely therapeutic.

With some international friends in Warsaw

We could walk more or less where we liked and we saw much of post-war Warsaw, still with many bomb-damaged buildings despite the reconstruction after the war. Dominating the centre of the city was the recently completed huge Palace of Culture and Science. It was a giant of a building, not liked by most Poles who christened it the "Russian wedding cake". It was clear that ordinary Polish folk were intensely patriotic and very pro-British, but they were reluctant to have conversations because of the presence of Russian soldiers who were everywhere. These Poles were also very Catholic, through belief and history. They were, very much in third place, reluctant communists.

During the two weekends we were in Poland, Richard, Alan and I took advantage of the free travel afforded to Festival participants. On the first weekend we took a train to the Baltic in the north and spent most of a sunny day on the beach at Gdansk, alongside Polish families. We bought ice cream and sandwiches and drank Piwo. Communist they might be, but those families were enjoying their weekend just as families in England would do. On the second weekend we explored the south of the country by taking a train to the mountain village of Zakopane, where we spent the day walking in the foothills of the beautiful Tatra Mountains. It was so quiet and the scenery was breathtaking. Two weekends of great experiences and all our travel paid for! We were glad we had seen more of Poland.

It was a memorable three weeks and we were sorry to leave. The Polish people had been very friendly, as far as they were allowed. The Russian military presence was very evident in the capital, but far less so in Gdansk and in Zakopane. I formed the impression that, for the majority of Poles, the Russian presence was heartily disliked and that, given an opportunity, there would be an uprising or organised protest against this foreign "occupation". On my return to UK I wrote an article saying this, and sent it to Edward Crankshaw at the "Observer". He decided not to print the article on the grounds that my forecast was "too fanciful". The following year there was the first Polish revolt against Russian rule, a workers' demonstration in Poznan, brutally suppressed. So much for the experts!

Our return train journey took a more southerly route and we spent a day at Auschwitz. As this was only ten years after the end of the war, the concentration camp had not changed much. It was a damp, cold day when we were there and mist hung over the marshy ground. It seemed an unhealthy place. We walked through the entrance gates close to the railway line. My thoughts went back to what it must have been like only 12 years before. We were shown the huts where the Jewish inmates were housed as well as the huge glass-fronted cages containing the discarded belongings of the prisoners: suitcases, spectacles, shoes, false teeth and clothes. The gas chambers were nearby. For all of us it was a harrowing experience. Some of the girls in our group were in floods of tears. As we left and re-boarded our train, nobody spoke. The experience left an indelible mark on us all. The camp was being retained so that future generations could visit and learn what atrocities had taken place there. Today the Holocaust Trust arranges for two 6th Formers from every school in the UK to visit Auschwitz with one of their teachers each year. It's a very commendable initiative. I have spoken to some of these students and I know what an impression their visit had on them.

On our return journey we were told that some Cambridge students had helped a young Polish lad to escape by hiding him under piles of coats on a luggage rack, and that he had survived all the regular searches. Did this happen or was the story a fabrication? Back in England, I parted company with Richard and the many other friends I had made. All, except Alan, my friend from Leeds, who was unable to return with us, as he remained in Warsaw, in hospital, having his stomach pumped out after too much vodka. I learned that he had returned safe and well a few days later.

One of the best things about Oxford was the friendships made. My two Yorkshire friends, Norman Goddard, from Barnsley, and Alan Wortley, from Leeds, both Grammar School lads, and both at St Catz, have remained friends to this day, as has Barri Bishop from Hastings. Alan also came to stay with me at my parents' house in Finchley. One evening we were walking through Soho, en route to a theatre. Being used to London I was leading the way, with Alan a few paces behind. We passed various clubs and strip joints, when suddenly Alan called out,

"Hey, Tony! That lady just spoke to you."

Alan had heard one of the girls of the night say, as I went by, "Hello, darling!"

I carried on; when we reached Shaftesbury Avenue, I turned to Alan and said, "That was no lady!"

Alan smiled and said he was definitely improving his knowledge of our capital city.

That incident led me to recall that a few years before, I had arranged to meet my mother in Soho on the corner of Brewer Street and Wardour Street, though why we had arranged to meet there, I have no idea. As my mother waited for me, and this was at lunchtime, one of the "ladies" came up to her and said, in a somewhat threatening manner, "Oi, duckie, you're on my patch."

Mother moved away a safe distance. When I arrived and she told me the story, she said she didn't know whether to be flattered or offended to be taken as a rival.

Another St Catz friend who came to stay at our house in Finchley was Ken Douie. Ken was of good stock, from a family with connections, with links to tea growing in Asia I recall. His mother had a daisy named after her. Ken was a character, rather overweight, often in bizarre, tweedy outfits and with a ruddy complexion, probably caused in part from his intake of port. My stepfather decided to walk to Finchley Central station to meet Ken, even though Ken had detailed directions. Halfway across the park opposite our house, Dad saw this figure coming towards him. It had to be him. They introduced themselves and walked back to our house. He was a most gracious guest, though I always felt he was doing us a favour by agreeing to lower himself to our humble level.

While up at Oxford, on another occasion I organised a party at my parents' house in Etchingham Park Road, Finchley, after receiving parental approval of course. Irwin ("Let's Go, Hartford!") Hermann was there, an American undergrad at St Catz, plus many of my friends, including Colin, who had managed to persuade some nurses from a London hospital to join us. His particular nurse, Dorothy, was in the back of the car as it pulled up outside our house with, on her lap, a large and expensive bottle of whiskey. As she emerged from the back seat, she allowed the very costly bottle to fall and break, spilling the contents across the pavement to shouts of dismay from Colin and her friends. That was to prove only the first disaster of the night. Shall I just say that, although we all had a good time, the lounge was not left in quite the condition my mother expected and she communicated her displeasure by letter the following week. Apologies and forgiveness duly followed, though memories took longer to fade.

My mother opened the front door of our house in Finchley one morning to find a body lying in the porch area. This turned out to be Roger Toseland, another St Catz colleague, originally from Kettering, who had arrived at our house very late, and rather than knock and wake everyone up, had decided to camp in the porch, where he said he had a very good night's sleep. Mother was becoming used to my university mates, and made him welcome with hot coffee. After all, she had said to me, "Any time any of your friends want a bed for the night in London, they are more than welcome." She hadn't meant the porch!

As I have said, I spent too much of my 3rd Year enjoying the company of Jane. On the river, when we went punting, full of good intentions, we always took a book to read, but it rarely got opened. Once, when punting with Alan, I fell into the river, but I was reassured when he shouted, "It's OK. I was the Leeds boy scout diving champion!" A couple of weeks before the final exams I fell in the river again. I arrived back at St Catz absolutely soaked, but many there seemed to think it was a suicide attempt! There was one benefit: I was given a free pint at the JCR bar.

Finals came all too soon, followed by the customary celebrations. Three years had gone far too quickly. Jane didn't want to continue our relationship as she had met someone else. I was distraught, but I had to return to Finchley, nurse my wounded pride and think about the future.

After finals, in which we had to sit 3-hour exams every morning and afternoon for a week in sweltering heat, came the results. I was awarded (if that's the right word) the equivalent of a 2:2 Hons. degree. In those days Oxford used the categories: 1, 2, 3 and 4 for their degree classes. Today, it's 1, 2.1, 2.2, and 3. I wasn't pleased or proud of the degree I had, but there were others who failed altogether. Alan Bullock wrote me a very encouraging reference saying that the degree class I was given didn't represent the quality of work I had produced or my level of historical knowledge and understanding. *Very good of him,* I thought, *but typical of the man.*

Alan Bullock was the Head of St Catherine's Society; more correctly his title was that of Censor. When I went up to Oxford, Alan Bullock's acclaimed book, *Hitler: a study in tyranny* had just been published. Later he was to write more, including his full-length biography in two volumes *The Life and Times of Ernest Bevin,* which is a masterpiece.

Alan Bullock was liked and respected by everyone at St Catz. He took a particular interest in the new undergraduates each year, and you knew that if you had any sort of problem, you could go and see him. He was known to say, in his broad Yorkshire, "What's the problem, lad? Money or women?"

On special occasions he would stand on the balcony at the front of St Catz and do his Hitler impression, which we all enjoyed. During Prelims he had one or two sessions with the 1st Year historians, but I felt it was a shame we never enjoyed the benefit of history tutorials or a seminar with him later on in our course.

He was determined that there should be a new St Catherine's College built, eventually to replace non-residential St Catherine's Society. He worked ceaselessly to bring this about, seeking wealthy benefactors who would contribute to his dream. Land was acquired and the Danish architect, Arne Jacobsen, was given the task of designing the new college. His mission was accomplished in 1962 when St Catherine's College opened and took in its first undergraduates, though the building work was far from complete. Today, St Catherine's has a modern, attractive and functional set of buildings, the College being Grade 1 listed, and it is one of Oxford's most popular and successful colleges, with renowned alumni in almost every field. Alan Bullock would be very proud of the college today, which has only recently celebrated its 50th anniversary.

13
Colin

At St Catherine's my best mate was Colin Barham from Hastings. We were both reading Modern History, both into athletics, and our social interests were similar, so we found ourselves at the same lectures, working in the Radcliffe Camera, sometimes sharing tutorials, running round the Iffley Road track or visiting pubs, curry houses or the cinema together. We had a similar approach to life, though Colin took his *joie de vivre* a bit further than I did. Colin gained something of a reputation for his relaxed approach to life, an endearing trait, some thought! We had many interesting encounters together, including the shared tutorial with Peter Dickson that I have already recounted. In several university vacations, Colin came and stayed with us in Finchley. My mother was very fond of him even though he used to eat us out of house and home! A particular favourite, I remember, was Branston pickle!

The favourite eating place for undergraduates in Oxford was "The Stowaway", situated down a narrow passage off the High with very basic amenities but with cheap, wholesome food. It was usually packed at lunchtime. Twice a week we dined in hall but on other occasions Colin and I often ate together. One evening we tried out a restaurant that was new to us.

"Looks a bit pricey," I said.

"Oh! Come on; let's give it a go," said Colin.

Colin might well say this, as he frequently came out without any cash, so the bill would be down to me. It had a well-appointed dining area; we were greeted and directed to a table.

We started with soup, which came with a crusty bread roll. Halfway through the soup, I called the waiter over and asked if we could have another roll, which, after a somewhat quizzical look, he duly brought to our table. Having eaten our soup and two rolls, we then glanced at the menu for the next course. Though very attractive, it was more then we could afford.

The waiter took away our soup bowls and side plates and said, "What can I get you now?"

"The bill, please," said Colin.

The waiter looked puzzled, then annoyed, but the bill came and I paid. We made a hasty exit.

We had a different gastronomic experience one Sunday lunchtime, when Colin and I visited a café in the High that we knew. We were directed to a table upstairs. We both ordered pork chop with all the trimmings: after all, it was Sunday lunch. It was good, and we followed it with apple pie and custard. When we had finished our meal, Colin said, "Do you know, I could eat that pork chop again!"

"Really! Seriously?" I said. "Shall we order another one then?"

"Why not!"

At which he called over the waitress and said, "My friend and I would like another pork chop, please."

We proceeded to eat a second plate of pork chop with apple sauce, roast potato, vegetables and gravy. It was as good as it was the first time, though we were now both rather full. Sitting back in our seats, replete, we saw our waitress coming towards our table, and she was carrying a tray on which were two bowls of apple pie and custard.

"What's this?" Colin asked.

"This completes your two meals, sir."

We hadn't realised that the two courses made up one meal.

"Very well," I said, "we'll do our best. Thank you."

The waitress placed the apple pie in front of us, and walked away. Colin and I burst out laughing.

"We'd better eat it," Colin said.

We enjoyed it, though we were now *complète totalement*! We decided not to order coffee, in case we had to have two cups each! After sitting for a while, Colin looked at his watch. It was 3.30 pm.

"Shall we stay for tea?" enquired Colin, always the jester. The story of our Sunday lunch went round St Catz to general amusement. On this occasion Colin paid for his share of our two meals!

One of Colin's traits was never having enough, or indeed any, money. Whether this was due to being impoverished, or forgetfulness, or a deliberate policy, remained unclear. During one term, Colin amassed a considerable bill at St Catz JCR bar. Despite regular requests, Colin always had some excuse until, finally, he was persuaded to write a cheque to settle the outstanding amount. The bar staff were delighted until, on closer inspection, they realised that Colin, now departed, had omitted to sign the cheque. He was a loveable rogue.

One of Colin's more embarrassing moments occurred late one Sunday night. He was living in Regents Park College in Pusey Street for one term. The College was primarily for those wishing to train for the priesthood, but they had spare accommodation for undergraduates from other colleges. Colin returned there on a Sunday night, very late and somewhat inebriated. The front door was locked. The only possible way in that Colin could see was via a ground floor window, one of which, he noticed, was not completely closed. Quietly, he managed to raise the window sufficiently to allow him to climb inside and slide on to the floor. The room was in almost total darkness but as he lay on the floor, Colin gently moved a curtain and saw a group of people, which was when he realised he had interrupted a prayer meeting. That was Colin!

One afternoon, a coach load of St Catz undergraduates travelled up to London for a concert at the Empress Hall. The trip was organised by Eric Silver. Louis Armstrong was performing and this was an opportunity not to be missed. Most of us visited a couple of pubs before the concert and everyone was up for a good time. Colin and I sat next to each other in the Hall.

"I think I had too much to drink," said Colin. "I can see the stage moving around."

"Surprising that!" I replied. "It's a revolving stage!"

"Satchmo" was brilliant, and after the concert we got back on our coach and headed back to Oxford. The next morning I went into St Catherine's and in my pigeonhole I found a note from Eric Silver.

"Thanks for leaving me in London," it said. "But don't worry, I caught the last train."

Without realising it, we had left Eric behind! He never held it against us; he was that sort of bloke. Another time, we all went up to London to hear Ella Fitzgerald sing. That was a memorable concert too, and we all returned together.

Colin always enjoyed his visits to my parents' house in Finchley. He and I often went for a run over Hampstead Heath, or to the theatre in London or to the local cinema. We always enjoyed a bit of mischief and when in Oxford Street or Regent Street, we would step off the pavement into the road (easier to do in those days) and stand and point up and gesticulate at a top floor window of one of the tall buildings. Other passers-by would stop and look up as we were doing, until a sizeable crowd had gathered, when Colin and I would then slip away. Those we left behind had no idea why they were standing there, staring up at a perfectly normal, boring building. It was silly, student humour, but fun at the time.

Just after we came down from Oxford, I agreed to support Colin in a special hearing he had to attend. Neither Colin nor I did National Service. As a footballer and runner, I was ribbed quite a bit about my D4 classification. Colin did have certain worthy principles, such as his attitude to war and fighting, so much so that he registered as a conscientious objector. Colin had to go before a Tribunal and answer questions on his beliefs. He also needed someone to speak on his behalf and convince the members of the Tribunal that he was genuine. Guess what! He chose me! We arrived one morning at Fulham Town Hall, not far from Stamford Bridge, home of Chelsea Football Club. Colin was interrogated and I was questioned as well. They believed him, and presumably me too, and Colin was granted exemption from National Service.

In lieu, Colin had to carry out certain other work. At first this was in a children's hospital in Westminster, which is where he met Agnes. At Oxford, Colin and I had made an agreement that neither of us would get married before we were 30. We both regarded it as binding. Then he met Agnes. Colin's version of events is that he met Agnes, got to know her and fell in love. Later, he found out that she was from a very wealthy Scottish family. Others tend to think it was the other way round: having discovered Agnes was from a wealthy family, he subsequently fell in love with her. When you knew Colin, you were bound to wonder!

Colin and Agnes are married in Scotland:
I was best man

Be that as it may, Agnes moved back to Scotland, Colin followed and worked for the Forestry Commission to satisfy the requirements for a conscientious objector. They lived in a somewhat remote cottage on the shore of Loch Awe, a beautiful location from which they were married, totally breaking the solemn agreement Colin and I had made. I was Colin's best man. Also at the wedding were my parents, plus Barri Bishop and Jim Waite, friends from St Catz. Barri and I were introduced to a couple of very attractive sisters, though I have to say that "mine" was even more attractive than Barri's! We went for a drive during which the car ran over and killed a rabbit. While Barri's "sister" berated the driver, my "sister" said, "It's only a rabbit!"

Colin's parents were flown up from Hastings courtesy of Agnes's father, who was a director of Carr's Biscuits and of one of Scotland's leading football clubs. The reception was held in a massive marquee at Agnes's parents' house at Bridge of Weir. Agnes's father was insistent he be told the football scores throughout the afternoon. It was a special occasion for everyone. Later Jim and I would return to Scotland, driving up from London in my tiny Standard 10, for the christening of Colin and Agnes's firstborn.

Although Colin is no longer with us, he and Agnes had a long and happy marriage and, as his best man, I went with my wife, Donna, to be with them 40 years later to celebrate their Ruby Wedding Anniversary. It was the same weekend in 1997 that Diana, Princess of Wales, died in a car crash in Paris.

14
Work Experience

So far my life had consisted almost entirely of school and university. My brief experiences in the world of work had been interesting, though not always successful.

After leaving school and before starting at university, I worked for the St Pancras Borough Council building department. Dad thought I could do with "toughening up" and he was probably right. It was here that I learned that you needed considerable skill to be an unskilled labourer. It was the summer when I was 18.

I arrived at 8.00 a.m. at the site, where a block of flats was being built. I met the foreman, who introduced himself as Joe. The first task I was given involved standing on a plank while cement was poured from on high into my wheelbarrow, pushing the now heavy barrow forward, which I found quite difficult, then negotiating two more planks and tipping the cement into a waiting trench. Unfortunately, in tilting the barrow to eject the cement, I forgot to hold on tight to the handles, and the barrow fell into the trench with the cement. Luckily, I had the presence of mind to let go, so I didn't join the barrow in the trench. When the guys I was working with saw this, a shout went up, a mixture of amusement and derision. My barrow was extricated with a large hook-like implement, washed in a shower and returned to me. I was allowed to continue and did so with no further mishap.

Mid-morning next day there was a long, loud blast on the foreman's whistle. Three brick lorries had arrived. As I soon learned, unloading consisted of a chain of men, throwing and catching bricks until they were neatly stacked on the site. I had never done this before but I was assigned position three, in the middle of the chain. Three bricks were thrown at a time. You got into a sort of rhythm: swing to the right, catch; swing to the left, throw. After a short while, I realised that most of the men were wearing gloves. I wasn't. Soon my hands were sore, red and bleeding. I began to drop some of the bricks thrown to me, and I was soon standing on a pile of broken bricks. The foreman yelled, "Stop!" I was removed from the line, partly, I suspect, out of sympathy, though chiefly so they wouldn't lose so many bricks. Looking back, it had all the elements of farce, though at the time it was more like tragedy. It had been a painful experience. I was sent home but, to my surprise, the foreman said, "Come back in the morning."

I didn't last long on my third day either. With both hands patched up with plasters, I was assigned to a different group and given a new task: helping to demolish some old buildings still on the site. As soon as the other workmen saw me near the top of one of these houses, armed with a sledge hammer, and thus eligible to earn extra, danger money, they objected. This foreman hadn't been told I was a newcomer, a greenhorn, so I was stood down. It was at this point that I decided that unskilled labouring was not for me. I collected my cards.

A few years later I was pleased to see that the flats in Torriano Avenue, not far from Kentish Town Station, were still standing, so my cement had clearly done its job. I took a very small amount of pride in that!

I went on to have some rather more successful experiences of work. I spent some of my university vacations in the Idris factory in Camden Town. I worked on the first floor in the soft drinks distribution warehouse. All day the squash, orange, lemon, lime, etc., was produced in the vast laboratory-like room next to ours and we stacked the crates as they were sent through to us. When our warehouse was full, it resembled a library with stacked shelves, except that, in place of books, we had different varieties of squash. Each stack was labelled: squash name and arrival date. Jock was our foreman; most of the other workers were Maltese. Jock was quite short, in his forties, with almost ginger, curly hair, and very obviously a Scot. "Jock, the stocky Scot", his mates called him. He was a very jovial character and we got on well. Every afternoon, and sometimes into the evening, the Idris lorries came into the yard below and the drivers sent us their order for different types of squash. They wrote out their order on a piece of paper and placed it in a tin, which we hauled up to our window by means of a length of stout string: primitive but effective. On receiving their order we fetched the required number of crates from the stacks on trolleys and put them on a conveyor belt, which sent the order down to the waiting lorry. We noted in our record book how much squash each driver had been given. Once that was done we dealt with the next order.

In the summer months we serviced a constant stream of lorries from mid-afternoon to late evening. Some lorries went straight out on delivery if their area was nearby, for example, London Zoo in Regents Park, only a 10-minute drive from the factory. Other drivers were loading up for an early getaway the next morning. It was hectic most afternoons but it made the time go by very quickly. In the mornings, when it was less busy, we processed the export orders, which were packed and secured in large, strong cardboard boxes, ready for dispatch all over the world. Places in West Africa, West Indies, Asia; all received "Export Quality" squash, as did HM The Queen, as Idris was "By Appointment".

First thing each morning we did a stock take. All crates of squash that had come from the factory next door had to be accounted for and a record kept in a book. The number of crates in and out had to tally with what remained on our shelves. Jock always did this and I helped. The Maltese guys weren't asked to help and spent a fair amount of time in our mess room, usually discussing their rabbits or Mr Churchill, who was a person they obviously revered.

"Mr Churchill – very fine man!"

Malta, an important base for the British navy during the Second World War, had bravely held out against enemy bombardment. George VI had awarded the island a collective George Cross. Two of our Maltese workers had been in Malta during the war. As I drank my coffee with them in the mess room at morning break, I was regularly told, "Mr Churchill – very fine man!"

Apparently, each year when Jock was away on holiday, about £100-worth of stock went missing. In my second summer vacation, I was asked to take charge during Jock's fortnight holiday, which the Maltese guys thought was a huge joke, though they cooperated without any problem, as I was the "main man". I enjoyed the responsibility. It meant a very early start, as some days I had to be at work by 7.00 a.m. while, on the busiest days, you didn't get away until eight or nine in the evening. I did the books each day; one morning I found there were five crates of lime cordial missing, which I couldn't account for. That's 60 bottles! I had a choice: I could record them as "broken", as bottles did get broken from time to time, though not usually five crates-worth, or I could note them as "missing". I did the latter and, although I was puzzled, thought little more about it. Just before lunch one of the directors, Mr Viney, came into our area and asked to see the books.

"Five crates of lime missing, I see," he said, looking at me as if he expected an explanation.

"Yes," I said, but before I could say anything else...

"I came in late last night and took them; glad to see they've been noted." He smiled. And he left. Was he testing me, I wondered, or did he genuinely need that amount of lime cordial? At the end of the fortnight I learned that there had been no loss or stock discrepancy at all on my watch and in my pay packet I found I had been given a bonus, as a thank you, of ten shillings! Big deal!

Working at Idris was good experience. During the mornings when it was often slack for us, I sometimes wandered into the adjacent factory area, which would be noisily turning out the bottles of squash. Here I had my first experience of factory women.

141

"I know what I'd like to do with him," one of them said loudly, so her friends could hear. Then in my direction, "Did you get it last night, sunshine?"

I was not used to such comments from women and didn't know how to respond.

"No! What a shame. Come over here then, darling."

Then another said, "Don't go there, pretty boy, you'll get the fucking clap!" And they all shrieked with laughter as I quickly made my exit. I was certainly broadening my education.

Sometimes Jock and I visited the floor below where the fizzy drinks were produced and stored, and where Jock's mate, Harry, was in charge. Harry was a cockney, who chewed constantly and had what I thought was a disgusting habit of spitting on the stone floor of the warehouse. On one of our visits, he offered me some of what he habitually chewed. I didn't know what it was.

Jock said, "I should be careful of that stuff," but I took some and began to chew. It turned out to be biltong. The juices are very strong and, as I didn't know any better, I swallowed them. The pain in my stomach didn't come on immediately, but when it did, I was in agony. Now I understood why Harry spat all the time: to get rid of the juices. He hadn't warned me.

As Idris was "By Appointment" to HM, one day I was given the opportunity to take an order of squashes, "Export Quality" of course, to Buckingham Palace, as the van driver's mate. It was good to get out of the factory for a while. In the royal kitchens we were offered beer "or something stronger?" I had never seen so much alcohol, mainly wines and spirits, in one place, stacked high along two walls of a very large cellar. We didn't stay longer than one drink, but just to be inside the Palace was a great experience. It was my royal appointment!

When I had joined Idris in the first summer vacation, so too had Sam, who became a driver's mate on one of the lorries. He had a mass of blond hair and was always smiling and joking. He could be quite cheeky, but he was popular and liked by everyone. I used to see him when his lorry arrived at our window for a supply of squash.

"Where you been today, Sam?" I shouted down.

"Regents Park," said Sam. "Saw the tigers in the zoo," he said with a broad grin.

I remember one Friday very well. There was a commotion out in the yard: lots of shouting and then silence. Jock and I rushed to the window. There had been an accident. Most people were standing stock still, hands to faces. Linda and others from the office were there, too, crying. Jock went down to find out what had happened. He came back a few minutes later, just as the ambulance drove into the yard.

"It's Sam," said Jock. I could see he was close to tears.

"What's happened?" I asked.

"He was behind his lorry, helping Joe reverse. It seems the lorry has crushed Sam against the wall. Joe couldn't have seen or heard him. They think he's dead."

We saw the ambulance take Sam away. Very little work got done after that, even though it was just before the weekend and normally a busy time. When I got to work on Monday, I learned that Sam had indeed been killed by his own lorry reversing. Someone said they had heard Sam shouting for Joe to stop, but Sam had made the mistake of being directly between the reversing lorry and the wall. Joe hadn't heard him. He was distraught, inconsolable. He never drove an Idris lorry again. At the inquest he wasn't blamed for Sam's death, though the firm was required to improve its safety rules and training of lorry drivers and their mates. Dozens of Idris workers attended Sam's funeral. Many found the occasion too much to bear. It seemed to me so sad that a young life had been cruelly ended almost before it had begun. We all missed Sam.

Part Three

Teaching

*"The mind is not a vessel to be filled,
but a fire to be kindled."*
Plutarch

15
KEGS Chelmsford

At King Edward VI Grammar School in Chelmsford, a very old and reputable boys' Grammar School, I would be teaching History and initially some English. Although I had taught girls at Hemel and in the first term in London, it only really occurred to me to apply to boys' schools. As a former pupil at a boys' grammar school in London, it seemed the natural thing to do. Chelmsford was the county town of Essex, best known for the extensive Marconi factory, and I soon grew to like the town and the area, with lovely villages close by, all with welcoming pubs. I started in 1958 on a salary of £608-6s-8d per annum.

I was still finding my way as a teacher. I had only had four terms of teaching: three in temporary posts and one on teaching practice, though they had given me practical experience of five very different kinds of schools. My role models were still very much the teachers I had had as a pupil; some I knew I didn't want to be like; others I could remember with affection and respect. I had answered one of my original three questions: I now knew that I wanted to be a teacher. Whether I would be any good at coping with children was still an unanswered question, though recent signs were encouraging. Whether I would be any good as a teacher also remained an unanswered question; time would tell. I was aware that to be a successful History teacher I had to be in command of the subject.

In theory the Oxford Institute of Education should have provided more guidance on teaching methodology and, especially, on how best to develop learning skills in young students. If this was covered I must have been absent or not listening, as I developed such skills very much as I went along. Perhaps it's the same for all new teachers. I dread to think what I would have been like without the four terms' experience I had managed to acquire. In my favour, I think, was the fact that I did, genuinely, like young people. I was later to encounter some teachers, indeed there had been some in my own schooldays, who gave the impression they did not like children at all.

I started at King Edward VI as an assistant teacher with a lot to learn, but I was quite confident. One thing I was initially really worried about was being asked a question in a class and not knowing the answer. I soon came to realise that it doesn't actually matter, and that you can gain respect from pupils by saying that you don't know. I was really pleased that the Head of Department, Tom Bromwich, gave me a Lower 6th A level History class to teach. He took the view that, as I had fairly recently been studying the periods of History that the 6th Formers were doing, I might as well be let loose on them. For that, I was very grateful, and it became a very rewarding part of my teaching. Tom taught one set and I taught the other, so we were able to compare notes. (Not literally! You know what I mean). There was an early hiccup. I taught the 6th Formers either in an old house on the far side of the playing field, or in some huts in a road opposite the main school. On two successive occasions, two of my students failed to attend, so I brought this to the attention of the Headmaster.

"They have absented themselves from my lessons, without any explanation," I complained.

"What do you propose to do about it?" the Head asked.

"Well, I don't know. Surely it isn't up to me, is it? They should attend the class."

"Perhaps you should look at what or how you are teaching them," he said. "The boys have chosen to take History. They should want to come. I suggest you make your lessons so stimulating that no one will want to miss them."

"Yes, sir."

I departed suitably chastened, but having learned a valuable lesson. My mind went back to A J P Taylor at Oxford. Nobody missed any of his lectures. But I had no illusions that I could be as inspiring as he had been. I don't know whether my lessons were an improvement from then on, but I didn't have any further absentees. I suspect someone, maybe the Head, had had a quiet word with the offending 6th Formers. In due course, several of the A level historians went on to read History at university, some at Oxford or Cambridge, so there must have been some interest stimulated.

I taught a range of classes below the 6th Form. I enjoyed the school trips that the History department organised for the younger boys. My favourites were Ingatestone Hall, a well-preserved Tudor manor house, a short coach ride from the school, and Coggeshall, a small town mentioned in the Domesday Book. At Ingatestone, the Priests' Hole always intrigued the boys, and the church at Coggeshall had a wooden carved sheep's head on the end of each pew, to mark the importance of the wool trade in the economy of medieval England. One year we had an American boy with us and he reminded our Essex lads that where he came from they had "no buildings as old as that".

Initially, I could not believe how tired I became. There seemed to be no let up. I had to get used to having a full timetable, with only the occasional "free" or "non-teaching" period. There was always something to prepare, books to mark, trips to plan, classrooms to get to on time, with seldom a moment for reflection or relaxation. For the first few weeks I often felt exhausted and the Staff Room became a haven of tranquillity from the bustle in the school although, after a while, at break and lunchtimes, I frequently spent any free time talking with the boys rather than in the Staff Room, which could become claustrophobic and smoky. Many of the staff were quite old, or seemed so to me, and I found we didn't have much in common to talk about.

Each day I returned to my digs, not far from the school. My landlord and landlady were lovely people and helped me to settle in.

Their daughter had just started at the girls' school down the road, and went off each morning proudly in her school uniform. Her father managed a shop in the town and was quite a character. Sometimes he got a bit muddled. We were talking about the trains from Chelmsford to London and he said, "They get so full each morning with all those computers."

Another time, becoming quite animated about our national defences, he told me, "We do need a nuclear detergent."

One evening, after a concert at their daughter's new school, Dad turned to his daughter and said, "In that last song, who sang the discount?"

As if I didn't have enough to do at KEGS, as it was known, in my second year I began teaching one evening a week at Mid Essex Technical College and School of Art. My class consisted mainly of apprentices who needed an English qualification, plus some older adults who wanted to improve their literacy skills, the latter proving more willing to work. For my two-hour class I was paid 37s 6d gross. It was a valuable experience, though not of course in monetary terms. I became aware, for the first time, of adults in the community who needed or wanted to return to education.

KEGS had an inner courtyard within the main part of the school. There was a raised walkway on all four sides of this small courtyard, which had grass in the centre. You soon came across this after coming in the main entrance. The school had a small boarding house, with a resident master to look after the boarders. This teacher had a small car, an old Austin 7, past its best days, but still in working order. One morning, as boys and masters arrived, they could not help noticing a car sitting on the grass in this inner courtyard. It didn't look damaged, and closer inspection revealed that it was not. *What was it doing there? And how did it get there?* A crowd of boys soon gathered to observe this unusual sight and were quickly ushered off to their classrooms. The boarding house master confirmed that it was his Austin 7. There was much interest and amusement, and then the Head arrived. He promptly ordered an enquiry, starting with the 6th Formers. Yes, it appeared that sometime in the night a group of 6th Formers, assisted by some boarders, had taken the Austin 7 apart, literally and quite expertly, and carried the parts into the inner courtyard, bit by bit, and there reassembled it. The boarding-house master confirmed that the car had not been damaged. It was another 6th Form practical joke. It was harmless, provided those responsible could do the job in reverse – which they did, in their own time.

On the whole, the behaviour of the boys at KEGS was good; after all, it was a prestigious grammar school and parents were keen that their sons should do well there. There were exceptions. Tom Keating, a lad I taught in the 4th Year, would not keep quiet or sit still in my lessons. I did my best; I talked to him, I gave him detentions, extra work, but it seemed to make no difference. One day he kept on interrupting and he infuriated me so much that I dragged him from his seat at the front of the class and bodily threw him out of the door on to the corridor outside. I thought maybe I had gone a bit too far, but at least now I could get on and teach the class, which is what they wanted too. I looked outside but he had disappeared.

Next day I was in the Staff Room at break and the internal phone rang, "Mr Elder, there's a Mr Keating wants to see you. He's in reception."

Well, that's it, I thought. *My teaching career ended before it has really begun.* I was genuinely very concerned as to the likely outcome. I walked, in some trepidation, down to the main school reception, where I saw a large man standing with his back to me.

"Mr Keating?" I said.

"Ah! Mr Elder? You threw my boy out of the class yesterday, I believe." Then he paused. I wondered what was coming next. "I want to thank you. It is just what he needed. He will not buckle down to behave and work. What you did will have done him the world of good."

"Oh! I'm pleased you think so," I said lamely. I was so relieved.

"Yes, I have given him a good talking to. He came home complaining at being thrown out and he had a bruise or two, but I told him it served him right. So, well done, you! You're new here, aren't you?"

"This is my first year, yes. I shan't be making a habit of throwing boys out of the classroom, I assure you," I said. "But every boy has to behave or the teacher cannot teach and the other boys cannot learn."

"Quite right," Mr Keating said. "Some of the other teachers should be more strict, in my opinion; then my lad would have a better attitude. You'll have no more trouble with him; I can assure you of that." And he shook my hand and left.

It is hard to describe the sense of relief I felt. The outcome was so unexpected. It was fortunate that I had encountered a parent who was prepared to support the teacher rather than their own child. I did know, however, that would not always be the case and I knew I shouldn't have used physical force to throw a boy out of the classroom. I never did that again.

In my first year at KEGS I was learning how to become a competent teacher. In doing so I observed other teachers, not by going into their classrooms, but more discreetly – or indiscreetly, if you include picking up on what some of the boys told me about some of their teachers. A few I admired, others I wasn't so sure. I suppose I was questioning the purpose and the practice of education and the role of the teacher and of the student within it. This was brought out at one of the staff meetings. Normally, these were dry affairs, with the Head and Deputy Head making announcements and most of the teachers hoping for an early getaway. One of the English teachers, a jolly, usually red-faced, rotund Welshman, David Jones, queried what we were all doing, and so voiced some of my concerns.

"The pupils are not empty pots for me to come along and fill up, pouring from a jug, facts and knowledge and all the answers until 'they are full'," he said. "We, teachers and pupils alike, should be searching for the facts, for true knowledge and understanding. We should be on a joint enterprise, working and learning together; it shouldn't be an 'us and them' scenario."

This was music to my ears but it was clear that several of the staff thought David Jones was a bit of an oddball. There was some discussion, but there was no desire for a common approach. That wasn't how things were done. Once the door of the classroom was closed, each teacher did his own thing, in his own way.

Many of the teachers at KEGS took a similar approach to those I had experienced in my own schooldays. The lesson content was about the subject, the facts, not about students developing their skills or their learning or doing things for themselves. Science and Art were exceptions but their approach was a minority one. One teacher spent every lesson dictating notes to his class of exam pupils. At the start of each lesson, he would say,

"Where did we get to? Oh! Yes, 'at the mouth of the Mississippi'. The city of New Orleans…" and off he'd go, dictating for the next 40 minutes. He had all his notes in front of him; he'd probably had them for years; all he had to do was read them out. All his pupils had to do was write it all down. *Is this education?* I asked myself.

Another teacher wrote his notes on the blackboard, for the class to copy. A lot depended on his handwriting and the boys' eyesight. I didn't consider this acceptable at all. I tried to stop myself from talking too much at each class. There was always a danger of lecturing to the A level students, in the belief that you had all the information and it was your task to impart it. Who was then doing the work, me or the students? I felt it was important to give them reading or short writing tasks. I also gave students issues to consider while working in small groups. Occasionally we had a proper debate. It was all very well them noting what I said, or what their text book said, but I wanted to know, as did the A level examiner, not only what they knew, but what their views and opinions were. Students need to be proactive if they are to question the available historical evidence. It's what historians do.

Towards the end of the Summer term of my first year at KEGS, I was summoned to see the Head, Nigel Fanshawe. He told me that I had passed my probationary year.

"Thank you very much, sir," I said. Due respect was the custom in those days.

"I am sure you will go on and be a successful teacher with a good career," the Head said.

Some members of staff had warned me about speaking out on

issues that I felt strongly about. I had been to see the Head a couple of times in my first year, but he obviously didn't object to this at all. If anything, he probably welcomed a young teacher with views of his own and with the confidence to voice them.

Boys at KEGS all wore the school uniform, including a school cap. There was even a discussion in one staff meeting about doing away with caps, but tradition and custom prevailed. The atmosphere at KEGS was similar to my own grammar school days: orderly movement about the school, intelligent pupils working in classrooms and a varied collection of teachers. Somehow, the way the place operated seemed to reflect the old, Tudor foundation and the long-established buildings. Was everyone conscious of the heritage? Probably not, but a sense of tradition was being inhaled on a daily basis. The main school hall reflected this, with high beams and a look of antiquity. I was supervising an exam there one day when a sparrow somehow got in and flew about, distracting the students. Even worse, the bird, probably frightened, deposited droppings on some of the answer scripts! The bird soon flew out through an open window and normality resumed.

There were some real characters among the staff. Il Duce was Jake Findlay, the Deputy Head, a major presence in the Staff Room. He was close to retiring, a large man, stern and much feared, especially by the younger boys, and also by some of the younger staff! But you could go to him with a problem and know he would listen sympathetically and give sound advice. He kept the place going on an even keel. And he told it as it was: I went to him one day requesting permission to leave school the following Friday at lunchtime as I wanted to get away for a weekend with some athletes.

"Are you sure it will be alright?" I said.

"Good Lord, young man, you don't think the place will fall apart if you aren't here for an afternoon, do you?"

This was Jake Findlay's way of saying, "Of course you can go. You're not indispensible."

Then there was Ralph Lee. What a character he was: an excellent English teacher by all accounts, but disastrously disorganised most of the time. He arrived back from a pub lunch one day to find that he had left the afternoon exam papers in the pub lounge.

We were discussing wives and girl friends one day and he said to me, "You know, young man, it's no harder to fall in love with a rich woman."

Many teachers had nicknames and Ralph's was "Isiah", as one eye was higher than the other! Each day the boys had lunch in a kind of large hut or prefab, with long wooden tables and benches with the kitchen at the side. Lunch was always a noisy affair, and the Master on duty would try to get quiet before the lunch began. One day Ralph was on duty, the boys were sitting in their places, so he picked up a spoon and banged it hard on the table to get quiet. Unfortunately, the spoon hit another spoon, which flew across the room, to loud, raucous cheers. Undeterred, Ralph stood on a nearby, unoccupied bench, so that he could better assert his authority. But he stood on the end of the bench, which promptly flew up into the air. He walked out at that point and another teacher took over.

Peter Pike was Head of PE. He was a tough, muscular, short-set guy who enjoyed his job. He was more often to be seen in shorts than tracksuit. He took pride in the fact that he had introduced boxing to the PE curriculum. This was not universally popular among the teachers, but Peter argued that boxing taught boys self-defence and self-discipline. Peter was pleased when I joined the staff, as he now had another teacher keen on sport and willing to play a part on the Games field. I got on well with Peter, though he could be something of a martinet in the gym.

At KEGS there were "fortnightly orders". All marks given to each boy by his various teachers during a two-week period were collated by the form tutor. When added together, a list, ranking the pupils, was produced, with someone at the top, and, inevitably, someone at the bottom. Each fortnight, each boy's parents would receive the details of how their son had fared, and this could be compared with his previous performance.

"You've done better this time, Simon. You've gone up from 15th to 10th. Well done!"

"What's the meaning of this, Jake? Last time you were 18th. Now you're 28th. That's almost bottom, isn't it? Explain yourself."

The general view among teachers and parents, and probably the boys too, was that these fortnightly orders were a good thing, producing more effort and a greater attempt to do well and gain high marks, plus what was considered a healthy spirit of competition. They were an established feature of the school and had come to be accepted. The amount of administration required to produce the results every fortnight was not that great. However, I recall one amusing incident. A form tutor had just completed his list: he had added up all the marks and produced his class order and was surprised to find one particular boy had come 3rd in the class, when he was usually much lower down. Then he realised what he had done: in error he had added in Stephen's date of birth to his marks! What was he to do? The list was all ready to go out. He decided to leave it as it was, but he wrote in his form tutor's comment to the parents,

"Stephen will have to work hard to maintain this position."

The boys at KEGS could be lively but I enjoyed their company. In one lesson with a 3rd Year class, I wrote "Portugese" on the blackboard. A lad put his hand up and said, "Sir, is that an acceptable variation of the spelling of Portuguese?" Better than, "You've spelt it wrong, sir," but cutting none the less. I corrected my mistake.

There was a boy in the same class whose name was Morris. Surnames, not first names, were always used in class. When his younger brother joined the school in the 1st Year, he was automatically labelled, "Morris Minor". Two years later a third brother arrived, to earn the sobriquet, "Morris Mini Minor". (I'm not making that up!)

I moved on from my first "digs" to a shared flat in Rainsford Lane with a Geography teacher, Mike Turner, who became a very good friend. Indeed we are still friends and in contact today, over 50 years later. We had a lounge on the ground floor, our own bedrooms upstairs and we shared kitchen and bathroom with the elderly house owner who had his downstairs room and his upstairs bedroom. It was a good arrangement, as the house was only five minutes' walk from KEGS, was close to the shops and main town centre, and we passed a café (or more often didn't pass) on our way home from school. Rainsford Lane was also on the way from the school to the cross-country course. Mike and I often ate out and he claims that I introduced him to Indian curry. It was while having a meal in a Chinese restaurant in Chelmsford that Mike came out with one of his classic one-liners. At the end of our meal, we asked our waiter if we could have some tea.

"Chinese or Indian, sir?" the waiter asked.

"English, of course," said Mike, in a deliberately superior tone.

Today, I suppose that remark might be thought unacceptable by some, but it was meant at the time to be humorous, as indeed it was. Mike and I still enjoy curries together.

In the summer of 1960, I went with my parents to the Olympic Games in Rome: it was an amazing experience and where I began my life-long passion for *gelati*! Peter Snell, Herb Elliot, Murray Halberg all won gold. We saw an interesting situation at the end of day one of the men's decathlon: after a heavy thunderstorm that delayed the Shot event, the 400m races began very close to midnight and officials were worried they might not be concluded during the first day, as required by the rules. It was my first visit to Italy, but certainly not my last. I loved the scooters, the noisy city streets, the food and the wine, the beautiful, expressive Italian language, in fact just about everything. We became used to hearing the vibrant and tuneful Italian national anthem, as it was played almost every night, its lively, stirring sounds, so evocative of Italy, competing with all the other city noises.

Soon after we had arrived at our hotel in Rome, we were taken downstairs to have a meal. After a huge bowl of spaghetti, Mum said, "That was lovely. I wonder what's for dessert."

"That was the antipasti we've just had, mother," we said. "The main course comes next!"

On another occasion, Dad and I went for a drink where the beer was served in German measures. When asked what beer he would like, "I'll have *eine grosse* beer," said Dad, showing off his limited German.

So I copied him. We thought we were getting a pint, not realising that the German *grosse* was somewhat more than one pint! Rome's packed trams could be fun, except when leaving the Olympic Stadium one evening, when everyone was soaked from a downpour and sweating from the heat: steaming, sweaty bodies, all in close proximity: not nice! One day, Mum attempted to cross a busy road in central Rome when the lights for pedestrians were indicating red. Suddenly a policeman's whistle rang out shrilly and Mum was hustled on to the pavement and lectured sternly, in Italian, to her considerable embarrassment, and to our amusement.

I was told that it was at the Rome Olympics that a young lady on her way to the stadium saw one of the athletes with a large kit bag on his shoulder and said, "Excuse me, but are you a pole vaulter?"

"No, I'm German, but how did you know my name was Walter?"

(Sorry! Had to include that).

Just before we broke up one summer, Mike and I had been told we would have to vacate our flat, so I left not knowing where I would be living the following September.

"Leave it to me," Mike said. "I'll sort something out."

On my return he informed me he had arranged to rent a thatched cottage at Howe Street, a few miles outside Chelmsford. This was out in the country, with cows just across the road. The cottage was great, though the beams were really low and we had to park our cars in a barn, 200 yards away. The cottage also had its own resident cat, who we learned was called "Will'm". He went with the cottage but was very independent most of the time. Near tragedy struck one day when Will'm sat too close to our drip-feed oil heater and burned off a large portion of his very furry tail. It was the smell that alerted us. Will'm only noticed that something was wrong when the heat reached the fleshy part of his tail. Ouch! He screeched for a while and ran round in circles but never went too close to the fire again. We enjoyed living outside Chelmsford as the air seemed cleaner and it took us nearer to some of the lovely country pubs in North Essex. It also meant that as the drive from KEGS to our cottage took, I suppose, 15–20 minutes, there was time for reflection on the day just gone. I have always found this useful, and have recommended it to other people whose jobs can be stressful. We should all try to find the time to think about our day: to unwind and to reflect on what has gone well, and to put into perspective those things that have not gone well. How did I treat people today? What could I have done better? What should be my priorities tomorrow?

Some of us used to make a regular trip to a pub outside Cambridge. My friend Barri Bishop, who had been at St Catz and who was now teaching on the coast at Westcliff, often came and joined us as we drove to "The Tickle Arms" at Whittlesford. It was an unusual pub. Named after the owner, Fred Tickle, it had a large double bed in the centre of the lounge; loud Wagner music would be playing; curried prawns would often be served at the bar, and the landlord insisted on "No Smoking". There was always an atmosphere of laughter and good fun, and we enjoyed our visits. We arrived one evening, a bit earlier than usual, to see a sign on the door, "Am having a bath. Will open soon."

The entrance door was closely followed by a second door.

"Treat it like a submarine hatch," Fred Tickle would say, especially in winter when he wanted to retain heat. "Close the first door before opening the second." Fred was as gay as you could be – "a touch light in the heels". If anyone asked for directions to the toilet, "Out the door, turn right, then right again – don't stop at the woodpile."

After a few pints at Whittlesford we would drive into Cambridge for a curry, usually at the "Taj Mahal". One evening, towards the end of our meal, Barri disappeared.

"Where's Barri?" someone asked.

"No idea. Thought he went to the loo."

"Maybe he went outside," Ian said. "I'll go and see." Ian also taught at KEGS.

Peering outside into the cold winter evening, Ian saw no sign of Barri. So I went to look for him in what I thought was the most likely place.

"Barri! Are you in there?" No answer, so I banged hard on the one locked toilet door. "Barri! Are you in there? It's me, Tony." There came a muffled cry, the sound of someone waking up! Barri had gone to the loo, no doubt for a perfectly legitimate purpose, and had fallen asleep!

"Come on, you old waster. We're going home," I said.

"Ok," said Barri as he emerged a few moments later, looking very much the worse for wear. How we drove back at night without mishap having imbibed several pints, I do not know. But we did so on several occasions, usually on a Friday, when we were tired as well as inebriated. "Don't drink and drive" had yet to become a slogan.

As I've said, nearly all the boys at KEGS were well behaved. One exception was an individual who was consistently untidy, rude, lazy and thoroughly uncooperative, so much so that after several warnings, he was suspended and later, expelled. The teachers didn't like him and it was mutual; even his peer group found him obnoxious. We all felt we were well rid of him. Several years later, I was with Penny Gardner, whom I was later to marry, enjoying a quiet evening in a rather smart pub by the lake at Hanningfield. We were reclining in a very comfortable settee in the large lounge. Several other couples were also enjoying their evening out. Suddenly a guy on the other side of the lounge got up from his seat and walked directly over to where Penny and I were sitting.

"Mr Elder, isn't it? How nice to see you."

I stood up and shook the hand being offered to me by this smartly dressed, good-looking young man. Then I realised it was the lad who had been expelled, whose back everyone at KEGS had been so glad to see. What a transformation! He told us that he had a very good job, was engaged, and we could see that he had obviously developed a taste for good suits. We chatted for a while and he went back to his seat and his attractive, lady partner. We didn't discuss KEGS, which was probably just as well.

At the start of my time at Chelmsford, I often drove home at weekends. I no longer owned my old grey Standard 10, nor my much-loved Lambretta, having marked my new role as a teacher with the purchase of an Austin A40. These journeys home involved the often hazardous North Circular Road where, some months before, I had had my windscreen shatter while driving in the centre lane of three: very scary! From Chelmsford, my journeys were partly to see Jenny and partly to take home some washing. Jenny and I continued to see each other but as time went on, these visits became less frequent, and eventually we realised our lives were drifting apart. Now that I had a permanent job, it would have been possible for Jenny to come to Chelmsford and we could have lived together. Her bank would have transferred her there, I'm sure. When we talked, we never quite got to that point. We had many discussions in our favourite Hampstead coffee house, listening to, among others, Helen Shapiro, singing, "Walking back to Happiness". The decision to split up was basically hers, though I had to accept that our relationship was going nowhere. The problem was, I was still very fond of her. Back in Chelmsford I played Del Shannon's "Runaway" (No. 1, and 22 weeks in top ten in 1961) endlessly, closely followed by "Are you sure?" by the Allisons (No. 2, and 16 weeks in top ten in 1961). If you know the lyrics of those songs, you'll know why they were so appropriate to my situation. I found it very hard trying to get over Jenny.

Looking back, the things I remember about my time in Chelmsford when not teaching or coaching are very varied. During the summer, some of us had a lot of fun taking part in the pram races, which involved two people, one inside the pram and one pushing, competing with other pram racers around a course which went out into nearby villages and included obligatory stops at a number of hostelries, an event enjoyed by all who took part. I have fond memories of several very inviting pubs just outside Chelmsford. And then there were the times when one or two staff from the Grammar School escorted some of our 6th Form students over to the Girls High School, just across the road, for an evening dance. Teenagers in those days were much more inhibited and it took some persuasion to get the boys to dance with the girls. Relationships were often warmer by the end of the evening.

I had much to thank King Edward VI School for: it had given me an excellent start to my teaching career, and I had learned a lot about teaching History and about myself. I had made lots of friends at the school, at the athletics club and in Chelmsford, a place I shall always remember with affection. After four years I knew it was time to move on.

16
Southend High School

Having spent four years as an assistant teacher, my next step was to take charge of my own department, so I looked out for Head of History posts. I didn't want to move far away, as I had several talented athletes who were still improving and I was about to become engaged. Out of the blue the ideal position was advertised in the *Times Educational Supplement*: Southend High School for Boys wanted a Head of History, and when I received the details of the school and the post, I discovered that they also wanted someone to take charge of school athletics! I could have written the job description myself. I applied, had interviews at the Council offices and at the school, and was appointed to start the following January with a grade C allowance of £485 per annum.

There were four single-sex grammar schools in Southend, which was its own education authority, not part of Essex Local Education Authority. At that time, rightly or wrongly, I didn't consider teaching in anything other than a boys' grammar school. I now had the additional responsibility of organising and running an academic department of the school, plus school athletics. In those days at Southend HS for Boys, all individual sports, football, cricket, hockey, as well as athletics, were looked after by members of the academic staff. It was the same up the road at Westcliff HS for Boys, though there the main winter game was rugby, and woe betide any boy found playing at school with a round ball! The PE staff had it easy in those days.

I found digs in Fairfax Drive at the house of Mrs Leslie. Recently widowed, she was happy to have a teacher living in the house. Shortly after I arrived, I was woken up one night by the sound of running water. Staggering out of bed – it was 2.30 a.m. – on opening my bedroom door I was faced with a stream of water cascading down the stairs. A flood of water covered the ground floor; the cat's saucer was afloat in the hallway. I had woken Mrs Leslie, who confirmed that the main water tap was under the kitchen sink. Wading through the water, I found the stop-cock and turned off the water but it took some time to take effect. Mrs Leslie said she knew of a plumber and, when she rang, he said he would come out in the morning. The stairs, downstairs carpets, the wallpaper and a cupboard with all the spare blankets were thoroughly soaked, so there would be a large insurance claim. I left at the end of the term as I had found a better place to live, a top-floor flat, right on the front on Westcliff Parade, overlooking the estuary, the house being the home of Mr and Mrs Beeney.

I was invited by the Head of Games at Westcliff High School for Girls to give a talk on the subject of training for middle-distance running. After this, I was approached by a girl, who asked if I would coach her. She was 16 and said she was a keen runner and a member of Southend Athletics Club. After a meeting in which we discussed what would be involved and what I would expect from her, I agreed to coach her for a trial period of a month. Fortunately, my predecessor at Southend High School, Rex Tregunna, who also coached at the Southchurch Park track, warned me.

"She's interested in anything in trousers," he said. "Be very careful."

Shortly after this, I went from the Southchurch Park track with a group of runners for a warm up run along the sea front and this girl came too. It was autumn and it was already quite dark by 7.30 in the evening. She managed to detach herself from the rest of the group and suggested we go down on to the beach. I told her I didn't think that was a good idea. Shortly afterwards, before the trial month was over, I told her she had better find a different coach. I doubt very much whether her real interest was in running. I had had a lucky escape.

I found it hard accepting that Jenny and I were no longer together. I had a couple of short relationships: Margaret was a teacher at the Girls' High School in Chelmsford; at the Lions' Club I met Sally who taught at a small private school. It wasn't the same. Then in July 1963 I went to a Conference for teachers of History at St Anne's College Oxford: "Factors in Recent European History". One of the first lectures was on the Holocaust. There was a collective intake of breath when lecturer, Elizabeth Wiskeman, rolled up her sleeve and revealed her concentration camp number on her forearm: it certainly gained our attention. At the conference I met Rene, an attractive young Irish teacher, with whom I soon struck up a rapport – there seemed to be an immediate mutual attraction. When the conference day was over, we spent time on the river and, with the punt tied up by the bank, I attempted to teach Rene the rules of cricket. It was midsummer, and we had a good time for a few days and then met up after the conference when she came to stay with my parents in Finchley. The relationship didn't progress, chiefly because I had started to develop closer ties with Penny and the Gardner family in Chelmsford. Penny was one of the athletes I was coaching. She was quite a lot younger but I became very fond of her. Had I not been so involved with Penny, I might well have developed my links with Rene. We never really explored how much we liked each other. As it was, she went on to marry a dentist and I would later marry Penny.

The person I was replacing at Southend High had been both Head of History and in charge of athletics, so the Head and Governors were replacing like with like. Rex Tregunna, a good Cornishman as the name suggests, had moved on to another local school, Belfairs HS, a Secondary Modern school, as Deputy Head. He and I were to become good friends. My department was actually History and Economics and, as I knew very little Economics, certainly not enough to teach it to A level, it was just as well that I had Hugh Gronow to teach the Economics.

Once again, I particularly enjoyed teaching the 6th Formers, many of whom had aspirations to go to university, some to Oxbridge. Several, such as Peter Callaghan, achieved this. There were soon 28–30 wanting to study History in the 6th Form, and, after some effort, I persuaded the Head, Mr Price, to split them into two classes. Even 15 in one class meant a lot of time spent marking essays, but on the whole the students worked hard and wrote well, which made the marking easier. The talent in the school could be seen in the 3rd and 4th Year classes, which were also a pleasure to teach. Quite demanding activities, such as debates and role-play, the top classes took in their stride. Monarchy v Republicanism was certain to arouse passions when we were doing the Stuart period. On one occasion, one of Her Majesty's Inspectors (HMI) visited my 3A class when we were having a debate on the trial of Charles I and he became so involved, he joined in!

The school was divided into streams, A to D, and in alternate years, A to E. The curriculum for streams A and B differed from that for the C and D classes. Latin or a second foreign language would be replaced with Woodwork or Metalwork for example. I found it strange that in a school that provided for the most intelligent 20% of the 11+ school population, it was considered necessary to divide them into four or five streams according to ability. Such matters were not aired at the generally bland, termly staff meetings, chaired by the Head, where to speak out or raise an issue was considered bad form. As a Head of Department, however, I considered it was not only my right but also my duty, to go to see the Head and raise any issues I felt strongly about.

Mr Price did not take kindly to any suggestion of change. It was said that he had made no changes in his first seven years at the school, as he needed to get the feel of the place, nor in his last seven years, when he considered any change would be a task for his successor. In the intervening 18 months, some said, those with a good memory, there had been one or two minor changes: all apocryphal no doubt.

I went to see Mr Price on several matters. I said that those in the C, D and E streams were underperforming, in my view, and that this was due to being labelled "less good" than their fellows in streams A and B.

"Nonsense," he said, gathering his gown around him, and retreating to the warmth of his favourite radiator, as he did when taking up a defensive position. "You can see from their results that they are not as able as those in A or B."

He would not see that this was as a direct result of the system imposed on them. I tried to get him to consider some form of setting. I pointed out that one of the best mathematicians in the third year was in the D stream, so he would never have the advantage of learning more maths by mixing with able students in the A stream. He wouldn't have it. And to be fair, the system of streaming was favoured by the majority of his staff. They had never known any different. One thing this did was to bring about some excellent results for the most able boys without the necessity for any outstanding teaching.

On another occasion I tried a different tack. It was at the time that CSE, the Certificate of Secondary Education was being introduced nationally as an alternative to GCE. This was designed for those pupils for whom GCE was considered too academic. At Southend HS every year there were some 5th Form pupils gaining very few GCEs, because, in my view, they had been demotivated by the system. Not only that: pupils in the C and D streams were considered by most of the teachers as "not very bright". I had looked at some of the CSE History courses on offer and thought they were interesting, quite challenging but not so academic.

"Could we consider introducing some CSE courses for these pupils?" I asked Mr Price. "If we are going to continue with the streams, could the lower streams be entered for CSE exams in some subjects?"

"Mr Elder" – gown and radiator again – "Can I remind you, this is a Grammar School." His exact words, verbatim. End of interview. Audience over.

I got into trouble with Mr Price on another occasion after one of my A level History lessons with the 6th Form. I had made some remarks, probably uncomplimentary, about the Freemasons, whose role in history, especially on the Continent, has not always been edifying. One of the 6th Form boys had gone home and told his father what I had said and the father had rung Mr Price and made a complaint. Mr Price wanted to know what I had said and what justification I had. I asked the Head whether the contents of my History lessons were now to be the subject of scrutiny by the Head, and he assured me that was not the case. He told me to be careful about what I said in future, which I found disconcerting. I later discovered that every head teacher in Southend, bar one, was a member of the Freemasons, as were the Director of Education and several other key public figures locally.

What I found particularly puzzling and thoroughly contradictory was what happened in the 6th Form. Every year we had a few pupils transferring to us at 16+ from local Secondary Moderns. These were youngsters who had "failed" their 11+ and had had to endure the less sunny climes of the Secondary Modern: "Less suited to an academic grammar school education". Yet here they were at 16, entering the most academically demanding part of the school, where, unstreamed, they were expected to survive with Southend High School's best brains, and possibly thrive – as some did.

Then there was Paul. He had gone through the school in the D stream. Expectations had therefore not been high and he duly obtained a few B and C grades in his GCE exams. He entered the 6th Form to study History, Physics and Maths. Here, when he was mixing with allegedly more able students, he not only held his own but became one of the high achievers and decided he wanted to apply to university. I was teaching him History, and his work was very impressive, but he wanted to become a journalist and his great passion was Physics. His 6th Form teachers forecast high grades for him at A level but, probably due to his unspectacular GCE grades, his potential was not realised and he received rejections from all the universities he applied to. When he received his A level results, he found he had achieved a grade A in all three subjects.

"What shall I do?" he asked me. "Shall I write to Bristol and Exeter and tell them about my grades? Maybe they'll accept me now."

"Well, you could do that," I told him. "But you gave them the chance to accept you, and they turned you down. With those grades, why don't you write to a couple of Cambridge or Oxford colleges and ask if they would consider you for admission this Autumn? I'm sure you'd like to go to Oxford or Cambridge, wouldn't you? And in the opinion of your teachers, you are very capable of doing well there."

"Yes, I'd love to go to Oxford or Cambridge. Do you really feel I could do it?" Paul asked.

"Definitely. I'll give you addresses if you like."

"Thank you very much," said Paul.

"But get writing quickly, as any spare places they have will soon be taken," I told him.

Paul went home that evening, talked to his parents, and prepared a letter, which he brought in to show me and his Physics teacher.

"Great," I said. "Get it in the post today."

Paul chose to write to two colleges at both Oxford and Cambridge. Within three days, he received a reply from Sidney Sussex College, Cambridge, offering him a place. Naturally, he and his parents were over the moon. He accepted by return. At Cambridge, Paul had the opportunity to develop his journalistic skills. He also gained a 1st class Honours degree and went on to edit a prestigious national magazine. All this from the D stream – where the teachers will tell you, "They're not very bright." I was so chuffed for Paul, but the system made me very angry.

Of course there are many examples of young men and women who "failed" the 11+ who subsequently went on to university, obtained degrees, and have highly successful careers. I was to have many professional friends and colleagues who did just that. Which begs the question: how many of those labelled as failures at 11, labelled as not being suitable for a Grammar School education, also had the ability to succeed, but accepted the verdict placed upon them and never did achieve? Wasn't it Michelangelo who said, "The greatest danger for most of us lies not in setting our aim too high and falling short; but in setting our aim too low and achieving our mark."

In other words, many of those labelled by the 11+ as "not good enough", accepted that verdict and lived down to it. I was beginning to feel strongly, not only about streaming into A, B, C and D but also about streaming into Grammar and Secondary Modern Schools via the 11+. This was a life-affecting judgment based on one test taken at the age of 11, often when the child was anxious, nervous, acutely aware of how much rested on their performance, both for them and for their parents. The key factor was the child's intelligence, defined as his or her IQ (Intelligence Quotient). In my view it was not possible to define or measure anything as complex as intelligence, and to determine a child's type of education based on this was not only mistaken but pernicious. I was developing my views on various aspects of education, and I began to see the iniquities of the 11+ during my time at Southend. I saw the strains, imposed on parents and young children, of the 11+ exam system. I visited Junior schools where to have a large proportion of pupils going to grammar school was a sign of success, so normal age-appropriate education was replaced by specific 11+ examination preparation. The teachers admitted that this was what they were doing; they didn't agree with it, nor like it, but felt they had no choice. And this was going on all over the country, and in some places, still is. My view was that this could not be right; there had to be a better way.

I had a History base at one end of a corridor, with Geography at the other end. Jimmy Alves, lovely guy, was a good Head of Geography, and naturally we discussed allsorts. He and I had different approaches to marking, which I found interesting, neither being right or wrong. He always marked work on the day it was handed in by the pupils. He said this was so it was fresh in his mind and so he didn't forget! I always marked work the night before I was due to see the class next. His argument was that he was always ahead and didn't have any backlog of marking to do. My reasoning was that by marking work the day before I had to give it back, what I needed to say to the students about their work was fresh in my mind.

I didn't find the duties of a head of department too onerous. I did a stock check of all the books in the department once a year. I revised the syllabuses being studied at 6th Form level and ordered in some new textbooks, and I made contact with folk I needed to know in some of the different examination boards. One didn't enquire too closely what teaching or how much good teaching was going on in other History classes by the two other members of the department. If there was some sort of an example to be set, I tried to make sure that my teaching was at an acceptable standard. Results seemed good and the Head had no complaints; in fact, I was promoted to a grade D after three years.

Down the road at Westcliff High School for Boys there was a dramatic start to one Monday morning, so we later learned. As the teachers began to arrive in their Staff Room, someone looked out across the playing field.

"What's that sticking up in the pool? It looks like the mast of a yacht," said one.

"You're right. It is," said another.

A group of teachers went to make a closer inspection. Leaning against the side of the small, open-air swimming pool was a small sailing boat. What's more the boat belonged to one of the teachers! *What was it doing there? How had it got there?*

The Head was informed. It was agreed that the most obvious place to start making enquiries would be the 6th Form. Their instincts were correct. Four members of the 6th Form confessed that it was their doing. For a challenge, they said, they had wheeled the boat from its moorings at the Yacht Club, brought it all the way to the school, and placed it in the pool. The Head was not amused. He did have some experience of previous escapades initiated by members of the 6th Form, however, and, after consultation with the owner of the boat, it was agreed that no further action would be taken, provided the boat was returned to its rightful mooring place without it being in any way damaged. And this is what happened the same evening.

While I was at Southend HS, we had a routine visit from HMI. Apparently they said that they had enjoyed the leisurely start to each day, an acidic example of how to be critical while appearing to be complimentary. Their visits to the History department lessons went well, but I was also accompanied out on to the field by an inspector when I had a Games lesson.

"Stop!" he said as we were walking from the school buildings towards the football pitches. "Look at those boys." He pointed to a large group of lads who were already out on the pitch with a number of footballs. "What are they doing?" he asked. It seemed to me obvious.

"They are kicking the footballs to each other," I said. "Waiting for me to come and take charge."

"No. Look again," he said, and I began to think I was failing in some serious way to meet an HMI objective. "They are warming up," he said. "It's an essential activity."

"Oh! Yes, so they are," I concurred, not revealing my scepticism. The reality was that the boys were pleased to be out on the field with the chance to kick a few balls about. I doubt whether the concept of warming up entered any of their heads. As an experienced athletics coach, I knew the importance of warming up before any strenuous sporting activity, but I thought it sensible to give the HMI his chance to put me right.

I soon realised that my teaching and, more specifically, the pupils' learning, would be improved if my blackboard was replaced, or at least augmented, by an overhead projector. Class brainstorming in the 3rd Year (what is now Year 9), for instance, on the rights and wrongs of Charles 1 and Cromwell, would be written up on the blackboard, as would anything that needed to be shown to the class as a whole. But what if one or more pupils were absent for one lesson or more? By the time they returned to school, the work had probably been erased. If I had an OHP, what I wrote could be retained. I could also prepare material and show it to the class on OHP sheets. In addition I had one class that was, shall we say, lively, by grammar school standards. Writing on the blackboard meant turning your back to the class whereas, when using an OHP, I could always be facing the class. A further argument was that an OHP allowed individual students to prepare something they could share with the class. This happened in Years 4 and 5, when working towards GCEs, and in the 6th Form. With an OHP the student could take away an acetate sheet, prepare their material and show it to the class next lesson. I decided to approach the Head and ask him if the History department could have an OHP.

First I had to explain to Mr Price what they were. I had found out that another school, where I had some teacher friends, had some, so I suggested that Mr Price and I might drive to Ilford County High School, talk to the Head there, see one in action, and maybe he would be persuaded. It was the first and only time I travelled in a car with Mr Price. We arrived and met the Head.

"I believe you have an overhead projector," said Mr Price.

"We have ten," their Head said.

We were shown one working in a History classroom and another in Mathematics. Mr Price was impressed; we returned to Southend; I got my OHP a few weeks later. It was put to very good use. I even invited the Head to come to a lesson to see it in action. This was almost a unique occurrence. The pupils were astonished to have the Head visit their lesson, and it was the talk of the Staff Room, but Mr Price realised that money had been well spent and soon mine wasn't the only OHP.

The other teaching aid I used at Southend that was new for me was a film projector. I showed short films on History, which the pupils enjoyed and from which they learned a lot. Quite often the machine decided not to work initially, but there was always one pupil in each class who was a self-appointed "expert" or "film technician", who always knew what to do. If the machine didn't start at once, Barry (he was in the 4th Year) would be out of his seat and at the front fiddling with wires and switches. Usually, it only took a moment for him to make it work, as he knew what he was doing. So much so that, when Jimmy Alves couldn't get a piece of technology to operate in a Geography lesson one day and he knew Barry was along the corridor with me, he knocked and asked if he could borrow Barry for a few moments! These lads knew far more than us teachers when it came to technology, and they were never shy in coming forward to show off their skills.

We had a singular daily assembly at Southend HS. The organ in the main hall played a hymn each morning, though it was rarely sung. The Head, suitably gowned, emerged into and spoke from a pulpit; the whole quasi-church occasion had an air of daily predictability and unreality. I usually took my place in an upstairs balcony with the senior boys, where I looked down on what I felt was a kind of ritual farce. The only assembly I can remember that had a notable effect on the boys and myself was the morning after the tragedy at Aberfan. The silence and the reflection were very genuine that morning.

The school was situated by the side of a not very busy dual carriageway and, not far away, on the same side of the road was Southend Hospital. The similarity in their appearance and their proximity gave rise to some amusing incidents. Occasionally one would meet someone in the school corridor and be asked the way to x-ray or the pharmacy. The temptation to direct such folk to the Head's room was usually resisted. Whether the hospital had parents looking for the Headmaster, I didn't discover. I know the 6th Form at one stage considered organising operations in the library but, fortunately (but perhaps disappointingly), this never materialised.

One thing that amazed and impressed me then and still does in retrospect about Southend HS was that the office was run by one lady, who was unmarried and who, I gather, had been at the school for many years. She arrived in her office every morning, disappeared punctually on her bicycle for her hour's lunch break, dutifully locking the office door behind her, and returning for her afternoon shift. She was the Head's secretary and finance chief, answered the telephone and dealt with personal enquiries as the sole office receptionist. No doubt the school has more office staff now, as secretarial and admin work has greatly increased, but what that lady did at that time was nonetheless impressive.

Many of the staff were what I would now describe as typical grammar school schoolmasters. One group met in the Staff Room every lunchtime, without fail, for their game of bridge, occupying their selected chairs and table, which was indisputably "their space". Among the bridge players in this all-male Staff Room, the only other competition seemed to be who could fart the loudest and most often. Obviously, their afternoon lessons required no thought or preparation. One of the language teachers, not a bridge player, could often be seen nodding off, sitting at his desk on the raised podium in his classroom at the front of the class. His pupils kept quiet as they could then read or do whatever they liked. This was an example of very able pupils doing well despite, or without, their teacher. On the last day of the Summer term, as the bell was sounding for the end of afternoon school, one member of staff could be seen, every year without fail, driving through the school gates towing his caravan en route for the Channel ferry. Some of the teachers worked very hard and did their best, especially for those sitting exams, but many others did the minimum. It was what they had always done. It was an easy life, as nobody checked up on them. The place seemed to be actually decaying around me. I became gradually more disillusioned.

I was fortunate at Southend HS to meet John and David Lloyd. Their father ran a tennis school in Southend and both boys were very promising tennis players. Each year SHS held its inter-house cross-country races in Belfairs Woods. One year, David captained our senior house cross-country team and did a remarkable job, running alongside the last two or three scorers for his team throughout the race until close to the finish when he shot off to finish near the front of the field. Our house won the team award, but David had sacrificed his own potential first place to make that possible. My role with John was to give him sessions of circuit training during lunchtimes and occasionally after school in the small school gym, as he needed to build up his general strength and stamina for his tennis. He was always keen and willing. On Saturdays, John, who was only 13 or 14, used to travel up to London for specialised tennis coaching under John Barrett. One Saturday the school wanted John to play soccer for the school 3rd XI, but he had a commitment to John Barrett in London. A dispute ensued.

"The school must come first," was the prevailing mantra.

"But which is more important," I said, "to play for the school 3rd XI or to receive tennis coaching at national junior GB level?"

"Representing the school has to be the priority," was repeated.

I said, "Surely we are trying to see that every boy has the opportunity to develop his talents to the full, whether they be academic, sporting, artistic or whatever. The school should be delighted when one of its pupils is so talented as to receive national coaching. Isn't that more important than playing for the school 3rd XI?"

Such views were greeted as heresy. John rose above the "little people" and became one of Britain's finest tennis players as well as Britain's Davis Cup Captain, and I am pleased to have been able to help him in a small way with his development very early on.

Southend had some promising young runners, Len, David, Andy, Mike and others, and they and I used to run out from the school some lunchtimes and train in a park just across the main road. Some of them went on to represent Essex Schools teams at cross-country or on the track. In the summer, we organised matches against other schools on our school field. On one occasion we didn't have a decent high jumper, so, to the consternation of our opponents, I drafted in someone from Southend High School for Girls to compete for us. Ann Wilson was an exceptional young athlete who went on to represent Great Britain on many occasions in high jump, long jump, hurdles and pentathlon, gaining three silver medals in the Commonwealth Games in Edinburgh in 1970, and competing for GB at the Munich Olympics in 1972. On this occasion, in the high jump, she beat all but one of the boys taking part in the match!

The annual sports day was an important occasion in the school year. Parents came to watch, teachers demonstrated timekeeping and judging skills, and inter-house rivalry was intense. Unfortunately, the facilities were not really up to the task. The track was grass, of course, and somewhat bumpy. Runners in the 100 yards had to negotiate the protruding roots of a large tree adjacent to the track. On one occasion one of the lads running in the 100 yards tripped and fell to the ground about 15 metres from the line, and all the judges, as one man, turned to look at him, to see if he was badly hurt, but in doing so, none of them saw who had come 1st, 2nd, 3rd. It was suggested that the race should be rerun, but it was decided to take the word of the boys, all of whom knew and could agree on the result.

I had driven up to Chelmsford most weekends to be with Penny. On one such visit we witnessed a clash between the Mods and Rockers, under the railway bridge in the middle of Chelmsford. There was no violence, just a stand off really, but I remember the colourful bikes and bizarre clothes.

One holiday, Penny and I went to South Devon in our recently acquired Hillman Estate, a lovely car in many respects but with some drawbacks. The first time we took it out, it rained, and the wipers promptly fell off into the road. We also noticed that a cold draught blew up Penny's skirt in the passenger seat, so I took it back to the car dealer.

"There's a piece missing," the guy said. So he took the required piece from a car in the showroom and fitted it into our car. "There you are, all sorted," he said. *What about the car in the showroom,* I thought.

In Kingsbridge we found ourselves stationary in a traffic jam on an uphill section of the High Street. In my mirror I saw a tractor approaching. To my amazement it didn't stop but ran straight into the back of our Estate where our cases were. Penny and I got out to inspect the damage. Standing in an adjacent shop doorway was a policeman. *Excellent, I'll have a reliable witness,* I thought. When I spoke to the Devon constable, who had obviously seen the whole thing, he said, "You can't expect tractors to have the same quality of brakes as a motor car, sir."

I couldn't believe it. We carried on with our holiday and later had the car repaired, but we decided to cut our losses and part company with the Hillman. I've had VWs ever since!

It was while I was at Southend HS that Penny and I were married, Mike Turner being my best man. One of her bridesmaids was Babs Horton, who I was also coaching. Although there was an age gap, Penny and I had fallen in love with each other and wanted to be together. I had been on holiday with Penny and her parents to the Lake District and I had always been welcomed into their home by her parents. I could foresee a happy future ahead for both of us.

Once we were married, for a short while we rented an upstairs flat just off Hamlet Court Road in Westcliff, before buying a small semi-detached house in Leigh-on-Sea in May 1967. Life was good. Penny continued to develop as a runner, doing well on the track and at cross-country. Before we married, she had come 2nd in the WAAA Championships Mile with a world-best time for an 18-year-old of 4 minutes 56.9 seconds. Unfortunately she developed a condition in one of her hips, which virtually ended her running career.

Penny Gardner wins 880 yards Melbourne Park, Chelmsford

After just over four years at Southend High School, I decided it was time for fresh challenges. Despite my critical comments about Southend HS, it did achieve successes with the most able students, and it had a good sporting record. I could now see many weaknesses in the 11+ system, and I wondered whether other grammar schools were failing to motivate their less able students. It was the middle of the 1960s and with Circular 10/65 the move towards Comprehensive Schools gathered momentum. I decided I didn't want to teach only the most favoured pupils, those with the highest intelligence, often with educated, fully supportive, usually middle-class parents, those who had managed to "pass" the 11+. I looked for advertisements offering challenges and opportunities in comprehensive schools.

Mr Price thought that I should apply for a suitable Headship, and I did make one such application, which led to an extremely interesting interview, the details of which I recount later. I was not convinced at the advice I was receiving. Yes, I wanted to obtain a post in a comprehensive school, but surely I would need some experience in such a school before being appointed a Head. Rex Tregunna, my predecessor, had moved from the grammar school to become Deputy Head in a secondary modern school. With that experience he progressed to the headship of a comprehensive school. Having just married and bought a house meant that I didn't want to move far away. The border with Essex was close and, by the late 1960s, Essex did not have the 11+. I soon saw an advertisement that caught my eye. It was a post of Head of Upper School in an 11–16 Comprehensive School just inside the Essex border. I applied and was granted an interview.

17
Appleton School

Having made my decision to leave Southend High School, I applied to become Head of the Upper School at Appleton School in 1968. Benfleet was just north of Canvey Island, down the road from Bread and Cheese Hill. The Appleton School at Benfleet had opened only three years earlier. Their oldest pupils were about to move into Year 4 (what we now term Year 10). The four-storey school building was modern, and it was so good to see teachers at the school without gowns. When I arrived for my interview I was given a warm welcome by the Head, Eddie Haynes, and other senior colleagues. *This place feels different*, I thought. My one reservation was that there would be no 6th Formers to teach, no A level students to prepare for university. Mr Price and others warned me about this: spending time away from older students would count against me in the future, I was told; furthermore the very best teachers didn't teach in an 11–16 school, and certainly not in a comprehensive school, so the quality of my colleagues would not be the same. I was advised to keep away, but here I was, about to be interviewed, and about to make my own judgments.

There were three others being seen. I was the first in and my interview seemed to go well. The Head and his deputy, Miss Jeffrey, were there, plus a couple of governors and a guy from Essex LEA. Mr Haynes asked me about teaching girls.

"This will be new for you, won't it? How will you cope, do you think?" he asked.

"Well, I did teach girls while on teaching practice at Hemel Hempstead," I said, "and I regularly coach girls at the athletics track, both at Southend and at Chelmsford. I am quite used to teenage girls so I don't think there should be any problem at all," I assured him.

To my great delight I was appointed. The job meant promotion. I was given a grade E allowance and my total salary was £2,206, a princely sum in those days. Also very important to me, I had made the key transition from grammar to comprehensive. I wasn't a Head, or even a deputy, as someone cruelly pointed out, but I knew I would be serving a very good apprenticeship. I was to take charge of the Upper School, Years 4 and 5. There was a Head of Lower School, and next year there would also be a Head of Middle School. We were the third tier, if you like, after the Head, then his deputy and the senior master. I had been at the school just over a term, I recall, when Eddie Haynes said to me,

"Freda, Roy and I have to go out; you're in charge!"

"Oh! What does that mean, exactly?" I asked, rather bemused.

"Well, we're not here, so you're the Head in our absence," said Eddie Haynes.

"But what do I have to do?" I enquired, feeling somewhat vulnerable and unprepared.

"You don't have to do anything," said Eddie, "except get them all out if there's a fire!"

"Oh! Right," I said, trying to sound reassured and more confident.

As things turned out nothing did happen, as Eddie knew would almost certainly be the case. Late in the afternoon they all returned to find there had been no coup!

Appleton was designated a 10-Form entry school, but because there had been a delay to building a new secondary school in the Rayleigh area, the actual intake had been 12-Form, so the 4th Year I had responsibility for consisted of 360 boys and girls. I had received no written job description, so after a few weeks I went in to see Eddie Haynes. He told me to sit down. Only later did I realise that this was the first time any Head had asked me to sit down in his room!

It was also the first time I had had a lengthy chat with any Head I had worked for and the first I had had with Eddie in his room since my interview. And another strange thing: up to now I had always felt I was working *for* the Head of the school; now at Appleton, again for the first time, I felt I was working *with* the Head and his senior colleagues. Subtle differences maybe, but significant in my view.

"Mr Haynes, I wonder if you could clarify what my responsibilities are. I don't want to tread on any toes, and I don't want to leave something undone that is mine to do."

Instead of telling me what my responsibilities were, Eddie Haynes said, "OK, fire away."

That took the wind out of my sails for a moment, but I said, "I take it that the 4th and 5th Year curriculum is down to me, that's my responsibility."

"That's correct," Eddie said.

"And by that, you mean I should liaise with all the subject Heads, to find out what syllabuses they are following, and what exam boards they are preparing for."

"Yes, and it will be a good idea to limit the number of exam boards being used by the school to two, otherwise the examination entries next year will be a nightmare."

"So some negotiation and persuasion may be necessary," I said.

"Indeed," said Eddie.

"And what about the quality of teaching and the learning outcomes?" I asked.

My experiences in the two Grammar schools had led me to believe that these should not be left to chance. Management and leadership should involve monitoring the quality of teaching and the quality and range of learning outcomes. So I asked Eddie if I had a role.

"Well, no one else will be keeping an eye on that, apart from me if it became a last resort. But I should tread warily," Eddie warned. "Sensitive area, and you're new. Might be a good idea to discuss this issue with them collectively, and set up a working group to deal with the matter of quality outcomes, with you as chair."

"Yes, thank you for that," I said. "What about the pastoral care of the pupils? There are 12 tutor groups; should I be monitoring what each tutor does with his or her tutor group?"

"Loosely, yes. You have overall responsibility for both curriculum and pastoral care as Head of the Upper School. They are answerable to you. But I'm sure I don't have to tell you that you have to work with these people. They are the ones who have to do the teaching and deliver on pastoral care. You should keep an eye on things, know what is going on, and intervene only when necessary. Most of them are very good – I appointed them! A few need monitoring more closely. You'll soon see who they are."

"Yes, I understand that," I went on, "but what about Careers advice and liaison with the 6th Form College and Colleges of Further Education? Who does that?"

"You do," said Eddie, with a smile, "working with the Essex Careers Service of course."

I began to wish I hadn't asked! It was becoming obvious that I was responsible for almost everything (no, cross out "almost"!) that happened in Years 4 and 5.

"One more thing," said Eddie. "Don't forget the GCE and CSE exams next year. We've mentioned exam boards. There's also the issue of doing the exam entries and conducting the examinations in May and June the summer after next. I'd like you to do that."

My head was beginning to reel and I wanted to get away and write all this down lest it be forgotten or something was overlooked.

"Yes, I see," I said lamely. "Thank you for spelling it out, and for the advice. I'll do my best."

"I know you will," said Eddie. "It sounds a lot, but you are more than capable. I have every confidence in you."

I got up and left the Head's office. I did go and write it all down, together with an anticipated timetable, my annual calendar, of when each bit of the jigsaw needed to be completed. I had never done that before. Yes, there was a lot to do, but I realised that I had never felt better. I had some real responsibility, with teachers and pupils depending on me to do a good job. Maybe I would be able to influence the education and future of these young people. When I thought about it, I realised I had never had such a one-to-one in depth conversation with the Head of any school I had previously worked in. Eddie gave me great confidence. I felt he had total faith and confidence in me. I felt I was an important part of the whole operation, and I was determined not to let Eddie down.

My weekly teaching programme gave me some History and also some English, which would be different, but I looked forward to that. I had a lighter timetable so I would have some time during each day to manage some of my areas of responsibility. I had also been given a 4th Year tutor group to look after. I'd been a tutor at Southend, but this would be different. Half would be girls and the 30 pupils would cover the whole range of ability. They were called 4T, and I was told that they had "seen off" their last two tutors!

"They can be a bit fiery," said Miss Jeffrey.

I must admit, I was just a little anxious about what to expect. I hoped that my experiences in the two London secondary moderns might come in handy.

My timetable included teaching my tutor group, 4T, both History and English. To my surprise and relief I had absolutely no problem with 4T. They were great: lively, willing to talk, ask questions, and they worked well if they were interested. As it was a mixed ability class, as I expected, I could tell straight away that some were very bright, while one or two were clearly close to the other end of the scale and would need help. I soon discovered that the able pupils were very willing to help the less able, which I had never experienced before. I genuinely enjoyed teaching them and being in their company. Even after all these years I can still recall Kay Hartless, Elaine Hares, Robert Hursk, Peter Jiggens, Jenny Green, Sally Hart, Timothy Lawrence and others who were in 4T.

As I started at Appleton School in September 1968, I decided to begin with a class project on the Olympic Games, due to start in Mexico in mid-October. 4T entered into this with real enthusiasm. I had hit the right note! I had some wall charts on the Olympics and the more artistic pupils created some more to decorate the walls of the classroom. Our project involved some research on their part: on the origin of the Games, on Mexico itself and its history, on the different sports in the Games, the British competitors most likely to do well, even on the effects of altitude on runners' performances. We even managed to examine the causes of the student riots and the harsh clampdown just prior to the start of the Games. And we looked at film of the "black" protest when Tommie Smith and John Carlos did a black glove salute on the rostrum after their 200m final. We discussed this and learned what it was all about. The Mexico Games saw the Fosbury Flop used for the first time in the high jump and some of the class saw it on TV and were amazed. They were even more astonished when we measured out Bob Beamon's world record long jump of over 29 feet! They were most impressed when I took in a postcard I had received from Mexico from Mary Tagg who was running in the 400m with Lillian Board. Mary was the brother of Mike Tagg who had beaten Malcolm Absolom in the English Schools Mile in 1965; she was also engaged to miler Andy Green who had been teaching with me at Southend, so Penny and I knew her quite well – thus the postcard.

Some of the pupils' written work contributed to their CSE English and the project was certainly cross-curricular, as it included elements of Art, Geography, History, Politics and Science as well as English. Several other teachers visited our classroom to see what we were doing, as word had got about! Naturally the class followed the Games on television and in the newspapers. They particularly enjoyed David Hemery's world record win in the 400m hurdles. I let it go on until Christmas, after which we concentrated on the specific requirements of the English and History exam syllabuses. It had been a good first term with 4T. I couldn't remember a term of teaching that I had enjoyed more.

I also enjoyed teaching the English Mode 3 CSE, used by schools in the South-East Essex area, called "Coming to Terms with People and Life". This was such an appropriate title for 14–16 year olds and it applied not only to their creative writing, but also to their literature, which for 4T included *Sons and Lovers* and *Macbeth* and some modern poetry. The History in the school was fairly standard fare: Greeks and Romans in the first years, Tudors and Stuarts later, then 20th century wars and their aftermath to examination level. I missed teaching 6th Formers, but I had so much else to do, I didn't have time to mope about that. Occasionally, I paid a return visit to my former colleagues at Southend HS, and they were genuinely amazed that it was possible to teach a class containing pupils across the whole ability range. It was beyond their imagination and their comprehension! I told them I enjoyed it, but they merely shook their heads in disbelief, so hung up had they become on rigid streaming.

Pupils were working towards exams in either the GCE or the CSE. Grade 1 CSE was equivalent to a GCE pass (grades A–C). Generally the most able pupils were entered for GCE exams, while those considered unlikely to obtain a GCE pass in a subject were entered for the CSE. Many pupils had a mixture of the two. The system worked pretty well, though it all had to be explained to pupils, and via letters and meetings to parents. As the school's examinations officer, I had to make sure that each subject head submitted his or her exam entries accurately to me so that I could send in the exam boards' forms by the required date. There were 360 pupils in the 4th Year, but this exercise did not have to be completed until the spring of the following year. I spent some time making sure the forms were clear and, as far as possible, foolproof.

The following year, Appleton's entry went up to 14 forms i.e. 420 pupils. So when the first intake of 360 went into the 5th Year and the second intake of 420 went into the 4th Year, I was effectively Head of an Upper School of 780 pupils! That meant 26 tutors and tutor groups to "monitor"; thankfully, the vast majority were doing a splendid job, with a Personal, Social and Health Education programme already in place. Tutors were also very good at dealing with issues and sorting out problems themselves. I rarely had to intervene to deal with "difficult" pupils or parents. Mind you, getting the whole year group into Assembly on their morning wasn't easy.

Another task that fell onto my plate was the organisation of the following year's "Option choices". Before the 420 pupils in Year 3 moved into Year 4 in the following September, each pupil would have to have made his or her choice of subjects to study in Years 4 and 5. English, Maths and PE (not an examination subject) were compulsory, so there were six more subjects that had to be chosen, one of which at least, it was decreed, had to be a Science subject. All this was in the days before the National Curriculum, of course. To carry out this exercise required liaising with Frank Whitnall, the newly appointed Head of Middle School, all the subject teachers, tutors, parents and, of course, with the 420 pupils.

It may be thought that having to organise this for 420 pupils would be a nightmare, but rather the contrary. Having so many pupils actually made the task easier, as it meant that several subjects could appear in more than one option block. Those who wanted to take two languages could do so. It meant that it was possible to let almost every pupil have the choices they made. This was before the days of computers in schools, so I had to do this job on pieces of paper, but it worked. It all had to be done as early as possible, so that the Deputy Head, Freda Jeffrey, could prepare the timetable, and so that advertisements could be placed for any additional staff we might need. The thinking behind all this, as I explained to a somewhat incredulous Heads of Department meeting one Tuesday afternoon, was that to give pupils the opportunity to choose the subjects they would study up to their exams would produce a more satisfied and motivated group of pupils. This was far better in my view than telling pupils what subjects they had to take, though of course each individual received advice, and we took on board the views of parents. Pupils were taking some control of their education, which was how I thought it should be. With that freedom came some responsibility, as I explained to pupils and their parents.

The biggest headache was the timetabling of rooms. We didn't have enough Science laboratories or Art rooms for all those wanting to take those subjects. We tried to discourage those subject heads who wanted to veto certain children from taking their subject and, to my relief and some surprise, by the end of the July term over 2000 individual subject choices had been sorted and each pupil, and their parents, knew what they would be studying the following September and for the next five terms. And each subject head had a list of the pupils that would be taking their subject to GCE or CSE level. Eddie Haynes was quite impressed that this exercise had gone as well as it had.

"Freda had said to me, 'it won't work'," said Eddie, "but I said, 'give him a chance, he says he knows what he's doing, and I trust him.' I'm glad I did."

Organising the examinations each summer was not straightforward. The 360 pupils in the first year's cohort, and the 420 in the second, could not all be fitted into the hall for subjects such as English and Maths, so the gym was brought into use, which upset the PE staff of course. Although the school leaving age was not raised to 16 until 1974, almost all our top year chose to stay to take their exams.

We had an interesting incident in my second year. Pamela, a girl in Year 5, had shown her ability in her first two years at Appleton, but after that she lost interest in schoolwork. When her teachers pointed out to her how much potential she had, she replied, "I wish I hadn't done so well in the first two years, then you wouldn't have known."

On the morning of the all-important English Language exam, Pamela didn't turn up. We knew she had the ability to do really well, so we didn't want her to miss it. The school rang her home, but there was no answer. The Head of English, John Garton, said he would pop round to her house and bring her in. I said I would go.

Eddie Haynes was in the exam hall when John and I were discussing what we should do. "Neither of you is going to Pamela's house on your own," he said, very firmly. Pamela, rather than doing well at her studies, had chosen to find other ways to spend her time, and she had something of a reputation. "It's much too dangerous. You don't know what you might get yourself into, if you go to her house," said Eddie. "I'll come with you, Tony. John, you see this lot start their exam on time."

The rules allowed a candidate to be no more than 30 minutes late for an exam, so Eddie and I hurried round to Pamela's house. We got no answer at the front door, so we tried the back door, which wasn't locked, so, after knocking and calling out, we entered.

"Pamela? Are you there?"

At first there was no response. Then we heard a voice, followed by a dishevelled looking Pamela, obviously just out of bed. Whether she had been on her own or not we didn't enquire. We talked with her in the kitchen, explained why we were there and, to our surprise, persuaded her to come and sit the English exam. It had been a strange event for us. It turned out well for Pamela though, as she earned herself a grade A.

From what I remember there was very little actual bad behaviour among the pupils in the top two years in the school. Yes, there was occasional truancy, and one girl, who was often absent, was suspected of either spending time in the shops and arcades in Southend, or of entertaining her boyfriend at home. On one occasion I was in the office when Marion rang her home. There was a quick response and Dawn explained why she was at home.

"She can't have getting up to any mischief if she answered your call that quickly," I said.

"She can if she has the phone where I have mine!" said Marion.

I was very impressed with Eddie Haynes, but at times he seemed to clamp down on very trivial issues. A group of pupils were in the entrance hall waiting for the coach to take them to a local theatre.

"You three girls, report to Miss Jeffrey's office. Your skirts are far too short," he said in a headmasterly, abrupt tone. It was the 1960s and many of the girls were wearing their skirts short if they could get away with it. The school had a policy: skirts had to be no shorter than a particular length above the knee. Miss Jeffrey would do the measuring if it was required. The three girls duly went to the Deputy Head's room and returned a few minutes later with their skirts slightly less short. Meanwhile the Head was berating a couple of lads for having their hair too long.

"I want to see you both in my office next Monday morning before school with a decent length haircut. Understand?"

"Yes, sir."

There seemed to me to be more important things to be concerned about than short skirts and long hair. When I raised this with Eddie Haynes, he said, "Of course there are. But if you make a fuss about so called trivial things, you won't have a problem with more important issues. Some schools happily allow smoking. What happens then? The pupils have to break another rule, so you get drug taking." I could see his point. "By clamping down on the little misdemeanours, you avoid the bigger ones," he said.

We couldn't accommodate all the pupils in the school hall for morning assembly, so year groups took it in turns. Sometimes it was taken by pupils; I recall one memorable, theatrical performance by three girls dancing to, "The Good, the Bad and the Ugly!" Members of staff often took assembly. One morning, one of the lady teachers was in full flow to a Year 4 assembly. Eddie Haynes and I were standing at the back of the hall as we often did.

"I don't know what effect she has on the kids," Eddie said to me in a whisper, "but she frightens the life out of me!"

As a Head, Eddie Haynes could not have been more different from Mr Price at Southend. He was often around the school, in corridors at break and visiting classrooms. He listened to what people had to say, though he was a forceful character. He usually wore a light grey suit, no gown of course, and it was clear that staff and pupils all respected him. He gave the appearance of someone who was doing a job he enjoyed, yet he stood no nonsense and was clearly "the boss". His Senior Management Team (SMT) consisted of himself, his deputy Freda Jeffrey and Senior Teacher Roy Musson. Eddie had brought both of them with him from his previous school. From time to time other senior people were invited to join the SMT meeting, including myself on several occasions.

Eddie had a good sense of humour. He, John Garton and I were discussing a lady member of staff one evening after school. She was a confirmed spinster, very prim, probably in her late thirties, who lived on her own and didn't seem able to understand the ways of the modern world. Her fussy manner often irritated the pupils. Even the clothes she wore seemed out of place. We were having a semi-serious discussion about this lady.

"I know what she needs," said Eddie, "but I'm not volunteering!"

Freda Jeffrey was middle aged and unmarried, and she provided the little personal touches and the warmth at senior level. She worked long hours and was very efficient. When an irate parent came striding into the school entrance swearing blue murder and demanding this and that, Freda would appear from her office and say, with a smile, "Come and have a cup of tea." And after a chat the anger would have subsided and the issue had usually been resolved.

Roy Musson, a smart, dapper man, should have been a waiter at the Ritz. He seldom raised his voice, but he commanded respect. I had only been at the school a few weeks when Roy introduced me to a term I had not come across before; we were walking up the main staircase and, as three lads went past, Roy turned to me and said, "Three of our toe rags."

Parents who had been allocated a place for their child at another school often sought a place at Appleton, even though we were full. One such parent kicked up a real fuss in the local paper, demanding that his daughter be admitted. Two other families jumped on the bandwagon. The local authority stood firm, so the parents wrote to the Prime Minister. Eddie Haynes received a letter from Margaret Thatcher telling him he must admit these three children. He replied to No. 10, saying that he didn't take orders from the Prime Minister, who had, he said, no authority over an individual head teacher. He could only be instructed in this matter by the local education authority. And there the matter ended. *Well done, Eddie!*

In my second year at Appleton I was given a small office at one end of the school. Next to my office was a common room for 5th Year pupils with its own small kitchen. From my office I was able to keep an eye on the common room, which was used at break and lunchtimes and after school. There were some study carrels at which pupils could work after school or during lessons if they had a non-teaching period. Occasionally the 5th Form committee organised a dance or disco, which I and other staff had to supervise. Next to my office was an entrance to the school, only to be used by staff and members of the 5th Year. As this wasn't always obeyed, I put a notice on the door, saying, "Staff and 5th Year pupils' Entrance Only."

One morning, a 1st year boy calmly walked in, so I said to him, "Hey!" And pointing to the notice, "Can't you read?"

"No, sir," he said, meekly. I could tell from his manner that he was telling the truth. I felt quite bad. One should not make assumptions, I reminded myself.

Also in my second year at Appleton one of the athletes I was coaching, Rita Ridley, of the Essex Ladies club, reached the final of the women's 1500 metres at the Commonwealth Games in Edinburgh. I had warned Eddie Haynes that this might happen and he had said that if it did, I could have the day off to go up to watch her race. An overnight sleeper to Edinburgh was expensive, so I did a deal with Rita's local paper, the Evening Echo, in Loughton, where she lived. If Rita won, I was to phone through to the paper an article the same evening describing the race and her victory, and in return they said they would pay all my travel expenses. I now had another reason for wanting Rita to win! My coaching friend and colleague, Frank Horwill and I travelled up to Edinburgh by overnight sleeper. That was an experience in itself as anyone who knew Frank can appreciate! Marea Hartman, Women's Amateur Athletics Association (WAAA) boss, kindly made sure I had a seat in the main stand. Rita won her race and became Commonwealth Champion, and after her race, all smiles, she was photographed having a chat with the Duke of Edinburgh. I quickly put together a piece for the Loughton paper and phoned it through to them; Frank and I flew back to Heathrow and I was in school the next day. Quite an eventful and whistle-stop 36 hours!

Looking back, I would say that my four years and a term at Appleton were among the most enjoyable of my teaching career. When I arrived, I already had ten years' experience, and although the amount of work at Appleton was often mind-boggling, I was still young enough to deal with it. One day when I was in my office after school, I became acutely aware of all the jobs and tasks I needed to complete by the following Monday: the list was horrendous; it seemed

Rita receiving her medal from the Duke of Edinburgh after her Commonwealth Games win 1970

overwhelming. *I'll never get all this done,* I thought. *So much to do, so little time.* (Who was it who said that? The White Rabbit? Or Peter Sellers?) When next Monday arrived, lo and behold, all the jobs had been done. It taught me that, however vast or numerous the agenda, it could be achieved.

It was at about this time that I learned an important lesson about managing tasks. To the expert this may seem obvious but to me it was a valuable insight to acquire: that one should distinguish between tasks that are important and those that are urgent. And act accordingly.

I also found I was much more at home in a comprehensive school set-up. I enjoyed working with disadvantaged kids, and from a quality of teaching aspect, I learned, for the first time, the need for differentiation in my teaching. Give a class of mixed ability youngsters a task and there will, obviously, be some very different outcomes.

What I worked out was that some tasks should be set differently or scaled according to the pupils' age and ability. After reading a chapter of *Sons and Lovers*, for instance, I began with fairly simple questions, which the less able could answer, then moved on to more complex issues with the more able. Advantages of this were that, initially, the less able had answers they could give, thus raising their self-esteem, and the less able pupils benefitted from hearing the answers given by the more able. Some of the youngsters were disadvantaged because they had less ability and less confidence than others, while some pupils (often the same ones) were from homes close to or below the poverty line; Benfleet was not an affluent area. There had been very little of this at Southend HS, and so my view of Grammar schools being elitist was confirmed. From my visits to other schools, I also came to realise that making generalisations as to which kind of school was the best wasn't helpful. There are good and bad schools, effective and less effective schools of each kind: Comprehensive, Grammar, Modern, and Independent, too. You could say the same of teachers – some are much more effective than others. And head teachers too. Eddie Haynes was the first Head I had worked with whom I admired. He provided me with a kind of template of what a Head should be.

At Appleton, John Garton, an impressive Head of English, became a good friend. We had similar views on teaching and learning. "It's not what you do in the lesson, that's important," John used to say, "it's what the children do."

I agreed. "Of course there should be some really good teaching going on every day," we agreed, "but the real test is to discover how much really good and lasting learning there is."

Coincidentally, it was about this time that I went on a local course at Brentwood on the subject of "The Effective Curriculum". What struck me most strongly was the message that the effective curriculum is not what is written down on paper to be studied or what the teachers teach; the effective curriculum is that which the children take away with them at the end of each day. I was coming to realise that totally teacher-centred classrooms were less effective then ones in which children, the learners, had made an input. John was a good teacher, but sometimes, if you went into his classroom, he wouldn't be doing very much at all but the children were busy and there was a lot of learning going on. John especially liked working with a lad called Kirk in CSE English lessons. Kirk was a family-damaged, black lad, cheerful, lively and mischievous, a promising young boxer, who could, and often did, produce imaginative writing. John loved him to bits.

John and I were both teaching classes that were reading *All Quiet on the Western Front*, a novel, which depicted vividly the horrors of war from a German point of view. One morning John had a phone call from the school office saying that a parent wanted to see him. John happened to have some time spare so he went along.

"I've come to complain," the parent said. John suggested they both sit down.

"I went up to my daughter, Susan's room yesterday evening, to find her in floods of tears. 'What's the matter?' I said. And she told me it was because of the book you had told her to read. Now I'm not having it. She shouldn't have to experience this," said Susan's dad, who was quite a burly character. Susan was a lovely girl, pretty, sensible and sensitive.

John thought quickly and said, "I'm sorry that you were upset," he said, "but I'm not sorry Susan was upset."

"What? What are you saying?" Dad was getting angry.

"Let me explain," John said. "Susan is a sensitive girl, as you, as her dad, well know. The book she is reading is part of the CSE English course, "Coming to Terms with People and Life". Some of the passages in the book can be upsetting, I agree. But frankly, I would be more concerned if your daughter had no reaction, or showed no emotion at all. Her tears show she empathises with the soldiers in the story and what they are going through. We want pupils to be shocked and upset by what they read. It shows they have feelings. And it gives them the chance to give expression to those feelings. It is an important part of Susan's emotional development and part of her journey to adulthood. I'm glad you told me."

Susan's father could see what John was saying. They talked some more about the book and about Susan's reaction, and they shook hands. John told me about this as he thought I should be aware that some pupils in my English group might have had a similar reaction. I was in complete agreement with John about this. Children cannot and should not be sheltered and protected from life's sadnesses, insulated from reality, nor, when they are older, from the horrors man has inflicted on his fellow men. A few weeks later, Susan, who knew her father had been to the school, told John, "*All Quiet* is the best book I've ever read. I felt so sorry for those men."

John had a difficult decision to make late one evening. He was driving home alone; it had gone 11 at night and it was pouring with rain. At a bus stop, he saw a girl standing in the rain. She was probably about 15 or 16, John thought. She was getting soaked and John knew that the last bus had gone. What was he to do? Girls are told not to get into cars when men offer them a lift; quite right too. *But what would happen to her if he drove on and left her there? Who might come along then and pick her up?* He had stopped the car; now he reversed back to the bus stop, where he got out.

"Are you waiting for a bus? The last one has gone," John said.

The girl looked cold and frightened, John later told me. She said nothing, understandably.

"Where do you have to get to? Where do you live?"

The girl told him where she lived, not far away and not far off John's route.

"Look," John said, "I know you shouldn't accept lifts from men you don't know. Your parents have probably told you that. I am a school-teacher. I have school-books in my car. I can't let you stand out here in the rain, and you don't know who might drive by next. No bus will come along now. Let me drive you to your home. Then I will come in and explain to your parents. What do you say?"

There was a pause.

"Yes, all right," the girl said, obviously somewhat reluctantly, and John made sure she sat in the back. Following the girl's directions, John drove to her home, where he was pleased to see lights still on. It was after 11.30 by this time.

"I'll come and explain to your Mum or Dad," John said.

They walked up the path; the girl used her key to unlock the front door and called out, "Mum, I'm home. There's someone here to see you."

John then explained what had happened and the dilemma he had found himself in. The mother said how grateful she was and she and the girl thanked him, and John drove home. He told me he was sure he had done the right thing, but he wished he hadn't had to put the girl into such a difficult situation.

Penny and I had moved into a small semi in Leigh-on-Sea and everything seemed fine. We had some good times and initially we were very happy. While I was at Appleton, we had our two daughters. Sally arrived in the December in my very first term. We had prepared a nursery room for the new baby and I remember that one way I found that I could get baby Sally to sleep was to sing or hum to her Lara's theme, from *Dr Zhivago*. I wonder if she remembers; I must ask her. Penny had Sally in Rochford Hospital, but Joanne, who was born just over three years later, she had at home. After Penny had given birth to Joanne, Sally came into the bedroom, looked at her mum, seemed surprised and said, "Where's your bump?" Penny pointed to the cot at the side of the bed, where Sally's new baby sister was asleep.

In 1972, I was promoted to Senior Teacher status; however, by then I knew I wanted to move my career forward and I began to apply for some headships and deputy headships. Although I knew I didn't want to move very far away and certainly not to the far north, one of the posts I applied for was in Bedfordshire. By this time, Penny and I knew that our relationship, our marriage, was not as good as it should be, nor as good as it had been. It was difficult then, as it is today, to explain exactly what went wrong. We were still very fond of each other, but the spark had gone. Penny had, probably still has, an independent spirit, and I was spending a lot of my time coaching, often coaching young women, which naturally aroused suspicions. Maybe Penny began to think she had married too young. Perhaps she had. I was interviewed in Bedfordshire and appointed Deputy Head in a 13–18 comprehensive school. With the future of our marriage so uncertain, it seemed foolish to attempt to sell our house in Leigh and move Penny and two young children to Bedfordshire, away from her friends and her parents, who lived in Chelmsford. I said I would return each weekend to see Penny and the children. Neither of us was sure we wanted our marriage to end; we agreed to see how things went when we were apart.

18
Houghton Regis Upper School & Community College

I had been appointed Deputy Head at Houghton Regis Upper School, to start in September when the school was due to open. I drove up to Bedfordshire several times between my appointment in January and starting in September. The school was still being built when I visited the site, amid the February mud and snow, to have discussions with the appointed Head, Stanley Robinson. The new school, a 13–18 co-educational comprehensive, was to serve a large, Greater London Council (GLC) overspill township between Dunstable and Luton. Houghton Regis was an old village, being transformed by the new estates. It may have been functional, but it wasn't beautiful. Dunstable, on the other hand, boasted the magnificent Dunstable Downs, part of the Chiltern Hills. Every weekend gliders and hang gliders could be seen testing the thermals. Nearby Luton had once been the home of hat making, but car manufacturing, in the shape of Vauxhalls, had taken over. Luton was industrial, with the airport a major employer. Houghton Regis lay in between these two towns, and most of the population had come recently from different parts of London, so had no roots in the area. I was looking forward to the challenge.

There had been four schools in Dunstable: Manshead and Northfields, both co-educational comprehensives, and a boys' school and a girls' school both on one site. These were being amalgamated to make co-educational Queensbury School. This reorganisation left the local authority with a spare head teacher, Stanley Robinson. He had been Head of the boys' school; now he had become Head of the new Houghton Regis Upper School. I failed to realise how inappropriate this was, and indeed how unfitted he was, until far too late. Stanley Robinson was an old-school gentleman who would have been at home as Head of a small, rural grammar school. He was from another age and totally unsuited to be Head of a new school serving a largely ex-London council population. I did not realise this at my interview or during our initial discussions in February. Stanley had been put in an impossible position: although it was, in fairness, inappropriate for him to become Head at Houghton Regis, what choice did he have? His headship in Dunstable had just disappeared; a replacement was offered to him. I don't know whether he realised how unsuited he was to meet the needs of the GLC community; he probably did his best. I could not have found a greater contrast than that between Eddie Haynes and Stanley Robinson.

At first I stayed with my old friend, Rex Tregunna, now living in Welwyn Garden City, a few miles away. His wife had just left him, so Rex and I were able to discuss my current marital difficulties. Rex and I had much in common. We were both historians, both had been Head of History at Southend HS, and we were both qualified athletics coaches, though Rex coached throwers. We often met up at the English Schools Track and Field Championships, Rex helping his throwers, while I would more likely be found in the warm-up area advising my own runners or those in our county team. Being slightly older than I was, Rex had already moved through the ranks and was now a Head. Most evenings we stayed in, either to chat or because there was work for each of us to do. We made occasional visits to the local pub, not many yards away. He was a good friend.

The overhaul of schools in Dunstable meant that several teachers who had been at Kingsbury, the now closed boys' school, came with Stanley Robinson to Houghton Regis. This could be seen as an advantage: a team of teachers coming to the new school at Houghton Regis, who knew each other and who had worked with Stanley before. I soon saw some of the disadvantages: that these folk assumed that life would continue much as before. New staff had some difficulty fitting in with them and I was one of these new staff. At first, I was greeted warmly. Stanley had brought his Kingsbury deputy with him, Ray Howard, and also joining the new school staff was Betty Howard, Ray's wife.

During the spring and early summer, Stanley, Ray and I had planning meetings in Linmear Middle School on the same site as the new school. Some teachers had already been allocated to us from other schools in the area, so we identified what staff we would have to advertise for. Stanley explained the way he saw the pupils being organised in tutor and teaching groups. The concept was exciting, the reality rather less so. I felt that we had the chance to create something different and impressive. Some of Stanley's proposals were certainly different. As the school was to have three main blocks, each with its own cloakroom, offices and classrooms, it made sense to plan for three houses, each with their own base. Stanley wanted the tutor groups in each of the three houses to be grouped together in pairs, so that, he explained, the paired tutors could work together, know each other and cover for each other if necessary. So far, so good. But Stanley wanted to call these pairings: A and Alpha, B and Beta, C and Gamma and so on. He prepared a timetable with these Greek hieroglyphics on, but this had to be hand-written, as he couldn't find a typewriter to cope with the Greek symbols! Some of Stanley's handwritten timetables were masterpieces – works of art! If you could understand them, that is!

Because we were opening in September with a one-year intake of some 240 13-year-olds, the school could not be adequately staffed to fill all the necessary positions. Several staff were asked to double up or take on additional or unaccustomed roles. I found myself in charge of the boys' football team, not a job I minded at all, as it got me out onto the field where I enjoyed the practices and the games, many of which we won. The lads and I got to know each other well, which was great. The school playing field had a large electricity pylon almost slap bang in the middle, which wasn't ideal at all: beneath the wires you could feel the vibrations and hear the noise. Apart from my deputy head duties, I would also be organising and teaching History to the intake pupils and starting a Careers department. Some of the building work was still unfinished when term began, and the field had no markings or football posts, so at first we played our matches away. In the first month a sponsored walk was organised over Dunstable Downs, which not only brought parents and staff together but raised useful funds. At the end of term we had a school disco, which was, to our surprise, quite successful. Before and during the first year all aspects of the school's day-to-day organisation had to be discussed, agreed and implemented. Everything was new. A Parents Group and a "Buy a Bus" committee were formed, as HRUS would clearly need transport for teams and visits, etc. Our priorities, apart from teaching and learning, were to unite the staff, involve parents, raise money and give the school publicity for all the right reasons. Often these targets could be combined, as through the Parents' Autumn Bazaar and the Summer Fête.

Stanley Robinson had some strange, eccentric ways and I spent the first three years trying to cope with these and to work with him. For example, staff regularly complained that the telephone system wasn't good enough, especially for making internal calls, and then one day I happened to discover a pile of brand new telephones locked in a cupboard in the Head's office. Why? On another occasion I found Stanley photocopying a bunch of keys. When I asked him what he was doing, he said he was trying out some new settings and keys were all he could find. But this was in the photocopying room with reams of paper. I thought it was very odd.

Another of Stanley's "strange ways" was particularly frustrating as it affected our ability to do our work. When material arrived at the school, from Area Office or from County Hall, or from a Government department, Stanley sometimes passed on to me or another member of staff only a part of what had arrived. We might be given pages 1 to 4, but not pages 5 to 7. Once I received pages 1–2, 5–6, 9–10 of a document, but not the intervening ones: 3–4, 7–8. The pages weren't numbered, so this wasn't initially obvious. At first I found myself not understanding what I had been given. I discovered what was going on one day: Stanley was out of his office, and I went in and found the "missing" pages. When I confronted him, Stanley said it must have been an oversight on his part. I wondered, was it deliberate? If so, why? Was he trying to make it difficult for us to do our jobs? If it wasn't deliberate, what did it say about Stanley's level of competence? We also discovered that, on at least two occasions, Stanley had sent an incomplete reference for a member of staff who was applying for another post.

Our pupils at Houghton Regis were no angels and many had a mischievous streak in them. At lunchtime many of the staff used to eat with the pupils, sometimes at a table on their own, on other occasions sitting with the pupils. It was good social interaction and generally conducive to pupils and staff understanding each other better. A story did the rounds, however, that when Stanley Robinson sat having lunch with pupils, it was considered a good game for one of the pupils to remove a potato from Stanley's plate. Several pupils had seen this happen, and at least four staff said they had seen it too, so it cannot have been a one-off prank. Though it is amusing, it shows the lack of esteem in which the Head was held and Stanley's own feebleness.

The behaviour of some of the pupils presented real problems, especially for those staff used to more acceptable behaviour from the mainly middle-class Dunstable children they had taught before. Ours were London kids: they and their families had no roots in the area and some had come from the poorest parts of the capital. For many, education was an alien concept, and school unwelcome when more fun could be had and money made in a local market. Kids played up in lessons; many didn't behave during break and lunchtimes; teachers were often the object of some very rude and occasionally violent, outbursts. The Heads of House did their best: Betty Howard (Bidwell House – blue), Ron Hodd (Poynter House – green) and Irene Shepherd and later Tony Fisk (Chantry House – red), and if their sanctions and advice didn't work there was always Ray Howard, deputy in charge of discipline, an unenviable role. Ray favoured use of the cane, which Stanley supported, though quite often any effect was short lived. All disciplinary measures taken were entered into the punishment book, but when the same names kept reappearing, you began to wonder if there wasn't a better way. Corporal punishment was not outlawed in state schools until 1986.

Occasionally, suspension or expulsion was applied. While this was sometimes necessary, either as a punishment for some serious misdemeanour or to enable teachers to teach their classes in relative peace, or to act as a deterrent, I always had concerns about it. The very children who were suspended were usually the ones whose daily attendance was poor. Having worked hard to get Alan or Sue into school, here we were suspending them. Another concern I had was that we were letting the suspended children loose into the local community, where they were free to run amok if they chose to do so. Shoplifting or causing general havoc, often with suspended pupils from other schools, were favourite pastimes. This was not only a problem at Houghton Regis; the number of daily truants and suspended children was, and to some extent still is, a national problem. What is required is positive leadership from the head teacher and governors to set up special units, manned by expert, experienced staff, with sufficient resources, to contain disaffected and badly behaved pupils within school, to discover the reasons for their behaviour and work to modify their attitudes so they might see the benefits of a decent education. This could be done without affecting the learning opportunities of the vast majority. It's not easy, but it's worth trying.

Each weekend I went back home to see Penny, Sally and Jo in Leigh. Often we went out on Saturdays and it was hard for Penny and for me, not being certain what the future held for us or indeed for our children. It wasn't a happy time for either of us. I missed the girls dreadfully, but try as we did, Penny and I eventually decided, after many arguments, lots of discussion and floods of tears, that our marriage didn't have a future. Neither of us was sufficiently convinced that to carry on would be the right thing to do. I was still very fond of Penny but not in the same way as when we had married. I was devastated at the thought of not being a dad to Sally and Joanne, not being there to see them grow up, but Penny and I agreed that for us to stay married just for the sake of the children would be wrong. I said I would always try to be there when special events took place in the children's lives, and this I always tried to do. Penny and I also agreed that neither of us would ever blame each other when explaining our parting to Sally and Joanne. I don't think either of us ever did. Our divorce was finalised in 1974, and I agreed to pay maintenance for each of the children until they had finished full-time education, which in Jo's case was twenty years later, the year I retired. I discovered that work was the best antidote for sadness but there seemed no way to remove the dreadful guilt I felt at the breakup of the marriage. I couldn't forget the good times Penny and I had had and I would look in the mirror each morning and see a guy who had let down his wife and children by being unable to keep his marriage going. That feeling, for me, never fully went away.

Our Community Tutor, Tony Pont, decided to spend a year doing a similar job in America on an exchange scheme. Paul Dulac, Superintendent of Schools in a part of Massachusetts, came to us as Tony's replacement. In the school and among the community tutors in Bedfordshire, Paul was a breath of fresh air. He was a lively, colourful soul with a broad New England accent, who liked his steak and his beer. His glass was always half-full, never half-empty and we loved having him with us. Tony and Paul had also exchanged houses and cars, so with Paul came his wife, Becky, and their three young sons. They were a delightful family and we were to spend some good times together. My deputy head's office was directly opposite Paul's, and one morning Paul called me in. He had been working on a particularly contentious issue involving expenditure on adult and youth services. That morning I heard an iconic expression for the first time.

"Tony," Paul said in his very distinctive accent, "the shit has hit the fan!"

I smiled as I sat down and he explained. I don't recall the details now, but I do remember the expression and the finality with which Paul expressed it.

As the first three or four years went by, the Upper School settled down. Having more new staff helped. Soon we had a 6th Form and once again I was able to teach A level History! As the school grew, we advertised for another deputy, hoping to appoint a lady. One who came seemed to have the edge over the others, but she had only ever taught in girls' schools, never in a comprehensive, and her subject specialism was Classics! Hardly ideal, it seemed. Having met Stanley, she asked me, with some diffidence, "I don't know that I should ask you this, but how can you work with him? Is it possible?"

Brenda Sullivan had picked up on Stanley's eccentricities, obviously far better than I had when I first met him, and she needed reassurance that she wasn't potentially walking into a madhouse.

"It isn't that bad," I said. "Quite a lot of the time it's possible to ignore Stanley, and just get on with what needs to be done. He won't interfere with what you are doing. I manage all right, and it would be good to have you with us."

Brenda decided to continue with her application, which had been in the balance, and she was appointed. She proved to be a real asset, as she stood no nonsense, neither from pupils nor from members of staff. Her somewhat brusque manner occasionally made her seem haughty, but it was only her manner. She even managed to teach a little Latin while she was at Houghton Regis. We worked together very well, and things got even better when Andy Rayment was appointed as Senior Teacher. Andy taught in the Technology department, and was very clear thinking and well organised, and was soon to occupy my office when I moved further up the corridor.

After my first term spent with Rex, I had moved into a pokey top floor flat in Elm Park Close, in the heart of the GLC overspill council estate. This had advantages as well as drawbacks. The main problem was I couldn't move without bumping into either one of the pupils or a parent. But it was very close to the school and living there helped me to understand the nature of the community whose children I was responsible for during the day. The flat was very small, so after a short while I decided to find somewhere with more room, and a house in Ullswater Road, in Dunstable, not far from Queensbury School became available. The owners of the house were moving to Zambia, but they wanted to retain their property by renting it out. After chatting with the estate agent, Steve Cook, I agreed to take it on and I set about finding three others to share the house and the expenses with me, as I was effectively paying the owners' mortgage. The husband was already in Zambia, so when I went to the house with my policeman friend, Tony, we met the wife, Kay. After showing us round, Tony and I said we would visit the pub, "The Glider", have a pint and a chat, and return with a decision. Tony had a policeman colleague who he said would come on board, and I knew one of the teachers at Linmear Middle School was looking for digs. After our pub discussion, I went and told Kay that I was willing to rent the house. With formalities completed and Kay en route for Zambia, I moved in and was joined by Tony, his PC mate, Derek, and also my teacher contact, Elaine. There were three bedrooms: the two young policemen shared one, Elaine had the largest bedroom and I had the smallest. We all got on really well and that first Christmas I cooked dinner for the four of us!

The following summer, Elaine moved out as she had acquired a boyfriend, so we had a vacancy. I placed an advertisement for a fourth person to share. Following a phone call, one evening there was a knock on the front door. A young lady was standing there.

"Hello! I'm Donna. I've come about the fourth person to share."

Donna liked the room and the house and she moved in. She was 25 and had grown up in Tonbridge, Kent, with her mother, older brother and younger sister. She had just given up a position as a live-in nanny to two young children in nearby Harlington. I found her rather shy, not initially very self-confident, but attractive and very easy to get on with. She certainly had my attention when she sunbathed in the back garden. Following my divorce, I was now single again. I explained the circumstances of my recent marital breakdown and she told me that her mother's marriage had ended many years before and that her mother had brought up her three children on her own.

I did some coaching while at Houghton Regis, though my school commitments prevented me from spending too much time with athletes. Sadly, I lost contact with those I had been coaching in Essex; I believe regular contact between athlete and coach is essential. This was the price I paid for putting my teaching career ahead of any possible career in coaching.

Debbie Buckley was a pupil at Houghton Regis, a member of Luton AC and a keen runner. I started to coach her in 1975 and she competed several times for Bedfordshire Schools in English Schools' Athletic Association (ESAA) Championships, both cross-country and track (see Additional Details). She trained at school and also on the roads in the evening, where she ran very strongly, with me trying to keep up on my bicycle! She raced well on the road, and competed indoors at RAF Cosford. Unfortunately Debbie didn't go into the 6th Form, so her athletics career didn't progress as well as it might have done, though she continued to run with Margaret Ashcroft, a senior Luton Athletics Club member who I also coached. Deby (as she now likes to be known) and I are still in contact.

Occasionally, I took Debbie and her sprinter friend, Janet, plus one of the lads from school, to the floodlit track next to Wormwood Scrubs in West London, now the Linford Christie Stadium, where we had a good training session with other athletes. One of these trips nearly ended in disaster. I was heading south in the middle lane of the M1, as the inside lane was congested. Ahead of me a lorry pulled out into the middle lane. As there were no cars behind me in the outside lane I moved over, maintaining my speed, in order to pass the lorry. Suddenly, without warning and with no good reason, the lorry continued into the outside lane. Why it did so, I have no idea, as there were no vehicles ahead of him in the middle lane. With him 50 metres in front of me, I braked hard, but couldn't avoid hitting the back of the lorry. I came to a stop in the outside lane, a dangerous place to be, especially with three teenage athletes in the car. I put on my hazard lights, got out of the car to see if it was drivable and, as it was, when there was a break in the traffic, I carefully manoeuvred onto the hard shoulder. The lorry had not stopped. A driver who was following me and who saw the incident rang the police, who arrived very quickly, almost as soon as I had reached the hard shoulder. I made a statement and we were allowed to carry on. The police tried to catch the lorry but without success; they said that the lorry driver may not have realised that he had been in a collision. Later, the police measured braking distances, and from what the other car driver told them, they were prepared, unusually, to inform my car insurance that the collision was not my fault. It was not an experience I would want to repeat; fortunately we were all unhurt.

I managed to persuade several of the senior girls at HRUS to run in the local schools cross-country race, after which they were astonished to find that they had been selected to represent Bedfordshire Schools. Shirley Bigwood, Pam Christie, Anne McMorrow and Kay Sanders all ran in the ESAA Cross Country Championships at Lincoln in 1978. Unfortunately, Debbie had left by that time or she would also have been in the team. None ran with any great distinction but they were all proud to have represented their school and county in a national schools event.

In 1975, Erwin Hartell contacted me. I had coached him briefly in Essex when he was 18 and a member of Hadleigh Olympiads. Then he had run the 800 metres in 1 minute 51 seconds and was ranked No.1 Junior in the UK. Shortly after that, he had taken a scholarship to Western Kentucky University in the States. Now in his early twenties, temporarily back in the UK and staying nearby in Bletchley, I organised some sessions for him in Woburn Woods: hill runs for strength and running technique, fartlek* sessions and, what he was really good at,

---

*"Fartlek" – literally "speed-play" in Swedish, is a form of training originating in Sweden in the 1930s, in which a runner alternates between longish steady pace runs, faster shorter runs, a few runs up hills, easy running to recover or even some walking for the not so fit. Ideally the runner decides what running to do in a fartlek session, though some coaches like to instruct the athlete how the session should be carried out. A fartlek run should be done in such a way that it meets the needs of the individual athlete. Fartlek enables a runner to experiment with different paces over a variety of distances and with varying degrees of effort, but without the constraints of a measured track and a stopwatch.

repeated fast runs of about a minute, with short recoveries, on a flat circuit of the woods. Erwin had a very fluent, economical running action and he was obviously a very talented athlete. That year he ran four times sub 1 minute 50 seconds for 800 metres and was a very creditable 3rd in the Amateur Athletic Association 1500 metres in 3 minutes 40.56 seconds (see Additional Details). When he returned to the States he told me he was going to take charge of the local radio station in Bowling Green. Now known as Swag, he runs successful shoe outlets under that name in Western Kentucky.

Athletics coaches need to obtain a coaching qualification if they are to have any status in an athletics club and to become insured. During the 1970s and 1980s I was asked to examine would-be coaches. This involved meeting up with the coach at their local track, observing them working with their athletes and asking them a few questions about their event speciality. Usually I was testing middle distance coaches, but sometimes it was a high jump coach I saw, as these were the two disciplines in which I had a senior coach qualification. The standard of these coaches varied enormously. Some were excellent, up to date with their coaching methods, knowledgeable and, from what I saw, very competent coaches with a good relationship with their athletes. My report would be sent in and these coaches would be informed they had qualified. There were a few, who, quite honestly, were awful, and throughout the time I spent with them I struggled to find anything I could commend. Occasionally the training they were giving their athletes was highly unsuitable. One fellow didn't include any warm-up in his sessions. These people did not pass and would either continue unqualified or give up, or possibly resolve to improve, though the personality of most of these unsuccessful coaches left a lot to be desired. It was work I enjoyed, linking with what I had done at Loughborough Summer School, of which more later.

Mum and Dad had retired from living and working in London and, against the advice of many of their friends that it was a crazy thing to do, they sold their house in Finchley and bought a lovely, thatched cottage, "Dingley Dell", somewhat isolated in the middle of Devon. Mind you, other friends said, "Go for it!" They were very happy there and got to know the neighbouring farmers, one of whom always stopped for a chat when his tractor came close to the edge of their garden. They did their shopping in North Tawton and became acquainted with many of the local pubs.

"Dingley Dell"

During summer and Easter school holidays, I would drive down to "Dingley Dell" and, with our relationship developing, I took Donna down to meet my parents. They liked her very much and we had a lovely time, visiting Clovelly and other parts of North Devon. The following year, we took Sally and Jo with us. They enjoyed the North Tawton Extravaganza, Sally riding horses and Jo taking part in the sack race. The "Countryman" was also a favourite spot for me as they served superb draught Guinness. Sally and Jo got on well with Donna, and the children loved playing on the sands at Instow and Westward Ho!

Back at HRUS, Stanley continued to aggravate Brenda and me, so as the school was not being led anywhere, we decided it was time to take some action. The Chair of Governors, Councillor John Kinchella, was aware of the situation. He was as frustrated as we were. I had already alerted the Area Education Officer, Peter Hopkinson, to the problems we faced. Deciding what to do wasn't easy. I had a loyalty to Stanley, as he was the Head of the school, and he had appointed me. But I also had a duty to the pupils, their parents, to the community of Houghton Regis, and to the staff. They all deserved better. After a lot of soul searching I decided to take the matter further. I asked Eddie Haynes for his advice. Eddie urged caution, but said I must do what I thought was best. I wrote a letter to the Chief Education Officer, Peter Browning, outlining in some detail the situation we were facing. For the good of the school, something had to be done.

Meetings were held, which naturally didn't involve me, and eventually a decision was reached: Stanley agreed to go on secondment to Cambridge for a year where, with some irony I thought, he was to study the connection between social conditions and juvenile delinquency. I was asked to become Acting Head. Stanley and I had no discussions about this; he just departed and we were left to our own devices. It is quite likely that he thought I had engineered this, and he preferred not to discuss it. Naturally, I was delighted to have been shown the confidence of the CEO and the Governors, and I set about trying to improve the way things were done at HRUS.

Three months after my appointment as Acting Head, Donna and I were married. We had been living in the same house, so we had got to know each other very well. We'd had one short break in Bournemouth, another to Whitby, which we thought was lovely, and we knew we wanted to be together: the mutual attraction had grown. I knew I was in love with Donna and she felt the same about me. Donna's mother, who had been horrified when she visited us to discover that her daughter and I were actually living together, was not overjoyed at her daughter marrying a divorcee, and because of my personal history we couldn't marry in church, which was a shame for Donna. John Garton, from my Appleton days, was my best man, and after our marriage and reception, we collected Sally and Jo and took them with us to Devon. As Sally and Jo were only 8 and 5 years old respectively, I didn't inform them that their dad had married again. I was sure that would have been insensitive and would have upset them. So Donna and I spent some time carefully removing confetti from our car before picking up the children! In Devon, Sally and Jo stayed with their grandparents, who were now living in Northam, near Bideford, while Donna and I had a few days honeymoon on our own at Port Isaac on the Cornish coast.

Donna and I are married 1977

Mum and Dad had had several years at "Dingley Dell" and they loved their cottage but, with considerable reluctance, when the gardening and the driving and the semi-isolation had become a concern, they had sold up and moved to Northam, near Bideford and Westward Ho!. They soon integrated with the local community and immersed themselves in the life of the village. In her seventies, my mother joined the WRVS and helped deliver Meals on Wheels to the local old folk! Dad joined the Northam and District Horticultural Society, regularly entering their competitions, with occasional success! They both joined North Devon Cricket Club, whose lovely ground at Instow overlooks the ocean. Here they spent many happy summer days watching cricket, with Mum often preparing the sandwiches for the players' tea. Fairlea Crescent became our holiday base and when we came down on holiday, the children enjoyed sampling tomatoes and beans from Grandad's vegetable garden. It was a very fulfilling and well-deserved retirement for them both. They were very happy and obviously very fond of each other.

Mum and Dad, Fairlea Crescent, Northam in Devon

The house had quite a large garden, at the end of which, beyond Dad's vegetable patch, was a sizable shed where I set up a mock shop full of cans and packets which were "sold" by Sally and Jo to visiting "customers". Sally was just over three years older than Jo, so she made it clear who was in charge. They both enjoyed their "work experience" in the shop, except when certain "customers" refused to pay the right amount or engaged in blatant "shoplifting". Sally would give chase to such "naughty people", telling Jo to take charge of the shop. The worst offender was "Archibald Carruthers-Smythe" (i.e. yours truly!). It was all good fun. They were both intelligent children: I've always believed that intelligence is the ability to perceive relationships between things. One day, aged about 4, Jo saw a single-decker in the town and exclaimed, "Bungalow bus"!

It was lovely having Sally and Jo with us in Devon. We took them to the Dartington glass factory in Torrington and they enjoyed Appledore's tiny cottages and the Lifeboat station, and the cobbles and the donkeys at Clovelly. The astroglide at Westward Ho! was a firm favourite. Every night at bedtime I told them a story, one I made up as I was going along. The stories always had an element of mystery, though they weren't frightening. Each night I left the story at a critical stage, so it could be resumed the next night. Even now they remember these stories! Well, not the stories themselves, but the telling thereof!

One of the joys of being in Devon was being able to get away from school, from where you worked, from teachers and, above all, from the pupils. However much you liked them and worked hard to educate them during the term, it was great to feel that you had "escaped". One summer morning, we parked up close to the beach and walked towards the pebble ridge. Suddenly a voice called out, "Hello, sir!" Unbelievable! One of our Houghton Regis 4th Formers and his family were on the other side of the road. Of course he was probably just as underwhelmed as I was. On another occasion I bumped into one of the staff while on holiday. Not easy to escape!

We visited many local places of interest, but Dad was not a great driver. He is the only person I know who drove better after two or three pints of bitter than when sober! Mum, on the other hand, was excellent behind the wheel, maybe due in part to her wartime experiences. She once told me that, when a lot younger, she had been attempting to drive up the steep Porlock Hill, near Lynton and Lynmouth, but her car couldn't manage it, so she turned the car round and drove to the top in reverse gear!

In most Houghton Regis families neither mother nor father had had any experience of higher education, yet I always argued that Houghton Regis children were capable of achieving success academically, if only they, their parents and their teachers believed this. There were plenty of sceptics however.

One day, not long after I had been appointed Acting Head, I was in the Area Education Office in Luton and I had an interesting conversation with Peter Hopkinson.

"Peter," I said, "you'll be pleased to know that Mark Rolfe has been given a place at Brasenose College, Oxford, to read Chemistry."

"What? Really?" He looked incredulous and had to sit down. "A place at Oxford for one of the Houghton Regis boys?" he said, looking totally gobsmacked.

"Yes, good isn't it? Don't be so surprised!" I said.

"Well that is amazing. Congratulations!"

"It's Mark and his teachers and parents who should be congratulated," I said.

"Well, yes, of course. I'll have to write a letter or two."

And Peter did. He wrote letters of congratulation all round. Several other boys and girls from that first intake of 1973 did well in their A levels and went off to different universities and other places of further study, as happened in the following years too. The Upper School was moving in the right direction.

When it became known that Stanley would not be returning, I applied for the headship and was appointed. Now I would be a head teacher in my own right, just as Grandad had been. 4th Year Commercial Girls seemed a long time ago! Naturally, my mother was particularly pleased. Leading a school would be a great opportunity and an exciting challenge; I looked forward to it. Although nobody said so to my face, I had the impression that, while some members of staff supported my appointment, others took a different view. Maybe some still harboured loyalty to Stanley. Some knew there would be changes. Bedfordshire LEA were very supportive, especially the CEO, Peter Browning, and also, at County Hall, Janet Darby. Locally, I had support from Peter Hopkinson and from the Governors.

Less good was an event in August that same year, 1978. I was looking forward to making a start as a Head in my own right. Donna and I had moved from Ullswater Road into an upstairs flat of our own in Chiltern Road. I decided to do a spot of gardening, though it was quite a hot day. I had only been digging a short while when I felt faint and had pains in my arms. I knew what this might indicate, so, with some difficulty, I climbed our outside steps and from the

213

bedroom rang our doctor's surgery. The receptionist told me to keep the front door open and to lie on the bed, "An ambulance will be with you shortly." I rang Donna at work to tell her what was happening. As I was being put into the ambulance, my friend and former housemate, Tony, happened to walk past and witnessed my departure. Lying in bed at Luton and Dunstable Hospital, I was sure I had died, as standing by the bed was an angel, all in white with blond hair; this turned out to be the lady doctor about to examine me. I had had a relatively minor infarction, but I was kept in hospital for two weeks. I was not to return to school for six weeks but I had to walk a short distance each day, and I remember how hard it was to walk 50 yards up the road and 50 yards back again.

The doctors were puzzled about my heart attack and so was I. I wasn't overweight, I didn't smoke, no family history of heart trouble: there seemed to be no logical explanation. I had just been appointed to a headship, but I was looking forward to that. As I reflected on what had taken place, I became fairly certain of the cause. My divorce from Penny had been four years earlier, but the guilt of leaving my two young children without their dad was ever present, even though I saw Sally and Joanne as often as I could. It is probably what triggered my heart attack.

Meanwhile Donna was enjoying her rehearsals and performances with Luton Operatic and Dramatic Society. She had done some singing when much younger and now she took part with great enthusiasm in *Trial by Jury* and *HMS Pinafore*. Great fun was had by all, performers and audiences alike, and the standard of acting and singing was very good.

I had a mixed time as Head at Houghton Regis. It was my first headship and many of the circumstances were far from ideal. Some staff didn't want to be 100% cooperative and found reasons to rock the boat. I never found out why the PE teachers were so antagonistic towards me. I thought it odd because I have always maintained that the PE department in any school plays a key role in influencing pupils' behaviour and attitudes, setting standards of fair play, respect for the rules, being part of a team and so on. John Jones, who was particularly objectionable, later sought me out to apologise for what he had said and done.

At times my approach didn't go down well with certain individuals. For instance, we had one particular pupil who was often difficult. 15-year-old Mary could explode without warning in a lesson or in a corridor, sometimes being rude or aggressive to fellow pupils or members of staff. Her Head of House, Ron Hodd, had worked tirelessly to support her, and the girl's outbursts had become less frequent. One day, Deputy Head Bill Stevenson came to me, saying that the girl must be expelled.

"What is it this time?" I asked.

"Mary called Mrs Bell (not their real names) a 'bloody, stupid, old cow'," Bill said, "in the lesson, in front of the class. We cannot allow or condone this. She has to go." I said I would talk with Ron Hodd and get back to him.

When I spoke with Ron, he said, "Please don't expel Mary. Of course she shouldn't have said what she did, and she should apologise. That girl has been cast aside throughout her life. Her mother rejected her when she was a toddler and she was put up for adoption. Then her adoptive parents threw her out. She now lives in a hostel. We are the one place she feels secure. I hate to think what will become of her if we also reject her. She has shown signs of self-harm and talked to me once about suicide. We have got to help Mary, not wash our hands of her."

"Thanks, Ron. I'll talk to Bill." I knew what we had to do. Bill did not agree and said we would get a reputation for being "soft" if we didn't take strong action. I had spoken with our Chairman of Governors, John Kinchella, who knew Mary from previous incidents. He agreed with me that we should follow Ron's advice. Ron and I met with Mary. She was full of remorse, and knew she shouldn't have spoken as she had. Mary apologised and Mrs Bell accepted her apology. Bill remained unconvinced and unhappy. Mary completed her time at HRUS and left us with some qualifications and the chance of a decent future. I'm sure we got that one right.

Some parents could be a problem. One mother came in regularly to see me with some complaint or other. She was usually intoxicated and was also known to be "on the game". I never saw her in my office without my secretary being present. One day I came out of my office into the entrance area to see a parent, who was "being difficult and aggressive" according to our office receptionist, only to be pinned against the wall by the collar by this large, beer smelling male. Several other staff appeared and the aggressive parent backed off. It was the only time I was subjected to a physical assault. Another problem we had for a while was bomb threats. A phone call would tell us that there was a bomb in the building. I would be informed immediately, so too the police. At first the whole school was evacuated until a search had been made. After a while, we were told not to take such drastic action, but always to inform the police, who would usually come and search. Nothing was ever found. Once whoever was ringing realised that nothing was going to happen, they stopped calling. It had been a nuisance and, at first, very worrying.

But there were lots of very good things that happened as well. Our annual school fête was always great fun and well attended, and the pupils enjoyed being able to throw wet sponges at Mr Harbour and Mr Fisk! One year the fête was opened by Gyles Brandreth, who introduced his lady companion as, "This is my present wife!" Tony Fisk, who became Head of Chantry House and was a teacher of Religious Education and Drama, in addition to conducting some really innovative school assemblies, also produced some amazing school plays and musicals. Tony was a creative and enthusiastic teacher who could develop often hidden talents in our pupils. He held all day Sunday rehearsals in the school hall and the hard work put in by him and the pupils was rewarded each opening night. Drama productions, concerts and musicals were testament to the performing skills of our pupils. *Oliver* was followed by *Eden*, produced in collaboration with English teacher, Roger Spalding, who wrote it. Others included a summer concert *London Suite*, a musical, *Agrippa*, then the story of Helen Keller, *The Miracle Worker*.

Godspell was another successful and very popular production, which Tony and I, with Peter Sargent and Janice Ashcroft, took to

Germany where it was performed at our twin town of Porz. Billy Smullen was outstanding as Jesus and John Fleming's drumming was amazing. Lisa Wilson and Suzanne Moore were memorable too.

Godspell rehearsals in Germany

The German school, Max Kolbe Gymnasium, Koln, visited us the following year and put on a performance of *The Threepenny Opera*. Everyone enjoyed their rendition of "Mack the Knife" and demanded an encore. Donna and I became good friends with Hans Buchheim, Head of Music at Max Kolbe and later stayed with him and his wife and children in their lovely house near Cologne. We visited Cologne Cathedral and walked one evening to a Rhine waterfront pub to hear some great traditional jazz. I found it amazing that Cologne Cathedral survived the bombing during the Second World War, as the main railway line and station next door was severely damaged by intensive bombing. Similar to the experience of St Paul's in London of course. One of the last plays put on while I was at Houghton Regis was *The Card* adapted from Arnold Bennett. There was always a concert at Christmas. Tony Fisk and Mark Wyatt showed just how much talent there was among the pupils of Houghton Regis, with several taking part in county orchestras or plays. Five HRUS pupils were members of the County Band that visited Germany in 1982.

Our productions were given a real boost after Mark Wyatt was appointed in charge of music. Not only did Mark's expertise support the plays and musicals, he also started the Houghton Regis and Community Big Band, which went from strength to strength, performing in school, locally and further afield. The band had its own logo and sweatshirts and became recognised throughout the county and beyond. Rehearsals were held in the evenings, which was no problem for the pupils as they all lived near the school and it enabled several parents to play in the band, providing an example and encouragement to the youngsters. Mark's youthful energy seemed to rub off onto our pupils and the community players. The school members of the band reached the final auditions for the Schools Prom, playing at the National Festival of Music for Youth in Croydon. Singing was also developed, Gill Camp being especially outstanding.

In addition to music and drama productions, a lot of other quality work went on in many subject departments. Geography field trips were popular, often producing impressive results. Occasionally we had a writer in residence for a term, and because we were a Community College, one writer held regular sessions in the local pub; very popular they were too. English and Drama teachers took pupils to theatre performances. The school library developed under the guidance of Judith Askey, and partly due to her introduction of Prestel, she became recognised as a leader in the field, so much so that Judith and I were invited to take part in an HMI presentation to schools in Lancashire. I made a point of visiting other schools in the area, partly to publicise HRUS, but mainly to pick up tips and learn from more experienced Heads. Geoff Cooksey at Stantonbury Campus was a good example. Geoff told me about his latest curriculum innovation – carpets! "Money well spent," he said, his argument being that carpets reduce noise and contribute to a more peaceful environment, thus facilitating learning and making teaching less stressful and movement quieter.

Another key development for us at HRUS was the addition of a sports centre, used during the day by the school, and available for community use in evenings and weekends. The new, large sports hall supplemented the school gym, and provided the opportunity for basketball, badminton, netball, indoor tennis, cricket nets and much more. The school and community swimming pool had opened in 1977. We had a joint management committee, consisting of County Council, Town Council and School representatives, which met regularly and usually harmoniously. The centre was popular and well used.

From very early days there had been a "Buy a Bus" Committee, led by Betty Howard, and after enough funds had been raised, we purchased an old London Green Line single decker, which I enjoyed driving, and the school later acquired two minibuses. All staff and any parents who drove the minibuses had to pass a rigorous practical test. There was no cinema in Houghton Regis, so we started a Community Film Club, with popular films being shown once a fortnight in the school Lecture Theatre. We were packed out the night we showed *The Boys from Brazil*. We also launched a School Bank with the help of Barclays. This opened at lunchtimes and was run by senior pupils who thus gained valuable, practical experience of managing banking and accounting. French and German exchange visits took place each year, and we had several visits from teachers from abroad, including Cyprus, Japan and India, plus a highly entertaining visit from a party of Jewish rabbis. Every year we held a Presentation of Awards Evening, one of my tasks being to find a suitable guest or celebrity to present awards and make an appropriate speech. Jimmy Greaves was our guest one year.

Another visitor was leading Labour Party politician, Denis Healey, who came to look round the school one day and have lunch in my room. Fortunately, the two events happened in that order, as I have never seen someone consume so much alcohol over lunch as on that day: lovely man, a raconteur par excellence and great company.

The 6th Form was our pride and joy. The 6th Formers contributed so much around the school, organising staff *v.* student encounters in a variety of sports. Our first Head of 6th Form, Nick Darlington, left at the end of 1981 after doing an excellent job with our older students. Some years later he led his own school in Switzerland where he and his wife went to live. We used to give 6th Formers "mock interviews" if they were being seen at a university or higher education college. One that I distinctly remember was conducted by our Head of Maths, Rod Young with a student from Vietnam, one of the "boat people". Rod gave him some Mathematics tasks, which Duc did with ease, even when Rod made them far more difficult. By the end of their session, Rod and Duc were having a high level Mathematical discussion! The standard of Maths of the Vietnam boat students was impressive. Duc gained a place at university without difficulty.

Donna and I had moved from the flat, scene of my heart attack, to a small, terraced house in England's Avenue on the northern outskirts of Dunstable, just a short drive from HRUS. In the summer of 1979, our daughter, Julie, was born at the Luton and Dunstable Hospital. Donna enjoys telling the tale of my mishap when I returned home after spending time at the hospital with her and the new baby. I was excited, happy but very tired. Back home, I decided to have a shower. Unfortunately I must have lost balance (I don't think I actually fell asleep!), and fell out of the shower, which was in the bath, taking with me the shower curtain and rail. I was also holding the shampoo bottle at the time and managed to spray the contents all round the bathroom. I ended up, bruised, on the floor. Not the ideal way to celebrate a new baby! But different!

The following summer, Donna and I had a very enjoyable and often hilarious holiday to Wales and the Lakes in a hired VW Camper van. We had assumed that each night baby Julie would sleep on the large, warm foam mattress above the engine at the back of the VW. Julie had other ideas, and wouldn't go quietly to sleep. So each evening, at about 7 p.m., Donna and I got into our double sleeping bag in the VW's large central compartment, and pretended to go to sleep. If Julie thought we were asleep, maybe she would sleep too. We lay as still as we could, eyes closed, trying not to laugh. For a while, baby Julie padded and crawled her way around on top of us, peering very closely in our faces, ensuring we were asleep. Eventually she wore herself out and collapsed, asleep. Then Donna and I had to extricate ourselves from the sleeping bag, so we could enjoy our evening, but without waking Julie! This became a routine every night, and at the time, Donna was three months pregnant with Robert.

Late one afternoon, having parked the van in a good spot, we raised the elevated roof and put up on the racks all surplus objects, cases, buckets, allsorts, to give more space at floor level. We made a cup of tea, always a priority for Donna, and sat down to relax. Realising that our neighbours were a large, noisy family with at least six children, we decided we would "move camp" to a spot on the opposite side of the site. I quickly started the engine and began to drive across the bumpy grass, only a matter of 100 yards. At that point bedlam ensued. Everything we had placed on the racks, including buckets and cases, fell to the metal floor of the van making an awful clatter. Our tea showered on to the floor. I had forgotten that we were in stationary, parked-up mode, and that one didn't drive a camper van with the roof up and the racks full. There was nothing we could do but keep going, a little more gently, until we reached our desired spot. Then we collapsed with laughter, cleared up the mess, pacified Julie, and reminded ourselves not to repeat that manoeuvre.

Other hilarious events on that holiday included Donna getting up in the middle of the night in high winds to lower our elevated roof, only to realise she was wearing her shortie nightie and not a lot else. Trying to hold down her nightie with one hand while lowering the roof with the other proved impossible, so Donna discarded her dignity and completed the task, during all of which, as was customary, I remained asleep, as did Julie. We returned safely to Dunstable and Robert was delivered the following February.

On several occasions Donna and I went, either with another couple or on our own, to Caesar's Palace Night Club on the outskirts of Luton. It was very popular, though I gather it has since closed down. A meal was followed by a cabaret. Brotherhood of Man, Peters and Lee and Guys and Dolls were all excellent. One evening we gave Donna's mother a treat by taking her, but we hadn't realised Freddie

Starr was top of the bill that particular night. He was at his prime and we thought he was great, but Donna's mother was not amused!

We almost had a disaster on a short break in France. One sunny afternoon in the centre of a small town we were standing outside a shop, deciding where we should go next. Donna was a few yards to my right and thought that Julie was with me. I assumed Julie was with Donna. Suddenly we realised that Julie wasn't with either of us. Panic! Frantically, we looked up and down the street, Donna calling out, "Julie, Julie," very loudly. Then Donna heard a faint cry, which she knew was Julie. In the distance, right at the top of the hill at the far end of the town, almost out of sight, we saw Julie, being led by the hand by a woman. In a few seconds they would have been gone. Donna ran, frantically, up the hill to the woman, asked her what she was doing, but couldn't understand what, in French, the woman said. What was important was finding Julie. Why the woman was taking Julie away, we never discovered. It had been a traumatic few minutes.

We had another scare on our way home. For our last night before driving to catch the ferry home, we had stopped at a small hotel. The bedrooms were separated from the dining area by a small roadway. Robert was still in a cot, while Julie, now 3, was in a small bed. Once they were asleep, Donna and I went to eat in the restaurant, returning every 20 minutes to check on the children. When it was my turn, I found the door open and Julie wasn't there. Her bed was empty. Rob was fast asleep, but there was no sign of Julie. After a moment's panic, I walked back along the corridor to raise the alarm. As I passed one of the rooms, I heard Julie's voice. The bedroom door was ajar. I knocked on the door. There was a youngish couple in the room and also Julie. She rushed over to me.

"I was in the corridor," said the English lady, "and saw this little girl. I thought she shouldn't be running around on her own in her jimjams, so I took her into our room. That was only a few minutes ago. I was looking after her."

I thanked the lady and carried Julie downstairs to where Donna was sitting at our table and told her the story. More recently we have been able to empathise with Kate and Gerry McCann after their little girl, Madeleine, was taken from their holiday apartment, and as I write this, is still missing.

Sally and Jo with Julie and Robert at Clovelly 1981

At Houghton Regis there was a cloud on the horizon. The Government of the early '80s was keen to spend less on schools, particularly as rolls were due to fall. The Bedfordshire CEO told the Upper Schools Heads at one of his termly meetings, "There are tough times ahead." The County Council published a Consultative Document on School Closure in July 1982. The following September we warned our parents about a possible closure of the school. They were horrified.

The letter confirming the decision arrived in July 1983. There had been many meetings and much speculation, the newspapers and letter writers had had a field day, so when we were told, the decision didn't come as a surprise: Bedfordshire County Council proposed to close Houghton Regis Upper School and Community College as well as John Howard School in the north of the county. We had opened in 1973 to serve the community of Houghton Regis; now we were considered to be redundant. There were several reasons for this decision: there was a surplus of secondary school places in South Bedfordshire; the government was encouraging local education authorities to eliminate surplus places wherever possible; it was inconceivable that any school in Dunstable would be closed by a Conservative-dominated county council education committee. The fall guy had to be HRUS. This was despite the fact that the population of Houghton Regis was 16,400 and growing, whereas Dunstable, with a population of 30,200 had three Upper Schools. In addition, HRUS had also been designated a Community College, the only one in South Bedfordshire, and there was a jointly managed Sports Centre on site. Was all this to go?

The county councillors voted on 7th July:

	For Closure	Against Closure	Abstaining
Conservatives	38	0	1
Labour	0	34	
Liberal	2	5	1
Independent	1		1
	41	39	3

Why two Liberals voted for our closure mystified everyone. It went totally against the policy of the party and, accordingly, the two were "dealt with" by their party chiefs by having the party whip withdrawn. But the damage had been done.

It was true that a number of Houghton Regis parents were sending their children to one of the Dunstable schools in the belief that they were "bettering" their families by so doing. They would be mixing with more middle-class children, it was argued. The parents who thought this were often the more ambitious ones with quite able children, so HRUS lost out both ways.

The strong and thriving Parents Association (PSFA), led by Pat Page, together with our Governors and staff, the pupils and the wider community decided that this decision would be opposed as strongly as possible. A public meeting was held in the school hall and 1,200 angry local people attended. As the local paper reported, "They spilled out of the hall into an adjoining drama theatre and outside on to the school grounds." A "Save Our School" committee was formed and the campaign was launched. Posters were printed, letters sent to county councillors and local papers. I was interviewed on Chiltern Radio. As the decision of the County Council had to be approved by the Government's Secretary of State for Education, Keith Joseph, it was decided that a petition would be organised to gather as many signatures as possible and taken to London. A march to London was organised.

"Save our School" march: Mr and Mrs Kinchella at the front

Letters to the local press protesting against the decision to close Houghton Regis Upper School and Community College came from a wide variety of local people. The Mayor of Houghton Regis, local Councillors and Clergy joined local Junior and Middle School head teachers in protesting. Letters of course came from HRUS Governors, teachers, parents and pupils, all angry, not only at the decision but the way in which it was carried out. Some protested from outside the area, such as the Trades Council Secretary from Leighton Buzzard, who described the closure decision as "an act of cynical political expediency and opportunism". Many ordinary members of the public added their voice. Our local MP, Conservative, David Madel, sat on the fence.

The Houghton Regis Interest Group had now been active for a few years. In this, representatives of nearly all the local statutory and voluntary organisations with an interest in the people and town of Houghton Regis met each month to discuss current matters of concern and to plan initiatives for the future. HRUS played a key part. I had always been keen that local commerce and industry should contribute to and influence the school curriculum wherever possible. Each year our older pupils went on work experience for two weeks, into offices, factories and other work places in Houghton Regis, Dunstable, Luton and sometimes further afield. In return we offered placements for business folk to spend time in the school, sometimes only a day at a time, occasionally longer. The volume of support for HRUS & CC among the wide local community was considerable. Ironically it was in 1983 that Houghton Regis held its first town Carnival on the green.

It was a difficult time for all concerned. Pupils who were in their first year didn't know what would happen to them. Pupils in the two Middle schools on our campus and their parents were in a quandary: *Do we send our children to HRUS next year? Surely not, if it is going to close.* But they could also see that the school wasn't going to accept the decision. Despite the unfortunate defections to Dunstable schools, there was still a great deal of loyalty among Houghton Regis parents. And if some members of staff chose, understandably, to leave, how were they to be replaced? Teachers don't normally apply for a position in a school scheduled to close. It was a difficult time to be a head teacher.

While the axe was hanging over us, we were visited by many more County advisors than usual and by loads of HMI! Local shops were targeted with posters and petitions. A group of us went to the House of Commons to meet the Labour Education spokesman, Giles Radice. We also had an audience with Education Minister, Bob Dunn, at the Department of Education and Science. In school we did our best to keep up everyone's spirits, while a walk to London was being planned.

Thirty of us set out on the first day of the February half term to walk from Houghton Regis to Downing Street. Our group comprised several parents led by PSFA Secretary, Pat Page, some teaching and non-teaching members of staff, several pupils who gave up some of their half-term to join in, and Rev Guy Buckler, a Governor who had done a lot to rouse local people to support "their" school. We didn't want too many taking part because of safety issues. The police maintained a discreet presence throughout. Taking the A5 out of Dunstable we passed under the M1 through Redbourne to St Albans, where Guy had arranged for us to spend the night in sleeping bags on a church hall floor. It had been tiring thus far and cold but thankfully dry. Spirits were high. As I settled down that night, I wished that Paul Dulac could have been with us. He would have kept us all in good spirits, but he was now back in the States. After another day and a night spent in Colindale, we made our way into London itself. In Downing Street we were all allowed to go to the door of Number 10 and hand in our petition, for the attention of the Secretary of State for Education.

Mini-buses took us back to Houghton Regis. We knew we then had several weeks to wait for the Secretary of State's decision yet the life of the school had to carry on. It was an anxious time. In March we held an International Fortnight: Tony Pont, back from USA, gave an illustrated talk about his experiences; Beech Hill School Steel Band from Luton played in a school assembly; Asian dancers from Challney Girls School gave a wonderful performance on another morning; one assembly focussed on Oxfam, while Japanese dancers and a group of Mexican artists visited us. The international food and drink evening proved very popular. At the beginning of the year we had decided to make an application for a Schools Curriculum Award. These were awarded across the UK to schools who could show benefits across the curriculum of links with business, commerce and industry. The assessors visited us at the end of March while we were waiting to hear our fate.

It was in June that the decision came: the Secretary of State's letter to Beds CC read:

"*The Secretary of State ... hereby rejects the proposals.*
The Secretary of State ... was not satisfied that the Authority's present

proposals were in the interests of the children involved. The Secretary of State was concerned that at a time when such population growth as was expected in the locality would be in the Houghton Regis area rather than Dunstable, the proposal would deprive Houghton Regis of its only upper school, concentrating upper school provision wholly in Dunstable. Moreover, Houghton Regis Upper School has been a successful school, and is housed in good, recently built premises. He was impressed moreover by the strength of local opposition to what was proposed, and was concerned that the public consultations conducted by the Authority fell short of his guidance in Circular 2/80. He was also concerned that the circumstances in which the County Council reached its decision to proceed with proposals for the closure of Houghton Regis Upper School might be contrary to the requirements of Schedule 12 of the Local Government Act 1972."

I could not have put it better myself! Remember: this was a decision of a Conservative Secretary of Education, a member of the Conservative Government, rejecting a proposal from Conservative county councillors. Our case must have been good!

We could all breathe again, while it was back to the drawing board for Beds CC. The community joined in a civic service at All Saints Church in July and this was followed by a celebratory concert at the school. The defence committee was not disbanded, just in case! We decided to bring out a new school prospectus, in which we were able to announce that HRUS had been awarded the Schools Curriculum Award! We were the only school in Bedfordshire to receive this accolade. Members of our 6th Form who had produced a short video on "How to make the best use of your library" discovered that it had won 2nd prize in a national student video competition and that the video would be put forward into the international competition hosted in Japan. I felt very proud of everyone's efforts.

The issue of falling school rolls was not going away of course and the CEO, Peter Browning, addressed this when he met with Heads the following June. Contraction of the system was essential and the CEO felt he should give the lead as to how this contraction was to be achieved. The problem affected the north of the county too, and he made suggestions for contraction there. Turning to the south, he proposed that Queensbury School should close, leaving Manshead and Northfields in Dunstable, plus Houghton Regis: a much fairer solution and he would be putting these proposals to the elected county councillors. His package of proposals was accepted by the Upper Schools Heads at their Standing Conference.

While at Houghton Regis, I played a part in several County education initiatives. There was a working party on disruptive pupils, a County Board of Studies topic: "Economic and Industrial Awareness and its place in the Secondary Curriculum" and I was Chairman of another which looked at Study Skills and how they might be developed in schools. A group of Heads looked into "Self Assessment and Evaluation in Schools", prompted by the pioneering work done by historian, Richard Brown at HRUS and the Report from the Heads' group was well received in many schools in the county. Maryland was the country house where many of the Heads' sessions took place and where Peter Browning held many meetings, though he also liked to call Heads together in schools. I enjoyed and valued greatly these contacts with other Heads.

I had decided that I had done all I could at Houghton Regis. The community estates were now well established and the community had a more settled "feel"; the school and community college had survived its big test. I had been there for 12 years and it was time to move on. I wanted a second headship. I looked at the details of several schools and applied to some, without a lot of conviction. Then I saw two headships advertised in Sussex. Both had strong community connections, one was in East Sussex, the other in West Sussex. At the first I was not successful (see chapter on Interviews) but, after a rigorous two-day selection process, I was appointed at Thomas Bennett Community School in Crawley, one of the post-war "new towns". I would be starting in January 1986. We would all have to move to West Sussex.

Looking back on my time at Houghton Regis, there were many more good times and memories than bad ones. The Governors were always very supportive, especially the long serving Chairman, chain-smoking, Labour Councillor, John Kinchella, and the Reverend Guy Buckler. The PSFA were always keen to help, especially their dedicated Secretary, Pat Page, who (I learned from her husband, Len), sadly died very recently. I had thoroughly enjoyed working with the local community, with the children and the parents. Many local families had a tough time, but the majority always wanted the best for their children. And as for the school: I felt we had achieved a lot. There had been initial difficulties, to be sure, but with the influx of new staff, attitudes and standards began to improve. We were fortunate to attract some outstanding teachers: Mike Harbour and John Bowman, English teachers, both of whom went on to be Heads of schools themselves, as did Brenda Sullivan. I have already mentioned Mark Wyatt and Tony Fisk, whose work in Music and Drama brought out the creative talent in so many children; and two teachers I was fortunate to work with in the History department: Richard Brown and Pat Cooper. Others who made a significant contribution to the life and development of the school were Viv Nunn, always calm and efficient, and Rod Young, an outstanding Maths teacher and Head of Department. The Heads of the three houses, Ron Hodd in particular, worked really hard on behalf of their pupils. Another very positive influence was Special Needs teacher, Carol Johnson. Community Schools often owe their efficient performance to the contributions made by folk such as caretakers and secretarial staff, and Houghton Regis was no exception. Maurice Richards and Ken Hanford shared our aims and contributed to our achievements, as did Pam Stone (now Pam Heath) in the school office. I was sorry to leave them and the many young people who had made all the hard work worthwhile. I was also sad to say farewell to the Houghton Regis community, with and for whom the Upper School had consistently worked.

Donna and I investigated houses in Crawley, Brighton, Haywards Heath and Horsham, but the house we liked best was in East Grinstead. As I still had a job to do at HRUS until Christmas, Donna organised the departure and once all was packed up and she had seen the removal lorries on their way, she set off with Julie and Robert. Apparently the highlight of their journey was 4-year-old Robert informing some nuns on the train about the new house he was going to live in! I completed the term at Houghton Regis while staying in Stevenage with my colleague and good friend, John Bowman and his wife Heather.

We were looking forward to living in East Grinstead, an attractive small town with several old, 14th- and 15th-century timber-framed houses in the High Street. East Court Mansion was impressive with a pleasant adjoining park. The town was home to the Queen Victoria Hospital where Archibald McIndoe had carried out life saving plastic surgery during the war. There was plenty of history here. Ashdown Forest was nearby, and the sea and the delights of the South Coast and Brighton were closer too. Donna would be only 35 minutes from where she grew up: Tonbridge, where her brother, sister and mother still lived.

One factor that influenced our choice of house was its nearness to a very good primary school, but when Donna made enquiries, she was told that the nearby school, Escotts, was full, so Julie and Robert couldn't go there. Also full was another school a further half a mile away. Donna was annoyed and upset, so she rang the local education office. She didn't say, "Don't you know who I am?" but with her husband a newly appointed Head in the area, she certainly felt like doing so. The only school with any places available was Blackwell School, which could only be reached, other than by car, by an uphill walk of about 20 minutes. But there was another problem. Robert had spent a term at school in Bedfordshire as a "rising 5" before we moved and was doing well. Donna and I assumed he would continue his schooling in West Sussex, but not so: we were told he could not take up a place at Blackwell until the following Easter; however, when Donna explained to the Head at Blackwell that Robert had already been attending school in Bedfordshire, he was allowed to start in January. Not long after this, Donna began working in East Grinstead, which involved walking with the children to school every morning before walking into town, then repeating the process in reverse each afternoon.

Meanwhile, Sally had done well in her O levels at Westcliff High

School for Girls and was now in the 6th Form studying A level Maths, Further Maths and Physics. She was playing hockey for Essex Schools and was beginning to think about going to university. Joanne was soon to begin her O level studies at Southend High School for Girls, her main interest apart from sport being Art. Jo represented Essex Schools at athletics and was also a good hockey player, captaining Essex Schools U16s, and later playing for Essex U18s, when they were chosen to represent England in a tournament in Holland. Whenever there were important meetings at their schools, I did my best to attend. I had helped Sally with her O level English Language, and she had moved from an "ungraded" in her "mock" to a grade A in the summer! Jo was in her school athletics team when they reached the final of the English Schools Cup in 1984, which took place in Derby.

There is no doubt in my mind that the original decision to close Houghton Regis Upper School and Community College was a "political mugging" and defied all rational argument. Although we won our battle, others who followed did not. The closure of Kingsland School, as HRUS had been renamed, occurred in August 1999. Why was the name changed? HRUS was not threatened with closure because of its name. It ought not to be like this: school provision should not be a political football, it should not be one of the games that politicians play, though recent events in Hammersmith suggest that this is still the case. Further reflection (in 2014) leads me to believe that before long there will be an overwhelming need for a secondary school once again in Houghton Regis. More houses are being built and the town has developed its own distinctive identity. It would be good if political consensus could bring this about. If Houghton Regis does get its secondary school back, perhaps it will occupy the same buildings as the first one – they are still there! – or they were when I was penning this.

19
Thomas Bennett Community College

The school to which I had been appointed had at one time been the largest comprehensive in Europe. Thankfully it was a more reasonable size by 1986 with about 1400 pupils aged 12–18 and a large number of adults enrolled on part time courses. The school was on two sites: Canterbury and Southgate/Ashdown. Apparently the original plan had been to build two schools, but during the building process it was decided that it should be opened as one school – a pity that decision hadn't been taken before building began, as having the school on two sites, albeit just 400 metres apart, always presented problems – for pupils, staff, timetabling, communication etc. etc.

Crawley was one of the "New Towns" created by the New Towns Act of 1947. Working in Essex I had been familiar with the features of new towns in Harlow and Basildon. The Chairman of the Crawley Development Corporation, Sir Thomas Bennett, gave his name to the new school, which was in the Tilgate neighbourhood, one of the community-based estates that characterised Crawley's development. Previous Heads of Thomas Bennett School had been Tim McMullen and Pat Daunt, the author of the superb little book, "Comprehensive Values", which should be read by anyone who doubts the wisdom or the value of comprehensive education.

My immediate predecessor was Jim Knight, who, shortly before he left, had carried out a major reorganisation, about which staff, pupils and parents were divided. Previously the Canterbury building had housed the "Lower School" and the Southgate/Ashdown the "Upper School". The change that Jim Knight initiated was to have half of all pupils in Years 2, 3, 4 and 5 (now called years 8–11) in each of Canterbury and Southgate, with 6th Formers based in the Ashdown building. Canterbury pupils would be in Parker and Wallis houses, with Southgate pupils in Hepburn and Roberts houses. The merits of this scheme were that pupils would remain in one building with a team of house tutors for four years up to their public examinations. The downside was that every teaching department would be divided. Under the previous arrangement departments had been split, but more logically into those teaching Lower School pupils and Upper School pupils. Feelings among the teaching staff were running high and when I arrived I was bombarded by folk on both sides of the argument: those who wanted to reverse the change and those who were equally adamant the changes should remain. Not an ideal introduction.

Jim Knight had left in the summer, so, for a term, the school had been led by Deputy Head Chris Roberts. As soon as I had been appointed, he, together with Liz Fletcher, the other deputy, based in Canterbury, plus Ieuan Thomas, in charge of Southgate, took me out to a nearby café in a park for a "get to know you" chat. I'm sure they must all have been keen to find out what the new guy would be like. For my part it was good to meet senior colleagues in an informal, relaxed manner. We got on very well and what soon became very evident was the enormous commitment these folk had to the school and its ethos. From that initial meeting I felt sure we would be able to work well together.

The Director of Education for West Sussex, Dick Bunker, whom I had known when we both worked in Bedfordshire, warned me that I might find some of the staff "difficult". Thomas Bennett teachers were quite used to expressing their views, and Dick Bunker was aware that some were strongly opposed to the recent changes. I thanked him for his warning and began to wonder what I had let myself in for. In the first week I called a meeting of all teaching staff to give them a chance to meet me. I made a few general remarks and then came the questions. I told them that I would not be making any quick decisions regarding the issue of the way the school had been reorganised, and invited those who felt strongly to come and see me. One teacher, Peter Hazelrigg, asked a very pointed question, to put me on the spot. I thought I dealt with it quite well, and afterwards Chris Roberts said it had gone well and that staff would have taken note. I considered I had passed my first test.

At Houghton Regis, as Head, I had my own personal toilet in a small cloakroom adjacent to my office. I didn't have this at Thomas Bennett, where I used the same toilet facilities as the rest of the staff, very much in keeping with the philosophy of the place. This had an unexpected advantage. One morning I was using one of the cubicles, when two teachers came in to use the urinals.

As I sat there, I heard one ask, "What do you make of the new Head?"

"He seems all right. Prepared to listen. Seems a reasonable bloke," said the other, whose voice I recognised as that of Peter Hazelrigg!

I didn't make a habit of using the toilets to eavesdrop on the staff, as that would only have given me a male perspective! It was an interesting initial feedback none the less.

I visited each of the Middle Schools who sent pupils to us, as it was important that I made myself known and that I continued to develop the links and good understanding that had been built up between the schools. A member of staff had specific responsibility to maintain those links, but I needed to show my face too. I wanted to meet the Middle School Heads and I knew they would want to meet me.

In the first two terms, I made a point of seeing every member of staff individually. These were not in depth meetings but a chance for me to get to know everyone. A few of these meetings were in my room; most were in classrooms. After a fortnight, I armed myself with a list of all teaching and support staff, and sat down to try to match the names to those I had met thus far. It told me who I still had to meet and alerted me to names I could not yet put a face to. "Headship" meetings (which I renamed Senior Management Team (SMT) meetings) were held each week, with agenda and minutes. I became aware that there were some issues concerning three or four "underperforming" teachers and I resolved to deal with this as quickly and as fairly as possible. Then there were the relatively senior members of staff who felt personally put out by the recent changes, one in particular who felt very strongly indeed. He was an experienced and very competent teacher, who felt that his professional development had been blighted by the changes in the school organisation. He felt that he could no longer do the job to which he had been appointed. He was probably right, but when changes in an organisation take place, this is what can happen. I had a few long chats with him. I was coming round to the view that the changes had to be given a chance to prove themselves, so he was likely to remain very unhappy and probably a thorn in our sides. I tried to offer him a way out. After a couple of weeks we had a conversation in my office, which went something like this:

"If you genuinely cannot work happily and give of your best in these new circumstances, you may want to consider moving elsewhere, perhaps with promotion," I said.

"But I don't really want to leave," he said.

"I don't want you to leave either. You are a good teacher and you still have a lot to offer. But what is the alternative? You say you can't work in the changed circumstances, and I don't want a disgruntled teacher, a senior one at that, not only unhappy but unable to work with his colleagues."

"So what are you proposing?" he asked.

"You are currently a Grade 4 teacher; you have an excellent record within your subject area and pastorally. Thomas Bennett would be the poorer without you, but why don't you consider applying for a deputy headship? I could support such an application wholeheartedly," I said. "It's a natural progression for you, anyway," I added.

There was a long pause.

"I'll go away and think about what you've said. Thank you for being understanding and for your support," he said.

I think that prior to my arrival, when he had complained, he had been told, effectively, "Tough. Changes happen. Get on with it."

A few days later we met again.

"Your suggestion really took me by surprise," he said. "I hadn't considered myself as deputy head material. But if you think I could carry out such a role, I'm prepared to give it a go."

Not long after, he made an application for a deputy headship. I wrote a supportive reference, which was a genuine statement of his accomplishments and what I believed to be his potential. I was told he interviewed well and he was appointed. I heard some while later that he was doing very well.

Dealing effectively with under-performing teachers or simply teachers who are unhappy or have a gripe is not always done well by Heads. Of course it isn't straightforward, but in the interests of the pupils, it is vital that this difficult task is tackled. Heads need to be on good terms with the union reps in the school, as these will be involved in whatever decisions are reached. Teachers "at risk" should have their performance monitored on a regular basis and should receive practical and personal advice and support. An individual mentor can be a great help. Headteachers' Associations will give advice on best or possible courses of action in different situations, but so many Heads either don't seek help or don't act on advice received, or more often, don't face up to the problem in the first place. A situation in which pupils are not being well taught, not learning or making the progress expected must be addressed. What is frustrating and difficult to deal with is the teacher who contributes little if anything to the general welfare of the pupils and the school, who doesn't arrive early and never stays late but whose teaching in the classroom cannot be faulted. We had one at Thomas Bennett. When I pointed out something that needed to be done, in the interests of the pupils and of the teacher's department, he agreed it was a task that needed to be done, "but not by me". Sand and ostriches come to mind! Then there was the Head of the school that our children attended. If a parent, or a teacher, went to him with a justifiable complaint or to make a constructive suggestion, his response was invariably, "I hear what you say." No action.

There was an NUT strike action during my first term. Being in sympathy with union aims and demands makes it easier for a Head to deal with the inevitable disruption such action causes. It didn't last long. Another issue that reared its head was that of "mothballing". Schools that had surplus places were required to put a certain number of rooms "out of action" so that the county could save money by not heating or cleaning such rooms. Understandable though this policy was, it flew in the face of our community needs, as there was an increasing demand for adult classes during the daytime as well as those in the evening. The rooms on the top floor of the Ashdown building were identified and a partial mothballing took place.

We were keen to develop the Certificate of Pre-Vocational Education (CPVE) at Thomas Bennett and one of my few teaching commitments was Travel and Tourism on this course. I don't think the Humanities department was too keen for the Head to teach within it, (I might have found out some of their secrets!), so the only History teaching I did was in my office with a couple of A level students who wanted to study the Tudors and Stuarts. Later I taught a Parenting Education course to some 4th and 5th Year classes as part of our Social Education programme. I was particularly keen that before some of them left school, youngsters should learn some of the realities of becoming a parent. Boys and girls were taught together and I focussed on the practical implications of parenthood. The course was well received. We had young mums come in with their babies and they discussed the many issues they faced. Being one of the founder members, I became closely involved with the newly created Parenting Education and Support Forum, which was based in London but aimed to support parents throughout the UK. As the vast majority of students in school will become parents sometime in their lives, it does seem to make sense to make them aware of the basic fundamentals of parenting. The pressure to produce the best exam grades possible often means there isn't time or willingness to include in a student's programme those things that will be of real importance to them in their lives, such as coping with and enjoying parenting, managing money, learning how to handle responsibility, being a good citizen and much more.

Unlike Houghton Regis, where we had to initiate all our systems, coming to Thomas Bennett I was able to continue the already excellent good practice, sending Parents Post home once a fortnight, producing a Weekly Memo for all staff every Monday and having a daily verbal briefing each morning in each Staff Room. Any papers I wanted staff to read, on current issues or proposals for discussion for example, went out on blue paper, so staff knew its provenance. In addition to the regular Governors' Meeting, there was also a Youth Wing Committee, which was a sub-committee of the Community Council. On site there was a Youth Wing which opened four nights a week, with a Playgroup in the Youth Wing during the daytime, where students in my parenting classes participated.

I instigated the practice of linking each governor to an individual subject department, allowing for visits and greater knowledge and understanding of what went on. Individual heads of department were invited to Governors' meetings to speak about their particular teaching area. I know some Heads believe that the less Governors are told and know, the better. I did not share that view. Governors can only make a useful contribution to the life and development of the school if they are well informed. As Head I had regular meetings with our Chair of Governors. Each one was invariably helpful and supportive and keen to understand the problems we faced. Some of our Governors took up my suggestion that they should spend an hour or two visiting the school, going in to lessons, having lunch with us, always having made an appointment of course. Meeting with staff and students helped Governors understand some of the issues that face any large comprehensive school. Staff and Governors welcomed the initiative. We all tried to work together in the interests of the pupils and the community.

Several things made Thomas Bennett special and it was these that had initially attracted me. The fundamental ethos of the school lay in the principle of equal value. This was applied consistently and in many different scenarios. As a general principle the doctrine of equal value was embedded in the way teachers related to pupils around the school, with a focus on the individual pupil. Many schools say they adhere to such ideals, but Thomas Bennett was the only one in my experience where such beliefs were put into practice so completely. There was no uniform, as we didn't want to promote uniformity. Instead each individual was expected to take responsibility for his or her own development and behaviour and to play a constructive part in the life of the class, the tutor group, the house, the school and the community. Of course from time to time some pupils behaved badly, but their attention would then be drawn to the "What is expected" poster, which was in every classroom and listed behaviour expectations, these having been drawn up with and agreed by the pupils themselves.

Although the equal value principle may be difficult to define in precise, practical terms, there was no doubt that having a belief in the principle underpinned many of the decisions that were taken within the school. I made the point once that streaming in a comprehensive school was a contradiction in terms. I was challenged as to what I meant by the statement. Anyone who had the equal value principle in their bloodstream would have understood. This example only relates to how teaching and classes within a school might be organised. But equal value embraces issues of gender, ethnicity, faith, background etc. Having a belief in the principle didn't mean that we were always successful in achieving our aims. Nor did it mean that all pupils were treated the same. Quite the opposite: in order to achieve equal value there were many occasions when children had to be treated differently. Thomas Bennett, a comprehensive, community college was in the best possible position to apply the principle. It was up to me and the SMT and the departmental and house coordinators supported by the Governors to achieve this. Incidentally I always took the view that equal value also applied to members of staff, teaching and support staff. They were not all treated the same, of course, as some were paid more than others and some had more responsibility, but those differences didn't mean that you had to regard any as of less value than others. I hope that came across, as that was certainly my intention and my belief.

Another feature of Thomas Bennett that made it special was the quality of the teaching staff. Many were outstanding, and I made it my business to visit their classrooms whenever I could. GCSE had just been introduced, which sensibly brought together GCE and CSE and, as well as being tidier administratively, it also signalled that all students could aspire to study subjects that led to a qualification at age 16. Following the union activities nationally, the 1,265 hours "model" was introduced. By this the teaching and other activities of teachers were supposed to be contained within a framework of 1,265 hours per year. How many hours should be allocated for this and that was all set out. It may have been a useful yardstick for some schools, but most teachers at Thomas Bennett worked far longer than laid down. For the few who wanted to be "picky" it could be used as a stick to beat the school, department and building managers with, but this rarely happened.

There were several excellent and well-led departments at Thomas Bennett. Chris Marshall coordinated the work of some first rate teachers in the English Department which was often innovative in its teaching approaches, taking students away on short intensive courses for example where they became immersed in an author or a novel. Craft and Design Technology (CDT), led by Tim Weekes, moved on from craft work, which many pupils did excellently, to computer-aided design, with some great results, but the outstanding department coordinator, I think by general consensus, was Chris Bilbrough, whose Art department was an example to us all. The quality of the artwork produced by students throughout the school was outstanding, and Chris worked so hard, quietly and unobtrusively, with both students and the members of her department. Her standards and expectations were so high. Her Art Room was always a joy to visit. And for all the time I was at TBCC, Chris was fighting off cancer and was frequently far from well. She was a lovely lady who, unfortunately, is no longer with us. Her former students and fellow Art teachers remember her with great affection, as do many more of us.

Another department where you could also guarantee high expectations and standards was Business Studies, led by Sandra Barnes, another lady who didn't tolerate slackness and whose students did very well. The Humanities department was always an interesting place to visit with much innovative work going on, and those students who caught the bug of individual research did very well. History, Geography and some Religious Education made up the Humanities programme, which, in the first years in the school meant that some real cross-curricular learning took place. Even at GCSE, the subject examined was Humanities. Many excellent teachers worked in the department over the years. Sue Rees, who also sadly succumbed to cancer, was outstanding, always fully in command of what she was teaching and uniquely aware of the needs and aspirations of each individual pupil.

At Thomas Bennett we had a sizeable minority of students (about 11%) from ethnic minority backgrounds, so we attempted to ensure that our curriculum was not predominately Anglo-centric. This was easier to achieve in some subjects than others. The issue was discussed at the regular departmental and house coordinators' meeting and we achieved some success in moving things in the right direction. An associated topic was the under-representation of Asian and other ethnic minority adults in our Community and Adult Education programme, as most of the classes were very traditional. This did change in time with classes such as Asian Cookery being well supported. The Multi-Cultural evenings we introduced, embracing dance, fashion and food, proved popular with parents, students and the wider community. One of our Governors was from the local Asian community.

Activities Week, which took place in the last or penultimate week of the Summer term, and was organised for the first time in 1988, proved immensely popular with students and most staff. It was introduced to make the final two weeks of the school year more meaningful and purposeful than it often was. Activities Week required considerable planning and organisation, which was usually coordinated by Ieuan Thomas. By this time, 5th and 6th form examinees were not around, so the week of activities was for those in Years 2, 3, 4 and Lower 6th. All staff were involved. Students were offered a choice of activities lasting a week: some were abroad, such as "Camping by the Italian Lakes", some were in different locations in the UK, such as "Walking the Cornish Coastal Path", while others were Crawley-based e.g. "Cycling in Sussex/Surrey", and a few took place in the College, such as "Photography" or "Creative Cookery". Naturally, a deciding factor for parents was cost, but rather than complain about this, many parents welcomed the opportunity being given to their children, when a family holiday might be out of the question. For many parents, we were giving their children what they couldn't.

Ieuan Thomas and Tim Weekes
load up for Activities Week

There were many benefits to Activities Week. Most groups consisted of students from different school years; some students came into contact with teachers they had never previously met; the experiences children had were usually new and exciting; staff, able to get away from teaching their subject, often enjoyed the activities as much as the children; and when they all returned to school there were many tales to tell and experiences to share in the last few days of the Summer term. It was also another reminder that education and learning also takes place away from school. Safety and an understanding of the responsibilities involved were key features. I held a meeting with all staff involved and made it clear that if those in charge of an activity followed all the guidelines laid down by our Governors and by the Local Authority, and something untoward took place, an accident for example, then they would be fully supported. If, however, those guidelines were not adhered to and there was an incident or event in which a member of staff could and should have acted differently, then the teacher was on his or her own. Union reps fully supported this. Pupils were also told of their responsibilities, to themselves and to others, including staff, in their chosen activity. Each activity invariably went smoothly, the only blips being occasional thoughtless behaviour, as is normal among teenagers from time to time. During each activity, pupils often had tasks to perform that gave them experience and responsibility, and the change in some pupils even in a week was frequently commented on by parents.

Building on the experience in my previous school, Thomas Bennett applied for and was awarded the prestigious School Curriculum Award in 1987, having had an extremely thorough assessors' visit. Once again it was good to have the valuable links between school and community recognised and celebrated. The Award ceremony took place at the Barbican in London, and I took with me the Chair of Governors, Bill Siddall, and two students who went up to receive the award certificate. As I had now been Head of two schools that had received this award, I was asked to become an assessor, and over the next few years I had the privilege of visiting several schools that applied for the award. There were strict criteria to observe, but I found each school really interesting to visit, and I was impressed by the variety of community and school interaction I saw. As you would expect, each school was different and presented individual features, for example a school in Hounslow, which had a vast range of different languages spoken in the school, had one family who had taken their two children on a year-long sailing cruise. Communication between ship and school was maintained electronically but the school did not want the pupils to try to keep up with the lessons going on in school as "they would be learning so much on their world cruise," said the Head. The school did let the pupils know what lessons were going on but, in return the travellers had to share their experiences with the pupils back in school, so everybody benefitted. Worldwide community education!

Thomas Bennett won the award again in 1992. It's a shame that the School Curriculum Award no longer takes place. Although many schools do work closely with their local community, it is a pity that more don't. In my view a good school draws on the resources and expertise available within the community and contributes to the welfare of that community. Thomas Bennett CC aimed to do both. A small example at Thomas Bennett was the Senior Citizens' tea that was organised each Christmas by the pupils in Hepburn House, when the interaction between the youngsters and the old folk was genuine and often quite moving.

All members of the 5th year at TBCC had two weeks' work experience in November, which was immensely valuable for them but a major headache to organise, a task that fell for many years to Sandra Barnes. If possible, all students were visited while on their work experience, usually by their form tutor or, failing that, by another member of staff. This was not only to support the individual student but also to make or strengthen links with the firms that were good enough to take our youngsters. Most of the work experience was local for obvious reasons, though personal contacts often led to some students going to London or a nearby town. I visited as many as I could. Our planned visit to one young man proved abortive as the firm's boss told us that he had gone in the removal van to Blackpool to deliver furniture. Another lad found himself on the runway at Gatwick helping to signal aeroplanes safely in to land. A girl assisted in an equine operation in a veterinary surgeon's theatre. We asked their "employers" to write a brief report and every year over 90% were positive and occasionally glowing. There is no doubt that putting young people into the work place is good for them and it can also help to dispel some of the myths that persist about young people in the minds of employers.

Students who gain excellent exam results at A level or in their GCSEs are rightly praised for their achievements, usually the result of ability, hard work, good teaching and support from parents. They reap the reward by going to university or, in normal circumstances, getting good jobs. Quite often the talents of those who are less successful in exams are overlooked. As a society we should be trying to provide all young people with opportunities to show what they can do. They are the country's future. Recently Sir William Haughey said "Even kids without A levels are a lot smarter than we give them credit for."

It is essential that we recognise what each school does to develop the talents and personal qualities of their pupils. Education is not only about examination results, important though these are. In most schools, so much individual and group activity goes on that is not easily measured but that contributes greatly to the personal development of every pupil.

I had meetings in my office with individual members of staff on a regular basis. The professionalism of the staff always impressed me; even when an individual was bitterly opposed to something or was very angry about an incident or a decision, their complaint was always articulated in a polite and reasonable manner. There was a plethora of scheduled meetings, not all of which I needed to attend, but there were many, including those in the evenings, where my presence was expected. It was part and parcel of the school's philosophy that every member of staff had a right to be heard and should make a contribution to the policies adopted, by the department, by their house or within the school. We reminded staff that they were members of a team, actually members of several teams. This was so different from my experience in other schools in which I had taught, in the grammar schools especially, where the views of individual teachers were generally seen as an inconvenience. Often I had meetings to attend away from school, usually within the county but sometimes further afield, such as at the Community Education Development Centre in Coventry or at one of the nearby universities. I never really liked being away from school. My life attending meetings had an interesting side effect at home. Donna went to see what our son and daughter were doing one day. Were they doing what most 6- and 8-year-old children do, playing "schools" or "hospitals" or with toys, cars etc.? No! When asked what they were doing, they replied, "We're having a meeting!"

For me the key meeting each week was that of the SMT. When I arrived, this consisted of myself, the two Deputy Heads, Chris Roberts and Liz Fletcher, plus the Head of the Southgate Building, Ieuan Thomas, the Ashdown Building director, Alan Davies, the Senior House Coordinator, Anne Mathieson, and our Community Tutor, Arthur Earl. Shortly after, new Deputy Heads were appointed: Diane Dockrell and Nick Sorensen. Each had their own areas of responsibility but we tried to discuss and reach a consensus on major issues in our meetings. As I believed in delegating responsibilities, often individuals would inform the SMT of decisions they had taken, and these were then endorsed and duly recorded. I didn't want the Deputy Heads to be tied up with everyday minutiae, sorting out individual disciplinary matters for example, though they were there to arbitrate or to support staff if needed. Deputy heads should have a strategic role in my view, concerned with review, planning and development, a role shared to a large extent with the Head.

The secretaries in each of the three buildings were important members of our team. The building directors could not have carried out their many responsibilities without the work done by these reliable and hard-working ladies. One advantage I had in my role as Head at Thomas Bennett, compared with Houghton Regis, was that my secretary's office was adjacent to mine. This enabled me to work closely with Brenda, my Secretary, who was always quietly efficient and reliable. She always knew where this file or that document was and effectively kept the machine running smoothly. I could not have done without her. After I retired and was working at home and needed a file, I would look out for Brenda, but, sadly, she wasn't there! Another essential team member was our excellent Bursar, Jean Tilley, whose office was close to mine. All financial matters were handled by her and she attended SMT meetings when major financial issues were being discussed or decided. Her advice, her calmness and efficiency were always valued.

Following the Education Act of 1986, we now had five days each school year for in-service training. These were the brainchild of Education Secretary, Kenneth Baker, so they were christened B-Days! They did prove very useful and some valuable and sometimes innovative in-house training was carried out. In April 1990, LMS started. This was not the rebirth of an old railway company, but a revolution, actually devolution, in the way schools' finances were allocated and managed. The introduction of Local Management of Schools was a real challenge as well as an opportunity as now the school had a much larger sum of money at its disposal each year. Instead of County being responsible for paying the salaries of our staff, for example, that task now fell to us. Our Bursar, the SMT and the Governors were all given training in how the new scheme might best be administered. Giving us greater flexibility in how we chose to spend "our" money was all very well, but was there going to be enough money? Time would tell.

During the second half of the 1980s, Health and Safety became an issue that could not be pushed to one side. Although IT in schools was very much in its infancy, there were initiatives, such as "IT across the curriculum". Teachers in all subject disciplines were encouraged to become computer literate and to promote opportunities for students to use IT in their studies. Our IT coordinator was Peter Hazelrigg, and subjects such as the Sciences, CDT and Mathematics led the way. This was the decade when computers were going to replace typewriters and there would be paperless offices. The first of these happened but not the second. Later we explored networking and linking Ashdown and Southgate buildings with Canterbury by means of an underground cable. Data protection affected all our records of pupils, parents and staff. Then the National Curriculum arrived. Staff at TBCC spent many hours analysing what had to be done and what the changes meant. The amount of bureaucracy that teachers were subjected to increased alarmingly. Despite the arguments in its favour, the effect long term has been to stifle curriculum innovation and it's no wonder that teachers are increasingly fed up with being told what they should do, especially when the instructions come from a source not known for knowledge or understanding of the processes involved in education, never mind its purpose.

We promoted Childline, which was launched in West Sussex in 1992. Some of our assemblies focussed on such organisations as Shelter and the Samaritans. We did this believing that children should understand the issues that made such bodies necessary. Amnesty International was a topic for a 6th Form assembly. We had a remarkable presentation in one assembly from David Kossoff, and we welcomed visiting speakers, including representatives of different faiths, to address our students. In one of my assemblies I played "Imagine" by John Lennon, and this, most unusually, produced a "thank you" phone call from the father of one of the boys, who said his son wouldn't stop talking about it. And speaking of phone calls, I had one from a woman who said she wanted her son to come to us as we were "the Christian school".

"I think you may be mistaken," I said. "Holy Trinity is the Church of England school in Crawley, and the Roman Catholic school is St Wilfreds."

"I didn't say, 'Church of England' or 'Roman Catholic'," the mother said. "I said, 'Christian'. Your school is all about fairness and equality, and the ethos of the school is Christian."

"Well, it's very kind of you to say so and to put it like that," I said. "Of course you and your son are very welcome to come and look round during the day when school is in session." This she did and the lad started with us the following September.

Occasionally a head teacher has to confront a very difficult situation or make a decision he would much rather not have to make. This was the case with Chris Roberts, one of my two deputies who had led the school for a term before I arrived and who had made a major contribution to the life of Thomas Bennett over the years. Chris was a Maths teacher. As a deputy head he didn't have a heavy timetable each week, but he was having problems with his classes. Furthermore he was not finding it easy to cope with the ever-changing educational landscape, crucial for a deputy. Chris was not contributing to the SMT. I also suspected that Chris knew he was underperforming, as although he hid it well, he was clearly an unhappy teacher. This was a situation I knew I had to confront.

I arranged for the two of us to go out for lunch one day and I plucked up the courage to raise these issues with him. He agreed with my analysis of the situation, and said he hadn't been enjoying work for some while. The question was: what do we do about it? Removing his deputy headship and reducing him to the ranks wasn't an option. I told Chris that he could probably receive an enhanced pension for taking early retirement in the interests of the service, if he was prepared to do that. He had agreed with me that it would be better if he left the school, not just in the interests of the school but in his too. Raising the issue had been painful for me, but, with some understandable reluctance, Chris agreed. It was a sad moment for both of us. We shook hands and returned to school. That evening I had a phone call from Margaret, his wife. For a moment I was fearful of what she was going to say.

"I just want to thank you, Tony, for what you said to Chris today. He has been so unhappy for such a long time, but he didn't know what he should do. You have lifted a weight off his back. I am so pleased. Thank you again."

Naturally, I was relieved that our lunchtime discussion had had such a positive outcome. Chris did receive an early retirement enhanced pension payment and he soon got a job working for an insurance company, which he enjoyed. When I saw Margaret some weeks later, she said he hadn't been so happy for years.

When Liz Fletcher left to take up a headship in Brighton, her successor was Diane Dockrell, who proved to be an outstanding replacement, though her role was different from the one Liz had had. Diane later went on to be a Head herself within West Sussex. Chris' replacement was Nick Sorensen, who proved to be another excellent appointment. Again, like Liz and Diane, in time, Nick left us to take up a headship in the West Country. Other TBCC staff who left to become Heads included Colin Taylor, Fiona Wright, Adrian Money and Sue Warren. It pleased me greatly that so many followed up their excellent service at Thomas Bennett by becoming Heads themselves. Talented teachers should be encouraged and given opportunities to flourish in the same way as the students one is teaching and the athletes one is coaching. Put your faith in them and give them chances to shine. It was always my policy to give senior staff wide-ranging delegated responsibilities: this was good for the school and provided valuable experience for the teachers themselves. Every single one richly deserved their promotion. Others, appointed during my time there, have since gained promotion, including headships and deputy headships, both within the school and in other schools.

I found the job immensely satisfying, though always challenging. I regarded it a privilege to be a head teacher, responsible for the welfare and development of students and teachers, and today, most Heads are doing a fine job, despite unhelpful, negative comments from Government and Ofsted.

All the usual school activities took place at Thomas Bennett: ski trips, foreign exchanges, Geography and Biology field trips, annual Art displays, Parents and Teachers Association dances – the list goes on and on. We also had a few that were less common: in addition to Activities Week, we also staged an annual Pop Mime, in which groups of pupils, dressed appropriately, mimed to their favourite pop group, in what was a competitive event, held in the main school hall, usually full to capacity, with a paying audience, with proceeds to charities, either local, such as the West Sussex County Youth Theatre, or further afield, such as Romanian orphanages, which were visited and supported by some of the 6th Form. I had the dubious honour of being chief judge, and expected to dress up for the occasion. It was all great fun, performances were often excellent and a lot of money was raised.

In Book Week, book swaps were organised; in Arts Week, the timetable was partially suspended to allow for arts activities across the school, often with visiting artists. Science Week was largely in response to Arts Week: "not to be outdone"! We made our own video, "Education for Life", to publicise the school. Early in the Autumn term our new Year 8 pupils spent two or three days staying in a youth hostel in order to gel and get to know each other and bond with their tutors. Able young Maths pupils spent some Saturdays at Sussex University with other talented pupils from across the county. Occasionally we suspended the timetable for a morning or afternoon for a particular year group in order to focus on a key issue, with outside speakers often contributing.

County asked if we would host a Hearing Impaired Unit, which we gladly did, with our staff receiving training and a small number of partially deaf children were integrated into classes and tutor groups. It seemed to work well; one consequence was that the teacher taking assembly had to wear a microphone, and on one occasion I forgot to switch mine on. A small girl in the third row realised at once and walked out to the front to point out my error! Amusement all round!

Traditionally, every other year, a party of 6th Formers, accompanied by two or three members of staff spent a month in India working with local people to improve some aspect of their community. One group worked on the construction of a theatre or performing arts area in a local school; another time, their task was fencing a school playground. The experience was invaluable and it led to some students returning to India after leaving school. Some 6th Form girls spent three weeks assisting in a Romanian orphanage. There always seemed to be something being planned; life was never dull for any of us!

Adults attended classes at Thomas Bennett in the evenings and occasionally during the day. There were dozens of classes and hundreds of adult students usually four days each week, sometimes on Saturday mornings as well. All this was organised and managed by our Community Tutor, Arthur Earl, and his PA, Beverly Parrett. While I was there, the responsibility for all this lay with the Community College Council. Our Head Caretaker, Alan Howson, renamed "Buildings Manager", had a big part to play in making sure all the rooms were cleaned and ready at the end of the school day, then ready for school use the following day. Caretakers are an often-maligned breed. Those I worked with (with one exception that I won't mention) were hard working, cooperative and resourceful, invaluable members of the team. Arthur Earl's annual exhibition of the impressive work done by adult students in the various classes served as publicity for next year's courses. Some adults joined daytime 6th Form classes, and some 6th Form students enrolled in evening classes. I was fully supportive of such flexible learning arrangements.

Ours was an open site, as we didn't think it was appropriate for a college that served the community to be fenced off, but occasionally youngsters with nothing better to do would cause problems in the evening. This led to one amusing encounter. Community Tutor, Arthur Earl, was outside one evening investigating some noise that was disturbing one of the adult classes. He found a 13-year-old lad and began to remonstrate with him.

"Don't you know who I am?" said Arthur, adopting his occasional bossy tone.

"Yes, you're the Head when the school's closed," the boy replied! Arthur and I enjoyed that.

As with most schools, we often had visits from individual inspectors, usually to take a look at a particular department or some aspect of the school's organisation or management. The visits were always cordial; sometimes we received feedback, but not always. After spending a day with us, one inspector popped in to see me.

"I hope you've had a useful day," I said, being both polite and in a spirit of enquiry.

"Yes, indeed. Do you know, I had the strangest experience this afternoon," the inspector replied. "I had spent the day in the Humanities department and I couldn't work out what it was that I was feeling. Then I realised. What I was seeing with the students and staff, the overall atmosphere, it was just as if I was in a university. No uniform, obviously, but students working to their own agendas, clearly taking responsibility for what they were studying, and the relationships between the students and their teachers, well, it had a university "feel". It was most impressive. And very unusual."

I thanked the inspector for his kind words, which were duly

passed on to the relevant staff and students. Was it just a good day? Probably, though a lot of what went on in Humanities (and at certain levels in other departments too) was as he had described. There were many teachers at Thomas Bennett who understood that pupils often learn more when left to work things out for themselves.

An Ofsted inspection was saved up for my very last term, the summer of 1994. The whole Thomas Bennett community joined in the preparation. We realised that we needed a large number of boxes for collecting and making available all the paper work that the inspectors would need to see. The local Tesco store was most obliging, so much so that one member of staff said to me, "They'll think we're sponsored by Tesco!"

We received a reasonable report: it recognised our strengths and confirmed to us our weaknesses, most of which we were already working on. All schools were meant to have a "daily act of collective worship", a requirement we interpreted somewhat freely. The Chief Inspector made an interesting comment on our assemblies, "You are not conforming to the law with regard to your morning assemblies, but I do like your assemblies. In fact I like them better than those that are laid down." He was referring to assemblies he and his colleagues had attended in both our main buildings, assemblies led by many different members of staff.

"Really?" I said. "I'm very pleased to hear that. Can you not say this in your report?"

"I wouldn't be able to do that," he replied, "that's just my personal opinion."

What a shame!

One contentious issue during the 1990s was staff smoking. One group said, "Smoking should be banned" but the smokers retaliated with, "We have our rights." Although I was on the side of the "Keep the Staff Room clean" brigade, I could see both points of view. There seemed to be no middle way. Neither the Local Authority nor the Governors would make a ruling. Our compromise "solution" was to have a small "Smoking Room" for break and lunchtime smokers. Although this left the main Staff Room "smoke free", which greatly pleased the clean air addicts, the "Smokers' Room" became foul and fetid, and every emerging teacher smelt even more noxious than if he (or she) had smoked alone. Latterly, and thankfully, the law has decreed that all indoor work places should be smokeless zones.

Just as athletes need recovery time after hard training, so do head teachers! In 1990 Donna and I took our two young children, now aged 9 and 11 on a holiday across the pond. First we went to Toronto, where we had a big family get-together at Stuart and Eileen's house and where our two met and played with Matthew, Erica and Bronwen, John and Kaili's children. Stuart was Donna's uncle, her father's younger brother, and John was one of his three sons. Then to Niagara Falls, followed by two weeks driving a hired Oldsmobile around New England, which was great fun. In Plymouth, New Hampshire we stayed with Paul and Becky and their boys, who we hadn't seen since Houghton Regis days. Julie and Rob had a wonderful time playing in and around Lake Winnipesaukee and Paul cooked us all a superb steak on his lakeside barbeque. We had a very hot day cycling around Martha's Vineyard, but as our next stop was New York, we returned our car to Springfield. From there it was a short air hop to New York.

Martha's Vineyard, USA 1990

In high winds and heavy rain our little plane took off. The weather was atrocious and the plane was tiny: standing in the middle you could touch both sides. In-flight catering was a packet of peanuts! It was only a half-hour flight to New York, but with the bad weather the plane rocked and rolled alarmingly and approaching New York the pilot circled for over an hour waiting for permission to land. The one stewardess reassured us that all would be well but Donna began to hyperventilate, becoming quite distressed. This alarmed the crew who thought she might be having a heart attack. They radioed ahead for an ambulance to meet the plane when it landed.

At JFK Airport medics came on board and escorted Donna into the ambulance. I was to travel to the hospital, together with Julie and Robert in a police car, which would try to clear the way through the busy, New York, rush hour traffic. Rob was in his element as he found himself sitting in the back of the police car next to a member of the New York Police Department who had a gun in its holster right next to him! Wow! The smile on his face said it all! The hospital was in the seamiest part of New York and Donna couldn't be seen straightaway, as two gunshot cases took priority. The police guy who had accompanied us to the hospital, said, "Don't let the children out of your sight, and don't let your hand luggage out of your grasp."

Donna was on a trolley, but as she was feeling better, she said, "Let's go."

We checked out, paid the charge imposed, and took a taxi to our hotel. A kind, local American lady told us what the charge should be for our particular journey.

"Don't pay any more," she said. Because of our unorthodox exit from the airport, the airline had our cases sent to our hotel.

Our first time in "the Big Apple" was brilliant. Highlights were Macy's, the Empire State, Schwarz toyshop, and the zoo in Central Park (where we were "taken for a ride" in both senses, by an Irish guy with a horse and buggy!), the Statue of Liberty and the Staten Island Ferry. McDonalds on Broadway, next to Wall Street, even had a pianist playing for the customers! We had to take a photo of that! We even went to a show on Broadway. It was a memorable holiday for many different reasons.

Donna was an excellent Mum for young Julie and Robert and it was good to have a holiday away together because my work, and the meetings, meant I made less of a contribution to bringing up our two children than I would, ideally, have liked. When the children were younger, it was not unusual for me to return home after they were in bed; both in Dunstable and then in East Grinstead, the major responsibility for looking after our children fell on Donna. Once Julie and Robert started at school, Donna was able to go out to work, part-time at first. Although Donna left school without any formal educational qualifications, she had had a variety of jobs: she has the distinction of having been Tunbridge Wells' first female traffic warden, she had worked in offices and children's homes, and in Dunstable and in West Sussex she had many different roles. Both at work and at home Donna has always been very organised, efficient and thorough: she likes to get things done, and employers appreciated these qualities, as does (most of the time!) her husband.

Soon after I had started at Thomas Bennett my eldest daughter, Sally, began her Mathematics and Computing degree at Loughborough University. As a regular Essex County hockey player, she was disappointed to find that the University 1st XI were nearly all internationals, so she settled for the 2nd XI and playing for her hall of residence, Cayley Hall. She enjoyed Loughborough, but in her final year she was struck down with an illness that put her in Leicester Royal Infirmary for several weeks. At alarming speed she developed a severe form of glandular fever and a virus attacked her spinal cord. It seriously interrupted her final year, but at least she recovered and was able to take her final exams and attend the Graduation ceremony to receive her BSc Hons.

Sally's younger sister, Jo, had taken a different route. After a year's Foundation Course in Art in Southend, she began a 3D Art degree course at Brighton University in 1991. Late one night as she was walking back along Western Road to her digs on her own, Jo saw two policemen walking on ahead of her, so she caught them up and said, "Would you mind if I walked along with you? I'd feel safer with some company!" Of course they readily agreed. Jo gained her BA Hons in 3D Art (wood, metal, ceramics and plastics) in 1994.

I decided in 1992 that I would study for a part-time Masters' degree from Warwick University in The Management of Community Education. For many years I had been promoting Community Education, trying to put aspects of it into practice at Houghton Regis and in Crawley. I had worked closely with the Community Education Development Council, based in Coventry, in particular with Phil Street. It may have seemed strange to some that I was starting a Masters' degree shortly before retiring, but I had never found the time before and when the opportunity arose, I couldn't turn it down. As it was part-time, I didn't have much time away from school at all – the occasional Friday for long weekend work courses. Having a heart by-pass in March 1993 proved only a minor interruption. I enjoyed the study programme and especially the work for my dissertation.

I receive my MEd at Warwick University 1993

As a secondary school Head, I often moaned to my middle school Head colleagues about the poor level of English and Maths of our 12 year old intake each year, to say nothing of their personal and social skills. They told me that they made the same complaints to the first school Heads. When I visited some of the local Heads of first schools they told me horror stories about their intake at age 5, many of whom had few of the basic skills: unable to read, do simple sums, use a knife and fork or tie their shoelaces and, in some cases, needed help going to the toilet. Many had not learned to share or cooperate and related poorly to their peers and to adults. It became obvious to me that some parents were not helping their children develop. I used this as the basis of my dissertation, whose title became: *The role of parents in the educational development of their pre-school age children and the perception that parents have of that role.*

Many years before, in 1967, the Plowden Report had established a clear relationship between children's home backgrounds and their success at school. My research involved interviewing parents with pre-school age children in different parts of Crawley as well as the first school head teachers. It found it immensely rewarding. One father I interviewed on the Broadfield Estate was obviously a very conscientious dad to his 3-year-old daughter, but during my interview he said to me, "I don't really know how to be a father. I'm not sure what a father is meant to do. You see, I never had a father."

I felt so sorry for this well-meaning chap. I wanted to spend time trying to give advice and to talk with him about the many roles of a father. But I couldn't. I was there to carry out an interview, make notes and use the data in my write-up. I explained that to him, though we did have a chat for several minutes which I hope reassured him. My dissertation was awarded a distinction making the hard work all worthwhile. I enjoyed the launch of the Parenting Education and Support Forum in London and have contributed in various ways since to promote the concept that it is in years 0 to 3 that parents have the most important roles in laying down a foundation for their child's future education and development.

I had decided to leave Thomas Bennett, to retire in fact, in the summer of 1994. In many ways I wanted to go on longer, as I loved the school, I enjoyed my job, my colleagues were great and I liked being with young people, but certain factors influenced my decision. My heart by-pass at St George's Hospital in London in March 1993 meant I was away from school for half a term, when Diane Dockrell held the fort in my absence. I knew I would be fitter following this procedure, but I was also finding it harder in school meetings to hear, or rather to decipher, what people were saying if they were not sitting near me. After 37 years teaching I was aware that I was probably not as effective as I had been. Statistics said that head teachers who retired at 60 had a longer life expectancy than those who went on to 65. Julie and Robert were teenagers, so I would have more time to spend with them if I were to leave. The decision was taken. Chair of Governors at the time, Dr Goodwin, was most supportive and I was given a first class farewell. Mary Russell, one of the long serving and active Governors, suggested that I should become involved in U3A – the University of the Third Age. She meant well, but I said I didn't want to spend my time with older people. Somehow I knew that my coaching of young athletes or teaching of students hadn't yet come to an end. But it was still very hard to leave Thomas Bennett, the staff and the children; I hoped it would maintain its beliefs and practices, even though changes were inevitable. The interviews held to appoint my successor proved abortive. Diane Dockrell became Acting Head again, this time for a term.

My leaving day July 1994

The Thomas Bennett of today appears to be an entirely different place. All the old buildings have gone and replacing them, on one site, is a brand new building, which is modern and looks, to my mind, very clinical, but then I don't work there any longer so it may be just as full of warmth and just as collegiate as before. Having all students and staff in one building must be an enormous advantage. There is now a school uniform, which, I'm sure, many parents welcome. The new school was the result of a Private Finance initiative, which affects how the building is managed. Lately, I hear that TBCC is "a maintained Comprehensive Secondary Academy". Some, at least, of the values that I associate with Thomas Bennett are still present, as recorded in a recent Ofsted report, which was very complimentary. The Government's Department for Education has said that academies can employ un-qualified teachers if they wish; hopefully the Head, Governors and Senior Staff at TBCC will ignore this and continue to appoint only fully qualified teachers. Yasmin Maskatiya has been Head for the last 13 years and though I have no direct evidence, I am told that under her leadership Thomas Bennett has maintained the ideals and ethos that made it special. Recently she has moved on. I understand there was no advertisement or interviews to appoint her successor, as this is done from within the ranks of the Academy hierarchy. All very strange! And as I heard of Yasmin's departure, I also learned that another stalwart of TBCC, Julian Grant, had been appointed Head of Sackville School in East Grinstead, the school our two children, Julie and Robert attended.

All schools should have qualified teachers, but more than that, they also want teachers who are competent and effective, excellent in the classroom. I read that top Mathematics graduates are to be offered £20,000 scholarships to teach in schools. This incentive should help able children particularly to excel at Maths and go on to become graduates themselves, provided that these new top grade teachers are also qualified and good at teaching. I recently heard of a school that was desperately short of Science teachers and had a new super Science graduate parachuted in, so to speak, to plug the gap. His knowledge was outstanding, but the pupils didn't understand him, as he had not learned how to teach. I was reminded of Ieuan Thomas, one of our Maths teachers at Thomas Bennett. Ieuan was originally a PE teacher who had retrained to teach Maths. Mathematics was not his specialism, so, as a result, when he was teaching a class of, say, 15 year olds who were finding Maths difficult, he understood and knew where they were coming from. He could help them overcome their difficulties. He had no trouble at all with classroom control and the children liked him. They knew that Mr Thomas understood when they couldn't grasp something, that he would be patient and try to explain to help them understand, or suggest ways they might work it out for themselves. I use Ieuan as an example because sometimes the very well qualified Maths or Science graduate cannot bring themselves down to the pupils' level. The teacher may be in the clouds but the pupils could still be at base camp.

As I retired, I was able to reflect. Thirty-seven years of teaching seemed to have flown by. Pre-PGCE, I had spent a year working and learning in four different schools. After my PGCE, I progressed from ten years in two boys' Grammar Schools to 26 years in three mixed Comprehensive Schools, the last two also being Community Colleges. I had worked in seven different local authorities. It had certainly been varied, always challenging but at the same time, enjoyable and rewarding. I worked with so many excellent teachers, with some of whom I am still in contact. Former pupils that I bump into normally recognise me better than I do them! And I definitely learned as much as I ever taught, if not more. I made the right choice all those years ago.

Paul Dulac, our host in New Hampshire

20
Interviews

During a long teaching career I applied for a number of teaching posts. Many of these applications were speculative and only some led to an interview. In several instances I decided quite early on in the process that this wasn't a job or a school for me. In one school while the candidates were being shown round, I took the opportunity to pop into the boys' toilets, often a guide to what a school is like. I was horrified: graffiti galore, much of it sexually or racially offensive, locks absent, plus broken urinals. Any school that allows such a situation to develop, apparently unchecked, was not one where I wanted to be. If a candidate withdraws, having been called for interview, he cannot claim expenses, so you go through with the interview, making sure your answers are such that the panel will select someone else. Eddie Haynes, my Head at Appleton School, told me that he once found himself in a similar situation, and in his interview he gave all the "wrong" answers, but was still offered the job! He had to turn it down.

Some interviews stand out for me, not all for the same reasons. While at Southend High School for Boys, and I don't know now why I did this, I applied for a headship of a secondary modern school in a south-east London borough. I was only a head of department, so I suppose I was dipping my toe in the water. To my surprise I was called for interview. There were only three candidates at the Council

Chambers where the interviews were being held, quite late in the evening, though earlier four of us had been shown round the school. I guess one potential candidate had seen enough. In my interview I sat on one side of the Council Chamber, with Governors sitting opposite. Both sides of the Chamber were raised and we were on about level three. Oddly, at right angles to me and the Governors, were the LEA representatives. The Chair of Governors was a youngish, attractive lady wearing a red suit, consisting of a jacket and a rather short skirt. During the interview she said,"Mr. Elder, what is your policy with regard to sex education?"

The response that came immediately into my head at that moment: *I think the Head and Chair of Governors should give practical demonstrations…* Although that might have ensured I wasn't appointed, there was always the possibility that my suggestion might have been taken up! I gave a suitably anodyne answer. I knew I hadn't performed very well, but I really didn't want the job. I had not been impressed during the tour of the school earlier in the day. Before the interviews had begun, the outcome was clear. Of the three candidates, I and one other had come from a relatively short distance away, so no large outlay on expenses there. The third candidate, a lady, was the Head of another school in the borough that was about to close. It was obvious that the LEA had this vacant headship earmarked for her. I knew that my references had not been taken up, a clear sign that I was not in the running as far as the LEA was concerned. After all three of us had been seen, we waited for what seemed an unaccountably long time for news of the decision. At last a door opened.

"Mr Elder, would you come through please?" said the clerk.

I was taken totally by surprise. *They must want me to clarify some point or other … or perhaps the Chair of Governors really does want to … no, can't be,* I decided.

Inside the chamber I was asked to sit down. The red-suited lady spoke. "Mr Elder, we would like to offer you this headship."

I was almost lost for words. I managed, "Oh I am surprised. Can I have some time to think this over?" Penny and I had not even looked around the area, not considered house prices or anything.

What I later discovered had happened was that, although the LEA wished to appoint their soon to be redundant Head, the governors had not wanted this and had ideas of their own. The governors wanted to appoint the best candidate that wasn't the LEA's choice. The clerk said that I could not have 24 hours to discuss with my wife, so I turned down their offer and the LEA, I gather, got its way. It had been an altogether bizarre experience.

Some years after this episode, while a deputy in Bedfordshire, I applied for a post in Sheffield. I had been particularly attracted by the details I was sent. How different my life would have been had I been appointed. The post was Director of Hurlfield Campus, which comprised the secondary school, a feeder school, a youth facility, a library and sports facilities. The challenge appealed to me and I was delighted to be called for interview. In the event none of those interviewed was appointed, but for me this interview stood out. Instead of questions being asked, and answered, with no comment, as was usually the case, on this occasion, the Chief Inspector gave me an interrogation. After every answer I gave, he asked me to explain, or justify what I had just said, or elaborate.

"What do you mean, 'streaming is incompatible with comprehensive education'?"

"In what circumstances would you want to teach boys and girls in different classes?"

And when I answered, he would come back and ask, "What is the justification for that?"

"How important do you rate effective communication within the school?" And when I said it was very important and was the key to good inter-departmental practice for example, he wanted to know how I would ensure good communication existed. "What have you done to make communication better in your school?" Then he went on, "What can you do to make everyone an effective communicator?"

We had a discussion, not a question and answer, on the subject of the curriculum, agreeing that the effective curriculum is not what is taught, but what each child takes away at the end of each lesson, each day, each term.

"So, how do you know what each child is taking away?" he asked.

We agreed there were some important questions to which there was no immediate or obvious answer. I really enjoyed the interview experience at Hurlfield, though it was gruelling and my interview lasted almost an hour. I felt we had a professional dialogue and that it had been good for both of us. I wish that more interviews had been like that.

As I said, nobody was appointed, and I didn't get to teach or lead in South Yorkshire. Wow! Wouldn't that have been different!

Despite my best intentions (and good references) sometimes I failed to convince a key individual of my qualities or suitability for a particular post. This was the case in Leicestershire. I had applied to become Principal of Groby Community College, a post which Cyril Poster was leaving, big shoes to fill. Leicestershire was one of a number of counties that had pioneered community education, so the County Chief Education Officer, Andrew Fairbairn, was keen to meet the candidates for this position, and assess their potential. He asked me about the community education work I had done in Bedfordshire and my philosophy. Despite my best efforts I was unable to convince him that community education at Groby would be in safe hands with me, which was very disappointing. I would not have minded living in Leicestershire at all, a lovely county … *Che sera sera.*

Mainly out of interest, partly for fun, I applied for the headship of Lord Williams' School at Thame in Oxfordshire, another county known for its community education work.

To my surprise, given my background and views on education, I was called for interview. This was the only school where my wife was expected to attend with me, no doubt to be scrutinised for suitability, prior to my formal interview. Donna held her sherry glass impeccably as I was sure she would. It reminded me of the Japanese culture where wives are very much involved in their husband's business world. I knew from the outset that this was not my kind of school. There was no social deprivation here, quite the opposite. Appeals to parents when improvements or new curriculum spaces were needed resulted in tens of thousands of pounds, if not more, rolling in. It was comprehensive, but I was told that the school produced more entrants to Oxbridge than any other state comprehensive and I can well believe it. It was a school favoured by many Oxford dons for their offspring. My answers in my interview probably confirmed to the governors my unsuitability. I know I would not have felt comfortable there: not my sort of people.

Just prior to my appointment to Thomas Bennett, I had an interview in East Sussex. This led to another somewhat bizarre occurrence. Five of us were being seen. As usual the key players were the governors of the school and the officers of the local education authority. The current and outgoing Head, who we knew had been very successful and was highly thought of, was moving on to another headship and his views obviously also mattered. It was normal practice for applicants to meet senior staff, including the existing Head, and their views on the candidates were usually sought though not necessarily acted upon. We were all interviewed and the selection panel made their decision. A little later we learned that the chair of the panel had asked the outgoing Head what he thought of the five candidates. This is quite a difficult position to put the Head in, but he said that he thought any of the candidates would be suitable and would do a good job, except one, whom he didn't recommend. Who was appointed? You've guessed it.

Of course in my capacity as Head, both at Houghton Regis and at Thomas Bennett, I have conducted many interviews myself, and it is interesting being on the other side of the table, so to speak. I always regarded the appointment of new staff as almost the most important thing I had to do. Central to a school's success is having the right teachers. I firmly believe that interesting people usually make the best teachers, and in interviews I tried to discover whether this candidate or that had done or were doing interesting things in their lives. At Thomas Bennett I usually asked candidates what they understood by Community Education, and the responses varied enormously. Questions about equal value also produced interesting replies! In my 17 years as a Head I can't remember making any really duff appointments, but I can recall many outstandingly good ones, too numerous to list. Two very different examples will suffice.

At Houghton Regis our original Music teacher left after a few years and we advertised for a replacement. It was a scale post, but there were very few applications from experienced people, and none that looked any good. I told the County Music Advisor that I would like to consider an application that had come in from a young man who had yet to begin his teaching career. To me he appeared promising. Faced with the dearth of good candidates, but with some reluctance, he agreed. This was how Mark Wyatt came to be appointed: he interviewed well, he was very likeable and he clearly wanted to take on the challenge that the post offered. He took charge of the Music department, though as a probationer, he could not receive the additional salary that went with a scale post. I told him he would be given serious consideration for this after a year if his work was deemed satisfactory, and it was. Mark made a great impression and Music took off. Our plays became musicals, the school orchestra grew, many more children had lessons from visiting peripatetic teachers, a choir was started and best of all the Houghton Regis Community Big Band was formed and played concerts throughout the area. Sometimes you have to take a chance – to follow your gut instincts. Mark was an excellent appointment and he went on to further heights in his career. I am still in contact with Mark and his wife, Gillian.

One of the key posts in a school that a Head needs to fill, and one that it is paramount to get right is the appointment of a new deputy head. The consequences of getting it wrong are too horrendous to contemplate. At Thomas Bennett, the Governors, the LEA and myself, had already made one excellent appointment when Diane Dockrell replaced Liz Fletcher. The following year we advertised for another deputy, when Chris Roberts left us. The Interviews took place over two days. In addition to the usual, formal question and answer session, we gave the candidates for this important senior position a somewhat different task. Those who went through to the second day were given a topic to think about overnight, and to return the following day prepared to talk for up to ten minutes on that topic to the other candidates, to enter into a discussion with the other candidates and to answer their questions. Diane and I were there as observers, noting aspects of each individual's performance. It proved a fascinating exercise. One of the four appeared to jump in with his opinion as soon as the previous speaker had finished, no doubt trying to be noticed and anxious to make an impression: "Look at me. I've got something important to say."

We noticed that one of the candidates listened to each speaker, but waited to hear what the others had to say before giving his views. He was assessing all opinions before saying anything, no doubt weighing up the pros and cons of a particular issue. Then his response was measured and thoughtful. This was Nick Sorensen, the one we appointed. During his time at Thomas Bennett he continued to display the same qualities, always prepared to listen and to respond only after careful consideration of all the relevant factors. He made a great contribution to the work of the Senior Management Team, and in and around the school his was a calming presence. He went on to be appointed a Head himself, as did Diane. Definitely another one we got right 100%. Fortunately I am still also in touch with Nick, who moved into the university world and has just completed his Ph.D.

21

Teaching in Retirement

Having retired after 17 years as a head teacher, I offered my services to Sussex and Brighton Universities as, with my experience, I thought I might be able to make a useful contribution to their education programmes with existing and aspiring teachers, but neither university was interested. I was really disappointed at this rejection as I should like to have assisted in their programme for the training of prospective teachers, but it was not to be. Following on from the work I had done with the Parenting Forum, I became involved with the Calouste Gulbenkian Foundation in London, where I worked with a group of like-minded professionals preparing and promoting material for schools to use in Parenting Education courses and programmes. The New Labour Government supported such initiatives but the topic never claimed a high enough priority to be implemented in all schools. The need to improve the quality of parenting in England remains, if children at Primary and Secondary schools are to be given the opportunity to reach their full potential.

I decided to take up the opportunity to do some examination marking of Key Stage 3 English scripts with Edexcel. The induction and standardisation process in London was very thorough and I was sent about 270 answers to questions on Romeo and Juliet. Despite the negative comments that are often made about marking examination scripts, I actually found the exercise enjoyable. I'm not sure what that says about me!

As always there were some gems among the scripts I had to mark: "it was mellowdremasstike" ... "jewel carriageway" ... "Cycologists" ... "Parretshoot jump". All genuine, I assure you, and my favourite, "Juliet could not marry Paris because she was already married to Romeo and to be married to two men at the same time is purgatory." My wife says that it can be purgatory being married to one man!

I moved on from Key Stage 3 to mark AS History papers for AQA, as I was about to start teaching some History to examination level in a local school and I thought it might be useful to gain an insight into the thinking of the examiners. For several years I marked scripts sent to me from schools up and down the country, and although the period given for marking is very tight and I had to keep to a rigid schedule each day for three or four weeks, again it proved to be a mainly satisfying experience. The standardisation process, when those marking a particular paper meet the Chief Examiner for that paper and agree the criteria for awarding marks, took place in Manchester, apart from one year when AQA, ill-advisedly in my view, moved the venue to Bolton. We shared the Reebok Stadium with a major darts event with TV apparatus everywhere. One unexpected benefit for me was a short but interesting conversation I had one morning when I bumped into the World Darts Champion, Phil "the power" Taylor. I preferred Manchester with its far better transport system. I enjoyed meeting the other examiners or markers, most of whom were full-time teachers, and I greatly valued the discussions we had with our Chief Examiner, James Staniforth, with whom I got on very well. I found the whole day a stimulating professional experience.

The standard of the scripts we received varied enormously: some were a joy to read and received full marks, while others were dire, with a few essays receiving no marks at all. We were encouraged to use the full range of marks. My most memorable quote came from an answer to a question about the French Revolution, "the king tried to escape from Paris but failed when his plane crashed."

When I had stopped chuckling over this gem, I realised that

this error or misunderstanding probably arose because the textbook covering these events talks about "the king's flight from Paris." Though one would have thought that an A level student might have known that aircraft were not flying at the time of the French Revolution!

Having done this for several years, I stopped marking for AQA when they decided to conduct the standardisation process online. By this method I had to attempt to allocate marks for handwritten answers that appeared on my computer screen when I could only read four or five lines at any one time. It also meant I was not meeting the Chief Examiner, nor the other examiners and no discussions took place. I declined to mark any more. I understand that to take matters further, the marking of actual scripts either is or soon will be conducted entirely online. No actual paper to read, and no opportunity to write comments on the scripts, which are always of benefit to candidates and teachers in the schools. Sad. Is this progress? I don't think so.

I had returned to my first love, teaching History. Initially, I spent a short while at Greenfields School in Forest Row. I had no desire to teach in a Scientology School, but I was intrigued, and my few months there were both interesting and bizarre. It was an oddly chaotic place inhabited by what to me seemed some very weird people. That's the staff, not the pupils! Though there were exceptions! The influence of Ron Hubbard loomed large, and some aspects of his philosophy and teaching I found positive and useful. The school did have some strange practices, and I decided I had had enough when I was required to be tested on my spelling! Teaching GCSE and A level History I met students with diverse abilities and motivation. Two able and interesting students, Edwina, who went on to do a degree in Archaeology, and Kay, who, in a very short space of time gained an A grade in both GCSE and A level History were exceptional. Edwina was from a Scientology family, whereas Kay wasn't. Kay was also an accomplished musician and secured a place at the Royal College of Music, before transferring to Cambridge. I am pleased to say I am still in contact with Kay.

Nearby, also in Forest Row, Michael Hall, a Rudolf Steiner School, wanted a part-time teacher for A level History. I applied, was interviewed and started in September 1999, five years after retiring from Thomas Bennett. Some of my former comprehensive school colleagues gave me some stick for my "defection" to the independent sector! I told them that Michael Hall shared much of the outlook and ethos of Thomas Bennett, with its prime focus on the all round development of each individual child and much else besides. I taught A level History at Michael Hall, part-time only, until the summer of 2011, as long as I had spent in any school in my career. I did have a couple of breaks, but Jo Reeves, who had joined the school shortly after I had, and who was in charge of History, kept finding ways of persuading me to return. During my time there I taught some interesting and outstanding students, many of whom went on to degree courses, often having spent a year "out" doing all sorts of worthwhile things around the world. There is no doubt in my mind that Steiner Education produces some uniquely capable and confident individuals. This was certainly my experience at Michael Hall, no doubt partly the result of the Steiner philosophy and curriculum in practice and partly due to the influence of some excellent teachers, plus some positive parenting I'm sure.

In accordance with Steiner philosophy every morning at Michael Hall School begins for every class with The Main Lesson and this carries on into the Upper School. This first hour of every day is devoted to a study of subjects that would not normally be found in a school curriculum, the content being geared to the age of the pupils. Those in the Upper School studying for A levels had Main Lessons on topics such as Philosophy, Astronomy, Economics, Politics, Modern Literature, Medieval History etc. Individual research and written work was expected of each student, so the Main Lessons were not merely lectures, and students emerged with a much wider knowledge and understanding of a range of topics. Those I was teaching said they found the Main Lessons stimulating and enriching, dealing as they did with subjects they previously had known little or nothing about.

I was fortunate to have only small groups taking A level History. Most of the students worked hard and many gained excellent grades.

I put across my view that to understand our lives today, young people need to have some knowledge and understanding of the past. "*How did we get to where we are today?*" As is often said, at the very least, this might prevent a repetition of the mistakes made by our predecessors. My aims in teaching A level History were always to foster an interest and enjoyment in studying the past, to develop in students a range of skills including effective reading, clear and useful note-making, and the ability to think for themselves, make judgments and write with confidence, relevance and conviction. I've always believed that good teachers develop the learning skills of their students. It pleases me that several of my former students tell me that they still have an interest in History: some went on to read History at university, but others who didn't still enjoy reading books with a historical flavour. It is also gratifying that I have been told by former students, now at university, that their studying and essay writing have been greatly helped by the work we did and by the study methods I tried to inculcate. Students in 6th Forms especially would benefit from some specific work on Study Skills, though younger pupils also need guidance on the most effective ways to read, to make notes, to organise their work and their time, to write with relevance and be able to assess the quality of their own work.

I always tried to provide my students with interesting and valuable experiences while they were studying History. A few years ago I took the students I was teaching to visit the Houses of Parliament. After a tour of the Lords, which was not sitting, we were allowed into the Commons' Visitors' Gallery. There was a boring debate in progress, when suddenly there was a flurry of action and the whole House began to fill up. Within a few minutes Prime Minister, Gordon Brown, appeared and as a hush descended he made a statement to the House on the recent G20 summit. The students were so fortunate to have had the opportunity of seeing both sides of the House full and to hear and see the Prime Minister of the country address the House. It reminded me of an occasion in my youth when I had been in the Visitors' Gallery and heard a young Tony Wedgwood-Benn make his maiden speech on the issue of Iron and Steel nationalisation.

Arranging for my students to spend a day researching their own special, individual, historical topics at Sussex University Library always proved popular and effective. The University Library staff were always very helpful and it was good for the students to have the experience of working in such a place. After the mysteries of the library catalogue system had been explained, the students were let loose and spent the best part of a day looking for relevant material in books and magazines, making notes, taking photocopies and having the occasional discussion.

One evening I took Katherine and Juliet, two of my A level students, to London to listen to a lecture given by Robert Fisk, Middle East Correspondent of *The Independent*. Katherine was researching and writing, for her A level coursework, an extended essay on the role of Britain in the Middle East and the extent of Britain's responsibility for the situation that has developed in recent years; it was natural to want to hear Robert Fisk, a renowned expert on the Middle East, and author of *"The Great War for Civilisation: The Conquest of the Middle East"*, a long but intensely moving and very personal account of the conflicts and mistakes in that always troubled region. As a bonus, my students were able to meet Robert Fisk after his lecture and when he heard about Katherine's essay, he asked if she would send him a copy.

Of course she was delighted. As I anticipated, Katherine's essay was outstanding as were her marks and grades. Katherine went on to take a Dance degree in London, while Juliet studied Social Anthropology at the London School of Economics. They both now have excellent jobs in London.

I also took my students to lectures in London which specifically aimed to enrich their A level History studies. Two of the best lecturers at these student History conferences were Edward Acton, Professor of Modern History at the University of East Anglia, who always pitched his lectures at the right level, as he understood just what A level historians needed and Robert Service, Professor of History at Oxford and a specialist in Russian History. I'm sure the students, coming as they did from a wide range of schools to these conferences, were often not aware of just how fortunate they were to be able to listen to such eminent historians.

These student conferences were held in a variety of locations in London, Senate House being one of the most popular. Normally these visits went off without incident. Once I took a group of AS level History students to some lectures being given in a hall not far from the centre of Camden Town. When we returned to Camden Town Tube Station there were several police with sniffer dogs in the main entrance area. We took the escalator down to our platform, but once there I realised that James wasn't with us, so I told the other students to stay where they were while I went up to find out where he was. I was told by one of the policemen that he was being interviewed in an office close by. I asked why, but he could not or would not tell me. I asked whether I could go in to be with James, as I was his teacher and he was my responsibility but was told I couldn't. After several minutes the rest of our group came up to find out what was going on. I passed on to them what I had been told. "Trust James!" someone said.

Twenty minutes later, one of the policemen who had been interviewing James emerged and spoke to me. He produced a form in duplicate, which recorded the details of the interview that had taken place. I was asked to read it and sign it. Apparently what had happened was that James, being friendly, had stopped to stroke one of the dogs when it would have been better just to walk on. The dog had detected signs of drugs, which is why the dogs were there. In the office James had been searched and was able to convince the policeman that he had no drugs on him, nor did he take drugs. I was told that sometimes traces of drugs can be found on people who might have come into fleeting contact with someone who was taking drugs or had drugs on them. Just sitting on a seat on a tube train could leave you with the trace of drugs, I was told. Armed with a copy of the interview report, we all made our way back to Forest Row, somewhat late, and where the far from shy James had a story to tell everyone!

Michael Gove, when he was Conservative Education Secretary, wanted to see coursework disappear, preferring to rely instead solely on end of course examinations to assess and grade students. This is such a retrograde step. Coursework, certainly in History and especially at A level, provides students with the opportunity to research a topic or an issue, to work independently and develop those very skills that they will require at university or in the world of work. Many of the students I taught at Michael Hall School produced excellent pieces of original work, the result of wide reading and careful selection of material, and covering some really interesting areas of historical study or investigation. Students who only sit end of course exams will miss out on this valuable experience. Instead they will be rewarded for having a good memory and being able to regurgitate what they have read or been told by their teacher. This was my experience at school. I thought we had moved on from that. Universities and employers don't want young people who only know a lot; they prefer them to be able to think for themselves, show initiative, take responsibility for their own decisions and demonstrate some flair – all the things that individual coursework can develop. The Education Secretary's "changes" bring to mind an old Athena poster, which proclaimed: "For every complicated problem, there is a simple solution – and it's wrong!"

Michael Gove decreed which books should be read by pupils in school. He also failed to see the advantages of AS being a stepping-stone to A level, as a bridge between GCSE and A level that has helped many students. His changes were introduced without any discussion or consultation with the professionals who work within the system. Teachers in schools and universities don't like these changes. Why do Education Ministers think they know best? Children's education should not be based on a personal view.

There has also been opposition to the Minister's National Curriculum plans, his "back to basics" campaign, in which children would learn "endless lists" of spellings, facts and rules; 9-year-olds would learn to recite poems and the History syllabus would be Britain based. It seems to me that all this is in line with doing away with coursework; clearly Mr Gove doesn't want to foster creativity or to encourage children to think for themselves. What he is proposing, according to a letter sent by 100 top professors and academics, is "rote learning without understanding". It's probably what Mr Gove did at school. Wasn't it Confucius who said, "I hear and I forget; I see and I remember; I do and I understand."

Hopefully the teacher unions will contest these proposed changes. As I am now retired I am an Associate member of my Association, which was SHA when I joined in the 1970s and is now ASCL, the Association of School and College Leaders. It is a superb organisation, which always gave me excellent information and advice when it was needed. It has recently launched a Great Education Debate and "the response," says Brian Lightman, ASCL's General Secretary, "has been impressive." More recently ASCL published Manifesto 2014, setting out what the Association believes and what it is calling for. I entirely agree with ASCL when it says that what is needed is a "shared vision for education". As I had found in Bedfordshire, education often seems to become a political football. There can be no real progress within our education system while decisions are being made and changes implemented by whichever political party happens to be in office or on the whim of whichever education secretary is in post.

Fortunately, as I write this, Mr Gove has just been relieved of his post. I hope that his successor will listen to ASCL and the other unions that represent the voice of teachers. The quality and effectiveness of children's education, now and in the future, is at stake. Although I am no longer involved, I am concerned for my grandchildren and the education they will receive. The changes that have been brought in have left the teaching profession with a dangerously low morale. It's extraordinary, isn't it, that while Mr Gove probably did want to see standards improve in the nation's schools, a series of doctrinaire policies are likely to achieve the exact opposite.

I had gained a great deal of satisfaction from teaching History in the first part of my career, and I returned to the classroom after my retirement with a sense of excitement and anticipation. There are those who say that teaching History cannot be very difficult. The past is the past; it is well recorded; all you have to do is to read about it or be told about it, after all it doesn't change. Therein lie several misconceptions. True, the past has gone and we cannot return to it in order to know it better. *Wouldn't that be fun!* But fresh details about the past are frequently uncovered and make us revise our knowledge or our interpretation. Issues such as the site of the Battle of Bosworth Field or the burial place of Richard III are examples.

Following the collapse of communism in Russia much new evidence came to light regarding the years of Stalin's dictatorship in particular. Files that were kept secret have become available to historians, and most of this is primary material. Now translated from Russian into English, the original documents and the commentary on them can be accessed by English historians, teachers and students. "The release of new archival material has opened up entirely fresh areas of historical research, sharply revising aspects of conventional wisdom." [Introduction, *The Soviet Union* Vol. 2, Edward Acton & Tom Stableford].

In his book, *The Wages of Destruction, the Making and Breaking of the Nazi Economy,* Adam Tooze gives evidence of large scale expenditure on rearmament from as early as 1933, the year Hitler became Chancellor. This view conflicts with that of A J P Taylor, generally accepted, that Hitler concentrated expenditure initially on domestic priorities and that he only began to think about serious military expenditure and rearmament in 1936 and 1937 onwards. Adam Tooze explains that this expenditure may have been "hidden" by his methods of financing it. His book also provides a fresh interpretation of the Second World War when looked at from a Nazi strategic point of view. These examples illustrate how nothing can be regarded as incontrovertibly certain: new evidence or a fresh interpretation may be just around the corner.

Historians are supposed to be impartial, but each one has his own personal, political, maybe religious or nationalist background, and this will inevitably influence what he writes. It may make their work more colourful and interesting of course. Students need to understand and allow for this when they do their research. Years ago I came across a book, entitled *An impartial history of the English Civil War – from the Royalist point of view.* Most writers of History are not so honest!

When A level History students at Michael Hall were working recently on individual extended essays on different aspects of African History, they and I became aware of how some recent events have been written about and interpreted quite differently by African historians as compared with versions by British writers. This is hardly surprising, but the differences for example in the accounts of the Mau Mau risings in Kenya were not trivial, their accounts were significantly at variance. And why wouldn't they be? Students should be alert to these differing interpretations and explanations of events. Then asking, "Why is this?" will lead to discussion, further questions and hopefully, more research. Students should be thinking, discussing, arguing, developing their minds and their confidence. They should not be passive receptacles of information, which is exactly what my friend and colleague Alan Jones was saying all those years ago in Chelmsford.

Our interpretation of the events of the past can often be improved when more material evidence becomes available. But time is often needed before an agreed view can become accepted. As one historian, when asked in the 1980s on the 2nd centennial anniversary, what he thought the main effects of the French Revolution had been, said, dryly, "It's too early to tell."

Teaching History, especially to more senior students, should be a two-way process. The teacher will not have all the answers, and even if he did, it is important that each student makes a contribution to the study of a particular country, period, person or issue – a contribution to each lesson too, ideally. By being involved, by doing something and taking responsibility the students should enjoy their studies and find History fascinating and interesting. The best A level History students that I taught were those who challenged what I said or what the book they were reading said. Such students were thinking for themselves and had the courage to articulate their views. Of course they listened attentively to what they were told and took in what they were reading, but in addition to being receptive and reactive, they had the confidence to be intellectually proactive. Often their questions and queries made me think more about the topic. Learning is a two-way street.

When they had a topic or an issue to research, I often told my students that they should think of themselves as detectives: where is the evidence, how reliable is this or that piece of evidence, what more evidence do I need to be convinced I have the complete picture? And when writing their essays, I said that they should make out their case just as a barrister would in court, using the evidence, making a strong case to the jury (in their case, the A level examiner), with a series of powerful points that were relevant and convincing. State your case. Build up your argument. Support it with evidence. Write a convincing conclusion.

Another aim of my teaching at Michael Hall of course was to ensure, as far as I could, that students secured good grades in their A level exams. I had been employed to teach an A level subject. However the philosophy at Michael Hall is that examination achievement rates second to involvement in the wider Steiner curriculum, as I discovered quite early on in my time there. 50% of the available lesson time in the upper school is spent on activities and learning that is not examined. As a consequence pupils are normally entered for only seven GCSE subjects. Some Michael Hall students have been admitted on to university degree courses without all the usual entry requirements, because the value of the Steiner curriculum is understood and recognised. When I began at the school, I hadn't fully appreciated this. In the Spring term, not long before important AS or A level exams, I found my students were unavailable for a week because of their play rehearsals. On another day I couldn't teach my class as it was a "gardening day" for the upper school! My initial frustration waned, as we found ways to cope with such disruption. When I attended the Class 12 play each year, which was consistently outstanding, I was able to forgive the interruption to my teaching programme.

Each year, after their A levels, the "top year" students at Michael Hall (Class 12) go on a visit to Italy. It's a traditional trip for which the students collect funds during the year, and it is partly educational, in terms of art, history, culture and language, but also a celebration of their time at Michael Hall. They all have an amazing time: one group was visiting the Vatican, the students were inside the Cistine Chapel, where there is meant to be silence, when one of the group asked a papal guard if they could sing. After an initial refusal, the students persisted, and were given permission to sing, provided their repertoire was suitable. I am told that what followed was quite extraordinary and indeed unique: the students began to sing and everyone in the crowded Chapel stood still to listen to the choir, who sang three songs, one a Negro spiritual. When they came to the end, the other visitors broke into polite applause. What a memorable experience!

After I had taught there for a few years, I was asked if I would become a member of the Michael Hall School Council, whose function was similar to that of a school governing body. We discussed all aspects of the life and development of the school, but Council increasingly felt that too many important school decisions were being taken by Council. What was needed was a decision-making body within the school, consisting of teachers who would effectively run the day-to-day operation of the school. I took a leading role in helping to set up this School Management Team as it was christened, though there were several opposing voices to such a development.

One of the problems that I identified at Michael Hall was that if Rudolf Steiner hadn't said it should be so, or hadn't written in support, then, according to some, it ought not to happen. Times and needs change however, and this innovation, the SMT, has gone from strength to strength. The School Council, now renamed the Trustees, maintains its role in whole school overview and strategic planning and prioritising, not least to do with finance. In addition there remains the College of Teachers, to which nearly all teachers belong, and which discusses and decides issues that primarily affect the teaching body. Clearly this group has to have a good working relationship with the School Management Team. Michael Hall has no head teacher and no hierarchy, so unless the situation changes, there are no senior teachers who, in an independent or state school, would make up the school's management team. It is certainly an interesting place!

In the 1960s, when I lived in Leigh on Sea, I had taught one student privately. Anne Rowse found that she couldn't fit History into her timetable with all her other subjects, and as she lived nearby and we knew the family, I agreed to teach her individually. She was able and conscientious and did well in her exams. I mention this because after I retired, I became involved in tutoring individual students who needed extra help with their AS or A level History. Over a period of about 12 years or so, I taught and helped a succession of students who came from a number of different schools in Sussex, Surrey and Kent. Working with an individual student is particularly rewarding as you have the time and opportunity to tease out their strengths and weaknesses and put into place programmes to bring about examination success. One advantage of teaching students at home is the access they and I have to all my many books, some of which might not be available in a school library: for example, the recently published documentary history of the Soviet Union by Edward Acton and Tom Stableford, which I mentioned earlier, has proved invaluable. There are many others, too numerous to mention. I am pleased to have been able to help students understand and enjoy History, do well in their exams and go on, many of them, to read History or a related subject, at university. Some keep in contact too which is nice.

22
Discipline in Schools

From what you read in the newspapers these days you might be forgiven for thinking that most children behave badly in schools in England and that the majority of schools have a discipline problem. While I can confidently say that this is nonsense, it is important to have a sense of perspective and to understand both the causes and effects of unacceptable behaviour in some schools today. What follows are my views, which are not the result of any specific research but which are based on my 40+ years experience as a teacher and on conversations with many teachers.

Recently, teacher Ann Maguire was stabbed in a classroom in Leeds. She is the first teacher to be killed by a pupil in a school in England. Each year at Teachers' Union conferences there are reports of aggressive and violent behaviour from school children towards teachers. Sometimes this behaviour can be persistent, and occasionally teachers have been the victims of an assault, which has resulted in physical or mental scars. Some teachers have had to leave the profession following such incidents. Of course such behaviour is totally unacceptable. Pupils sometimes harm each other and assaults with weapons now appear to be more common. Exclusions of pupils for bringing knives or other weapons into school, primary and secondary, are on the increase, so we are told. While only a small minority of pupils are guilty of such behaviour, the trend is worrying.

Children today experience violence in their lives in many contexts. Films, television and violent computer games are obvious examples, but there are reports in the papers every day of violence from road rage to muggings and indiscriminate killing. Children growing up in such a society cannot avoid being affected. Sadly some children experience violence in their own homes, either physical or verbal, and some parents do not always provide the best examples for their children during their formative years. When some parents, indeed families, promote inappropriate and anti-social values and behaviour, their children are receiving messages and examples, which they often reproduce at school. These influences make the teacher's job even harder. I sometimes wondered why certain pupils behaved the way they did, until I met the child's mother or father; then I knew. From being angry and annoyed at the child and its behaviour, I became sorry for him or her.

It is undoubtedly true that the children who go to school today come from a far more aggressive and less tolerant society than was the case years ago. Schools now have a more difficult job. It used to be the case that if you were punished at school for some misdemeanour you would hope your parents didn't find out as, if so, you would most likely receive a clip round the ear, be grounded, or have further punishment. Often today the parent will support their child and blame the school. In a case recently, reported in the Daily Mirror, a 14-year-old girl was suspended by her school for downing ecstasy and vodka at school, then hallucinating and vomiting. Her dad is reported to have said, "Girls will be girls. She's at that age. There's not enough teachers to monitor the pupils." No thought that it might be due to poor parenting. No apology to the school.

The vast majority of children go to school wanting to learn. They much prefer a well-ordered classroom to one of chaos and mayhem. They want to have a good relationship with their teachers who they want to be able to respect. Of course some pupils will be high-spirited and will want to have fun but as long as they know where the boundaries lie, they will be fine. And, naturally, adolescent teenagers will bring their own problems for teachers and parents alike; it also helps if each teacher understands each of his or her pupils and their individual background and circumstances. With so much else expected of teachers today, this is not always easy, but with an effective pastoral system in place it should be possible and it greatly increases the chances of a good relationship between teacher and pupil.

To try to ensure that discipline is maintained, many primary and secondary schools draw up a Code of Behaviour, which lists expectations of behaviour and the sanctions that will be applied if the Code is broken. Pupils should be involved in drawing up this Code of Behaviour, as there will then be much more chance of compliance. Children prefer to be allowed to participate rather than be told what they must do. Consent and participation is far better than instructions, directives and being given orders. Many schools have School Councils where the contents of such a Code can be discussed, and it is important that junior pupils as well as senior students have their say. The emphasis should be on everyone seeing the school as a community to which each person contributes. The Code will certainly say that all teachers have a right to teach without hindrance and that all pupils have a right to learn and to work undisturbed. There should be respect for each other and for the school itself, as well as other details relevant to each school.

The school should inform and involve parents when drawing up this Code of Behaviour, as they need to know what the expectations of the school are as far as their children's behaviour is concerned. This might be done via the Parent Governors or through the school's usual means of parental contact. Some schools draw up a contract relating to the school's expectations which parents are asked to sign. Whatever an individual school decides to do, it is clear that getting the parents on your side is more than half the battle in ensuring pupils' acceptable behaviour; only then can effective learning take place.

Some specific individual issues need addressing if acceptable behaviour throughout the school is to be the norm. One of these is bullying. If a school turns round and says, "We don't have any bullying here," I would suggest they are likely to be kidding themselves. Regrettably, bullying is endemic among groups of young people, and I would suggest that some bullying goes on in most, if not all, schools. These days bullying can take on new forms, such as cyber bullying, which can be very insidious and harmful. The school may have a separate policy statement regarding bullying or it may be included in the Code of Behaviour, or possibly both. Recently we have learned that Susan Boyle was bullied at school, as was Olympic Gold medallist, Jessica Ennis. Their examples also show that individuals can rise above school bullying in their adult lives, as I'm sure many others have.

In each school it is essential that any person being bullied knows to whom they can go to tell them what is happening, a particular teacher perhaps. Every teacher must know what the school policy is in order to deal with what they have been told. The school must also deal with the information and confront the pupils who have been accused of bullying and find, if possible, a satisfactory way of resolving the issue and ending the bullying. This is never easy or straightforward. Parents will almost certainly need to be involved, though bullying often originates from disputes between families. Children who are the worst affected by bullying are those who haven't been able to tell anyone about it, or those for whom the issues weren't resolved. It is an issue that is never going to go away, and teachers and parents should both be on the lookout for any signs of unusual behaviour or unhappiness that might suggest that a child is being bullied.

Regrettably, there is more explicit exposure to pornography today than there was a few years ago. As one teacher said recently, "Before, parents would just put a block on the home computer – but now, with smartphones, kids are walking around with computers in their pockets." Young people are being put at risk by such access to pornography, and some experts feel it is affecting attitudes and relationships between the sexes. Recent cases of very young children committing acts of sexual assault and even rape appear to confirm this view. All this doesn't make the task facing schools any easier. A recent Netmums survey found that two-thirds of parents believe today's children have lost their innocence by the time they are 12, because of exposure to online pornography. This is an issue for parents as well as schools obviously. Some would argue that it is also an issue for Government, since child protection is at stake. The latest insidious craze among young children is what is called sexting, which can cause great problems for teachers and parents. Some primary school children have been excluded for overtly sexual behaviour towards fellow pupils and many parents do not know the best way to respond when they discover that their child has been sexting. What a world we currently live in! Although inappropriate use of technology can now be detected in many schools, the systems are not 100% effective, as security falls down when using a 3G network on a mobile phone.

Another issue that schools have to look out for is sexual, physical or emotional abuse of a child in their care. Every school should now have a designated Child Protection Officer, whose job it is to deal with any suspected or reported cases. It will probably be an individual teacher who will suspect that a child is being abused, but it must be the Child Protection Officer who follows up any such suspicions. Sometimes this is difficult or not possible, yet in the interests of the child some action needs to be taken. Such a situation occurred in one of the schools in which I was working.

It was late on a Friday afternoon, getting on for five o'clock. The pupils had all gone home, except for one girl (I'll call her Susie, not her real name), who Mr Scott found sitting on a bench in the school corridor. Susie was a pretty girl, quite small and rather timid for her age.

"What's the matter, Susie? Why haven't you gone home?"

Susie didn't answer but started crying. Susie was in Year 9, so 13 or 14 years old.

"Stay there," said Mr Scott. "I'll find Ms Hunter, your Head of House. OK?" Susie nodded.

Bob Scott found Claire Hunter (not their real names) and explained. Ms Hunter came down immediately to speak with Susie. She asked the same questions. Bob Scott decided to leave the two of them together as Susie might talk more freely with Ms Hunter if they were alone. With some obvious reluctance, Susie then began to explain why she hadn't gone home.

"My uncle is living with us at home at the moment," Susie said, very quietly. "He keeps doing things to me. I don't like it. I can't go home or I know he will do it again."

Claire wanted to ask what it was that Susie's uncle had been doing and how long this had been going on and whether her mum or dad knew or suspected anything. But Claire Hunter knew that she shouldn't begin to ask Susie questions about what had been going on. If anyone was to do this it had to be the School's Child Protection Officer or someone from Social Services. Claire went to the nearest office and rang Jayne Byford's phone. She had gone home. Claire rang Social Services, but it was after 5 p.m. on a Friday and there was no answer. Here was a dilemma. Claire knew or felt she knew that it would be wrong to tell Susie she should go home, after what Susie had said. For a moment Claire wondered if Susie might be making this up, but she knew enough about such matters to know that children who say such things should be believed. *Why would Susie be still in school at 5 p.m., crying, unless there was good cause?* thought Claire. *What was she to do? She could take Susie home with her, but would that be right? She would be protecting Susie, but in doing so, would she be exceeding her responsibilities?*

Claire decided she shouldn't take Susie home with her. She knew the Head was going away for the weekend so she couldn't contact him either.

Almost as though Susie knew what Claire Hunter was thinking, she said, "I could go and stay with Miranda, my best friend."

Claire gave Susie a hug. "That sounds a great idea. Would Miranda's mum and dad mind, do you think?"

"No," said Susie. "I've had sleepovers there before. Miranda knows anyway."

"What? Miranda knows about your uncle?" said Claire.

"Yes, I told her last week."

"And what did Miranda say?"

"She said I should tell my mum," Susie said.

Claire thought that Susie going to stay at Miranda's was the best way out of what was a serious and difficult situation. When she later told me the story, I agreed that she had found the best solution in the circumstances.

"We'd better ring and check with Miranda's mum that this will be all right," said Claire. "And if it is, we'll have to let your mum know where you are." Claire rang Miranda's mum, and let Susie speak to her.

"Yes, of course you can come here for tonight," said Agnes, Miranda's mum. She didn't ask any questions, so Claire guessed that Agnes might have worked out the reason for Susie making such a request. *Had Miranda told her mum?* Claire then rang Susie's mum and explained that Susie wanted to go and stay with Miranda for the night. Susie had a quick word with her mum, who said that would be quite all right. Claire was pleased with this, but it made her wonder whether Susie's mum knew what had been going on.

Claire drove Susie round to Miranda's house. She didn't feel that she could begin a discussion; she thought it best to leave Susie to do whatever explaining needed to be done. She did say to Susie, "I'll be following this up in the morning," though Susie didn't know quite what this meant. Claire was satisfied that she had placed Susie in a place of safety for the night. That had been her overriding priority. Pyjamas and toothbrush seemed of less importance. The issue of her uncle would have to be taken up by the relevant authority.

The reason I include this story is to illustrate how difficult and delicate some situations can be for teachers in schools. Whether Claire acted within the letter of the regulations is, in my view, immaterial. Faced with a 13-year-old girl in tears not wanting to go home for fear of suffering more sexual abuse, Claire had to take action and she did what seemed best and possible in the circumstances. Susie's accusations were followed up and appropriate action was taken by Social Services and other bodies.

The latest danger facing young girls, which schools need to be aware of, is sexual abuse carried out at specially arranged parties by gangs who have targeted girls via the internet. It beggars belief that such practices are going on in what is alleged to be a civilised country. Most recently we have learned of the awful catalogue of abuse of girls in Rotherham. This ought to be a wake-up call for the whole country. In the midst of all this, teachers have a key role to play. Girls who are involved and who go to school will often show signs that can be detected by alert teachers and schools. Unusual behaviour, signs of self harm, changes in appearance, suddenly being at odds with their family, unexplained absences, even going missing from home can be signs that should be followed up.

Many schools these days have a "buddy" scheme in place. When I was visiting schools as an assessor for the Schools Curriculum Award I went to two schools where such a scheme operated, and in both of them I met both senior and junior pupils who were taking part. The scheme was proving to be extremely effective. Each child, when they entered the school, was allocated a more senior pupil who acts as a buddy, looks after them, gives guidance, shows them the ropes, answers their questions and listens to any concerns they may have. It is someone to talk to if need arises. It helps to dispel the feeling of being overwhelmed by the size and complexity of a new school. This kind of scheme makes a contribution to having an orderly school with happy, motivated pupils. Well-chosen senior pupils can soon pick up signs that there is something wrong, such as bullying or unhappiness at home, and act accordingly. Happy, confident, well looked after children work better, behave better and achieve more. Good behaviour in schools is essential if effective teaching and learning are to take place.

The care and welfare of pupils is also the responsibility of schools, and these days there seem to be more things to look out for. A recent report by The Children's Society shows that many children today are arriving at school hungry. Over two million children are living in poverty in England today, a terrible indictment on our government and society in general. Fortunately, starting in September 2014, all pupils in the first three years of primary school will receive free lunches, provided local authorities can pay for them, and this should go a long way to improve not only learning, but also self-esteem.

Children need to feel safe and happy in a well-regulated and caring environment.

The bottom line, of course, is that the responsibility for acceptable behaviour within the school and for the care and welfare of pupils lies with the head teacher, supported by the teachers and other adults who work in the school. Today, this is a huge responsibility, because they don't start with a blank sheet: they have to work within the cultural and social environment of the local community, which may be largely favourable or unfavourable. And it seems that more responsibility is being placed on schools while funding is continually being reduced. As I have said before, the key lies with the parents. The task of educating children effectively and maintaining good order throughout every day in each school, would be made many times easier if schools and teachers had the full backing of all parents, and if all children had parents who were good role models.

Part 4

Coaching

*"Each great human accomplishment
begins with a dream."*
Terry Orlick

23

Athletics Coaching – the early years

I started to enjoy athletics at school and joined Highgate Harriers at the age of 15, in the days when Andy Ferguson was the club star. As a young man I was a very average middle-distance runner but I competed for Highgate Harriers in some club fixtures: some cross-country races and a few road relays including a short leg in the London to Brighton road relay, a race that sadly no longer takes place, and I took part in several 880 yards and 1 mile races on the track. Particularly enjoyable were the handicap meetings that were held, usually on bank holiday weekends. Local families would come along and if the weather was fine, everyone had a really good day out. The club went each year to one of these at Aylesbury, where in each race you were given a handicap start according to your previous best time. It was good fun starting off, say in a mile race, with less good runners ahead of you, who you set out to catch, and better runners behind, who were chasing you. The best runner started on scratch, and to win he had to catch and pass everybody. You ran round the grass track to the noise of the hurdy-gurdy and the aroma of onions from the hot dog stalls. Winners received prizes and, at Aylesbury one year, one of our club members, a very popular, young black 440-yard runner, won a large sofa, which, with some difficulty, we managed to hoist on board the club coach. When we arrived back in London, we helped him unload his prize in Maida Vale where he lived. I can still see him sitting on his sofa on the pavement as the coach drove away with everyone on the coach waving and cheering! I've no idea how he got it home.

Completing a relay leg for the club

Living in North London and later in Finchley, I trained at the Parliament Hill track, in those days a cinder track. I had just come down from Oxford and was taking part in a club meeting at the track and my mother happened to be watching from the elevated path from which you could look down at the track. I was running in an 880 yards race and a lady standing next to my mother, turned to her and said, "It keeps them off the streets, doesn't it?"

Just along from the track, in South Hill Park, was the "Magdala" pub, where we occasionally went for a drink after training. It was outside this pub where Ruth Ellis, the last woman to be hanged in England, shot her boyfriend. After the court case and Ruth Ellis's execution in 1955, the pub, understandably, acquired considerable notoriety.

Athletics matches – on the track, the country, or indeed on the road – wouldn't take place were it not for all the officials who voluntarily give up their time to help run the meetings. There are occasional mishaps. At one meeting at Ladywell Park track in South East London the timekeepers were standing on an inclined grassy slope in a line directly opposite the finish, so that they could time each runner at the end of the race. A 100 yards race was about to start. The timekeepers were ready. The starter fired his gun. The timekeepers reacted to the flash of the gun by starting their stopwatches. One elderly timekeeper at the top of the bank then lost his balance and fell, toppling over and rolling down, quite gracefully, to the bottom of the slope. Still clutching his stopwatch, he got to his feet, got back in line and timed the race. Heroic and amusing! "Over in a flash," you might say!

During my teenage years, Mum and Dad had taken me many times to London's White City Stadium to see athletics matches. We saw sprint star McDonald Bailey set a new British Record of 9.6 seconds for 100 yards in the AAA Championships when we were at White City in 1951. Another favourite, Gordon Pirie, set a British Record for 6 miles at the same meeting, and other stars of those days included the elegant 440- and 880-yard runner, Arthur Wint, steeplechaser John Disley, hurdler Peter Hildreth, pole vaulter Geoff Elliott and many more. The best occasions were probably when foreign teams and athletes competed, such as the London v Moscow floodlit match in 1954 when Chris Chataway defeated Vladimir Kuts from Russia and broke the 5,000 metres World Record. The whole of the White City crowd was on its feet when Kuts was overtaken, very close to the finish.

One Saturday, there was an important inter-club cross-country race with over 150 competitors taking place over Hampstead Heath. Not far from the track, the finishing funnel had been set up as usual. The officials stood facing the direction from which the first runners would be approaching. But it was mid-winter and foggy. Unbeknown to the officials, the runners had gone off course.

"They should be here by now," one of the officials said, looking at his watch.

Suddenly, Dad spotted the first two runners but they were approaching the finish from entirely the wrong direction. They were behind all the officials not in front of them!

"Go round those trees over there," Dad shouted as he waved and pointed to a clump of trees about 100 yards to the right. The runners knew they were not on the correct course so were pleased to get this late instruction. All the other runners then followed and the race came to a satisfactory conclusion, even if the run-in to the finish had been a sudden invention. Some quick thinking had saved the day.

Highgate Harriers in the 1950s. My Dad far left.
I am in the middle at the back.

Though I still have many happy memories of White City, there was one less happy event, which occurred on the evening when Trevor and I had taken some boys from Hitchin to the London-New York floodlit athletics match. Our party were all sitting on the back straight in a very crowded White City. I knew that my mother, a keen fan of athletics, was in the main stand opposite. My parents and I had been to the European Championships in Bern a few years earlier. This was where, on a visit to the glacier at Grindelwald, I went for an uphill road run and discovered for the first time the effects of altitude on my breathing and heart rate. Though this wasn't an issue with runners and coaches at that time, I became only too aware of it as I struggled to run up this Swiss mountain road! But back to 1957 and the White City. Dad was an athletics official, having joined Highgate Harriers when I did as a young teenager, initially to support me, but later because he enjoyed his involvement very much. He often played a prominent part in the News of the World athletic promotions at the White City, and he became an official not only with Highgate Harriers but with Middlesex AAA (Amateur Athletic Association) as well.

On this occasion he was in the centre of the field, judging the hammer event. Most of the throws that night were around 180–190 feet, so the officials, whose job was to note where the hammer landed so the throw could be measured, were standing behind the 200-feet line. Up in the stands we were watching the races taking place on the track. Suddenly there was a commotion and we noticed that a crowd of people had gathered in the middle of the in-field. Then an ambulance drove onto the centre and someone was put on a stretcher and into the ambulance, which drove away. I soon realised that the casualty was Dad. I later learned what had happened. Mike Ellis, then British record holder, had unleashed a throw that went close to or beyond 200 feet, and the officials "lost it" in the floodlights. All the other throws had been below 200 feet, but this one hit Dad full on, fortunately on the upper part of his left arm. He hadn't seen it until too late. Had it hit him on the head, or even in the chest, the 16-lb hammer or its chain would have killed him.

Most of this I learned later. My mother went with my dad to Hammersmith Hospital. He lost a lot of blood and most of his upper arm was smashed: tendons, muscles, bones etc. Mike Ellis was, naturally, very upset, and visited Dad in hospital. Dad did recover, and as he said later, it was fortunate it hadn't been his drinking arm! One thing that upset him was that by interrupting the flight of the hammer, he had prevented it from being measured accurately! I had to return in our coach with the boys to Hitchin but I visited Dad in hospital the following evening. He was able to go home some days later, after he had been patched up. The arm never fully recovered, though Dad made light of any discomfort he had. It is interesting that Mike Ellis threw a British National Record that night and Athletics Weekly commented, "… he had one no throw of about 208 feet." I wonder if that was the one that hit Dad and couldn't be measured.

It wasn't long before my interest turned away from competing and towards coaching. I had done some coaching at Highgate Harriers and with Middlesex AAA before moving to Essex and I was already qualified as an AAA Honorary coach in all athletics events when I arrived at KEGS. While I was there I took and passed the written and practical exams that gave me the Senior Coach award in middle-distance running and a little later in high jump as well. These were the years when I first attended the Loughborough Summer School as a fledgling coach, learning from Chief Coach, Geoff Dyson and, in my case, with a special interest in middle-distance running, from national coach Jim Alford too.

Very soon after I arrived at KEGS I began to organise a cross-country team. I posted a notice on the PE notice board asking for those interested to meet after school the following Tuesday with running kit. Over 20 turned up, so we changed and ran to the cross-country course. This meant going along and across a few roads, so I was glad to have one of the PE teachers with me. I could be at the front with some of the seniors while Dave brought up the rear. This way we didn't leave anyone behind, nor have anyone run over. The jog to the course was the warm up. There was a mixture of ages with us, and as the older boys knew the course, which was fairly flat, mainly grass with an occasional stile, they led the way. We had a good session and ran back to school about half an hour later. It was the start of regular training runs, some for seniors and some for the new 1st Years who, I soon realised, had considerable talent.

The school already had a senior cross-country team and, in my first year, I took two senior teams and one intermediate, 24 boys in total, by coach to a match at Buckhurst Hill. They all acquitted themselves well, but as we set off to come home, I was to learn a very valuable lesson.

Our coach left Buckhurst Hill and we had been going about five minutes, when one of the boys said, "Sir, where's Fry?" I realised, by not checking or counting the numbers on the coach, I had left one of the boys behind. Fortunately, we had not travelled far.

"Can we turn round, driver?" I said. The coach driver was very obliging and we returned only to find the place deserted. All the other coaches had gone; the hall where the runners had changed was empty; there was no sign of Fry, one of our senior runners. Once again I could see my career ending prematurely. "Teacher leaves runner stranded" ... "Boy left to find his own way home" ... "Still no sign of missing schoolboy"... These were the headlines I saw in next week's local paper, or maybe the nationals.

No mobile phones in those days, so all we could do was to drive back to KEGS, then work out what to do from there. We arrived back at school and there was Fry! Relief all round.

"How did you get here?" I asked, amazed but pleased.

"When I saw our coach leaving," Fry said, "I quickly cadged a lift on the Braintree School coach that I knew would have to come near or through Chelmsford. Their master kindly dropped me off here." Quick thinking ... initiative ... good lad!

I apologised to Fry and, from that day, I always made a point of knowing how many students I was responsible for, and counting heads before moving off or going anywhere. Basic, I know, but the new boy had to learn – the hard way.

A different kind of problem occurred on another cross-country trip. I was driving one of the school minibuses, with Peter Pike driving another. I had 12 young lads on board. We were on a two-lane dual carriageway approaching a roundabout on the A12, heading towards Ilford, when my accelerator wouldn't come up from the floor, so I wasn't able to slow down. *Help! What was I to do? Foot on the brake wasn't any good. Keep going around the roundabout at the same speed? No, impossibly dangerous, with 12 young boys on board, all someone's children.* I thought of bending down to try to release the accelerator pedal. *Too dangerous*; I had to keep steering.

I hadn't said anything to the boys; I didn't want to alarm them. One scared person was enough. I even thought of asking one of the boys to go down and try to lift up the pedal, which was obviously stuck. I had all these thoughts in about two seconds. What I did manage to do was to use the welt at the side of my right shoe to lever the left side of the accelerator pedal up sufficiently to slow the bus down. We thus negotiated the roundabout, safely if a bit fast, but the problem remained for the rest of the journey. I still had not said anything to the boys, so I decided to keep going. When the pedal went down, we went faster, but every time we needed to slow, I had to repeat the side of shoe technique. We arrived safely and the boys trooped off to the changing rooms, none the wiser. Peter's minibus followed me in and I told him of the scare we'd had.

"You did well," he said. "Let me take a look." Peter would probably have been a car mechanic if he hadn't become a PE teacher, and he soon saw the problem. "The spring's gone," he said.

He managed to repair or replace the damaged spring, and I had no trouble on the way home. An experience I could well have done without. The boys remained totally unaware of how close to disaster we had been. On reflection I was quite proud of the way I handled the crisis: I didn't know I had such sangfroid!

Each year new boys made up the 1st Year cross-country team, which went from success to success, winning Mid-Essex Schools Championships with several individuals being selected for the Essex Schools teams. I was also coaching at Chelmsford Athletic Club, usually at their Waterhouse Lane hut, which served as club cross-country HQ, and many of the school runners became members. Bill Farnham, a very promising runner who was to come 4th in the ESAA Senior Boys' Cross Country race at Birkenhead in 1962, was soon followed by John Archer, Chris Joslin, Bob Chapman and others. John, a dark-haired, tall, rangy runner was ranked 3rd best youth miler in UK in 1962 with 4:18.5 and also ranked in the top 6 in UK at 880 yards and 1500m steeplechase, as well as ranking 5th best Junior at 880 yards in 1964 with 1:53.3. Twice he finished 2nd in an English Schools final. [Further details can be found in the Additional

Information]. Chris didn't have John's natural ability but he ran many good races for his school and club in the 1960s. Bob Chapman was one of the original members of the KEGS 1st year XC team that I put together. As he got older he developed into a very good junior athlete on the track and cross-country. His best year was 1965 when he came 17th in the ESAA XC for senior boys in March, but bettered this when finishing 5th in the senior boys track mile at Watford in July with the amazing time of 4:10.4, which ranked him 5th of UK Juniors that year. The first four in the UK rankings were the four who beat him in that race!

I was also coaching a group of young female Chelmsford AC middle-distance runners, aged 15–17, and each week they had a session on a road circuit into Writtle and back into Chelmsford. The favourite circuit was 4 x 880 yards with a continuous slowly run (not jog) recovery, so that in all they ran about five miles. When I didn't run with them, I followed in my car, so I could see how each one was running and time each 880 yards run. Having done their warm up, and before starting the first fast 880 yards run, the girls would take off their track suits and any other warm outer garments and I would put these in the car, ready to hand them back when they had completed their 4th run. One particular evening I was following the girls, with my headlights on, when I was stopped by a police car.

"Do you mind telling us what you're doing, Sir?" asked the officer, obviously suspicious of a guy following scantily clad girls in his car with the headlights full on.

"I'm following those girls," I said. And then, maybe unwisely, I added, "I've got their clothes in the car." And, showing him my stopwatch, I said, "Could you let me go, as I'm timing their run and I need to be there at the end when they finish."

The girls wondered where I'd got to when there were no headlights showing them the way, but they carried on to the designated finish by the Britvic factory. The police officer accepted my story and let me drive on, but he followed so he could see what happened when I met up with the girls. He saw that all was well and he drove off. When I explained to the girls what had happened, they thought it was hilarious and giggled all the way home.

I began coaching with Essex AAA, organising training weekends at Wickham Bonhunt, in North Essex and at different club locations, such as at Colchester, Thurrock and Basildon in addition to Chelmsford. The weekends at Wickham Bonhunt were in the winter, for athletes from different clubs in Essex who were doing their basic build up work for the following summer. Group running sessions would be followed by short athletics films and film strips on my old 16mm Specto analysing film projector. Sometimes we had visiting coaches and discussions about training. The weekends were popular and enjoyed by all. Very recently I was at an "Athletes Reunited" meeting in London organised by Tony Maxwell, of Woodford Green AC, a former athlete whom I coached, and Ronnie Howe came up to me and said, "I remember you – Wickham Bonhunt!"

One particularly cold Friday evening in January, I set off to drive to Wickham Bonhunt. It had been snowing and the roads were quite icy. I drove carefully, passing gaunt, leafless winter trees, on through the flat, white, North Essex countryside, when suddenly, in the distance ahead, I saw a swinging light. Slowing down I realised that it was a torch being waved about by a policeman standing in the middle of the road. Carefully I slowed right down. Ahead I could see a large furniture van, which had collided with a tractor. Both were now stationary and almost blocking the road. I tried to stop, but despite braking, my car continued to slide slowly on the slippery surface. I had no control of the car. The policeman leant against my car bonnet, but the weight of the car pushed him backwards, slowly, towards the rear of the van. To avoid becoming squashed between my car and the van, he let go, nimbly slipping sideways. My car then slid slowly into the van, bringing it to a halt. I got out, almost slipping over on the ice, thanked the policeman, who had had an impossible task, and inspected the front of my car. At that moment, another car was seen approaching. I could see the whole motor ballet being repeated, but this time, on seeing the resolute policeman's torch, the car driver managed to steer on to the grass verge and bring his car to a halt avoiding a collision with my car. Although in January it was normally dark by this time, nearly 7 pm, because of the snow, we could see perfectly well. My car was not damaged and we agreed that it should be possible to drive on. With the help of the policeman and the other car driver, my car was pulled back sufficiently to allow me to continue on my way. I was only half an hour late arriving at Wickham Bonhunt!

Occasionally in the winter months I took the athletes I was personally coaching to Camber in Sussex for weekend training camps, where we stayed in chalets and bungalows used in the summer for holiday lettings. The sand dunes were excellent for toughening up middle-distance runners, though it could be quite cold running barefoot on the dunes and in the sea in the middle of winter. Bob Slowe, Dick Corbett, Peter Bushell and young Alan Alderson from Highgate Harriers came, as well as others, Cliff Redman from Watford and Brian Hill-Cottingham from Chelmsford, later to gain an England vest for cross-country. The training could be tough but we had a lot of fun. We took our provisions with us; we divided into two groups and while one group made breakfast on Saturday morning, the second group had their pre-breakfast five-mile run over the dunes. On Sunday the roles were reversed. The two main training sessions on Saturday and Sunday took place in the morning and afternoon, the period after lunch being "rest time". The runners were getting in five sessions in two days and "crash" courses such as this made a big difference to a runner's overall level of fitness, once they had "recovered"! Not all the sessions were on the dunes. The firm, flat sand was ideal for faster running and for technique work. We did runs, barefoot, in the sea, where a good, high, knee lift was essential. One weekend we ran from Camber to Rye and back, as Catholic Mary insisted on going to Mass in Rye so she ran there! Trying to melt the frozen margarine on the bars of the electric fire, one of the lads fused all the lights! Yes, we had a lot of fun.

*Camber Sands with John Sullivan, Brian Hill-Cottingham, me, Pete
Bushell, Alan Alderson and Bob Slowe*

Bob Slowe, who I coached for a while, went on to run for
Highgate Harriers for many years, and later held many club positions
including President and Club Secretary. He tells the story that in
1988, when he was running as a veteran in the London Marathon,
he was the 2nd placed over-50 competitor with a time just outside
2½ hours. But in the commentary on the BBC, Ron Pickering had
said, "And here comes the vet, Bob Slowe from Highgate." Next day,
one of Bob's friends said to him, "Vet? I always thought you were a
lawyer!"

Brian Hill-Cottingham, one of the senior athletes at Chelmsford,
and already very successful, asked if I would coach him and I readily
agreed. He had a lot of talent and trained regularly and efficiently.
He ran well on the country and some of his road-running sessions
were exceptional. One that I organised for him was 4 x 1½ miles
with decreasing recoveries, which I used to time and monitor on my
bicycle. The rationale was that 1½ miles is half of 3 miles, so Brian
could get used to running at the required pace for, initially, half the

racing distance. The first of these runs would be relatively "easy", just as in a race, but as the time of the recoveries decreased, maintaining this speed became increasingly difficult. Naturally in a race you don't get any rest after running half the distance! Running 4 of these runs meant that Brian was operating close to race pace for double the race distance. Of course he did many other training sessions: longer runs to build up his aerobic capacity, shorter runs faster than racing speed.

When Brian joined our sand dune weekends, he was always very hard to catch! One of Brian's best racing performances was finishing 2nd to Gordon Pirie in the 1961 AAA 3 miles in 13:39.91. The previous year he had run for England in the International Cross Country race in Belgium and with colleagues such as Basil Heatley, Stan Eldon, Gerry North and Frank Sando, Brian came a very creditable 21st. Brian was a prolific competitor, racing with distinction on the track, cross-country and road, one of his best ever performances being his 2nd place in the 9 miles Hogs Back road race near Guildford in 1961, running 45:56 to winner Martin Hyman's 45:54. One of Brian's training companions and racing colleagues was the American, Buddy Edelen, better known as a marathon runner, who spent several years in the UK, winning the Polytechnic London marathon, and making lots of friends among the Essex running fraternity. Buddy was a lovely guy, liked by everyone, either for his guitar playing or his friendship when running or when sinking a Guinness. He and Brian had many friendly duels, interrupted from time to time by one Mel Batty!

One athlete who impressed me at that time was a young lad called Mike Erith, one of our Camber sand hill runners. He attended the local secondary technical school in Chelmsford. We were genuinely "tripartite" in Chelmsford in those days! He was a promising 880 yards runner, but what impressed me was the way he fitted so many things into his life. He worked well at school and was quite ambitious; he delivered groceries on his bicycle each Saturday morning and he later owned a motorbike, which he personally maintained; in his spare time, his hobby was campanology, as if training 3 or 4 times a week wasn't enough. How he fitted it all in I never knew. When he had some "free periods" in the 6th form, he asked me if I would have a word with his Headmaster to see if he might run during some of this non-teaching time. Mike also told me that he wanted to go to Oxford or Cambridge, which was unheard of for a student from a technical school. I spoke to his Headmaster and he readily agreed to Mike training in his non-teaching periods, and he also supported Mike's application to Oxbridge. In 1966, at the ESAA Championships at Blackburn, the Essex Schools team won the aggregate trophy and it was a proud moment for Mike, as Essex Boys captain, to go with Ann Wilson, the Girls captain, to receive the trophy from Barbara Castle MP for Blackburn. Mike went up to Cambridge to read Natural Sciences, transferred to medicine, trained in London, and later become a highly successful GP. I am pleased to have played a small part in Mike's success story. We met up again not long ago at a British Milers' Club training weekend in South Wales.

There was no cinder track in Chelmsford when I began teaching at KEGS in 1958. Grass had to do for training and for matches. With Tom Morris, Essex Coaching Secretary, I helped to organise coaching courses for young athletes on the grass at Melboune Park in 1960. I had been invited to become a member of the Chelmsford Sports Advisory Council and I worked with other keen sports enthusiasts to improve the basic facilities, not only for athletes but across the board in all sports. The local council was supportive and within their financial constraints, did what they could. The cinder track at Melbourne Park became a reality in 1961 with the opening match being held in April 1962. The following year, Essex Schools hosted the English Schools Track and Field Championships at the Chelmsford track.

At Chelmsford, I also met a young lad who was a very promising high jumper, which was when I decided to become qualified as a senior high jump coach. At that time the main high jump techniques used were the straddle and the western roll. The Fosbury flop hadn't been invented. To improve my knowledge of high jump I sought the advice of Arthur Gold, who regularly coached at the Parliament Hill Track, my Highgate Harriers base when I was in London. He was very helpful and encouraging and I learned a lot from him. He told me the story of when he was competing for Great Britain in a match against USA and an American high jumper, after watching some of Arthur's warm up jumps, had come up to him and said, "Hey, I sure like your style, Arthur, but I guess I like my height better!"

One of the problems in high jumping in those days was the landing area, which was usually a sandpit often with unprotected hard sides. Injuries could and did often occur, particularly with the straddle technique in which the jumper usually lands on their back. I coached Steve Hayward at Chelmsford for a while and was asked by National Coach, John Le Masurier, to coach some high jumpers in London. Later, I spent a fortnight at the Loughborough Summer School working with John Bailey, analysing film of the Russian Olympic champion Shavlakadze's high jump technique. It was interesting work and we presented a paper on our findings to a senior coaches' conference at Crystal Palace, but I never had the same buzz from high jump coaching as I did from coaching middle-distance runners.

While I was teaching in Chelmsford, AAA Chief National Coach, Geoff Dyson, came and had lunch with me at King Edward VI School. I had attended several of his lectures and we had met at the Loughborough Summer School. He and Southern National Coach John Le Masurier were looking to appoint another National Coach, and I was "headhunted" and asked if I would be interested. I was very tempted to apply for what was, after all, a very prestigious position in British athletics. If appointed I would be able to continue coaching almost full-time and expected to coach some of the best athletes in Britain. Travelling to GB matches and major championships was another inducement. National coaches were also paid, unlike the many voluntary coaches up and down the country, so it would have been a career move. If I had gone for this, I would have given up teaching, which, admittedly, I had only just started, but which I now assumed I was going to make my career.

Difficult decision though it was, I decided not to apply to become a AAA National Coach. One thought I had was that I would be away from home quite a lot and, as I was shortly to become engaged, I was concerned that this would put a strain upon married life. As events turned out my marriage didn't survive anyway, but I wasn't to know that when this career decision had to be made. Instead I stayed in teaching, not something that I ever regretted. Scot, Tom McNab, was appointed National Coach and, in the many years since, I have had no doubt that his was an excellent appointment and that he did a far better job than I could have done. I coached with Tom on several courses and we became good friends. He is a somewhat "larger than life" character, with a great sense of humour and an ebullient personality. In addition to being an excellent coach, Tom has also become an author, an expert on ancient games and a playwright. His play, "Berlin", based on the 1936 Olympics, has been performed in several theatres. Tom still writes for Athletics Weekly, and contributed an excellent critique of the techniques and tactics used at the World Athletics Championships in Moscow.

Jim Alford, in order to take up a coaching position abroad, had already resigned his position as National Coach in December 1960. I was sad to see Jim go as he was a lovely, quiet man from whom I had learned a lot. The only positive aspect of Jim's going was that Ron Pickering was appointed National Coach for Wales in his place. There was a lot of argument going on in the higher echelons of the AAA concerning the role of National Coaches, indeed over the role of coaching generally. The AAA "top brass" were extremely reluctant to recognise the role of National Coaches and especially that of the Chief National Coach, Geoff Dyson. Geoff was outspoken and forthright and his candour and directness clearly upset the old guard amateurs in the AAA. He was also an outstanding coach and a great motivator, both of athletes and coaches. When he eventually resigned in 1961, having been National Coach for over 14 years, he spoke of the constant undermining of his position by "a handful of powerful and entrenched AAA officials." Other National Coaches were to follow.

I continued to coach in an amateur capacity and enjoyed it immensely. At this time I was writing a chapter on middle-distance running for a handbook called *Athletics* which was published by

Nelson in 1963 and received very favourable reviews, in Athletics Weekly for instance: "a really first class book … this book is a must for everyone interested in coaching athletes" (P.W.Green). Coaching and teaching naturally go together; at least they did for me. Helping young people achieve their aims and realise their potential, whether athletic or academic, was what I wanted to do.

24
Training Runs

My very first training runs were with Highgate Harriers, soon after I had joined the club. A group of us used to meet at William Ellis School, close to Parliament Hill, on a couple of weekday evenings, the school being only a short walk from my home in Boscastle Road. Our coach on these evenings was Charlie Warner, a lovely, cheerful guy, who took us through a few exercises before we set off on our road runs. In the winter evenings running on the roads, or more accurately, on the pavements, was all we could do. It was too dark to run on grass and tracks were seldom lit in those days. We were all very fond of Charlie, who made the whole evening fun, so we always wanted to come back for more. Derek Adams, Alan Corfield and Billy Mutler were among the lads I ran with. Some more senior runners went off on their own, going further and at a quicker pace than we could manage. Over the years, as we got older, we were able to join in and run with the likes of George Brown and George Harrison. A favourite route for them, from the school, was past Gospel Oak Station, across Haverstock Hill near Belsize Park, along Eton Avenue to Swiss Cottage and down Avenue Road to Regents Park, then round the outer circle and back home. The pace was never easy, but on one particular evening I managed to keep up with George Harrison the whole way, which for me was quite an achievement! George went on to have a very successful career as a senior athlete and later became a very good coach.

On winter Sunday mornings we ran on Hampstead Heath, setting off from the Parliament Hill track. This could be a short five miler, past the Hampstead ponds and Kenwood House, or if we went through Ken Wood, crossed the Spaniards Road and ran round the Heath Extension, it became 7½ miles. Runners from several clubs, Highgate, Shaftesbury, Wigmore etc, would all set off for their training run, together with the occasional boxer, trying to get fit or lose weight. One such was young Terry Downes, a regular visitor, who amazed us by the amount he wore when he ran in order to shed the pounds. After a run when he was removing layers of clothing, all you could see was steam! Later, Terry went on to win the World Middleweight title. The purpose of these runs, in the dry, the wet or the snow, was to gain endurance by running at a steady pace; there was also a social element: we chatted as we ran, at least for the first half. They were enjoyable and by the finish you felt you had achieved something.

Running on Hampstead Heath on my own one weekday, I suddenly heard a shout, "Stand still!" I thought this instruction was probably addressed to me, so I stopped, but as I wasn't completely immobile, the command was repeated, but with even greater volume and insistence, "STAND STILL!" Then I saw the large Alsatian dog. *Maybe the command applies to the dog as well,* I thought. A chap came up to me, apologised and explained that he was a police dog handler and training this particular Alsatian to chase people who were running away! But the dog also had to learn when to stop, and this he hadn't yet done, so it was important that I stopped otherwise the Alsatian would have brought me down. The dog was brought under control so the policeman said I could continue my run.

When we lived in Finchley, during university vacations, I sometimes used the flat grass of the Heath Extension, close to Wildwood Road, to do some fast interval running. I also went for runs on my own on the roads often up to and round Mill Hill and I obtained permission to run, on weekdays only, on the local Finchley golf course, quite near home. The undulating grassland was excellent, much kinder to feet and body than running on roads. I promised I would keep off the greens. Occasionally there were people playing golf during the day, and I was careful to keep out of their way. Two elderly ladies caught my attention one afternoon, as they seemed to be taking a long time to complete one of the holes. Then to my surprise, one of the ladies spoke to me, "This isn't a running track, you know, young man," she said, unaware I had permission to run there. I felt like saying, in reply, "It doesn't look much like a golf course, either, the way you're playing," but I didn't.

Over the years I was to have many memorable training runs. At Oxford, a favourite was running in Bagley Woods, reached by running along the river towpath towards Iffley. The woods were especially welcoming in the spring when there was a carpet of bluebells.

Sharing digs with Tony Weeks-Pearson led to many joint training runs. Tony was from Hastings and reading English. He was a year ahead of me and was a very good runner, far better than I was. Tony gained his Oxford blue and represented the university each year on the track and in the cross-country match with Cambridge on Roehampton Common. He was quite short and wore glasses, in fact not unlike Sydney Wooderson, also a Blackheath Harrier and an even more famous runner. Before he went out from his digs for a run on his own, Tony used to play Wagner loudly on his record player to motivate him and give him power and inspiration for at least the first two miles, or so he used to say. *Tristan and Isolde* was his favourite. I had moved to digs across the road when we set off one Sunday morning. I had told my landlady what time I would be back, so she knew when to have lunch ready. Tony and I had had a good steady run for about ten miles, just under the hour, when we came to a crossroads, where we should have turned for home.

"Let's go on down to that village," Tony said, indicating a road that would have added a good three or four miles to our run.

"No, we agreed the distance," I replied. "And I've told my landlady I'll be back at 12.30. I'm going back."

Typically, Tony stormed off on his own, very cross with me, that I should decline the chance of an extra few miles with him. He did speak to me later in the week!

One winter Saturday, the university had a cross-country match with two visiting clubs, one of which was Blackheath Harriers. I had volunteered to be a hare for a section of the course, to show the runners the way. I had to wait at a certain point on the course, then set off when I saw the runners coming and keep ahead until we came to the next hare. I had about a mile to run. I had several problems: I couldn't start running until the leaders in the race were in sight and therefore quite close, the surface was wet and slippery on this particular Saturday and I hadn't chosen the best shoes, so I was slipping all over the place. To make my task even harder the race was being led by one of Blackheath's best Junior runners of that time, John "Kipper" Herring. I was sure I was going to be caught. I struggled on, slipping and sliding, trying to keep ahead, but I could hear and sense the runners getting closer. I just managed to reach the next hare as "Kipper" Herring sped past, giving me a grin as he went.

During my term at Didcot, when I sometimes went into Oxford to train with Oxford City AC, I ran with Phil Porter, whose favourite route regularly took us up Headington Hill, a long, steep hill to the east out of Oxford. It was hard work but enjoyable. Sometimes I found it difficult, as soon as we had finished, to drive back. Some years later I remembered this when I was at a Loughborough Summer School. British and Yorkshire miler Derek Ibbotson was there and ran with the middle-distance group through the campus, regaling us with his tales. When he went for a training run over the moors back home, he said he would often return to his car and be too tired, literally, to lift his hand to turn the key in the ignition. Getting the car started could take some time. I never got quite that tired from my training runs, but then I didn't break the British or World mile record!

Another famous runner I had the privilege to run with was Peter Snell, triple Olympic gold medallist: 800m at Rome, 800m and 1500m at Tokyo. Along with a number of other New Zealand athletes being hosted by Essex Beagles, Peter took several local club runners out on a training run over the fields near Chigwell. Sunday morning training runs can be "easy" or "steady" or on occasions really quick. On this particular day, running with the group that included Peter Snell, several of us realised that one person's steady pace might be too quick for others. Peter ambled along in his easy, long, relaxed stride at what for him was a very comfortable, easy pace, while many of us were running hard to keep up. He began to tell what turned out to be both an amusing and a long story. We were all keen to listen but, each time he got to a critical part, he seemed to go a bit quicker. It was probably deliberate! As the miles went by, I was trying to run close enough to listen and trying my best to keep up! And I wasn't alone. I have to admit I didn't hear the end of the story, but it was a great experience and a privilege to run in a group with such a famous athlete.

25

Athletics Coaching – the next phase

In the 1960s, I was coaching young athletes at school and also at the Southchurch Park track in Southend. I was still travelling to Chelmsford and coaching there at least once a week, and I began to develop a squad of runners who met with me every Wednesday at the Hornchurch track, home of Havering AC. Some of the athletes I was coaching came from the London area, and it was good to get everyone together.

At Hornchurch, the London based athletes included Malcolm Absolom from the Eton Manor club, Tony Maxwell of Woodford Green AC, Clive Ridley of Walthamstow AC and the Lincoln twins, Rita and Iris. Malcolm was at an East London school but ran for Essex Schools, coming 2nd in the ESAA Senior Boys' Cross Country race at Colchester in March 1965 and he was in the Essex Schools team in the summer too, as was Bob Chapman, from King Edward VI School, Chelmsford, both running the mile. The Senior Boys' Mile at Watford became a memorable race, with the leading five runners entering the final straight together. Chris Stewart from Somerset won in 4:08.7 with Mike Tagg of Norfolk 2nd, Malcolm 3rd and Bob 5th. Malcolm was given 4:10 and Bob ran 4:10.4, which were amazing times for schoolboys. Bob's time in 5th place would have won every other Senior Boys' One Mile race in the 1960s except one. Malcolm had a fine career as an athlete on the track, on the road, and over the country [See Additional Details].

The Lincoln twins, Rita and Iris, were from Loughton and members of Essex Ladies AC. Ron and Madge Merrie had started the girls on their athletic career and I met the twins when I was coaching at Lilleshall for the WAAA and they asked me to coach them. Both ran cross-country and middle-distance races on the track and it was obvious that not only were they talented but they absolutely loved running. They were identical twins and for a long time I had great difficulty telling them apart. Both went on to become international runners, Rita finishing 2nd twice and 3rd twice in the International Cross Country Championships, winning the Commonwealth Games 1500 metres in Edinburgh in 1970 as well as representing GB on numerous occasions on the track, and several times setting new British records for the mile and 1500m. Iris was more an 880 yards runner and narrowly missed out on selection for the 1968 Olympics, finishing one place away from selection in the trial race. Rita also never gained Olympic Games selection, mainly through illness and injury at the wrong time. In what was almost a repeat of Iris's experience in 1968, Rita had a trial race for a place in the GB team for the Games in 1972 in Munich. The race was held in Middlesbrough on a cold, wet day on a very cut up cinder track. Joan Allison and Joyce Smith had already been selected, but because of a bad back injury, Rita had not trained or raced well that year, so she had to compete for the final place in the 1500m team when far from fit. Sheila Carey won the race in 4:16.8 with Rita 3rd in 4:18.6. Sheila was selected and Rita's hopes were dashed. One has to add that in Munich, Rita's British Record for 1500m was broken, first by Joyce in the heats and semi-final, bettered by Sheila in her semi, but then taken to an amazing 4:04.8 by Sheila in the final when she came 5th. [40 years later at the London Olympics the women's 1500m was won in 4:10.23!]

When coaching the twins there were track sessions at Hornchurch and Ashton Playing Fields, Woodford Green, but it was in her runs in Epping and Hainault forests that Rita developed the aerobic base that enabled her to do so well at cross-country, and also laid the foundation for the track season. Often she would push herself too hard and I had to find ways to control the intensity of some of her sessions. Instead of a 45 minutes fartlek run, in which she would often run too hard for too long so that the quality was lost towards the end of the session, we devised a form of "interval fartlek", where she ran 3 x 15 or 2 x 20 minutes of fartlek, with a good 5 minutes easy running in between. It was quite difficult to get Rita to run a long way "comfortably"! She was a joy to coach. This foundation running in the forests enabled her track sessions to be done at specific paces. It is no good trying to run on the track at required speeds if the necessary groundwork hasn't been done.

If you want to become a successful middle-distance runner, first you have to get fit enough to train, and to train regularly. Then, preferably with your coach, you have to plan a programme of training, which will establish the essential aerobic base, by gradually increasing (a) the distance you run in a single session, (b) the frequency of the runs, and (c) the pace at which the runs are performed. It's easy to remain "aerobic" running slowly. The challenge is to remain "aerobic" while running a lot faster. Each of these variables should be increased one at a time. These basic fitness elements will be improved every year you train, as will your total weekly mileage. Only when this base of aerobic fitness is established can athletes begin to think about running at the speeds needed for their event. Among coaches there is often discussion about quantity v quality when it comes to weekly or monthly training.

I was at a health club in East Grinstead many years later when Seb Coe appeared. We chatted and he said, "Are your runners doing loads of miles each week?" And when I said, "No," he said, "Good!" Although the number of miles being run by developing athletes will and should increase each year, there should be some quality running all year round.

"Speed must be retained throughout the year," said Seb Coe.

It is also possible to "lose" some aerobic fitness during the summer, if the concentration is solely on faster running, so many coaches will recommend including some aerobic running during the summer months.

We divided Rita's training into "easy" sessions (often "recovery" runs after harder sessions), "medium effort" sessions (as it is important to train the body to run "comfortably"), and "hard/tough" sessions. These were integrated into running at different paces, similar to Frank Horwill's five-pace theory, which was published in the 1970s. For Rita, the paces were: (1) slower than racing pace, (2) at the desired racing speed, and (3) faster than racing pace.

Easier runs are needed to give the body a chance to recover from really hard sessions; it gives the athlete the opportunity to learn to run "comfortably", without strain. Jim Ryun, the famous American miler, used to have an "easier" run each morning, to give his body a chance to recover from the hard or fast session the previous evening and to enable him to do the next tough session. Too many British runners devote too much training time to running slower than their intended race pace. Easier runs can be done every day, as Kenyan runners do, with the important proviso that some faster and harder running is also done each day. Getting used to running at intended race pace is fine, but often the recovery times taken are too long. Runners must get used to decreasing their recovery times in training while running at race pace. It is a key variable that should be worked on. A fundamental objective is to learn how to run at racing speed, comfortably, without strain.

It is also essential that the middle-distance runner trains at a faster speed than intended race pace. Again there are several reasons for this. The fast twitch muscle fibres need to be regularly brought into use. A middle-distance runner cannot have too much speed, so it is good to develop it. The last part of many races requires the runner to accelerate in order to win the race, as Mo Farah has demonstrated. Training at faster than race pace makes it easier for the runner to maintain intended racing speed. Fast running will involve running distances such as 150, 200 and 300 metres, even 400 and 600 metres, much faster than racing pace. There are all sorts of ways these distances can be run or combined, on the track or on good grass, to produce valuable training sessions. "Tempo" runs are often included in a middle-distance runner's programme. These are runs where a fast pace is maintained for maybe five or ten minutes, but where the runner is running anaerobically towards the end of the run. The aim is to extend the runner's aerobic threshold as far as possible.

While it is important to do some really fast running, it is also vital that this is done correctly. Learning how to run fast correctly will take time. Running tall and running relaxed are two essentials. Correct posture should be checked by the coach and if necessary, corrected. The sprinter who wins is the one who stays running fast and relaxed the longest. So too the middle-distance runner and the 5K and 10K runners.

The 1500m runner should also race at distances below and above 1500m. It is much easier to run the first 800m of a 1500m "comfortably" if you have recently raced a fast 800m. For a similar reason if the 1500m runner occasionally races 3000 metres or even 5K, the 1500m distance doesn't seem so long. When runners, such as Mo Farah, can accelerate at the end of a 5000 metre race, it is not just because they have great speed, it is also because they are so well prepared that they have not found the pace up to that point too demanding on their cardio-vascular system. They are fitter than their rivals or have managed to run the race more economically. They may be less anaerobic than their rivals at that crucial final stage of the race or they are better able to handle their anaerobic condition. Essentially they have been able to stay closer to being aerobic.

The most important thing to remember if one is coaching young athletes is that they should enjoy it! As time goes on, more enjoyment should come with improvement and success. Even with senior runners it is sensible for the coach to satisfy himself that although the training is tough and often painful ("It's only pain!" Franz Stampfl), the runner is gaining satisfaction from what he is achieving. All runners who train really hard will probably ask themselves from time to time, *"Why am I doing this?"* And this is where a sensitive and sensible coach can often be very helpful.

I always encouraged Rita, and others I coached, to run the first half of races as relaxed as possible, and to run the second half of the race faster than the first. Not only was this good, physically and psychologically, for Rita, it also meant that she was often increasing the pace just when her opponents were becoming fatigued. Running relaxed doesn't mean running slowly. Iwan Thomas, GB 400m record holder, told me once that for him the most important thing in racing 400 metres was to run the first 200m fast and relaxed. It is one of the most difficult, but also most important things for a track runner to learn: how to run really fast and stay relaxed. Ron Delaney, the Olympic 1500m winner in Melbourne in 1956 said, "Seek to master the art of feeling relaxed when running." Sprinters have to learn how to be powerful and relaxed at the same time. I remember a coach saying to me that he told his sprinters when they were on their blocks, "Relax, relax, relax" i.e. no tension.

In addition to her considerable success on the track and also on the country, wearing the British (and England) vest with distinction on many occasions and setting new standards with her UK 1500m records, Rita also enjoyed racing on the road, and special favourites of hers were the annual Nos Galan races, organised by Bernard Baldwin and held on New Year's Eve in Mountain Ash in South Wales. Scores of athletes would descend on this small Welsh village every year to contest the four mile race in which runners started in the old year and finished in the new. The streets were lined with torch bearing local lads and lassies and there was a great atmosphere. Of course in those days this was coal mining country and sometimes the runners used the pit-head showers, though on one occasion when we were there, a shift ended and we saw the coal-black, exhausted miners emerge from their lifts and disappear into the showers themselves. Local Mountain Ash folk enjoyed acting as hosts to the visiting runners. Several of the athletes I coached ran in these Nos Galan races until the races were eventually brought to a halt by the police. Several years, Rita and I went down to South Wales, sometimes in my VW camper van, so she could run in the one-mile race, in which she invariably won or came 2nd. The other surface Rita loved to run on was, of course, the sand, and she relished the challenge of the sand hills, which helped to toughen her up for her competitive races. Sadly, in recent years, Rita contracted cancer and despite putting up a tough fight, she died in February 2013. As former editor of Athletics Weekly, Mel Watman wrote, "Her blond, smiling presence lit up the sport during her heyday in the 1960s and 1970s."

Rita's identical, twin sister, Iris, whom I also coached, now lives in Australia, having married Australian marathon runner, Tony Cook. After moving her base "down under", Iris ran several marathons in the 1980s, including the London Marathon, all under 3 hours. After many years, I met up with Iris again, sadly, at her sister's funeral.

At Hornchurch, my group included not only Rita and Iris and senior middle-distance runners, Tony Maxwell and Clive Ridley, but also younger, female athletes. These included sprinter Christine McFarlane and hurdler Jacqui Philp both from Chelmsford AC, Jackie French from Southend AC, Christine Brannon from the local club, Havering AC, plus several others, including Lonnie Perry from the Basildon club. I tried to organise sessions so that each athlete had the appropriate training, bearing in mind the time of year and their individual racing commitments. I always enjoyed those Wednesday evening sessions.

I also coached several other athletes at this time. Andy Davis was a black, US Air Force man, based at USAF Wethersfield. I met him at the Chelmsford track and he asked me to coach him, as he wanted to compete in the US Air Force European Championships in the 440 yards hurdles. He was a big, strong lad, not the most elegant of runners, but powerful and quite quick. His training consisted of running and some hurdling practice. He told me he did plenty of strength work at the base. Each time I met him at the track, he would greet me, "Hi, Coach!"

As part of his preparations we entered him in the 880 yards in the Essex County Championships, to be held at the Eton Manor track in East London. He was eligible to compete, and despite finishing the race in lane 6 because other runners moved out to try to prevent him coming past, to everyone's surprise, Andy won. He didn't run for Essex in the Inter-Counties because as nobody knew of him, his name hadn't been entered.

Before he travelled to Germany to race the 440 yards hurdles for which he had been training, he took me to one side at the track one day.

"Hey, Coach. I have a question for you," Andy said. "Is it OK for an athlete to have sex before a competition?" he asked with a big grin.

I told him I wasn't too experienced in such matters, but maybe I could help. It had been reported that Herb McKenley, the Jamaican 440 yards runner, had had sex on more than one occasion prior to an important race and that it hadn't done him any harm, as he had won. I told Andy that there is no evidence that having sex would lessen his chances of running fast or winning. But I also told him that loss of sleep would be harmful and would almost certainly adversely affect his performance on the track the following day.

"OK, Coach," Andy said. "I'll follow your advice. I'll try not to lose any sleep." Andy grinned and shook my hand.

A few days later he went to Germany and though disappointed not to win, was delighted with the silver medal. I didn't ask any questions about his amorous activities. He also won the USAF European 880 yards title, setting a new record time. Andy was well liked in the Chelmsford club and he is remembered as a cheerful, friendly guy, and a talented runner.

Jacqui Philp was another hurdler I coached, first at Chelmsford, then increasingly at Hornchurch. Although I was primarily a middle-distance coach, I enjoyed coaching a hurdler. She was 14 when I first met her, and we worked on her hurdle technique until she was usually very proficient. It was while coaching Jacqui (and also when coaching high jumpers) that I learned how important it is to watch the athlete from a number of different positions. I watched Jacqui hurdling from behind, from the side and in front, in order to detect any flaws in her technique. I would watch what her arms were doing and also her legs, as well as her head and body position throughout. We worked on all aspects of the event: the start obviously *("Get to the*

First Hurdle First!" – Geoff Dyson), as well as the rhythm of the event and maintaining speed off the final hurdle. With Jacqui we did loads of starts to four or five hurdles, timing them, often with a flat sprinter for company.

Jacqui did lots of drills, and her hurdling improved as she got taller. Sometimes she ran over five hurdles with the hurdles spaced further apart, doing five strides in between each hurdle instead of three. This was to develop the feeling of arriving at and crossing each hurdle at greater speed. She also worked on all ten hurdles, because there are ten hurdles in the race, so it would be foolish only to work on five. As her coach I tried to teach her to have maximum concentration at the same time as maximum relaxation: difficult but essential.

In 1967, Jacqui competed for Essex Schools in the English Schools Championships at Peterborough, in the Intermediate Girls' 80 metres hurdles. In her final training session at Hornchurch something had gone wrong in almost every run she did over the hurdles. There were about five key points of technique we regarded as essential, and always one or more went wrong. Even in her heat at Peterborough, she didn't have an error free run. She knew that to get everything right meant maximum concentration. In the semi-final Jacqui not only got everything right, she won the race and set a new ESAA Championship best time of 11.5 seconds. She went on to win the final in 11.8 seconds. It was the culmination of lots of hard work for a very able and dedicated young athlete and a fitting reward. As a Senior Girl Jacqui continued to represent Essex Schools as a hurdler, coming 2nd in 1968 and 3rd in 1969. She was also an excellent Pentathlete, winning several titles and being ranked in the UK [see Additional Details].

Later Jacqui took part in WAAA training and coaching weeks at Lilleshall, where she had the benefit of Fred Housden's coaching. While training at Crystal Palace she was given advice by the experienced international American hurdler, Willie Davenport. "You have a good technique over the hurdles. Now you must learn to run faster," he said. Jacqui went on to become a PE teacher and for several years was herself an Essex Schools team officer, passing on her experience to other young athletes.

Jacqui Philp (lane 2) at Crystal Palace watched by coach Fred Housden

I had been asked to coach on coaching courses for a number of years. The very first one was for Middlesex AAA and was held at the Paddington track. My group consisted of about a dozen 13- to 14-year-old, keen, young middle-distance runners. It was absolutely pouring the morning we arrived, so with the cinder track totally awash and unusable, I decided to take the youngsters on a run to Hyde Park instead. This involved running down the Edgware Road to Marble Arch and then into the park, where we did a short fartlek run for about 30 minutes. When we set off to return to the track, two of the boys said they couldn't run back so, as I had come prepared, I gave them the money to return by bus! This they did, in their wet running gear, meeting us just as we got back. Luckily the showers were working that day. One of the group, Bob Ellis, became a very good senior club runner for Thames Valley Harriers in the years following and he always says that he puts his career as a runner down to that run to Hyde Park that day – he has never forgotten it! About ten years later Bob moved up to Yorkshire to teach, and of course to run, and he had some excellent races on the road and country. He became involved with Yorkshire Schools athletes and quite often we met up at the English Schools Cross Country Championships. I saw Bob recently at "Athletes Reunited" in London and he had just retired from his role as Secretary of West Yorkshire Schools AA. From small beginnings …

I had another, very different, experience later at the same Paddington track. I was there coaching a couple of my athletes from Highgate, when who should I see on the trackside but Mihaly Igloi, the famous Hungarian coach. What's more he had with him two of the trio of World Record holders he coached, Sandor Iharos, Istvan Roszavolgyi and Laszlo Tabori, who had been setting tracks alight in the mid 1950s. I introduced myself; he was very gracious and we talked about coaching.

He asked me, "How many athletes do you coach?"

I said, "About ten or twelve at present."

He laughed. "How do you expect to be successful, coaching such a small number? I coach as many as a hundred," he said.

I didn't respond to this, but I thought that you cannot give individual coaching to a hundred athletes; that isn't coaching as I understood it. But he had been highly successful with his record-breaking runners, so maybe as a consequence of that, many flocked to receive schedules of training from him.

"What session are your athletes doing today?" I asked him.

"I watch them in their warm up, then I decide the session," was his reply.

I found this interesting. I would always know what my athletes were going to do on a particular day when we were at the track, but I had to recognise that maybe he had a point. An athlete can arrive at the track in a variety of conditions: he may be very tired from a day's work or study; he may be a bit under the weather, perhaps with a cold or he may have a slight injury; the track may be in a poor state or it may be a very windy day. Any of these factors could affect the training session, so in future I tended to follow Igloi's example, and though I would have a planned session, I was always prepared to modify it.

I felt I had been privileged to talk with such a famous and experienced coach and to watch his athletes train. I had a similar opportunity at the Commonwealth Games in Cardiff in 1958, when I had a short conversation with Percy Cerutty as we were leaving the stadium. Percy Cerutty was the enigmatic, inspirational Australian coach of such athletes as John Landy and Herb Elliot, believing in doing things nature's way, advocating tough sand dune running rather than track running, as practised by Elliot's great rival, Merv Lincoln, coached by Franz Stampfl. Just to be in Percy Cerruty's company for a few minutes and to exchange a few thoughts on running, was a fantastic experience for a young fledgling coach. Herb Elliot set a new World Record (3:54.5) for the mile in Dublin that year and I was in Rome to see him win gold at the Olympic Games two years later. Herb Elliot never lost a mile race throughout his career.

Running on sand and up tortuous sand hills might be the key to success, thought many athletes and coaches, and it soon caught on in this country. I was one of the team of coaches at two training weekends organised by Tony Ward held on the dunes at Braunton in Devon in 1963. We were billeted at RAF Chivenor nearby. Each day there were punishing runs, or climbs, up the sand hills, which toughened up the athlete, physically and mentally. The following year I was at Merthyr Mawr in South Wales helping to organise and coach on a similar training weekend, the first of many I attended there. In those days the coaches in addition to myself were usually Frank Horwill and Harry Wilson.

With Harry Wilson and Tony Ward at Braunton Sand Dunes

Following my first taste of sand dune running at Camber in Sussex in the mid and late 1950s and early 1960s, later I took my group of athletes instead to Winterton in Norfolk to dunes that Robbie Brightwell and Ann Packer had trained on prior to the Tokyo Olympics. In fact it was Robbie and Ann who had recommended Winterton to me. There were miles and miles of flat sand backed by what appeared to be almost pristine sand dunes. Some days in the winter we would see nobody on the beach or dunes all morning: we had it all to ourselves.

Occasionally there were horses being exercised on the flat sand and sometimes we met dog walkers who looked at us in bewilderment. Running up sand hills is tough; it tests and develops many aspects of a runner's armoury: legs, arms, heart and lungs as well as determination, what Geoff Dyson liked to call, "intestinal fortitude"! Running barefoot in shorts in the sea in midwinter can be quite challenging, as can really fast runs on flat sand repeated two or three times with very short recoveries! But it was also great fun as well as character building. They were great weekends.

Jacqui Philp and Pete Fulcher show good form on the sand hill

Iris and Rita attacking the hill

I coached on many courses for young athletes during the 1960s and early 1970s.

The Crystal Palace National Recreation Centre had opened in 1964 and I coached on the first ever course held there, which was a Southern Counties Young Athletes weekend in May.

In Essex, I was organising training weekends, some at Wicken Bonhunt, others in different parts of the county, including one at Grange Farm, Chigwell, on the weekend in November 1963 when John Kennedy was assassinated. Yes, we all remember where we were when that awful event took place. The previous year I had been elected to the committee of the Athletic Coaches Association, with Harry Wilson as Chairman and Dave Evans as Secretary. It was a well-meaning initiative but I think most coaches, who are voluntary anyway, don't have sufficient time to devote to developing a national organisation such as that. Another initiative, in 1969, was the formation of the Essex Federation of Coaches, the brainchild of Derek Hayward, to bring together the coaching of athletes in Essex AAA, Essex WAAA and Essex Schools AA. I think it was the first of its kind in the country. A Young Athletes weekend followed in April 1971, which I helped to organise at the University of Essex at

Colchester with Tom McNab as Chief Coach.

A particular training weekend that I remember well, back in the early 1960s, was one held at Motspur Park and led by Chief National Coach, Geoff Dyson. I was one of a team of coaches and had a group of 17- or 18-year-old lads to look after. They did a track session on the first day, at the end of which, Geoff Dyson came up to me and asked what we were planning to do the following day, and would it be all right if his 14-year-old son, Tim, joined in. I told Geoff that tomorrow I planned to have a fartlek session using the excellent grass in the park.

"That should be fine. Tim just wants to have a go. He knows the others are older. Just let him do what he can," Geoff said.

The next day, Tim joined in the fartlek and, by cutting a few corners here and there, he was able to keep up most of the time. He did well, though it must have been tough for him. When I next saw Geoff Dyson, he told me that when Tim got home he went up to his room and lay flat out on his bed. His mother, slightly concerned at this unusual behaviour went up and asked him if he was all right.

"Mum," he said, "I'm exhausted! And I've just had the best day of my life!""

Geoff didn't have to tell me how pleased he was that his son had linked extreme physical endeavour with a sense of enjoyment.

26
Loughborough

In the 1950s and early 1960s Loughborough College of Technology (as it was then) hosted a summer school for a variety of activities, including athletics, which in those days was organised by the AAA. Summer School participants not only enjoyed a week or fortnight learning more about their particular interest or activity, but also met, during breaks and evening leisure time, people who were there on completely different courses. For some folk this was their summer holiday. Athletes and coaches would rub shoulders with artists, literature buffs, basket makers, swimmers, in fact all sorts from different parts of the UK and abroad. One year our group noticed several nuns and, when approached, they seemed friendly and good company if a little wary and reserved when coming into contact with boisterous sporty guys. One young, attractive nun caught the eye of Ben in our group and he said he was going to have a chat with her at dinner. We told him that his prospects of taking her for a drink or having a date were very limited, but he said he would try his luck. At the evening meal we kept out of his way. He reported back later and said she had been excellent company at dinner, but had courteously declined his offer of a "coffee afterwards".

My first experience of the Loughborough Summer School was as a student coach in the late 1950s. The AAA ran courses for intending or new, inexperienced coaches. Middle-distance lectures were given by Jim Alford, and there was some practical work and several demonstrations by international athletes. I learned a lot in those early days from National Coaches, Jim Alford, Lionel Pugh, Bill Marlow, Denis Watts and John Le Masurier. In one lecture, Chief National Coach Geoff Dyson was asked by a rather naive young man, "Mr Dyson, what are your views on breathing?"

There was a short pause. "I recommend it," was Geoff Dyson's put down.

It was either the same guy or one similar who got confused as he must have misheard or misunderstood Geoff Dyson when he was lecturing on high jump technique, as in his notes he had written C of E, whereas Geoff was talking about the C of G (centre of gravity). In one of Jim Alford's lectures, held in the small upstairs room in the athletics pavilion, I was sitting next to Geoff Gowan. We were both making notes, noting the points being made by Jim, when Geoff suddenly took away my notebook and scribbled something on it. He handed it back and I saw that he had written, "I should like to see more original work here!"

In those early years I was billeted in either Rutland or Hazelrigg hostel, close to the Fountain Lawn. They are still there, but no longer used as halls of residence. In the evenings a group would get together in one of the hostel rooms and have a party, just an informal get-together with a few drinks, to which some local people sometimes came. It was here that I met Eileen, who lived in Loughborough and was an art student at the College of Art in the town. She had dark hair, was slim and attractive and good fun to be with. We went out a few times while I was there and later she came and stayed with us in Finchley. One evening Mum and Dad and I were going to a Highgate Harriers dance so Eileen came too. I well remember my Dad's face as Eileen came downstairs ready to go out wearing a hooped skirt. He had never seen anything like it! Eileen looked great and had made a special effort to impress, which she certainly did. My friends at the club dance were definitely envious that evening. Eileen graduated, moved to London, had some of her own printed fabrics displayed at Liberty's in London, and though we met again, our lives took different paths: she now lives near Leicester with her doctor husband and has two grown up daughters. I still hear from her every Christmas.

After I had gained my Senior Coach award and my coaching experience had become recognised, I was asked to join the staff at the AAA Summer School. In the early 1960s I was lecturing and helping would-be coaches become more confident. The two weeks spent at Loughborough in August were always very enjoyable and there were some memorable and amusing incidents most years. Some evenings, with Denis Watts, one of the AAA national coaches, we used to visit the hot dog stall in the centre of Loughborough after a busy day at the track. Often we called in at The Generous Briton on the way and sometimes on the way back too. I got to know all the National Coaches, each with his individual expertise and personality. Denis was good company, but he didn't hold his drink too well, and we would make sure his metallic wastepaper basket was close to his bed when he retired to his room.

Scottish coach, John Anderson, (later of "Gladiators" fame) and I had been working together one day and we returned to our hall of residence, William Morris Hall, very tired from the day's exertions. His room was opposite mine on the first floor. Adjacent was the bathroom.

"You bath first, Tony," John said. "Give me a call when you're out."

"OK, John, will do." I had my bath (there don't seem to have been any showers in those days) and then knocked on John's door.

"Bathroom's free, John. I've finished."

"Thanks, Tony. Would you start the bath running for me?"

"Sure." I turned on the taps and shouted through his door to John, "Your bath's running." I went into my room, finished drying, got dressed and went downstairs to the refectory, which was just across from our hall. It was while I was having my meal that I became aware of a commotion. Apparently there was a crisis in William Morris Hall.

"You've never seen such a mess," one guy said as he came in for his meal.

Apparently water had poured from the first floor through the light sockets, run all along the corridor and flooded the corridor downstairs. The lady in charge was not happy. It would appear that after I told John his bath was running, he fell asleep. The bath had filled, then overflowed, with disastrous consequences. It was quite a serious mishap, and John and I did our best not to laugh about it, as it had caused so much turmoil.

John and I did have a genuinely amusing incident in Leicester one evening. We had gone for a curry in one of Leicester's very good Indian restaurants. We looked at the menu, and both decided on a chicken vindaloo.

"Chicken vindaloo – very hot, Sir," said our waiter in wonderful Indian English.

"Yes, we know," we said, no doubt in a somewhat dismissive and superior tone.

What happened next is that the waiter must have gone into the kitchen and said, "There are two guys out there who claim to know that vindaloo is hot. Can we show them just how hot vindaloo really is?" Because when our chicken vindaloo arrived, John and I said it was the hottest we had ever known. We had each ordered a beer, but now we had to ask for water to put out the fire!

"Everything all right, Sir?"

"Oh Yes! Wonderful, thank you."

One of my good friends in those days was Ron Pickering. I had known Ron when he taught PE in Essex. He had been appointed National Coach for Wales in 1961. He was three years older than me, a larger than life character as well as being large! He was tall and swarthy, an extravert who was seldom without a smile or a grin. Ron and I were strolling round the campus one day and happened to walk into one of the gyms where a chap was conducting some form of exercise with a group of women. There were leotard-clad ladies at the top of the wall bars, and one had just come down from the top as we entered.

"No, no, Deirdre," the instructor said. Ron and I watched and listened with interest. "Go back up again, and this time, jump down more slowly." Ron and I made a quick exit.

In the days before he became a National Coach Ron and I found ourselves in a group of coaches who were trying out as many athletic events as possible. We sprinted OK and our hurdling wasn't too bad, but we both came a cropper at the pole vault, where our efforts were abysmal. Ron had some difficulty at the steeplechase water jump too, as his large frame wasn't really suited to negotiating such obstacles. Our throwing and jumping was quite good, Ron being much more proficient than I was. The day was good fun, we laughed a lot and we both appreciated how much skill some athletic events require – which was the main purpose of the exercise – and valuable knowledge for coaches to have.

In 1963 Ron was at the summer school with Lynn Davies, the Welsh long jumper he was coaching. Lynn was a very talented athlete and Ron, who was an inspirational coach, had high hopes for him. One evening Lynn had borrowed a friend's motor scooter, but he stalled the engine at some traffic lights in Loughborough and couldn't get it going again. As luck would have it, a member of the local constabulary was passing. Lynn explained, but the PC wasn't convinced.

"Are you sure your friend gave you permission to take his motor scooter, sir?" Lynn and Ron had to go down to the local police station, where the sergeant in charge told Lynn he would have to return on a certain day to answer charges.

"But I can't come on that day," said Lynn, "I'm long jumping at the White City for Great Britain then."

"Hmm; well you're for the high jump now, laddie," he said with obvious amusement. The scooter owner came forward and the whole matter was cleared up amicably.

The following year Lynn won gold at the Tokyo Olympic Games and has subsequently become President of UK Athletics. Also at the summer school one year Lynn had his girlfriend with him. The two of them plus Ron and I were at one of Loughborough's swimming pools. I had never learned to swim, chiefly because when I was younger, I had been told not to get water in my damaged ear. However by the time I had fallen in the river several times at Oxford, there seemed no point in not trying to learn to swim. I didn't find it easy at all. The previous year at Loughborough, Bert Kinnear, GB's top swimming coach, had tried to teach me to swim.

"You have negative buoyancy," he said, as I kept sinking!

Lynn's girlfriend, Janice, said she would try to teach me. While Lynn and Ron were busy elsewhere, she asked me to place my body horizontally in the water and move towards her. I tried, but my feet and legs kept dropping. She was wearing a swimsuit and was in the water at the shallow end of the pool.

She said to me, with great patience and obviously keen to succeed, "Hold my hands and I'll pull you towards me."

I tried but this didn't work as my legs just would not stay horizontal. (Negative buoyancy!)

"OK," she said, "come nearer, hold on to my shoulders and now try."

I should explain that Lynn's girlfriend was extremely attractive and I had no difficulty in accepting her suggestion that I hold onto her shoulders and let her pull me towards her. We tried this for several minutes. It was undoubtedly my most enjoyable swimming lesson, but, regrettably, my lack of buoyancy proved too great an obstacle. She didn't teach me to swim.

Towards the end of my "lesson", Ron and Lynn reappeared, and when I got out of the pool, Ron came up to me and said, with a big smile, "You devil! I've been trying to get that close to Lynn's girlfriend for ages! How dare you!"

Ron said that on one visit to the States, he was at the track with Bruce, his host, who was coaching a young high jumper, Ben. Whatever the coach did or said, he seemed unable to get Ben to jump any higher than 6ft 8in.

He had a chat with Ron and then said, "I know, I'll ask Matt to come and have a look at him." Matt was the chief athletics coach at a nearby university and a good friend.

That afternoon all three coaches were at the high jump area

watching the sophomore jump.

"Your run up can be improved," said Matt. "Try to accelerate in your last three strides," and when he did this, Matt said, "Great. That's better. Now make your take off more positive. Drive UP!" Matt gave a little demonstration. As soon as he tried this, Ben sailed over 6ft 10in. Bruce was delighted; so was Ben. The three coaches later went inside to have a chat about high jump technique.

What impressed Ron was how natural it was for Bruce to contact another coach and ask for his help, and then let him advise his athlete.

"That doesn't happen much, if at all, in UK," said Ron. "But it should."

Ron was much in demand as a coach. He told me about two athletes he had somewhat reluctantly agreed to coach by post. Ron had sent the long jumper details of the technique he should be trying to develop, and received regular feedback from the athlete. Ron thought that he ought to go down to Devon to see for himself how the lad was getting on. They met at the track and after a warm up the long jumper took a few jumps from a shortened run up.

"Your run up and take off are both fine," Ron said. "Your form through the air is also quite good. But your landing is dreadful. Why is that, do you think?" Ron asked.

"I'm sorry," the long jumper said. "I lost the last two pages of your letter."

Ron, who loved a good story, even if it was against himself, told me about the discus thrower he had also agreed to coach by post.

"I don't seem to be able to get this right at all," the guy wrote to Ron.

Ron repeated all the basic advice, about maintaining good balance at the back of the circle, pivoting over the left foot, while keeping the right arm back holding the discus out straight during the movement across the circle etc. Eventually Ron went to see him too, only to find that he was a left-handed thrower! No wonder he couldn't get it right. Ron had to laugh!

I was able to tell Ron the story that a coach in Essex had told me. He had been approached by a young man who wanted to improve as a 440/880-yard runner. So the coach met up with him one Sunday morning and gave him a number of sessions to do, five in all: a week's programme in fact. Late on Monday night the coach received a phone call from the athlete.

"I've done the training you gave me," he said.

"Which session have you done?" asked the coach.

"I've done all that you set me," he replied.

"That was for the week!" the coach said, unable to contain his amazement! This guy had done a week's training all in one day. It made the coach realise that one shouldn't make assumptions. What the coach understood to be obvious wasn't so to the athlete, who was clearly very inexperienced. It also made the coach consider whether he was giving his athletes enough to do if one guy could do a week's training in one day! Mind you, he didn't know what sort of state he was in.

"I should have a couple of days rest to recover," the coach said.

The two weeks at the Loughborough Summer School each year were always instructive and enjoyable. I met many of Britain's leading athletes and coaches and I learned a great deal and gained a lot of satisfaction in helping new coaches develop their knowledge and coaching techniques. Every year new friendships were made and old ones strengthened. I don't know when the annual Loughborough Summer School ceased to function, but it seems a shame they no longer take place.

27
Lilleshall

One of the National Recreation Centres was situated at Lilleshall in Shropshire. It's where Alf Ramsey took the England football team to train before the 1966 World Cup and it has been used by many different sporting bodies to prepare teams for major championships. Lilleshall Hall is a lovely old building set in some beautiful grounds. There are lots of good grass fields, some woods to run in and a small, dedicated surface for sprinters, hurdlers and other track runners to use. The Women's AAA held courses there each year for young, talented, aspiring athletes. Each one was billed as a "Potential Olympic Athletes Course" and was sponsored by Bovril and the athletes were organised for the week in event groups for specific coaching and training. I was fortunate to be invited to take charge of the middle-distance athletes each year from 1963 to 1968. In that time I met many of the country's leading female 800 and 1500m runners. In addition to group sessions with the individual coaches, there were lectures and fun activities, such as inter-group hockey or basketball matches, in which the middle-distance group always seemed to come last!

Many international athletes of the day came to these WAAA courses, either as coaches or as visiting lecturers or sometimes to give demonstrations to the young athletes. On one course I went out for a meal and drinks as a foursome with Robbie and Ann Brightwell, plus Janet Simpson. They were all GB Olympic runners and I felt very privileged. I had met Robbie and Ann several times at meetings and training courses; remember, they were the ones who had told me about the sand dunes at Winterton. Janet Simpson was a sprinter, very attractive with dark hair and a bubbly personality, and a friend of Ann's; I didn't know her prior to our evening out, which turned out to be very enjoyable.

One activity I have special reason to remember well. Among the international stars attending was Mary Rand, GB long jump record holder, the pin-up lady of the women's team, whose jumping legs were not only powerful but also, by general agreement, considered to be gorgeous. Together with some others from the British team, she took part in some tests in the gym while at Lilleshall. One was the Harvard Step Test, a test of cardiovascular fitness, which involves the athlete stepping up and down at 30 steps per minute on to a bench 45cm in height for 5 minutes. The athlete's pulse is taken at the end of the stepping activity after 1 minute, 2 minutes and 3 minutes, each time for 30 seconds. The fitter you are, the quicker your pulse returns to normal. I was assigned to take Mary Rand's pulse. So there I was, watching Mary, in her tight shorts and singlet, stepping up and down for five minutes, making sure she fully extended each leg on the bench as she stepped up (what a shame it was only for five minutes!), then, when she had finished and was sitting on the bench, after one minute holding her wrist and taking her pulse. This was then repeated at two minutes and three minutes, and a strange thing happened: as Mary Rand's pulse steadily came down, mine steadily went up! Not something one easily forgets. Mary of course went to Tokyo the following year and, like Lynn, took the Gold Medal in the long jump, her distance of 6.76m being a new Olympic and World Record. She also gained Silver in the pentathlon and Bronze in the 4x100m relay: a lovely lady and an outstanding athlete.

One year all the young female participants were asked to take a hand-grip strength test using a grip dynamometer. One of the girls in the javelin group had an incredibly high score of 42Kg and we wondered why this was. We asked her about her training, the other sports she did, but we couldn't fathom out how she came to have such remarkably high grip strength.

"What other things do you do, when you're not at college?" she was asked.

"I work in a pub five nights a week," she said.

"What, pulling pints?"

"Well, yes, and serving other drinks," the young javelin thrower replied. Case solved! The action of pulling pints each evening had given her well above average grip strength, very useful when throwing the javelin. So when looking for future javelin throwers, perhaps clubs and coaches should check local bar staff!

There are many tests a coach can give an athlete, from endurance tests, such as the Balke Test and the Kosmin Test for middle and long distance athletes, to strength tests for throwers, jumpers and sprinters. Then there are physiological tests carried out in a sports laboratory. With such tests, a coach, and the athlete, can become aware of any weaknesses there may be. A coach should ensure his athletes are working to rectify any weaknesses, and he or she can't do this if the weaknesses haven't been identified. It's much the same for a teacher, who should be aware of any specific weaknesses that any of the children in the class have. I used to require A level students I was teaching to complete a self-assessment form in which each one had to rate his/her ability or level of performance against a set of criteria. Later in the term the procedure was repeated so that the students could assess in which areas they had made improvement. Self-awareness is important for students and athletes, and also, of course, for teachers and coaches.

Some young men and women become very proficient at some of the tests. One young man at KEGS regularly did 60+ press-ups in a minute, almost as a party piece. Another lad of 16, admittedly training to become a pole vaulter, could often be seen climbing up a rope in the gym, upside down – legs highest, hands lowest: very impressive. I was running a course for young athletes at Marlborough College one year and the group was in the gym, circuit training. Suddenly, a middle-aged guy, possibly a hiker, stepped into the gym from the road outside. He watched the athletes working for a few minutes and when the circuit had obviously finished, he put down his rucksack, walked over to one of the beams we had been using, and did 25 pull-ups using one arm only. Then he picked up his rucksack, smiled, and walked out. I had no idea who he was. After he had gone some of the lads tried to do one-arm pull-ups and most couldn't do one.

Back to Lilleshall! In my group each year I had some really promising runners, with whom it was a privilege to work, athletes of the calibre of Mary Hodson, the Lincoln twins, Margaret Moir, Joan Page, Rosemary Stirling, Sheila Taylor and Anita Webb (these being their unmarried names of course!). I always told the girls that they must tell their coaches what they had done and what they had learned at Lilleshall, and discuss all of it with their coaches. If an athlete came who didn't have a coach, I gave more in-depth advice but always told them to find a coach. Why? Because young runners especially need the guidance of an experienced coach who can prepare a suitable training programme and monitor their progress. The coach can plan each week's training, which, when the athlete is a bit older and more ambitious, will form a part of the training programme for the year. A coach can also contribute to the athlete's mental development, by encouraging a positive attitude and by being there when the athlete is depressed or injured or just going through a bad patch. If the runner is to be successful over several years, there are many other aspects on which the coach will be able to give guidance, such as diet, running technique, racing tactics etc.

Lilleshall WAAA Course 1966 Robbie & Ann Brightwell & baby at front plus coaches and athletes

Several times in the 1960s and 1970s I went to Lilleshall independently with a group of athletes I was personally coaching. Sometimes they came with their "other halves" so that when the hard work had been done for the day, we could socialise. We stayed at Lilleshall Hall in accommodation not normally used for courses and we made our own arrangements for eating. There is so much grassland and woods to run in that just to get away and train in a different environment was a stimulus for the weeks ahead.

At Lilleshall: at back (from left) two "other halves", Carol and Liz, plus athletes I coached: Iris, Penny and Rita; at front, Dennis Colton, Tony Maxwell, Malcolm Absolom, Pete Fulcher, Clive Ridley and me

I also coached at the CCPR Centre at Bisham Abbey and on courses at Crystal Palace, some with Frank Horwill, when we all had to be up early and ready for the pre-breakfast 30 minute run, which at Crystal Palace was around the local roads. I coached on the WAAA "National Scholarship Course" sponsored by Birds Eye, which lasted a week at Crystal Palace. Timsbury Manor in Hampshire saw a special middle-distance get-together in 1964, organised by members of the International Athletes Club with support from Frank and the recently formed British Milers Club. Some of Britain's leading middle-distance runners were looking forward to getting in some good training in the hills and woods of the local countryside. I was there along with Rita Lincoln, Penny Gardner and several international runners. One training run descended into farce when the runners became lost in the Hampshire countryside. One group had gone off in one direction, while a rival group decided a different route would be better. Both groups became hopelessly lost, but eventually everyone found their way "home", though it had been an overly long outing. I always believed that UK middle-distance standards would rise if the best runners could train together on some sort of regular basis. At that time most athletes had jobs which made getting together difficult, but the occasional weekend course went some way to meeting that aim.

At one Lilleshall course I was approached by National Coach, Denis Watts.

"Tony, I'm in a bit of a jam. I wonder whether you might be able to help me out."

"Well, yes, if I can," I said. "What's the problem?"

What he explained and what I agreed to do turned out to be, for me, a training and coaching experience to log forever in my memory bank and a personal encounter to savour.

"I've arranged to be at a training session at Cosford tomorrow with one of my athletes and I just cannot make it, as there's a bit of a crisis back home. Could you possibly go down to Cosford – it's kind of on your way home," he smiled, "and conduct the session for me? I would be so grateful. I don't feel I can ask anyone else, and I know I can totally rely on you." RAF Cosford was near Wolverhampton and had an indoor 200m track. It was on my way home. I had known Denis for years and we were good friends.

"Yes, I'll be pleased to do that. Who is the athlete and what session have you got planned?"

"It's Lillian Board," Denis said, "and she is due to do some 300s." I think I probably gasped!

Lillian Board had already represented England at the Commonwealth Games in Jamaica in 1966 where she ran 54.7 for

400m, coming 5th. She was then only 17. She ran for Great Britain later that year. In 1967, she won the WAAA 440 yards and reduced her 400m best to 52.8 representing the Commonwealth v USA when winning in Los Angeles. She had a very successful season, winning several 400m international races, including the European Cup 400m in 53.7. She also raced at 200m and 800m. 1968 was Olympic year and Denis was asking me to take a session with her. Wow!

Lillian was an extremely talented athlete as well as being very attractive with neat, short blond hair. She was to become known as "the Golden Girl of British athletics".

"She needs to do some 300s," said Denis, "but not too fast. 6 x 300 with two to three minutes recovery should be fine. But don't let her run them faster than 43 seconds. 44 would be ok, but definitely no faster than 43."

"I'll do my best," I said, as I wondered how one could stop someone like Lillian from running faster than 43 seconds.

The next morning I drove down to Cosford, only a short distance from Lilleshall. After explaining who I was and why I was there, I was allowed in and walked into the indoor athletic arena. I had met Lillian before when she had attended the WAAA course at Lilleshall in 1966, though she had been in the sprints group and probably would not have remembered me. I saw her warming up on the far side of the arena. I walked across.

"Hello, Lillian. I'm Tony Elder. Denis has asked me to come here today for your training session, as he couldn't make it."

Lillian smiled, and said, "Yes, I know. Denis got a message to me. And I remember you from Lilleshall."

"Oh! That's good," I said. "Did he tell you what the session is?" I asked.

"Yes, he said I was to do some 300s and that I wasn't to run any faster than 43 seconds!" Lillian said with another smile.

"Yes, he told me that too," I said. "Six 300s with a recovery of two to three minutes. If that's ok, then carry on with your warm-up and tell me when you're ready," I said.

Lillian went off and ran several more easy laps of the tight 200m track. When Lillian was doing some loosening exercises, I went over to her.

"I don't know what Denis says to you," I said, "but I always think the important thing in a session like this, is not to strain or try to run quicker than your body wants to, but to do the times running as comfortably and as relaxed as possible."

"That's what he says," Lillian replied. "I'll do my best. I don't know that I'll need as much as three minutes in between each one though."

"We'll see," I said. "If you reduce the recovery too much, you may find it difficult to run the times without any strain."

Soon, she was ready. Lillian took off her tracksuit, revealing a club top, white shorts and those lovely, athletic legs. She then did several strides to loosen up some more and get the feel of the pace. As she moved, I saw just how smooth and effortless her running looked. She moved beautifully and I felt privileged to be there to witness her running at such close quarters.

"OK I'm ready," she said.

"Good; I'll time each one and also the recovery and tell you when to start the next one."

Running 300m at Cosford involved doing a lap and a half so I noted exactly where each one would finish. Lillian ran the first 300 looking tremendous: 41.5 secs! It looked so easy.

"A bit fast," I said, as I began to time the recovery. Lillian jogged away. "I'll tell you when there's 30 seconds to go," I said.

Lillian only had 2½ minutes recovery and she wanted to start again before that. She ran the 2nd one in 41.8 seconds. I was a bit concerned that she wouldn't complete the session still running well and at the required time. I needn't have worried! She did slow a little but not much: the last four were 42.0, 41.8, 42.4 & 42.0. All faster than 57 seconds 400 metre pace but well under the 43–44 secs that Denis had asked for, so when I sent him the details of the session, I apologised for failing to keep her in the 43 zone, but I said how easy and relaxed Lillian had looked. No strain at all. Denis thanked me and said that the times were good.

"She has obviously wintered well," Denis said, "perhaps she is going to have a really good summer."

"Thank you so much for coming down to time my session," Lillian said, after her warm-down.

"It's been a pleasure," I said. "I've enjoyed seeing you run and I'm sure you're going to have a good season, especially with the Olympics later in the year." We said our goodbyes and went our separate ways.

In the Mexico Games which were later in the year, not till October, Lillian, still only 19, set a new British record at 400m of 52.12 but was beaten into 2nd place by the French athlete, Colette Besson, by 0.09 seconds. The following year, Lillian ran 800m in the European Championships held in Athens and won in a new championship record of 2:01.4. Also in Athens, Lillian ran the final leg of the 4 x 400 metres, which the GB team won in a new World Record of 3:30.8.

Sad to say, her running career, which held so much promise, never developed from that point. Lillian was awarded the MBE in January 1970 but she became unwell during the year. Competing in the WAAA Championships in June, despite being in pain, she finished only 3rd in the 800m in 2:05.1 and was obviously only a shadow of her former self. She never ran another race. In September she was diagnosed with cancer of the bowel and stomach. She went to a clinic in Munich hoping for a cure but she died on 26th December 1970. She was 22. What a sad end for such a lovely and talented young athlete.

28
British Milers' Club

In the early 1960s British middle-distance running was not in a very healthy state. Many British milers would attempt to run the first three laps as slowly as possible and then try to win with a blistering sprint over the final 300, 200 or 150. As a consequence of this, when they met foreign opposition they were usually unable to last the pace. Middle-distance coach Frank Horwill decided that something needed to be done. He wrote a letter in 1963 to Athletics Weekly, in which he asked if anybody would like to join him in attempting to improve the standard of British middle-distance running. He had several replies including one from me. Frank then founded the British Milers' Club and I was one of the first coaches to join, though not technically a "founder member". Frank had begun to coach in 1961.

On BMC courses when he had become a world-renowned coach and I was one of the coaches working with him, he liked to say, "The first lecture I ever attended on the subject of middle-distance running was given by Tony Elder." This was true, as I had begun coaching a few years before Frank, and the lecture he referred to I had given at the LCC College of PE in Paddington Street just off Baker Street in 1960. Geoff Dyson had lectured there in 1955. My lecture was one of a series covering different sports, and I remember one of the other coaches I met at those Paddington Street lectures was Mick Jagger's father, who was a prominent basketball coach. I was a member of the

BMC's first committee, which met in August 1963 at Bowater House in London, just opposite Harvey Nicholls. In 1970 I was elected Vice Chairman with Harry Wilson Chairman and Frank Horwill National Secretary. Later I became a vice-president and life member of the BMC. I still receive BMC News – 50 years later.

Frank Horwill

To meet its aims the BMC attracted a membership of mainly 800m and 1500m runners, male and female, of all ages. There were entry standards and a joining fee, and races were organised, nearly always with a pacemaker, with the aim of encouraging and helping runners to run faster. Regional secretaries came forward who put on races and training courses in their areas. Athletics "officialdom" didn't take kindly to the formation of the BMC or to its intention of putting on races, as this they considered was their prerogative. The leading members of the AAA and BAAB, folk such as Harold Abrahams and Arthur Gold, saw the BMC as a threat, a rival and an interloper. Frank, not one to walk away from an argument, had some fierce battles with these officials, who represented the "old school" and were averse to anything new that might deprive them of their special place in charge of British athletics. (My thoughts went back to Geoff Dyson and the problems he encountered with these same people).

The BMC survived these "attacks" on its existence and its role and several initiatives took place. In March 1971 to support BMC funds I helped Cecil Smith put on a sponsored football match at Harlow in Essex, in which a team of International Athletes played Ex-Spurs All Stars. The athletes secured a very creditable 2–2 draw, thanks chiefly to inspired goalkeeping by Chelsea manager, Dave Sexton and Tom McNab. Later that year Cecil and I worked together to organise a mile race during half-time at Stamford Bridge, which was something different, the race being won by Maurice Benn in 4:10.0. I put on a training course at Hadleigh in Essex, and all over the country aspiring young middle-distance runners joined the BMC, as its aims and activities were publicised in Athletics Weekly. All members of the BMC received a copy of the BMC News quarterly. As races were put on by the BMC, usually organised by the Regional Secretaries, the BMC membership grew and the performances of British middle-distance runners improved. By the 1980s British athletes held World Records from 800m to 5000m, Sebastian Coe (1500m) and Steve Ovett (800m) won Olympic titles, Steve Cram set World Records at 1500 metres and One Mile, Dave Moorcroft set a World Record at 5000m: all were members of the BMC.

As the years went on, Frank continued to pursue his aim of seeing British standards rise. The BMC News regularly contained articles from Frank addressing different aspects of middle-distance running; the races that were staged became better in quality, so that today, in addition to Regional races, there are Gold Standard and Grand Prix races. Pacemakers are usually used to ensure the pace is appropriate for the assembled field of runners, and at most BMC events lots of personal best times are achieved. Residential courses for young athletes have also been held for many years and, more recently, the BMC Academy has been started and is now run by David Lowes specifically for young athletes. On these courses athletes are able to train together to a high standard and learn from the coaches. Many visiting coaches also attend eager to learn and to contribute to the BMC.

I was a coach and member of the BMC from its inception but, although I helped in the early stages, it was not until I had retired from full-time work that I was able to take a major part in BMC residential education and training courses. From 1996 to 2005 I took part in BMC courses in various parts of the country, working with Frank and other leading coaches, and meeting some very promising athletes. Occasionally there were amusing incidents. In March 1998 the BMC held a course at RAF Uxbridge. To meet security requirements, on arrival on Friday evening each one of us had to report at the gate, to ensure no unauthorised person entered the RAF station, all quite understandable. What the RAF authorities didn't know was that at 7 a.m. on Saturday morning all the athletes and most of the coaches would run out through the gates for the early morning 30-minute run. The poor guy at the gate saw this horde of runners stream past. Worse still, after 30 minutes a mass of bodies ran back into the camp without any checks done at all. RAF security was temporarily suspended at that moment. No harm was done and we could see the funny side of it, even if the RAF Uxbridge "top brass" didn't.

The BMC training courses for young athletes, to which I contributed, were held in the spring at Ardingly College in West Sussex, where the training and the lectures were geared to the forthcoming track season, and in the autumn at Ogmore in South Wales, where athletes often began their winter training by tackling the sand dunes, including the Big Dipper, at Merthyr Mawr. This is described by David Lowes (in BMC News Spring 2009) as "a stunning environment and an endurance athlete's paradise ...without doubt one of the most awe-inspiring venues in the UK for gut-wrenching sessions!" He goes on to describe the Big Dipper, the "massive sand hill of strength sapping soft sand which gets steeper the longer you run." I can certainly vouch for this. Last time I was there I had difficulty walking up it! It gave me quite a sense of pride at the BMC course one year when the first runner to the top was Craig

Ivemy, a lad I was coaching. An additional feature at Ogmore was the session at Southerndown beach, with flat, firm sand, ideal for faster running. Although the Ogmore weekend is tough, the scenery and surroundings are stunning and the runners enjoy the challenges and undoubtedly benefit from the experience. Many come back for more!

I coached on several BMC courses

Since suffering a spinal thrombosis in November 2005, I have, unfortunately, been unable to take any further part in these courses. And even though the founder of the BMC, Frank Horwill, sadly died in January 2012, these courses, and others like them, continue to be held, organised by David Lowes (Chairman of the BMC Academy), Rod Lock and others. BMC races are held at certain key venues such as Wythenshaw and Watford during the year and participation in the Grand Prix races is much sought after. The young athletes' BMC meeting organised by Mike Down at Millfield School every May always sees scores of athletes achieve new personal best times. The success of the BMC owes a lot to Frank Horwill whose brainchild it was, and to his enthusiasm and fanaticism, but the club has been kept going by the work of a series of dedicated Regional Secretaries and, of course, by a constant stream of new members. These days when an 800m or 1500m runner needs a fast time to qualify for consideration for a place in a GB team for a major championship, they look for a BMC race.

Today the BMC News, (which has reached volume 11) containing photographs, informative articles, news of members' performances and up-to-date ranking lists, is published twice a year and is sent to all members, who today number about 1800. Many people have contributed to the continued success of the BMC over the years, none more so than Pat Fitzgerald, the ever present Treasurer and Administrator plus the current President, Norman Poole. There were special races and events in 2013 to mark the 50th anniversary of the founding of the BMC.

[A list of the BMC Courses I attended from 1996 to 2005 can be found in the Additional Details section at the end of the book.]

29

Nos. 27 & 28, Nos. 3 & 4, Nos. 79 & 80

[Before and after Retirement]

In June each year, following the County Schools Championships, a selection committee of teachers meets in every county in England to pick its best schoolboy and schoolgirl athletes to compete in the English Schools Track and Field Championships, held in July when over 1600 boys and girls aged 14 to 18 take part. A similar exercise takes place in March when the ESAA Cross Country Championships are held, when there are close on 2000 runners, as each county can bring eight runners for each of the six races: Juniors, Intermediates and Seniors for boys and girls. At both events, which are hosted by different counties and held at different venues each year, each county schools team is led by a team manager and a number of team officers.

Although Southampton was the first English Schools Track and Field Championships I attended (while teaching at Hitchin in 1957), the first time I went to an ESAA Championship as a County Schools team officer was at Chelmsford in 1963, though I did go to Hull in a private capacity the previous year, taking with me two lads who I

354

hoped would make the Essex Schools team the following year. This turned out to be an adventurous weekend. When we reached Hull late on Thursday evening we erected our blow up tent on a smooth piece of grass close to the Humber River. We slept well after our car journey until I was woken in the early hours by Mike, who had his head poking out of the tent flap, saying, "Hey! Look, Tony; we're surrounded by water!"

My swift visual survey confirmed that Mike was quite right: our situation was indeed circumfluous; we were marooned and in danger of floating off somewhere: North Sea? When we had put our tent up, we hadn't realised that the Humber is tidal! Fortunately, although the tide was coming in, the water had not yet become deep, merely lapping on all sides, so we swiftly dismantled our tent, collected all our belongings and waded, barefoot, to the bank, rather wet, but none the worse for our tidal mishap. It was not yet 6 o'clock! We had to laugh. We stood on the bank and watched as the water rapidly became deeper.

"I'm ever so glad you woke us up, Mike!" I said. Nobody seemed to be around where we were, so we stood by the river-bank and changed out of our sleeping attire into daytime apparel. We had found the whole episode hilarious.

That visit to Hull had two other interesting moments. In the main street I suddenly saw Rick Gardner, triple jumper from Chelmsford and captain of the Essex Schools team that year, driving down the road in a rather large, smart car. He stopped when he saw us.

"What are you doing in that?" I asked.

"My host lent it to me; said I could take it for a drive," said Rick. He was grinning from ear to ear, obviously feeling very proud of himself. I wondered what Sidney Rose, team manager and boss of Essex Schools, would have said had he seen this, strict disciplinarian that he was.

After day one of the Championships, on Friday evening I took my two aspiring athletes, who had come with me to get the experience of an All-England Schools, to a large pub, where I had been told the Essex Schools team officers would be meeting. We were sitting quietly in one corner when Sidney and the others came in.

He didn't see us straightaway. When he did, he said, in a stern voice, "What are those athletes doing here? Members of the team have no business to be in a public house. What's going on?" He looked accusingly at the team officers with him. He was angry, as only Sidney could be.

I went over to him and explained, "These boys are not part of the Essex team, Sidney; they are here with me, to spectate at the Championships." Though I was not at that time a team officer, I knew Sidney and the team officers quite well, so he calmed down and apologised, quite gracefully for Sidney, actually.

The following year, 1963, at Chelmsford, I had become one of Sidney's Essex Schools' team officers. The Championships were being held on home ground: Essex being the hosts. It required a major feat of organisation putting on the ESAA Championships, but by the day, all was ready. I had several middle-distance runners taking part: Penny Gardner finished 2nd in the Intermediate Girls 880 yards, John Archer 2nd in the Senior Boys 880 yards, Malcolm Absolom 3rd in the Intermediate Boys' Mile and Mike Erith (my water look-out in Hull!) came 5th in the Junior Boys 880 yards. 1963 was the year Ann Wilson, from Southend, won the first of her five ESAA titles, the Junior Girls' high jump.

Sixth place in Penny's race was taken by Mary Hodson (2:21.1), who then had an amazing rise to Olympic selection in 1964. Mary was in my middle-distance group at the WAAA course at Lilleshall the following year (that's what must have made the difference!) and at Hendon won the ESAA Senior Girls 880 yards in 2:13.6. In August she ran 2:10.4 in the Edinburgh Games, then 2:08.7 at Blackburn, and still only 17 years old running for GB v France in September she not only ran 2:05.3 but beat Ann Packer! Ann of course sensationally won the Gold Medal in Tokyo in the 800m in a new World Record, whereas Mary went out at the semi-final stage in 2:07.1, the youngest member of the GB team.

But I digress! It was at the Essex Schools selection meeting that year that I again clashed with Sidney. We were discussing selection of the senior boys and we came to the 880 yards, which John Archer, whom I coached, had won. John had run for Essex Schools before.

"He's the lad I saw coming into the stadium arm in arm with his girl friend," said Sidney to the meeting. "I don't like seeing members of the Essex team behaving brazenly like that." Apart from the fact that I could see nothing wrong in John's behaviour, and accepting Sidney's very old-fashioned view of such matters, I felt I had to take him up on his error. "Sidney, when you saw John walking into the stadium where the County Schools Championships were going to take place, he wasn't a member of the Essex team. He doesn't become a member until we select him today."

We all had to get used to Sidney and his ways. Thankfully he also got used to me and we became good colleagues and firm friends. Although he lived in leafy Brentwood, he was the Head of a boys' secondary school in a fairly rough part of East London. He told me that one morning as he was walking from the train to his school, he saw that someone had scrawled on a nearby wall, in large letters, "ROSE IS A BASTARD".

He said to me, "When I saw that, I knew I was winning!"

When choosing the County Schools team to take part in the ESAA Track and Field Championships, a maximum of three athletes can be selected for any one event. More usually only one or two are picked. Essex has always been a strong county for athletics, due in part to the number of strong athletic clubs in the county. One year when the selectors met to pick the County Schools team, in the senior boys' triple jump no less than four athletes had bettered the ESAA National Standard set for that event. It was the only time I ever experienced this. The selectors could only pick a maximum of three for that one event, so the lad who came 4th with a National Standard performance, could not be selected. I can't remember whether he was entered for another event, say the long jump, or left at home. In any other county, with his performance, he would have been selected.

I was an Essex Schools team officer at the ESAA Track and Field Championships for the next ten years, up to 1973. During that time Essex won the major county title twice, at Blackburn in 1966 and at Motspur Park in 1969, over 40 individual athletes won their events, some winning several times, Linda Knowles and Ann Wilson for example. Several athletes I was coaching performed well. One of these, Jacqui Philp, from Chelmsford AC, not only won but set a new Championship record of 11.5 seconds. in her semi-final of the 80 metres Intermediate hurdles in 1967 at Peterborough – the only time an athlete I was coaching set a new ESAA Champs Best Performance. I coached athletes who came 2nd on six occasions and three athletes who came 3rd, plus several others who represented Essex Schools. Main highlights for me were Jacqui's win and her record in the hurdles and the remarkable Senior Boys' Mile race at Watford in 1965. The ESAA Championships at Watford were memorable, partly because this was where one of the stands collapsed in particularly high wind, but also for the extraordinary Senior Boys' Mile race, described earlier. Fancy running 4:10 for the mile as a schoolboy, as Malcolm Absolom did and only coming 3rd!

In the winter the ESAA Cross Country Championships are held, each county, in theory, taking its turn to be host. In the 1970s and 1980s the Girls' and Boys' XC Championships were often held on different weekends and at different locations. At Colchester in 1965, ever-present Malcolm Absolom was narrowly beaten into 2nd place by Norfolk's Mike Tagg. In Bedfordshire, from 1973, I soon became a County Schools team officer, and the same thing occurred in Sussex after 1996. One of my memories, I can still see her now, was watching Paula Radcliffe run away with the Senior Girls Cross Country race at Bristol in 1992 with such assurance and determination. I think many of us knew we were watching someone special that day.

In the early days, athletes and team officers were billeted in local homes. The host county would ask local schools if parents would act as hosts to one or two counties. For the cross-country this would usually be for one night. Our coach would arrive at the host school at teatime on Friday if it was cross-country. We would unload and be shown into the school hall, where the host parents were waiting to meet us. After a drink and a bun and brief words of welcome, each runner would be introduced to their host family and would go off to their home, with instructions to be back at the school by a certain time next morning so that the team could go off in their coach to do an on-foot pre-race inspection of the course. Many friendships were made during those weekends, and it's a shame that because of child protection issues, such arrangements had to come to an end. In recent years athletes in summer and winter have often been housed in university accommodation, which can be soulless and gives nothing like as individual an experience of a host town or city. It was often an education for our youngsters to live in families very different from their own. One year, a girl from a very affluent family was accommodated in a Durham miner's small terraced house – quite a valuable culture shock; it could work the other way too.

There were often some amusing moments on these trips to different parts of the country. The Essex Boys Cross Country team went to Sheffield in 1967. Quite often the team officers went out for a meal or a drink on Friday evening, availing themselves of the services of the team coach and their driver, who in the 1960s was invariably Norman Tiffin, of Tiffin's Coaches, Brentwood. On this occasion we had a good evening out and getting on for midnight began the drive back to our respective digs, all fortunately close together. The boys who would be running the next day had all been told to be indoors and in bed by 10.30. Our driver, Norman, a lovely guy, who we all got to know well over the years, wasn't too sure which road he should be taking. None of us was much help either. We drove around in what we thought was the right part of Sheffield for 15 or 20 minutes. We all knew our individual addresses of course, but not precisely where our road was. Embarrassing! It was soon to become even more so. Up ahead I saw a lone figure walking in the direction our coach was slowly taking. It was Dave Browne, a lad from my school in Southend! He was obviously making his way back to his host family – at nearly midnight! And he was due to run in the Junior Boys race the next day. I also remembered that he was billeted in the same road as I was. He seemed to know where he was going. There was nothing else we could do. We stopped the coach, opened the door and I said, "Hello, David. Would you like a lift?" He got in. No mention was made of the time. He unwittingly guided us to where we needed to be. We were extremely grateful, though we didn't tell Dave that. He also had a good race the next day.

On arrival at the school and on first meeting our hosts, everyone, athletes and team officers alike, took a good look at the locals. At Track and Field, this would be on a Thursday evening, as the summer Championships last for two days. The boys would be looking out for some pretty local girls, the girls seeing what the male talent was like. Most of the team officers were married so we didn't have the same interest, except on one memorable occasion. Standing at the back was a lady, probably in her early thirties, wearing a smart red suit: jacket and skirt. She stood out from the crowd, as she was extremely attractive and her skirt was quite short.

"I wonder which lucky lad is going to stay with her?" fellow team officer, Dave, said to me. Each athlete was paired up with his or her host family, "Cheers; see you in the morning," until there were only two or three left. The lady in red was still there. Dave and I were due to be in digs together and we began to think that maybe we were going to get lucky.

And so it turned out. There was only the team manager left when our names were called and the lady in red came forward to greet us. Dave and I said nothing to each other but we each knew what the other was thinking. We walked outside to her car, a low slung, open top, sportscar. Well, it would be, wouldn't it! The angle at which the driver sat made the skirt even shorter, and Dave and I only just managed to squeeze ourselves into our seats. Our expectations for the weekend had changed considerably. Janice turned out to be a young mum, who was an excellent host and Dave and I had a very enjoyable stay. Nothing untoward took place, of course, though when the senior boys found out who we had been staying with, we did have some probing questions to answer in the morning!

We were in Leicester one March for the Cross Country races and another team officer and I were billeted together. Our host turned out to be a local vicar in a nearby village. We climbed into his somewhat ancient, rickety car, my friend in the back and me in the front. We drove off into the country, through distant fields on which the evening mist was already descending. We finally arrived at the vicarage. I went to open my door.

"Oh! You won't be able to open the door," said the vicar with a sly grin, "this is my courting car!" He laughed, came round and opened the door on my side. I think he had been joking.

We were shown into a library, while the vicar chatted with a local couple shortly to be married.

"You must be hungry after your journey," said a lady who we took to be the vicar's wife. This was both a statement and a question, to which we said,

"Yes, we are rather hungry."

"I'll get you a meal shortly," the vicar's wife said.

We waited for what seemed ages, but the vicar's talk with the about to be married couple having ended, we were shown into a room with a table in the centre, where we sat down. The wife then brought us our meal: scrambled eggs on toast! I'm surprised we didn't wake our hosts during the night with the sound of our stomachs rumbling!

In 1980, the Bedfordshire team shared a coach to Newcastle for the Boys Cross Country Championships with the Buckinghamshire team. Unfortunately the Bucks coach was not modern by any stretch of the imagination and the journey took longer than expected. As we approached Newcastle in a snow storm, already late and struggling up a steep hill, two of our lads came to the front and said to the team manager, Graham Baker, "Would you like us to get out and push?"

On another occasion the team coach broke down on a motorway. The driver managed to park the coach on the hard shoulder and rang for a replacement coach. We hadn't been sat in the coach more than a few minutes when a large lorry roared past, extremely close, so much so that our coach shuddered, leaving several of the girls very frightened. Fortunately, just where we had stopped there was a high, grassy bank with a flat section at the top, so the team manager told all the athletes to leave the coach and go straight up to the top of the bank. The athletes did this and sat on the grass and behaved impeccably as we waited for another coach to appear. After a few minutes a police car drew up and we were told we should all get back in the coach, as it was too dangerous to have "so many youngsters loose on the motorway." We told the policeman that it was far more dangerous to be in the coach. He didn't agree and repeated his instruction. Our team manager refused to comply, saying that the safety of these athletes was his responsibility and that he would guarantee their good behaviour where they were. The traffic police officer said he would have to take some details and make a report. Having noted who we were and taken some names, he drove away. We had to wait nearly three hours for our replacement coach, but when it arrived, all the athletes got on without incident and their bags and cases were moved from the broken down coach to the new one. We set off for our host school and, as far as I know, no more was heard from the police. I think it is more accepted today that to sit for any length of time in a vehicle on the hard shoulder of a motorway is extremely dangerous.

As a Deputy Head, and later, Head, in Bedfordshire, I didn't have much time for coaching athletes, though one youngster I did coach was at my school. Debbie Buckley, mentioned earlier, was a keen and talented runner. Representing Bedfordshire Schools, she twice reached the ESAA Championship final in the 1500m. Debbie's dad and I drove up to Durham in 1975 to watch her run. Dennis Johnson became County Schools Team Manager in 1976 and led the track and field team each year, with team officers, Dawn Daley, Graham Adamson, Jenny Sudworth and myself, plus others from time to time.

Dennis was an excellent team manager, always very organised and his enthusiasm had a positive effect on the athletes and his fellow team officers. The tone was set at the team meeting on the Thursday before the team set off. Here the members of the team got to know each other, Dennis gave an inspirational talk and sometimes a film was shown. Being also a coach, specialising in high jump and multi-events, he could speak with authority to the athletes. Quite often this team meeting was held at my school at Houghton Regis.

In those days in order to become a coach, you were tested at a track by a more experienced coach, and Dennis recently reminded me that when he had his first test to qualify as a coach, I was the one who tested him, at the Thurrock track, when we both worked in Essex. Dennis is still coaching and taking an active part in track and field in Bedford, and also with the County Schools teams.

Bedfordshire had at least one winner in each year I was a team officer from 1976 to 1981. After Cannock in 1976, Hendon, the following year, was memorable for several reasons: Dennis and I were billeted together in somewhat strange circumstances, as our sleeping arrangements involved spending the night, effectively, on the floor. Dennis, close to midnight, would be counting up the number of points we had won on the Friday and working out what we were likely to win on Saturday.

"Couldn't you do that in the morning?" I seem to remember saying. In those days teams didn't return home until Sunday, even if they didn't have far to travel, so on the Saturday night I took Dennis and Jenny to my favourite curry house, the Shahbag in Hampstead. 1977 also saw a certain Steve Cram win the Intermediate Boys' 1500m for Durham.

Winners and those in 2nd place in the Intermediate Boys' and Girls' age group were normally selected to represent England Schools in the annual Home Countries Schools International, although, as she recently reminded me, when Jacqui Philp won in 1967, it was the seniors who were selected to represent England Schools, so Jacqui missed out. Unfortunately I didn't go with the team to Birmingham in 1982, (when Houghton Regis Upper School was facing the possibility of closure), so I missed seeing Sue Jordan win the Junior Girls' 1500m in a new record time. I became Chairman of Bedfordshire Schools AA in 1978 relinquishing this position in 1984 when I was about to leave the county, and I was later honoured by being made a Vice President. I return to Bedford as often as possible for schools events being hosted at the Bedford track.

Moving to work in Crawley at the start of 1986, I found Sussex Schools a very different set up. After one County Schools

Championships meeting at Brighton, as a senior coach and with several athletes from my school with a good chance of being selected, I decided I would go along to the selection meeting being held directly after the Championships. Essex always held their selection meeting on a Sunday. I was about to enter the hut by the Withdean track to attend the Sussex Schools selection meeting, when I was told I couldn't go in. The then secretary, Roger Wardale, said that this was because I didn't represent anybody, I wasn't a team officer and I wasn't a district representative. In Essex and Bedfordshire teachers were welcome at the selection meeting. Only certain people had the right to vote, obviously, but others could attend, either from interest or because they might have some information about an athlete, useful to the selectors. Naturally I was somewhat miffed to be told I couldn't attend. I wondered how many other folk had been put off by this policy and discouraged from becoming involved. After all, as with other counties, Sussex Schools AA could always do with more teachers to contribute to the work of the County Schools AA. Sussex Schools do things differently now.

I did go to the Sussex Schools AGM, where I found that the Independent Schools had a much larger influence than had been the case in Essex or Beds. I still went to several ESAA Championships but it was a few years before I became a team officer in Sussex. I was able to give more time to Sussex Schools AA after I retired in 1994: organising training sessions for the schools' cross-country runners at Ardingly College, and with Martin Bilham at Ambersham. I also helped to update the Constitution and then, as Chairman from 1996 to 1999, I attempted to improve the overall efficiency of the organisation. My view was that although we were all amateurs, we should always strive to act professionally. I continued to carry out a detailed analysis of the team's performance at each ESAA championship, as I had in Essex and Beds.

After I had retired I went to the ESAA Championships with the Sussex Schools team as team officer each year from 1995 to 2005 and we had individual winners every year bar one. Claire Smithson won the discus event four times, twice setting a new championship best performance while Sam Redd won the javelin on three occasions. As in Essex and in Bedfordshire, I had athletes I was coaching in Sussex Schools teams on several occasions, though my only winner was Craig Ivemy in the Intermediate Boys' 3000m event at Nottingham in 2002.

Our usual Sussex Schools team manager, Mark Sheridan, was unavailable in 2001 so I was asked if I would take over as team manager for the summer Track and Field Championships to be held at Exeter. I had never actually been the team manager before, but I accepted the offer and I took the opportunity to hold some relay practices, something Sussex didn't do, unlike Essex and Beds, where the preparation of the relay teams was one of the pre-championship highlights. I can still recall the sessions of relay practice the Essex team officers, including myself, organised at the Ilford AC track where there was a very high standard of coaching and of baton passing. When a relay team I had prepared and trained were about to compete at the English Schools, I know how nervous I got: disappointed when things went wrong or ecstatic if the team made the final or even won. The Essex and Beds team officers were often qualified coaches, so the athletes had excellent training for the relays. So in 2001, as team manager, I arranged to meet some of the Sussex sprinters at the Brighton track for relay practice. This led to an interesting encounter. The mother of one of the Junior Boys was sitting at the front of the stand, and I went to speak with her.

"I'm Wade's mother," she said, referring to the lad who had won the Junior Boys' 100 metres in the County Champs with an excellent performance. "He's more interested in football really, you know."

"Well, we think he could have a future in athletics, as a sprinter," I said. "He was very impressive in the County Schools Champs. Obviously, he has to decide, but just think how difficult it is to get into the top flight as a professional footballer." Wade's mum was listening. I went on, "If he reaches the final at Exeter, which we think he could, he would be in the top eight sprinters in his age group in the country. Is he good enough to become one of the top eight footballers in his age group in England?"

"Yes, I see what you're saying," she said. "We'll just have to wait and see."

Wade Bennett Jackson did make the final of the Junior Boys' 100 metres at Exeter. Not only that, he came 1st! He was the All England Champion, No 1 in the country at his age. And in the next few years, as he developed, he went on to represent Great Britain as a sprinter. The relay practice went OK: I had high hopes that they would do really well at Exeter. It was not to be: my Junior Boys were disqualified in their heat as one runner went off too early.

"Obviously they hadn't been coached well enough!" my friend Dennis would have said!

The Sussex team did very well at Exeter, amassing 146 points, their highest total for years and finishing 3rd among the Group B counties. I had a good team of athletes and good support from the team officers with me. Nevertheless I was quite chuffed. Mark Sheridan returned the following year!

Each year a different county takes on the responsibility of organising the ESAA Cross Country Championships. The ESAA Committee member whose role it was to try to persuade an individual county to do this was my old friend, Derek Hayward. We had been good friends since Essex days. Derek had played a major part in preparing the jumping facilities for the ESAA Track and Field Champs at Chelmsford in 1963. So when he rang me, somewhat out of the blue, early in 2000, because of his current role for ESAA, I had good reason to be apprehensive. As I feared, he asked if I thought Sussex would like to hold the XC Champs in 2002, as London were doing 2000, and Essex were earmarked for 2001.

"We have nobody lined up for 2002," Derek said.

I told him I would get back to him, as this "offer" or "poisoned chalice" would have to be discussed by the Sussex Schools AA Committee. I knew that if Sussex were to put on these Championships, it would very likely fall to me to organise them. And that is what happened!

Once I had told the Sussex Schools AA Committee that I would be willing to do the organising, they agreed that Sussex would do it.

Fine! I did have some idea of what I had agreed to take on.

I had been to many ESAA Cross Country Championships over the years and I went along to the 2000 races held at Parliament Hill Fields, but this time in a different capacity, as I was taking notes and talking to those in control of the different aspects of the organisation. I had become the organising secretary, and stalwart Sussex folk, such as Ray Hopkins and Mike Carrington had willingly agreed to help. Overall control and responsibility is retained by ESAA, whose Championships they are, but it's the local people who do all the work! At PHF I learned a lot from observing what London Schools had done and by talking with Richard England, the London Schools Secretary, and others.

I planned to visit the 2001 Championships to be held in Hylands Park, Chelmsford in Essex, but for the first time ever these could not be held as planned, owing to the outbreak of foot-and-mouth disease. Essex had to put all their plans on hold and agreed to host the Championships the following year. Consequently we put all our preparations back a year as well. Deferring to 2003 gave us more time to prepare.

Our first task was to find a suitable venue. We looked at the advantages and disadvantages of several Sussex racecourses, Goodwood, Plumpton and Brighton, and also the South of England Showground at Ardingly, but the best course, certainly for the runners, and the one that we selected was Stanmer Park, Brighton. It had the added advantage of being easy to access by road. Brighton and Hove City Council and West Sussex County Council were both extremely cooperative and gave us considerable help financially. The University of Sussex, adjacent to Stanmer Park, kindly said we could use their campus for coach and car parking. Changing facilities for 2000 athletes presented a problem, so we decided to have two huge marquees where boys and girls could change for their races.

An important part of the organisation of these ESAA Cross Country Championships is to keep all 45 counties informed of all the arrangements, so they can make their plans, their travelling arrangements for example, and so they can keep their athletes and schools informed. This we did. We sent out preliminary information to all counties early in the Autumn term with further details both before and after Christmas. It also works the other way: each county has to let the local organiser have certain key information, such as their travel details, expected time of arrival, number of packed lunches required and so on. We asked that the forms containing these details be returned three weeks before the event. 29 counties replied on time, eight came a few days after the deadline, four arrived ten days late, one arrived the day before the event and one reply came in on the Monday after the Championships! Two counties never replied at all. This doesn't make the Organising Secretary's task any easier. Presumably these defaulting counties had never organised the event themselves.

The nearby University Sports Centre, where Karen Dunster, Head of Centre, and Paul Newman were a great help, was used for officials, for the press and other media, for storing the 1,000 packed lunches that had been ordered, and for the presentations. Martin Kemp, from Phoenix AC, who knew Stanmer Park very well, agreed to work out suitable courses for each of the six races that would take place on the day, and we sent each county some maps of the course. Every one of our course marshals was experienced and handpicked. We invited local Sussex officials to do the officiating and they were delighted to take part in such a prestigious event. A multitude of other tasks had to be done in the months and weeks leading up to the event, such as carrying out a risk assessment, detailed liaison with the police, St John Ambulance, the RAC, seeking advertisers and sponsors and preparing the programme, booking the catering outlets, ordering the portable toilets, obtaining a public address system and walkie-talkies for key officials and course marshals, plus many more tasks too numerous to detail here. One major issue was arranging security for the site. Because the marquees took so long to put up and take down, our security team was involved overnight on site for eight nights, involving considerable expense. We found hundreds of adult and young volunteers, some to sell programmes, some to greet and escort each visiting county team from the coach park to the ground, which involved a trek through part of the University campus.

The local organising committee met several times on site with ESAA officials to keep the officials informed and satisfied that all was going well. They seemed to be pleased with the preparations being made.

Then came an unexpected exocet! Not long before the day of the Championships we were informed that UK Athletics (UKA) would like to hold their Cross Country 4000m trial races for senior men and women on our course on the same day! Just like that! Although this would involve rearranging the already scheduled timings of the six races, we agreed to this request, as it would give the young athletes a great opportunity to see many of Great Britain's top cross-country runners in action. I showed the UKA representative around the course only to be told that he didn't like the hill that was part of the course Martin Kemp had planned and which had been agreed by ESAA for the schools' races. He thought it was too severe! I had to smile! I said that the Junior Girls were going to run up it, as were all the schools athletes and we certainly weren't going to change the course at this late stage. Reluctantly he agreed and the senior GB men and women managed to cope with the hill. Because we couldn't have the senior athletes changing alongside the schools' runners, separate changing areas had to be found, though I learned that many of the senior runners came changed.

On the day, the major problem was car parking. Officials had their own designated car park. The coaches were all neatly and correctly parked within their appointed area, with athletes and their team managers making their way, escorted, to the changing marquees. Cars were arriving from all directions, but the university had only casually referred to the fact that on the day of the XC Championship it was also a University Open Day! In the spaces we had assigned for spectators' cars were Open Day visitors' cars. Nightmare! To compound the problem, we had been told, from the experience of previous years, to expect 800–900 cars but on the day just under 2,000 arrived! We made use of Brighton University car parks on the Falmer Campus across the A27, which they said we could use in an emergency. We also had to divert cars into Stanmer Park itself, the one thing we had wanted to avoid. Several of us, Ray Hopkins in particular, felt our blood pressure rise, but eventually every car found a space to park and the races got underway.

There were several things on the plus side: thanks to Dave Bedford, London Marathon supported the Championships and spectators found that they could easily follow the runners making their way around the course. The races all went off smoothly and the presentations were made in the Sports Hall, where printed results of all the races were available to county team managers and the public. Sussex won the Group B Boys' trophy and overall (boys and girls combined) Sussex came 3rd in Group B. Two of Sussex Schools' best runners, Craig Ivemy and Charlotte Browning, ran well. Craig, who I was coaching, was very proud, as Sussex Schools' Captain, to be presented with the Group B Boys' trophy, and by Mike Carrington, long-serving official of Sussex Schools, who, sadly, is no longer with us.

Many counties responded to our request for feedback. Of the items on the evaluation sheet, 102 were rated "excellent" or "good", 18 "satisfactory" and nine "could have been better", with one "poor" (packed lunches!). We had many complimentary comments both on the day and subsequently. Both St John Ambulance and several counties said it was very helpful having a doctor present all day, something that doesn't happen at every Schools Cross Country Championship. It had been a mammoth enterprise, certainly not without its headaches, but for me it had been not only stressful but also very enjoyable, a job well done by all concerned. I had lots of help from folk within Sussex, Ray Hopkins in particular. Julie, Robert and Donna all helped, and I was grateful for the contribution they and many others made. Several of us returned to Stanmer Park on Sunday to clear up the mess left in marquees and on the ground generally. The marquees, metal fencing and start and finish scaffolding were all taken down and removed. Officials from Kent Schools AA had been observing all day Saturday as it was their turn to stage the races the following year in Moat Park, Maidstone. We held a "Thank you" buffet at Ardingly College in May for all the officials and helpers.

In due course, as the local, organising Secretary, I attended an ESAA Cross Country Committee meeting, in Chesterfield, and made my report including the financial statement. I think the ESAA officers were pleased with the show that Sussex Schools had put on. One interesting side issue: the Championships had undoubtedly been a great success, so, since then, whenever Derek Hayward rings me or we meet him somewhere, Donna is afraid he is going to ask Sussex, which could be me, to stage another Championships!

Many Great Britain international athletes had their first taste of major competition in the English Schools Championships. The Track and Field Championships is a remarkable event, run with almost military precision, because of the large number of athletes and events to get through in the two days. Over the years ESAA has had to rely on sponsors to support the summer and winter events, but the Championships still go on very successfully each year. Mishaps are rare, though on occasions some of the ESAA officials can be somewhat officious. ESAA plan and promote many inter-school and inter-county competitions and these involve a significant amount of organisation and commitment, nationally and locally. All the work is carried out by amateur, unpaid, volunteer teachers who, by and large, love what they do, though they seldom receive the recognition they deserve.

My life-long involvement with teaching and coaching came together, quite naturally, in Schools Athletics: at school, county and English Schools level. As a team officer at the English Schools Championships, one's role is primarily to look after and support the athletes in the county team, encouraging them to have the confidence to perform at their very best and to enjoy the whole experience. (Rather like teaching A level history really!) Being County Schools Chairman in two counties gave me the opportunity to lead, support and thank all those teachers and others who play such a valuable and often unsung part in encouraging our boys and girls in the sport of athletics. It has been a privilege and immensely enjoyable.

The numbers? I'm sure you will have worked them out, but just in case you haven't: in the summer at the ESAA Track and Field Championships, Essex Schools' athletes run in numbers 27 & 28 (3rd string – if there is one: 29); Bedfordshire Schools' (now Beds & Luton Schools) run in 3 & 4 (3rd string: 5); Sussex Schools' compete in 79 & 80 (3rd string: 81).

30
Coaching after Retirement

There was no time for coaching athletes while I was at Thomas Bennett, though each year when Sports Day was held at the Crawley track and I saw the talent on show, I was frustrated at knowing I hadn't the time to coach. I had always said that if I coached anyone it would mean 100% commitment. So when retirement came in 1994, I decided I would take up coaching again. This involved informing the UK athletics authorities and being CRB checked and receiving my UKA Coaching Pass. During the next ten years, I became a member of the National Coaching Federation, Sports Coach UK and the Athletics Coaches Association of the UK.

I went along to East Grinstead Athletic Club (EGAC) whose base in the summer months was Sackville School, where there was a 400-metre track marked out, but it was very hard, similar to the old cinder tracks. I began helping young athletes along with the other club coaches, chief of whom was John Rogers, a senior coach, now re-designated "level 4", like myself, though his speciality was the sprints – formerly a runner with Woodford Green AC, he said. In April 1996, I met Tony Read, a 14-year-old Imberhorne School pupil. He was quite tall and keen to be coached. As is usual for lads of his age, he had a string of personal bests over the next two years. He competed for Sussex Schools in the 1500m in the ESAA Championships on two occasions, just missing out on a place in the final at Exeter in 1998. Tony ran well on the country and he was also a decent high jumper. Then in October 1998, at the age of 17, he rang to say he wasn't going to continue with athletics! I have since discovered that this was when he first met his girlfriend, Jo, whom he has since married.

John Rogers suspected that I had tried to persuade Tony to join Crawley AC, which, of course, I hadn't. He even went so far as to visit and quiz Tony's parents, who told him it was nonsense to suggest I had tried to persuade Tony to leave East Grinstead AC.

John Rogers and I had an uneasy relationship. I never knew why, though it may have been because my arrival meant that he wasn't the only senior coach at the club. John didn't believe in giving athletes too much work to do, and he thought that the training I gave my middle-distance runners was too severe.

We also fell out over Georgina Hayward, who was a promising young high jumper. I began coaching her in the winter of 1997 when she was age 14 in Year 9 at Sackville School. She improved her technique and competed indoors at Crystal Palace and outdoors for the club and for Sussex during 1998 and into 1999. Her run up, take off and bar clearance all needed further improvement, so I began filming Georgina, in training and in competition. This was common practice and would help me analyse her faults and also enable Georgina to see herself in action. Her mother spoke, not to me, but to John Rogers about this. I was told that Georgina was put off if I watched her jump in competition and she didn't want me to film her either. When her mother raised these points with John Rogers, he agreed with her. He wasn't able to support his fellow club senior coach. I stopped coaching Georgina.

I coached several other athletes at the East Grinstead club. One of the problems for the young athletes was that there were no top class athletes in the club for them to look up to. Nobody with a British vest, no runners, jumpers or throwers to provide inspiration. The club seemed to lack ambition. I suggested that the club produce a monthly or quarterly magazine for members, to keep them up to date with matches and other developments. Why couldn't we have an occasional social for young club members, sausage and mash and a disco, as at Chelmsford in the old days? I argued that the club should have a liaison officer to link with the local schools; I even offered my services for any of these roles, but not one of my suggestions was taken up. Mediocrity ruled.

About this time I met up with Mark Rowland. Originally with Phoenix AC in Brighton, the same club as Steve Ovett, Mark had run brilliantly in the Seoul Olympics in 1988, when he split the Kenyans in the 3000m Steeplechase, finishing in bronze medal position in a time of 8:07.96, still a British Record, which no British runner has since even got near. Mark came along to one of the EGAC circuit training sessions at Imberhorne School, mainly for young athletes. At my suggestion he brought with him his Olympic medal, which naturally impressed the youngsters. Mark was appointed Athletics Development Officer for Sussex AAA in 1996 and two years later he set up The Athletics Youth Foundation (AYF), "to help young people in the pursuit of academic and athletic achievement", by combining coaching in athletics with an academic education. It was based at Lewes Tertiary College. Mark's role was Director of Coaching. As part of the AYF programme to identify promising young athletes, the North Sussex Athletics Academy was launched, bringing together for a series of coaching sessions, a group of some 50 young athletes with potential. Mark asked me to coach the middle-distance group, which met at the Crawley track and at Broadbridge Heath track in Horsham. It was at these sessions that I met Craig Ivemy.

Craig lived in Hailsham and was a member of the local athletics club. He was 14 when I first met him; he was very keen and enthusiastic and had already won the Sussex Youth Cross Country Championship and the Sussex Youth 1500m title and finished 11th in the English Schools U15 Cross Country at Parliament Hill Fields. He was obviously talented and his coach at Hailsham AC felt she couldn't take him further so was pleased when I agreed to coach him. He was a great lad to coach as he always trained very conscientiously and cheerfully. He had a number of notable successes but his running career was blighted and prematurely brought to a close by a series of injuries. I supervised the running he did on the Hailsham recreation ground, in Abbott's Wood nearby, or in Stanmer Park in Brighton. In all of these grass based sessions he often looked impressive. He occasionally trained on the road. He did his track sessions at Lewes or at Broadbridge Heath track at Horsham where he often joined in with Mike East or Hayley Tullett, both GB internationals, who were being coached by Mark Rowland, and here his training times showed what talent he had. Craig also joined them and others in some great sessions on the excellent grass in the grounds of Christ's Hospital School, so he was in good company. He regularly attended Regional Squad Training Days, organised by Neville Taylor and held at St Mary's College, Twickenham, with running sessions usually held in Bushey Park, a short distance away. All the training was geared to produce good racing performances.

Craig Ivemy (at the front, facing us on the left, attacking the big dipper at Merthyr Mawr

I got to know Mark Rowland well. Mark brought all his racing and training experience to his coaching. He and I had many in depth conversations about different aspects of training. Although I had not had anything remotely approaching Mark's success as an athlete, I had been coaching for a long while and Mark recognised this. I formed the impression that while I had a lot to learn from Mark, initially he thought he could learn something from me. It is sometimes felt that all that former athletes do, when they take up coaching, is to reproduce what they did as athletes. Mark was certainly not like this, though he knew there were lessons he had learned from his own racing days that he could apply now that he was coaching.

I was extremely fortunate to have been with Mark as he coached his athletes, British international runners and others. As I came to know him better I saw what made him such a good coach. Quite rightly, he believed in the importance of planning the training and racing programme of his athletes. He kept detailed records and an analysis of each runner's physiological profile as their training developed. He took the technical, scientific aspects of coaching and monitoring athletes to a new level, relying on the expertise of those doing the testing in the laboratory to give him the data on which he could assess his athletes' priorities and determine their training programmes. At trackside he was calm and organised. He had an excellent relationship with his athletes. They had great confidence in him. He helped his athletes prepare for competition by analysing the conditions, the other competitors and their likely racing tactics. It was a privilege to work alongside him. I was not at all surprised when he landed the position of Chief Track Coach at Eugene, Oregon, in the States. Their gain was GB's loss.

Craig finished 6th and 4th in successive years in the National Cross Country as an under 17; his best run in the ESAA XC was as an intermediate when he came 5th at Chelmsford in 2002; this earned him a place in the England Boys' XC team, when he also came 5th in the Schools' International at Derby, a race he should have won. In 2003, he was captain of the winning Sussex Boys' XC team when finishing 10th in the ESAA Senior Boys XC at Brighton. He regularly ran in the Inter-Counties XC and, in 2003, had what Mark Rowland regards as "Craig's best race on the country" when he took the lead with less than a mile to go, broke away from the others, eventually being caught and finishing 3rd. In 2003, he ran for an England XC team in Belgium and finished in 5th place. He was always "there or thereabouts".

His best year on the track was 2002 when he won the English Schools Intermediate Boys' 3000m race at Nottingham and followed this up by winning the AAA U17 3000m in Birmingham. The same year he represented England Schools in Glasgow and the following year he got his Great Britain Youth vest when he ran in the European Olympic Festival of Youth in Paris, finishing a disappointing 5th in the 3000m, because he was too cautious. He ran for GB in an U20 International in Manchester in 2004, came 2nd at Gateshead in the ESAA Senior Boys' 3000m, and achieved his best time for 3000m in a London Grand Prix U20 invitation when he finished 4th, in 8:24.61. The following winter he was thrilled to be going "down-under" to run for GB in the Commonwealth Youth Games in Australia, where, again disappointingly, he couldn't produce his best as his shin problems recurred the day before the Championships.

Going up to Loughborough University should have given him a passport to better training and competition but he spent most of his time there seeing physios, doing cross-training, swimming and running in the pool, having MRI scans and blood tests etc. He saw all the top physiologists such as Nick Webborn at Eastbourne, John Fairley, Neil Black and Mark Buckingham, and diligently did all the exercises he was told to do, but was unable to rid himself of what were essentially biomechanical problems, caused either by the way he ran or by his body make-up, maybe a combination of the two. It was disappointing for Craig and for me as I am sure he had the talent to succeed as a senior athlete. Some of the lads with whom Craig had close races have gone on to do well as seniors, athletes such as Keith Gerrard, who won the English National Cross Country title and Andy Vernon, now a British international on the track and a recent medallist at the European Games. I am sure Craig could have been up with these guys, but it was not to be.

Obviously, the role of the coach is to advise and help the athlete become the best he or she can. This involves planning and supervising training programmes, but it also includes preparing the athlete to race well, to achieve their best possible performance in given races. Some athletes genuinely don't believe they can do well in a particular race. They lack confidence and perhaps as a form of insurance, put themselves down. It is part of the coach's task to help an athlete remove such negative thoughts. Winning at County level or at National level requires a runner to be confident that they are going to be successful. All kinds of strategies can be employed to achieve this. Taking a good look at your opponents and how they are likely to run is a good move. Having a plan yourself is advisable, though you may have to modify your pre-race plan if the race turns out differently from how you expected.

I tried to persuade Craig to visualise himself running the race in the days beforehand. The best example I know of someone who did this was David Hemery, before the 400m hurdles final in Mexico in 1968. He visualised himself in the final, running in lanes 1 to 8, and each time he won! This almost certainly helped him, as he ran brilliantly, setting a new World Record in winning the race. The best example of Craig carrying out a pre-race plan and winning a race after visualising himself winning was the ESAA Intermediate Boys' 3000m at Nottingham in 2002, when he ran away from the rest of the field, Halberg-like, with almost half the race still to run. Unfortunately Craig didn't have the confidence or self-belief to do this on other important occasions.

At about the same time that I was working with Craig, I was also coaching three female runners: Gemma Viney, who lived in Tonbridge, Kent and was a young member of Blackheath Harriers, Emma Satterly, a former Loughborough student, now a PE teacher and a member of Phoenix AC in Brighton, and Iona Robertson, who lived and worked in Oxford and was a member of Headington Road Runners. They were all middle-distance runners who raced on the track, road and cross-country.

Gemma was a fluent and relaxed runner who I thought could have matured into a good senior athlete. We parted company when her boyfriend, Mark, had views about her training, which differed from mine.

Emma found it hard to combine being a PE teacher with a regular training programme. When our coaching relationship ended, she soon found herself another coach. She became an enthusiastic and efficient team manager for Sussex Schools and Sussex AAA.

Iona had asked me to coach her at a coaching day in Oxford to which she had invited Frank Horwill and myself. My role with Iona was mainly advisory, as she enjoyed doing other less conventional forms of running. She had a spell with the SAS in the Borneo jungle being filmed by the BBC and later joined up with the Scottish Triathlon squad.

These three athletes being geographically so spread out also made it difficult for me to see each of them on a regular basis. I was disappointed that I was unable to take any of them further than I did.

Every successful coach will have developed a good athlete-coach relationship with each of the athletes he or she coaches. To do this requires the coach not only to understand the personality of each individual athlete being coached, but also to be aware of his (or her) own personality characteristics. After a race at White City, back in the 1960s, I was standing at track-side with Harry Wilson, later coach to Steve Ovett, and he said to one athlete who he coached and who had just finished his mile race, "That was rubbish!" Harry probably knew he could say that to this particular athlete. Another runner might need to be treated more gently. Some humour can be useful: one lad was always at the back on one of the training courses, so much so that the coach finally said to him, "I've got a stopwatch here, not a calendar!"

The ideal is to have a young athlete who you can take all the way to international and then world class as a senior. It is what Peter Coe did with his son, Sebastian Coe. This development will take many years in which the coach plans and monitors the training programme of the athlete. Regular discussion and assessment between athlete and coach will take place. Each will listen carefully to the other. Along the way, potential and actual obstacles have to be avoided or negotiated, such as injuries, illnesses, school and college obligations, girlfriend/boyfriend distractions, pressures from parents, setbacks and disappointments etc. This runner must also possess outstanding ability or at least outstanding potential. And this potential has to do not only with physical attributes, though these are vital. Mental toughness and self-belief are also sine qua non. What Dyson called "stickability". I remember Mark Rowland telling me that after he had run for Great Britain and therefore become an international athlete, he realised that there was more to do, more steps to take, if he was to become world class. This is something many international athletes don't realise. Those steps are partly mental and partly physical, but they will take you into new and, for you, uncharted territory.

It's a very lucky coach who can find such an athlete and take them from schoolboy or girl to world class. This is something that Tony Minichiello has recently done with Olympic Heptathlon Champion, Jessica Ennis of course. A story is told about Jesse Owens and his coach. After Berlin in 1936, when Jesse Owens had won four gold medals, someone came up to Larry Snyder, Owens' coach, and said, "Oh! You're Larry Snyder, the famous coach of Jesse Owens." And Snyder replied, "No, I'm Larry Snyder, coach of the famous Jesse Owens."

The coach can, and should, plan, guide, inspire, criticise, praise, but it's the athlete who does the work, who has the desire and translates the plan into action, putting in the hours and the miles, who endures the pain, and who is presented with the medals. As Frank Horwill used to say, "An athlete's success is ninety per cent down to the athlete and ten per cent down to the coach." He was referring to senior athletes. For young athletes the ratio would be different, as Frank agreed.

Obviously, such talented athletes are rare. Most of my time as a coach, I have been trying to help athletes become the best that they can, or the best that the other demands on their lives allows. There is satisfaction in this, for the athlete and the coach. As Brendan Hackett says in his excellent book, *Success from within*, "For many, success means winning. But success is about more than winning; it is about being the best you can be." Or, as a former athlete I coached,

Tony Maxwell, recently reminded us (with thanks to Ian Thorpe), "Losing is not coming second; losing is leaving the track knowing you could have done better." However much the coach is able to do for an athlete, it is from within the individual athlete that success will come – from innate ability, hard work and self-belief.

Since retiring I have taken part in some in-service sessions for teachers. One that was held in Chichester involved PE and non-PE teachers from a number of local schools. The theme was the role of teachers in schools in coaching runners, both sprinters and middle-distance runners. I have also contributed to various athletics magazines, writing articles on aspects of coaching for the BMC News, the Coach magazine and other journals many years ago, including Track and Field News. I've kept in touch with Mark Rowland, and it was good to catch up with Mark when he returned to London for the Olympics.

I received a rather strange invitation from UK Athletics in 2002 to apply for the post of National Coach (part time) for High Jump. "To develop Great Britain's next generation of World Class high jumpers...." I suppose I was flattered but as I hadn't done any serious high jump coaching for many years, I can only assume that they were either desperate or all former senior high jump coaches were invited and sent an application form. The position involved specific and wide ranging responsibilities, all for £2,500 pa. I didn't apply.

Sadly, my illness in 2005 has prevented me from further coaching.

Being a Londoner and also an athletics coach, I was thrilled when it was announced (the day before my birthday!) that London was to host the 2012 Olympic Games. Along with thousands of others, I failed to obtain any tickets to watch athletics in the Olympic Stadium, which was disappointing, but the TV coverage was brilliant. Highlights for me were Danny Boyle's superb Opening Ceremony and all the athletics, especially of course, Mo Farah, Jessica Ennis and Greg Rutherford, our gold medallists. Rob and I drove to Cardiff to see a quarter-final soccer match in which Team GB lost to the Republic of Korea on penalties. Donna and I watched some hockey in the Olympic Park and volleyball at Earls Court. Later I went to Greenwich and saw two sessions of wheelchair basketball including the GB team, who were great. I managed to see some Paralympic athletics in the Olympic Stadium. Many thought it was the best Games ever. The volunteer helpers and guides were superb, and London's transport system rose to the occasion, confounding the pre-Games pessimists. Having been to the London Games in 1948, I am really pleased that I was able to see some of the 2012 Games. How difficult will it be to get tickets for Rio in 2016?!

Part 5

Life Goes On

*"It's not the years in your life that count.
It's the life in your years."*
Abraham Lincoln

31

Making the most of Retirement

In September 1994, it was strange not to be going back to school. I think most retirees feel disoriented at first. *What should I be doing?* I asked myself. I needed a rest! Never having been one for gardening or golf, I learned (more) about washing machines and the weekly shopping. Not very exciting, you say, but it was different. "A change is as good as…"

Rather more exciting and constructive, we planned a family holiday for the following summer. In all probability this would be the last holiday we would all have together. We followed up our New England holiday, five years previously, by going to the West Coast of America, and we had an amazing time, travelling over 3000 miles in our rented Buick Century. This was Julie's GCSE year, while Rob was 13 going on 18. Rob navigated brilliantly and with great enthusiasm the whole way, as Donna, having recently had an operation, preferred to sit in the back. Rob and I decided we would try to spot car registration plates from every state in USA. We listed all 50 states and ticked them off one by one. Our route took us south from San Francisco, past Monterey and Carmel, Clint Eastwood country, where I was reminded of *Play Misty for Me*, before we turned inland to the Grand Canyon, Lake Powell and Las Vegas, where we stayed at Caesar's Palace. Temperatures were 110 in the shade in Death Valley and we were advised to turn off the air conditioning otherwise the engine wouldn't cope. Our return to San Francisco took us through the vineyards of the Napa Valley and the Redwoods. We spotted our last State number plate on the last day's driving!

Before heading home, we visited Alcatraz and rode the city tramcars. On our last evening Donna and I took a walk over Golden Gate Bridge, and roughly halfway across we leant on a parapet to look down on a massive ship passing beneath us. I then noticed that exactly where we had stopped a couple had carved their names inside a heart. The names were Donna and Tony! How about that!

GCSE results awaited: we had a mad dash from Heathrow to Julie's school arriving just in time for her to pick up her results; all was well, her results were good, and now Julie had the 6th Form to look forward to. Moving from Bedfordshire to West Sussex in late 1985 had been good for Julie and Robert. As they progressed at school, first at Blackwell Primary, then Sackville, they made many new friends and discovered new interests. West Sussex, though consistently Conservative as a county council, had the good sense to have all their local authority secondary schools fully comprehensive. In East Grinstead, where we lived, both Imberhorne and Sackville were very good schools.

Both Julie and Robert enjoyed sport and music. Julie played hockey, while Rob at first preferred football, playing for the Crawley Town youth team, before trying his hand at hockey. East Grinstead had, and still has, a first class hockey team, and Rob enjoyed the game, playing for his school and the club, then Sussex Schoolboys and having a trial for the South of England team. Rob was an attacking mid-field player in soccer and hockey, making some memorable passes to set up goals for the forwards. He kept up his interest in soccer, followed his Dad and Grandad in becoming a Chelsea supporter, so the family loyalty goes back a long way! "Come on, you Blues!"

Rob: hockey practice   *Rob (front 2nd left) with some of Sackville*
School cricket team

Fortunately, Sackville School, as well as fostering sport, also had an excellent reputation for music. Julie discovered she liked playing woodwind and reached Grade 8 playing jazz saxophone. Rob took up the trombone, initially because next door to us lived Jamie, a few years older than Rob, and he played the trombone. Rob attended the County music school and played with the West Sussex Youth Concert Band, performing in several concerts and travelling to Hamilton, Ontario with the band at age 12. He played to Grade 8, but he could not be awarded this as Grade 5 theory eluded him, despite teacher, Steve Dummer's best efforts. Later with some friends he formed a jazz group, "Jagged Jazz", which played at several local venues, where the young band members could earn themselves some beer money. Julie's and Rob's musical talent can probably partly be traced to my mother, their grandmother. It is said, isn't it, that these things can miss a generation – well they certainly did in my case: my musical talent lies in listening, which I do quite well!

Understandably, neither Julie nor Robert continued playing instruments after leaving school. They had had their fun and enjoyment, and it was time to move on. I do recall taking Rob to a concert at Haywards Heath, where Chris Barber and his band were playing. In the interval, the band members came out to meet the audience, and Rob met Chris Barber.

Rob playing his trombone   Julie practising her saxophone

"What do you play?" Chris Barber asked Rob, aged about 13 at the time.

"Trombone," said Rob, which of course was Chris Barber's instrument.

"Trombone! You're not thinking of taking it up seriously, when you're an adult, are you?"

"I don't know," replied Rob. "I might."

"Oh! You don't want to do that," Chris Barber said with a chuckle, "take up something much easier, like coal mining!"

Julie played hockey for her school and East Grinstead Ladies. After A levels, she went up to Loughborough to read Sociology. She had researched various universities and, after one visit where she met some of the Sociology tutors, she said to me, "I couldn't possibly be taught by those people; they were so dull, so boring."

Loughborough's reputation for sporting excellence was one reason she chose to study there, though you stood no chance of getting into the University hockey team unless you were a current international. Julie played for her hall, Cayley Hall, coincidentally the same hall in which Sally had lived when at Loughborough. Julie didn't have the distraction that afflicts most university undergraduates, looking out for potential partners, being in the right places "to be seen", being dated and trying to cope with all this while studying, because for her three years at Loughborough she had a steady boyfriend back home. She had met Chris while she was in the 6th Form and he visited Julie occasionally at weekends, and their relationship has strengthened as they are now married. At Loughborough Julie made several very good friends with whom she is still in contact. She enjoyed her three years there, had a lot of fun and came away with a First Class Honours degree.

Rob also did well at school, being made Senior Student in Year 11, in which role he represented the school in a number of ways. His work experience at Gatwick was quite memorable. He was assisting passengers on a normal day, keeping in radio voice contact with his supervisor, when the alarms went off. Rob was in a lounge area where there were several wheelchair bound passengers, but he had lost radio contact. Nobody knew what the alarm signified, so Rob decided to take the initiative, to act as he thought best, and moved these people carefully to a place of safety, as he perceived it. Staff in his department at Gatwick were impressed by this and Rob received a commendation. On another occasion Rob was taken by plane on a trip to Bristol and back. At one time he had considered a career in the Air Force but in the end didn't pursue it.

Rob's arrival in the 6th Form coincided with a new Head of 6th Form. From the outset they didn't get on. Mr McIver knew nothing of Rob's record at the school, and he also knew very little about how to relate to 6th form students. Instead of treating them as adults, as the school's brochure proudly claimed, he had them picking up litter from the playground and doing other menial tasks. Rob became disillusioned; his work suffered and, when I gave him the choice: "Work hard towards your A levels or stop wasting your time and everyone else's and leave," he said, "Could you write the letter now, Dad?"

I told him he would enjoy three years at university but he wasn't convinced, so he left school without any A levels, but confident he would do as well as his graduate sister and half sisters, which he has since proved in abundance. One irony was that a year after Rob left school, so did Mr McIver, as the school discovered he wasn't what he claimed to be and shouldn't have been appointed in the first place.

On Rob's 21st, he had a celebratory meal in Brighton, but what followed was an incident that will always stay with me. Approaching midnight, Donna and I drove home in our VW Passat with Julie and Chris in the back. An enjoyable evening was about to turn into disaster. It was pouring with rain as we made our way up the dual carriageway of the A23 away from Brighton. I was driving carefully, well within the 70-mph limit because of the atrocious weather and road conditions. I had only had one drink in Brighton, a small beer at the start of the evening. Suddenly, in my headlights, I saw a figure immediately in front of the car. I had no chance to take any kind of evasive action. I braked but the car hit the man, who shattered the windscreen and then very nearly came through it, but was flung on to the grass verge to the side of the road. Shaken, I stopped the car. Another car halted just ahead of me. Donna was in a dreadful state of shock. Chris said he would walk back to see if the person was alive or dead. As a fireman he was used to dealing with the results of road traffic accidents. He came back to say the man was definitely dead. I was sat rooted to my seat. I couldn't believe what had just happened.

The police soon arrived. I was asked to get out of the car. I was breathalysed and made a statement. I explained that this person had been walking in the middle of the inside lane. Yes, I explained, he had been walking away from us in the direction of Crawley. The driver of the other car that stopped confirmed that he had seen what had happened. He said that I had stood no chance of avoiding the man. My VW was in quite a mess, certainly not driveable, so Chris's dad, Richard, who lived not far away, kindly came and gave us a lift home. The police impounded my car anyway. An ambulance took the dead man away.

Of course I felt dreadful that I, or the car I was driving, had killed someone, though my feelings of guilt were lessened by the fact that nobody could say it was my fault. A police sergeant later told me that the dead man was well known to the police and other authorities in Brighton. It transpired that earlier that evening he had been kicked out of the hostel where he had been living, because he had taken drugs into the hostel. The assumption was that he had decided to walk to Crawley where he had friends. But why walk in the middle of the A23? Had the dead man been a family man with a wife and children, I know I would have felt far worse. The police sergeant, knowing the man's record, said, "You have done a favour to the women of Sussex."

I attended the inquest where I answered the coroner's questions. The dead man had apparently come from the North of England. His mother was at the inquest and shouted "Murderer!" at me, which upset those of my family who were there. The police took no further action as far as I was concerned. My car had been found to have no faults. Driving past the spot where the accident happened always brings it all back.

My old Oxford college, St Catherine's, periodically holds a reunion, called a Gaudy, for alumni from selected years and, in 1997, I returned and met up again with many of my former college mates.

A relaxed Ian McNaughton, Barri Bishop, Colin Barham and me

At the Gaudy: Norman Goddard, Alan Wortley and me

With Donna

Since then, for a few days most summers, Alan, Barri, Norman and I have travelled up to the Lake District to stay with Dr Ian Davidson, known to us as Scott, who lives in a delightful old cottage, conveniently close to an excellent pub, "The Blacksmith's Arms", and with views of the beautiful Cumbrian hills. When we all get together it is as though no time has elapsed at all. We appreciate his hospitality. Our cups are often full, we eat well and the conversation ranges from the nostalgic to the contemporary. Scott takes us to many of the local hostelries, which he has known all his life, and he often drives us out to one of the lakes or into the hills or down the coast. As you might expect, there are plenty of amusing incidents. Recently Scott took us to Millom, where we walked over the sands stretching out towards Haverigg.

Then he said, "Let's go to the harbour." *That'll be good*, I thought, *small fishing boats nestling close to the harbour wall, fishermen busy with nets, lots of crying gulls – the usual sights and sounds of a harbour.* Not a bit of it! As Scott's car pulled up and we all got out, he made straight for "The Harbour"! The local pub! They did a good pint and excellent sandwiches, but it wasn't the harbour I had envisaged. That's Scott for you. We value these friendships, which have survived, with some minor interruption, for over half a century.

Norman, Barri, Scott, Alan and myself at one of our "get togethers"

Since my retirement Donna and I have been fortunate to enjoy several holidays abroad. We first went to Africa in 1997, when we stayed in Johannesburg with Martin and Gerri and their children, Howard and Caitlin. Martin and I are grandsons of sisters. Their lovely house had barbed wire on the perimeter walls, the house and main gates were alarmed and for additional security they had a contract with a private security firm, all because of the high level of crime. What a shame that South Africa, such a beautiful country should have such social problems, so much poverty and crime. Sadly, quite recently, Martin has died. With Howard now married and Caitlin completing her medical studies, Gerri has moved into a smaller home.

From Jo'burg we made our way to Cape Town by rail, not on the expensive Blue Train, by the regular service with overnight sleeper, which was a great experience and a brilliant way to see the changing countryside. From Cape Town, a city we like very much, we drove along the beautiful Garden Route to Port Elizabeth in our hired VW Polo. Here we met Heather and her mother, Sheila, and visited Addo Elephant Park, where we learned that cars must give way to dung beetles on park roads. We have returned to Africa several times. It's what they say Africa does, "It calls you back!"

We first saw "The Big Five" at Mala Mala, a private game reserve close to Kruger National Park. It was on this holiday that we drove up into the Drakensburg Mountains, passing native villages and several dead animals by the roadside, only to realise, when we were miles from anywhere, that neither of us had brought our mobile phones. It was just as well we didn't run into any trouble and our hired VW was reliable.

The Masai Mara is a very special place for us: the vast open plains and the beautiful wild animals are simply stunning. On one visit we were staying in a safari holiday lodge and one evening we were walking back to our apartment after our meal and noticed a herd of zebra strolling about on the campus. We were told they would not harm us if we gave them a wide berth, which we did. We also avoided their smelly "calling cards". Back in our room, Donna and I soon went to bed, eagerly anticipating tomorrow's activities. In the middle of the night we were woken by a loud banging noise. We thought some animals might be investigating the construction site next door. Then we realised the banging was on our front door. We thought it best to lie low and after a while the banging stopped. In the morning we learned that some lions, attracted by the malodorous zebra, had wandered on to the site. It was a lion that had been banging on our apartment door! We agreed that it had been a good decision not to open the door!

On the last occasion we visited Masai Mara, we were privileged to be present as the wildebeest made their migratory crossing of the Mala River in their thousands. We had seen this many times on TV, but to be there and witness such an amazing feat, and to film and video it, was awesome. Seeing all the wonderful animals in their wild and natural environment is very humbling: you have to remind yourself that you are in their world, an intruder almost, certainly a respectful visitor.

In Kenya one year, Donna felt quite ill and a doctor was called. He spoke very good English, diagnosed gastro-enteritis and prescribed antibiotics. Donna soon felt better. We were returning from Africa by plane. It was the middle of the night. Donna went off to the toilet. After what seemed a very long time, Donna hadn't returned. I thought I would go and see if she was all right. I found both toilets unoccupied. *Strange*, I thought. There was no sign of Donna. *Where was she? Had she sat down somewhere else? Had she got off? People don't just vanish on aeroplanes – do they?*

As I puzzled the options, a steward said, "Can I help you, Sir?"

"Well, I'm looking for my wife," I said.

At that moment, I saw a pair of feet on the ground protruding from the stewards' quarters. I walked closer and there was Donna, lying on her back on the floor. She spoke and was obviously unwell but seemingly not seriously so. An announcement was made (at 2 a.m., when most passengers were asleep), "Is there a doctor on board?"

Within a minute, three doctors arrived! The first was a lady, from the northeast of England, who examined Donna and decided she was probably dehydrated, but nothing worse. "Drink all this water before we land and you'll feel better." This she did. Apparently, Donna had collapsed when entering the toilet. It had been a strange episode for both of us.

Paul Dulac, who had spent nearly a year with us at Houghton Regis before returning to his work as a Schools' Superintendent in Massachusetts, had always wanted to work abroad.

"Would you write a reference for me, Tony, if I applied for a position abroad?" he asked me.

"Of course, Paul. What job and what part of the world do you have in mind?"

"Africa, maybe, or somewhere in Asia. Probably not Europe. I'll see what comes up."

Sometime later I received a request to say how suitable I considered Dr Paul Dulac would be for the post of Director of The International School in Beijing. Which is how Donna and I found ourselves on the way to China in 1999 to stay with Paul and Becky in their apartment in Beijing, as Paul got the job! My recommendation must have helped, hence our invitation!

Beijing: what an amazing place! We found Capitalism was well developed in this huge Communist city; Donna's favourite place was the Pearl Market, close to the huge and somewhat intimidating Fish Market. We enjoyed bargaining with the street market-stall holders by means of a pocket calculator! One evening, we had tickets for a Chinese concert of music and acrobatics, but first we needed to eat. In the restaurant we chose, the menu was in Chinese and none of the waitresses spoke English. A line of six waitresses stood, in very short green skirts, close to our table, as if on guard but smiling in unison, observing our efforts to eat the very unappetising dish we had ordered. What we needed was some rice.

Suddenly a different lady appeared at our table, looked at us and at what we had been trying to eat, and said, "Wouldn't you like some rice?"

We left soon after, still hungry. In the theatre next door, there was a small café, where we each devoured a banana split. The Chinese acrobats were amazing!

It was quite late when Donna and I arrived back, by taxi, to Paul and Becky's apartment. Quietly, so as not to disturb Paul and Becky whose bedroom was on the 1st floor, we raided their kitchen, as we were still very hungry. Feeling better, we locked and bolted the front door and went quietly up to our room on the 2nd floor. It had been an eventful evening for us and we were glad to climb into bed.

A short while later I said to Donna, "Are you sure Paul and Becky are in? We've locked the front door. Suppose they're still out."

"Oh! You could be right," Donna said.

"You'd better go and see if they are in, hadn't you?"

"What? You mean..."

"Yes. Go down and have a look in their bedroom, see if they are there! It's better if you go."

"OK, I suppose..."

Donna went quietly down the stairs, as she didn't want to wake them, and with some trepidation, peered round their bedroom door and into the room. They weren't there! Donna came back upstairs to give me the news.

"Paul and Becky aren't in yet, and we've locked and bolted the front door! They won't be able to get in!"

We quickly made our way down to the kitchen floor when we heard what sounded like Paul and Becky approaching. The front door was quickly unlocked and unbolted and, yes, there were Paul and Becky, back from their evening out! We told them the whole story, which they found hilarious. What an adventure! On top of everything else that night!

Paul's position as Director of the International School gave him the services of a driver, and Paul loaned him to us for a couple of days. He took us to the Great Wall, where we walked for quite some way, while contemplating with a sense of awe the amazing geography and history of China. We visited temples where devout Hindus were able to pray undisturbed by the authorities. There had been some relaxation, we were told. We also attended a performance at Paul's school of *Grease*. It was a great week and over far too quickly.

Visiting Beijing – we walked part of the Great Wall.
Donna took the photograph

When Robert was finding his way after leaving school, he worked abroad for a couple of summers for Mark Warner, first on the Greek island of Lemnos and the following year in Punta Licosa, south of Salerno, in Italy, where he organised and supervised sports activities for holiday makers. Donna and I took the opportunity to visit him and spend time enjoying each location. We love Italy and have had several holidays there. Rob and Clare chose to have their wedding at Bellagio, on the shores of Lake Como, which was magical.

Rob's and Clare's wedding at Bellagio, Italy

Donna was born in Canada, and we have visited Vancouver and the Canadian Rockies, Toronto and London, Ontario, in each of which, some of Donna's relations live. Donna's father, Melton, was in the Canadian Forces, and we visited his grave in Toronto. Donna took her mother, in her 80s, to the Rockies, and they went up in a helicopter to view the Rockies from above. Quite recently Donna and I had a trip which began in Chicago, took us to Memphis and Nashville, where I sat at the piano in Elvis' recording studio, and then on to listen to jazz in Bourbon Street in New Orleans. It doesn't get much better than that…

In Europe, in addition to Italy and our annual visit to Switzerland to see my daughter, Sally, and her family, we have enjoyed visiting Prague. As we were crossing the Charles Bridge, we heard an old man playing the Harry Lime theme from *The Third Man* on the zither, one of my favourites. Recently we were fortunate that our few days in Prague coincided with a memorable performance of *Nabucco* at their magnificent Opera House.

Our first cruise, organised by Saga, took us to the cities and ports of the Baltic. A more recent cruise took us from St Petersburg down the rivers and through the lakes and locks to Moscow, where I fulfilled another ambition by visiting Red Square. It was extremely hot so I didn't join the queue to visit Lenin's tomb, but that omission gives me a reason to return! Most recently, we explored the coast and fjords of Norway with Hurtigruten, travelling into the Arctic Circle as far as the Russian border.

Now that Donna has retired too, her main hobby is photography, and a few years ago she joined a photographic safari to Alaska, where she photographed grizzly bears catching salmon in Katmai National Park. The group got quite close to the bears, who weren't interested in humans, as they had come for the salmon. Donna has always wanted to see polar bears, so last year she went on another trip, organised by the same US company, Joseph Van Os, this time to the Arctic, north of Longyearbyen, on board an old Russian trawler, to photograph the wildlife, including polar bears. She had an amazing experience and took some great photos. Next year she is planning to visit Antarctica. Wow!

Donna's photograph of grizzlies catching salmon in Katmai, Alaska

Donna's photo of polar bears in the Arctic, in Svalbard

32
Hospitals: fun places?

It wasn't fun being in hospital over Christmas when I was 12, but all the children brightened up when nurses came into our ward carrying a large cooked goose, which two surgeons, suitably gowned, proceeded to carve in front of us. And, in that same hospital, it was no fun for the nurse who knocked a phial of penicillin off a trolley onto the floor of the ward, where it shattered, as penicillin was then a new and expensive wonder drug in short supply: the poor girl disappeared in tears.

Lying on my back in a hospital bed in November 2005 for the best part of two weeks, unable to move my left leg at all for the first week, certainly wasn't fun either. One night I even wondered whether I would ever walk again. As I lay in bed, wide awake, I could not move my legs at all. I began to panic. It was 2 a.m. when a young nurse came and reassured me that I would be fine. Being admitted to hospital on a Friday wasn't a good plan either, as all investigations had to wait until Monday. Worse still, doctors and consultants couldn't find out what had occurred to bring about my loss of mobility below the waist. I still had feeling in my legs, which the doctors said was a good sign. After a plethora of tests, including an ECG, blood tests, a brain scan, several CT and MRI scans, a lumbar X-ray and a lumbar puncture, the specialists concluded I had suffered a spinal thrombosis, caused, they later discovered, by a slight tear in one of the inner walls of the aorta, and resulting in damage to the central nervous system, which is why feet and legs, lower back, bladder and bowel wouldn't work properly. In week two, an excellent physiotherapist forced me to get out of bed and hobble about on crutches, and I went home soon after. Rehab sessions at the Queen Victoria Hospital in East Grinstead helped me regain some mobility and balance. The whole spinal thrombosis experience plus the two weeks in hospital I wouldn't recommend, but there were some lighter moments.

Wednesday, five days after I had been admitted, it is 7 a.m. A tall, young, fair-haired nurse approaches my bed. She is carrying a large sheaf of papers.

"I've come to prepare you for your operation."

"What operation is that?" I ask, surprised.

"To do with your prostate. You're having your stones removed."

"I haven't been told about any operation."

"You must have been – I've got the paperwork here." This was said somewhat dismissively as if I was not quite able to remember. *These older patients …* She moved closer.

"But I haven't got stones. Are you sure you have the right person?" I said.

Nurse looks again at her paperwork and checks the name.

"Oh! I'm so sorry," she says. "Your name is similar." (That's all right, then!) Nurse leaves me and walks across to a bed on the other side of the ward and starts the conversation with another patient. Good job I was awake and alert.

One morning in the second week, just before breakfast, I was sitting up in bed as the nurse came round the ward with the drugs trolley. The lid opened rather like a bureau lid. She stopped by the patient two beds along to the right from me. She turned towards the patient and said, "Is it the little red ones you have, Mr Walker, or the little white ones?" Well, you have to be sure, don't you!

Not so amusing was the occasion when a nurse began to give a patient opposite me in the ward some breakfast. Above this patient's bed was clearly written, "NIL BY MOUTH". Fortunately, a staff nurse saw what was happening and took the nurse, and the breakfast, away. The nurse was new and her English wasn't good, I was told.

These incidents, which, while amusing, were also, shall we say, unfortunate, were the exceptions. East Surrey NHS Hospital looked after me very well, both then and on the subsequent occasions I have had recourse to return. During my two weeks' stay, I chatted with a young lady who came in each morning to sweep and clean the ward. I learned she was from Prague and had a Chemistry degree. I guessed she was in her mid 20s; she had a nice smile and was very polite.

"I want to work in a hospital," she said.

"But why this? Why cleaning?" I enquired.

"It is all they would give me," she said. "I would like to train and become a nurse or a doctor but I need money now to live." Her English was excellent. I told her I understood. Each day she came. She was a very efficient cleaner of the ward. I wonder if she ever managed to become qualified or whether she is still cleaning.

I also had a young nurse arrive at my bedside one morning to take my blood pressure etc. She said, "You were my Headmaster, weren't you?" Indeed I was. Whether I received better treatment as a result of this recognition, I'm not sure.

While I was lying in bed in hospital, I was visited by a succession of doctors, some of them specialists, who frequently asked me, "How are you feeling?" I found this interesting. Doctors and nurses with all their knowledge and experience, and despite all the modern techniques and sophisticated equipment, still ask that question, because they need to know what the patient is experiencing in terms of pain, tiredness, feeling better etc. The reason I found this interesting was because that is what I regularly did as a coach, when my athletes were training. As a coach, I could see what the athlete looks like, how well they are running, how fast etc., but I need to ask, "How do you feel?" to get the complete picture. Just as the coach will tell the athlete to "listen to your body" and don't ignore what it is telling you, the doctors and nurses who came to see me told me what I should do and what I shouldn't do until I was a bit better. So a doctor-patient relationship is not that different from a coach-athlete relationship. The expert needs feedback from the patient or athlete for the partnership to be effective.

Leaving hospital after two weeks, I was soon able to resume my History teaching, though for a short while my students from Michael Hall came to my house for their lessons. Carys even visited me in hospital as she had an exam imminent, so we had a lesson in a day room! Gradually my legs recovered enough mobility to enable me to walk, though with a stick.

The following April I had a replacement right hip inserted at Gatwick Park Hospital. In July I returned to Gatwick Park, a private hospital, for an operation to reduce the size of my prostate. In bed after the operation, I had my legs held down by straps at night to prevent movement, which could have been damaging. So if I needed to get out of bed in the night to visit the toilet, I was told to "press the red button". I woke at 2.30 a.m., needing the loo, so I rang for the nurse to come to "release" me. All remained quiet. At 2.45 I pressed the button again, as my need was increasing. No one came. What was I to do? I gave it one final shot, and at 3 o'clock the nurse came, undid the clamps holding my legs and I walked carefully, but with some urgency, to the toilet. It was the same West Indian nurse who had put the clamps on the previous evening.

"I rang you half an hour ago," I said to the nurse. "You took all that time to respond. Suppose it had been an emergency," I said. "What then?"

"Oh! If it had been an emergency, I would have come sooner," she said. Right!

I am fortunate that the long-term damage from the spinal thrombosis wasn't worse. My consultants have been excellent, as has the osteopath who has regularly treated my back; the acupuncturist, plus physiotherapy and hydrotherapy treatments, and the medication, have all contributed. Although it was the tear in the aorta that caused the problem, the heart has only needed attention twice. I was told when I had a quadruple heart by-pass in 1993 that it would last for 15 years, and so it turned out. My angina returned in 2008, so after seeing consultants again and having an angiogram, I was given stents by Dr Swanton at the London Heart Hospital. My cardiology consultant at ESH, Dr Banerjee, said, "Keep exercising; it's better for your heart than any medication."

While I was in hospital in London, recovering from having the stents inserted, I glanced at my records and saw that a trainee nurse had calculated I was "seriously obese"; her calculations were correct, but she had measured my height as 1.32m i.e. 4'4"! Obviously she wasn't in the habit of observing her patients. Even when this gave her a BMI score for me of 45.96, which is seriously obese, she didn't query it. My correct BMI at that time was 24.97, based on my correct height of 1.79m. Let's hope that the mistakes these people make are not any more serious.

33
Families

Maybe it's because I'm a Londoner
That I love London so;
Maybe it's because I'm a Londoner
That I think of her wherever I go.

I was brought up as a Londoner – not a Cockney, as I never heard the sound of Bow Bells! London was my home from before I went to school until adulthood. I spent many teenage years exploring and enjoying the sights and sounds, yes, the smells too, of London. Red buses, noisy underground trains, black cabs, famous buildings, streets and parks, I loved them all. For years, I felt part of a great family that was made up of Londoners. Living in London and, later, close to London, I have always regarded as a privilege. In addition to all the historic buildings, museums, churches and other places, there are so many advantages to living near London, not least the theatres and concert halls where one can experience the thrill of superb performances by the world's leading artists.

I have already said how I went to Sadler's Wells while at school, just round the corner from the Angel. For years, I have enjoyed operas at Covent Garden and the London Coliseum, home of the English National Opera. *La Bohème* remains my favourite, though several others run it close. As for orchestras and conductors, my mother was a fan of

Adrian Boult and Malcolm Sargent, the one, austere and masterful, the other, precise and painstaking. I saw Adrian Boult conduct one Beethoven symphony at the Royal Albert Hall without once opening the score in front of him. My mother liked the comment she claimed was attributed to Malcolm Sargent, who interrupted an orchestra rehearsal one day, as he was seeking competence if not perfection, to say to one of the lady cellists, "Madam, you have between your legs an instrument capable of giving pleasure to thousands, and all you can do is sit there and scratch it."

I saw both of these great conductors in my youth, but the conductor I have come to admire most is Simon Rattle. He has such an air of authority. At one of the promenade concerts at the Royal Albert Hall, the orchestra sat ready and waiting, the wait seeming overly long. Perhaps the conductor wasn't quite ready. The audience also waited. At last, Simon Rattle came out to the usual tremendous applause, took his place on the rostrum, and then stood for what seemed ages, until there was total quiet throughout the Hall – literally complete silence – before raising his baton and beginning the symphony. Patience, timing, control: perfection.

I remember two amusing incidents in London theatres: many years ago I was fortunate to see Sammy Davis Jnr. He was his usual brilliant best. He began to sing,

> *"Pack up all my cares and woe*
> *Here I go*
> *Singing low*
> *'Bye 'Bye, Brown bird."*

The audience let out a collective gasp of surprise.

Sammy Davis stopped and said, "Well, you know how sensitive I am … being a short, black, one-eyed Jewish boy!" Laughter filled the theatre.

The other occasion was at the Royal Albert Hall where there was to be a performance of Khachaturian's violin concerto, which I love. Just before the start of the concert, the audience was told that unfortunately the violinist had been taken ill, but at short notice they had found a replacement, James Galway, who would perform the concerto on the flute. Gasps of surprise and disappointment were heard, and I for one was sceptical, not knowing what to expect. We need not have worried. James Galway's performance, in what is a difficult yet beautiful concerto, was superb and he received loud and prolonged applause and was called back several times. He asked if the audience would like an encore, whereupon, to a rapt and silent hall, he played "Danny Boy". More cheers and applause followed, when suddenly from the Upper Circle, timing her moment, a woman with a very Irish voice cried out, "God Bless Yer." It still brings tears to my eyes.

A more recent and very memorable London theatre performance I attended was Patrick Stewart and Ian McKellen in *Waiting for Godot* by Samuel Beckett. I had seen this play when I was in my 20s and found it hard to understand. The second time, nearly 60 years later, it remains something of an enigma, but what performances! Actors at the height of their powers – an amazing theatrical experience!

I have many memories that are London based. In July 1951, when I was in the 6th Form at Owen's School, I happened to be walking along in front of the National Gallery, when I saw a small crowd of people gathered around a car that had stopped by the kerb in Trafalgar Square. Being inquisitive, I went over. The car owner had the car radio on and everyone was listening to the commentary on the fight at Earls Court between British boxer, Randolph Turpin and Sugar Ray Robinson for the World Middleweight Title. We all listened intently, cheering when Turpin landed a good blow. We kept shouting and saying, "Come on, Randy!" as if he could hear us. When the fight ended and the MC announced that Randy had won and taken Sugar Ray's World Title, we all clapped and several of the crowd went across to the pub, no doubt to celebrate. I remember that occasion vividly.

My other notable memory was of a state funeral. The procession was making its way slowly up Whitehall to the sombre sound of slow beating drums, horses' hooves clip-clopping on the tarmac and occasional barked military orders. I was standing on the pavement at the top of Whitehall, near Admiralty Arch not far from Trafalgar Square. Where I was the crowd was about four deep. I can picture it all and hear the sounds to this day. Suddenly, interrupting the near silence of the occasion, from a top floor window came the sound of Gracie Fields singing, "*Now is the hour, for us to say goodbye...* "We all looked up and there she was, at the window, and somehow, her singing that particular song seemed very appropriate. It's another London occasion, a very poignant moment, forever inscribed on my memory.

Now on to proper families! Having obtained their degrees, my eldest daughters, Sally and Jo started work. Sally took a break after Loughborough to recover from the illness that had put her in hospital. She spent much of the spring and summer of 1991 working abroad for Mark Warner. She was recuperating, earning money, gaining experience, confidence and independence and having a great time. On her return to the UK she thought she would make use of her Mathematics and train to become a chartered accountant with KMPG. It was a mistake: she hated it. Sally remembers a visit I paid to her in her London flat, when she was agonising about what she should do. She wanted my advice. Apparently I said, "I think you've already made up your mind." She says, "I guess I just needed confidence to make my decision." She left KMPG and, soon after, joined Dunnhumby, where she used her computing skills working on data analysis and became a Managing Consultant.

Jo thought she wanted to teach, so she spent a year in schools, including a spell at Thomas Bennett, to get the feel of being a teacher before embarking on a PGCE Primary Course at De Montfort University in 1995. Jo taught in Milton Keynes; then, in 2000, she married Rob, who she had originally met among the peas and carrots in a local supermarket, while doing part-time jobs. It was at their wedding that Sally met Mark, whom she married four years later. Rob and Mark had been at Westcliff High School together, Rob coming from Canvey Island, where he and Jo were married, and Mark from Leigh-on-Sea where Sally had grown up.

Both now have families of their own. With Rob, Jo has moved about, living and teaching for a while in Scotland. Jo and Rob's first child, Ethan, was stillborn, which, of course, was a tremendous and tragic blow for them both. Jo has since had two more children, Molly and Reuben, and lives near Shrewsbury where she teaches, and

Jo with her dad

Sally with her mum, Penny

where Donna and I try to visit as often as we can. Sally has two girls, Zoe and Neve, and she and Mark live in Switzerland, just outside Zurich, where the girls have the advantage of speaking and learning two languages as they grow up. Donna and I visit each year before Christmas, and Sally usually comes over to the UK at some time during the year.

My first wife Penny's family were lovely. Her dad was from Kirkby Lonsdale and when I knew him, before he retired, he worked in the Visual Aids department for Essex Schools in Chelmsford. He was a great guy with a grand, Northern sense of humour. One rather irritating neighbour used to visit their house and regularly outstay their welcome, so Ron Gardner would hold up and read The Times to block out any visual or verbal contact. When watching the weather forecast, he often said, "Fist and Mog again!"

Penny's mother, Marjorie, was lovely, and always made me most welcome. She could be very understanding. Early one evening, before we were engaged, Penny came round on her bicycle to the flat where I was living in Chelmsford for a bite to eat. One thing led to another and we realised, too late, that it was too dark for Penny to cycle home, so I took her home in my car. It had been nearly midnight, so next day I felt I owed her mother an apology.

"I'm so sorry to have kept Penny out so late yesterday. I do apologise."

"Oh! That's all right. It's surprising how the time flies when you're having fun!" All said with a smile. Very understanding.

The Gardners had a little dog, a poodle, called Tuppence, after Penny of course!

Penny has an older brother, Rick, once a good triple jumper, and a younger brother, Anthony, who had a dreadful accident some years ago. Driving home down the M11 late at night, he collided with a large stationary object in the middle lane. It was a trailer that had become detached from the rest of some showground apparatus. The accident has left him permanently disabled, having to be looked after by a team of nurses in his specially adapted bungalow. Such a tragedy for a young man. Penny visits him each week. She has not remarried following our divorce and still lives in the house she and I bought in the 1960s. We are on good terms and see each other from time to time. After all we do share two daughters and four grandchildren.

Donna's mother, Phyllis, met and married Melton who was serving in the Canadian Forces, so she became a (Canadian) GI bride. Donna and her older brother, Owen, were born in Toronto. While in Canada, Phyllis contracted poliomyelitis, and had to return to the UK with her family. With Phyllis recovering, Melton went back to Canada to sell up, returning to England in the summer of 1953. For whatever reason, towards the end of the summer he vanished, leaving

Phyllis with very little, except a new baby, Norma, born towards the end of the year. Phyllis and her three young children lived on her parents' farm until she was able to purchase a small terraced house in Waterloo Place in Tonbridge. Melton had returned to Toronto and in effect the marriage was over.

When I first met Donna, in 1975, she told me about her early life on her grandparents' farm and being brought up by her mother on her own in Tonbridge. She also said that her father, whom she hadn't really known at all, had just died. Donna's situation was not unlike my own, therefore. Hardly any knowledge of our respective fathers, brought up by our mothers, though there were differences. I had had a stepfather and my mother had told me absolutely nothing about my father. Donna's mother never had a partner or remarried after her husband died, and she spent a lot of her children's early years denigrating their father, blaming him for the collapse of her marriage.

When we got to know each other better, Donna told me she would like to find out more about her father and the Harding family in Canada. Her father, Melton, had been one of eleven. One of his brothers, Stuart, one of Donna's uncles, lived in Toronto with his wife, Eileen, and close by were two of their children, Mark and John, with their families. Another son, Robert, lived on the other side of Canada in Vancouver. Donna was keen to go to Canada to meet them all. This we did in 1990, staying with Stuart and Eileen, as described earlier. Phyllis was none too keen that her daughter was making friends with the family of her former husband, but Donna wanted to discover the truth behind some of the stories she had been fed and grown up with, and she wanted to meet and bond with other members of her father's family. It was no great surprise to find that the Hardings were a great bunch. Donna and I have been back several times and we learned that there were two sides to the story and that Melton was not the complete villain he had been painted.

Our two children, Julie and Robert, get on well with Sally and Jo, their half-sisters, especially as they all now have children of their own. They have visited each other and they communicate regularly.

Sally and Jo now also have a very good relationship with Donna, their dad's second wife. Julie works in recruitment, specialising in recruiting Human Resources managers in the South of England. Quite often she's in the gym. Her husband, Chris, a fireman with Surrey Fire Brigade, plays football and golf and supports Chelsea too!

Julie's and Chris's wedding in Sussex

Julie's work has been interrupted of course by the arrival of Isla, now 4, and more recently, Lucas. Isla is lovely: feisty, intelligent and loving. Donna and I have recently moved to Horsham, so as grandparents, living nearby, we have looked after Isla quite a lot. Their second baby, Lucas, was diagnosed before birth with a hole in his heart. The specialists wanted to delay the essential operation until Lucas was older and stronger, but at five weeks old there was an emergency and his operation was brought forward. One week after being admitted to the Evelina Children's Hospital in London, Lucas had a five-hour operation to deal not only with the hole in the heart but also leaking heart valves. It was a very stressful time for everyone. Lucas survived his operation and has progressed well. As I write this, he is 2 and Donna and I have been looking after him once a week, as we did Isla, so that Julie could return to work. He is a very cheerful and loving little boy, often smiling. Chris recently ran the London Marathon to raise money for Evelina Children's Hospital. Together with a golf tournament Chris organised, he will have raised a considerable sum of money for ECHO, thanks to all the generous sponsors.

Rob and Clare have Sophie, who is a loveable, thoughtful little girl, now 3 years old. After having several different jobs, Rob began working at Keysource in Horsham ten years ago. Keysource is a company that designs, builds and manages data centres for organisations and businesses throughout the UK. Rob has been instrumental in the development of Keysource and he has recently been made a director of the company, which, of course, brings a lot more responsibility and work. The company is looking to expand, perhaps abroad. Before they were married, Clare's work involved looking after young children, so she is ideally suited to care for Sophie and for their most recent baby, Jack. All my grandchildren are special to me of course, but I was delighted when Rob and Clare had a little boy. As my daughter, Jo, said in her text to me, "The Elder name lives on!" Donna and I often see Sophie and Jack, as Rob's family, like Julie's, live only a short distance from us. As I write, Jack has just had his first birthday. I now have eight grandchildren! As Rob said, "You only need three more and you'll have a football team!" I asked if he was volunteering! … His expression gave me my answer!

Donna and I have had some good holidays in Europe, at first with the children to places such as Val Andre in Brittany, then later to Crete and Cyprus. More recently, without children, we've been to other parts of Europe. Normally these holidays have gone without a hitch, but there has been the occasional hiccup. On one occasion we caught Eurostar at Ashford, but found that the seats we had reserved were occupied by two young ladies.

"Excuse us, but you are sitting in our seats."

"Oh! Sorry, but we sat here because two men were sitting in the seats we had booked."

"Well, you should have asked them to move. You can't sit in seats

Julie and Robert with Mum and Dad

Our "Horsham" grandchildren: (left to right) Sophie, Jack, Lucas and Isla

we have reserved."

A steward appeared and spoke to the two guys.

"We have tickets that show we are in the correct seats," they said.

At this point, the train began to move out of Ashford Station. The steward examined their tickets. "Yes, Sir," the steward said, "but your tickets are for Brussels; this train is going to Paris." The Brussels train had left its platform a few minutes earlier and our train was already on the move. They had been in the right seats but on the wrong train! Presumably, when the train reached Paris, they found a connection to Brussels.

We've twice had a similar experience. One was on an aeroplane when we were merely spectators. A few rows in front of us, a married couple found two men sitting in their seats. After a somewhat heated discussion it turned out that the two men had been allowed to board the wrong plane. This time: correct seats – wrong plane! They were ejected by embarrassed stewards. With all the checks on tickets and boarding passes, we were amazed that this could happen.

The other incident did involve us, but in a London theatre. Donna and I were sitting in our seats in the Dress Circle waiting for "Curtain up", when a couple came and told us we were in their seats. I checked our tickets, which were correct, then looked at theirs, which were for the Upper Circle. Correct seats – wrong level!

Quite recently, Donna and I visited and stayed with Anne and Peter in London, Ontario. Anne is one of Donna's cousins, being the daughter of Norman, one of the eleven Harding brothers. Donna has been in contact with Anne and Peter for many years and they have stayed with us in the UK. While we were there we found some old photographs and, as a result, went to Yonge Street, Toronto, and found the very shop that Donna's grandfather had owned, above which, in the flat, Donna's father had very probably been born. Donna revisited her father's grave in York Cemetery in Toronto. Donna's mother Phyllis is now 91 and in quite good health, though her eyesight has deteriorated. Donna feels more at ease now she knows about both sides of her family.

My mother, Freda, had always been active and had enjoyed sport all her life, as a good tennis, netball and hockey player when younger, at St Paul's Girls' School and in local clubs. Later she was a knowledgeable and enthusiastic spectator. Before the war she had often watched tennis at Wimbledon and rugby at Twickenham, and post war, with Dad and me she had watched athletics at White City and soccer at several London grounds. Her sporting hero was Fred

Perry and she had little good to say about the modern British tennis players she saw on TV. Mum was an ectomorph, tall and thin, and moved around at speed. Going shopping with my mother you had to walk quickly to keep up! At home she enjoyed reading, gardening, letter writing and listening to music. When younger and living in London, she was a regular at the Proms, and enjoyed trips to the theatre. I never knew the impact that her wartime experiences had on her, as it wasn't something she spoke about. She and Dad were devoted to each other and enjoyed their retirement to "Dingley Dell" in Devon in 1969 and then, when they needed to be nearer to shops and neighbours, to Northam, close to Westward Ho! in 1977. She always looked forward to visits from her family, especially her grandchildren, Sally, Jo, Julie and Robert, and her step-grandchildren, Dad's other sons' children, Kaeyya, Ashley, Martin and Simon.

Mum's hearing and her arthritis deteriorated as she got older, but she seldom complained and she kept her sense of humour and an alert mind and an interest in the world around her. Sadly, in her 80s, she was showing clear signs of Alzheimer's. She and Dad were still living in Northam in North Devon. Although we visited them in the summer, Mum and Dad used to drive up to us in East Grinstead for Christmas, until the year we learned that, on their way to us, Dad had fallen asleep and driven their car into a field on the opposite side of the road, the A272, thankfully avoiding a collision or any injuries. Some kind folk helped them get their car back on the road and they continued their journey. Fortunately, Dad told us of this incident so, thereafter, we always drove to Devon and brought Mum and Dad back with us for the Festive Season.

The Christmas of 1990 at our house was horrendous. Donna and I experienced at first hand the dreadful effects of Alzheimer's. Mum's condition was far worse than we had realised. In our house she really didn't know where she was, accusing us of changing the furniture in what she imagined was her house. She had always enjoyed opera and operatic voices, so I put on our video of the Three Tenors, which I knew she would like. She drew up a chair in front of the TV, put on her smart gloves, and sat watching and clapping, fully believing she was at the theatre. It was both amusing and very sad. At times she was aggressive and her language was not only loud but not like my mother at all. When she became incontinent and obviously far from well, we had to call the doctor, who gave her sedatives, which calmed her down. There were times when she seemed quite lucid and held a normal conversation, but Donna and I realised that inviting Mum and Dad for Christmas had been a big mistake. We drove them home to Devon without too much stress. For her own safety and as respite for my Dad, she was later taken into Bideford Hospital.

The following February, for Dad's birthday, I decided to drive down and take him out for lunch to "The Commodore", a hotel and restaurant on Instow seafront, a favourite place for both of us. With Mum in hospital, it was sad, and, unbeknown to me, Dad was also far from well. We had a super lunch; as we'd gone in, I had told them that it was my dad's birthday, and a waitress brought a lighted sparkler to our table, which pleased him no end. We had a good chat; he was missing his beloved Freda, my mum, more than he could say. They had been together for 50 years. A month later, he too was in hospital. Donna and I drove down each weekend to see them, both in hospital though not together. At the end of March the hospital authorities allowed Mum to be brought into the same room as Dad.

As I was leaving his bedside, I said, "I'll see you next weekend, Dad."

"I don't think so," he said. He knew he hadn't long as he had cancer of the stomach. "Of course I will," I said cheerfully.

The following weekend we all went to the hospital. Young Robert, aged 10, held his grandad's hand as he passed away. It was the day of the Grand National.

We knew Mum could not return to their bungalow in Fairlea Crescent so, a short while after Dad's funeral, which Mum attended very bravely, though I'm not sure she was fully aware of whose funeral it was, Donna and I arranged for her to come and live near us in Sussex, in a residential home at Chelwood Gate. We debated whether she should come and live with us, but common sense plus lots of advice told us that this wouldn't be practicable. At Chelwood Gate she received the expert help she needed, we visited her frequently and she even spent a few hours with us at our house from time to time. When we went to see her, Mum didn't know who we were. She enjoyed sitting out in the extensive gardens, enjoying the flowers and the spring and summer sunshine. I hated leaving her: it was very sad, but she was being well looked after. Donna and I spent several weekends in Devon sorting out all their belongings and arranging for the sale of their bungalow. It was while we were there, in August, that I received a call telling me that Mum had died. She had outlived Dad by four months; she was 85. I was so sorry not to have been with her at the end. We had been through a lot together and I loved her dearly. Her funeral service was held at Worth Crematorium, Crawley. Her ashes, together with Dad's, are in the Kingsley Garden section at North Devon Crematorium in Barnstable. We visit when we can. Though they are no longer with us, we have loads of photographs and our memories. But we miss them.

When Donna and I began sorting through Mum and Dad's paperwork, we discovered all sorts of interesting details. I was reminded of *The Bridges of Madison County*. There were things that Mum thought it best not to tell me; many things that I then realised I should have asked about while she was still alive. But now, too late.

I knew of course that Mum had taken Bob's name just after the war. From my first days at Owen's School my mother was Mrs Hayland. This didn't bother me at all. There was never any suggestion that I should change my name. What I did not know, and was never told, was when my mother and Bob actually got married. I suppose in my teenage years I assumed that Mr and Mrs Hayland, Mum and Dad, were husband and wife. Looking through their papers I discovered that this had not been so: they married in 1967, when I was 32, but I wasn't told, nor did I receive an invite! *Why not, I asked myself? Did they think I would disapprove?* After they had been together for over 20 years! Perhaps they were embarrassed at not telling me that they had not been married all those years when I was growing up. Ten years later, in 1977, Mum informed me, in Donna's presence, that my dad, my biological father, had died in 1964. *Why hadn't she told me at the time?* I'm not even sure why she told me this, as she had kept so much other information to herself. Later we worked out that my mother and Bob got married when they did, because they couldn't do so before, as Mum was never divorced from my dad, and Bob's wife (yes, he had a wife that I didn't know about! Though I had met his son, Eric), was also still alive. Once their married partners had died, they were free to marry.

I then began to think more about my real dad. *When had he returned from abroad? Had he and my mother been in contact with each other? Had he ever asked about me?* He knew he had a son; it seemed unlikely he would have had no interest at all in what that son was doing. *Did he know that his son had been to Oxford University and was a teacher?* From the papers, Donna and I discovered that he had died in the Isle of Wight in January 1964 aged 57. We decided we would go to Ventnor and do some detective work. At the undertakers we were told where he had been buried and that his funeral had been paid for by a Mr Elder. This set us thinking. *Who could this be? Maybe my Dad had fathered another son with someone else; then I'd have a half brother.* All sorts of thoughts rushed through my mind. I knew my dad had a sister, who had married, but *did he have a brother?* I didn't think so. We were puzzled until we discovered that the person who had paid for the funeral had been his father, my grandfather, who as far as I can remember I had never met. Thomas Coutts Elder actually lived on until the age of 104, living out his last years in a home in Brighton. Donna and I went to my dad's burial site, but there was nothing to mark his grave, no headstone, nothing; just a patch of grass. We found out that my dad, Douglas Rodney Elder, had worked in Boots the chemist, in Ventnor, in their photographic department. There he had met and made friends with a young lady, whom Donna and I decided we would visit. As soon as she saw me, she nearly fainted. Apparently I looked remarkably like my father! We spoke for a while, and yes, they had been close friends, but as far as she knew, my father had had no other children.

Looking further into the papers that my parents had left behind I found out that when my mother married my father, she was already pregnant. To be an unmarried mother in the 1930s was considered a disgrace, especially if you came from a good family. As my mother's father was a retired headmaster and a local magistrate, it would have been unthinkable for her to have a child out of wedlock. I had never been told any of this, but putting two and two together it seems possible that Freda, my mother, and Douglas, my father, had an affair, a fling, whatever, and she became pregnant. My grandad will have told his daughter that she would have to marry the father of her unborn child, which she did. My grandad therefore avoided social disgrace and so did she. I have no idea whether my mum and dad were fond of each other, whether there was any love or whether their coming together had been purely for sex. Maybe my dad did what he had to do in the three or four years before being posted abroad, then left my mother to bring up his son by herself. The war intervened, Bob came on the scene, and my dad chose to play no further part in my life. Either that or my mother wouldn't let him. Perhaps my dad did try to make contact with me via my mother but wasn't able to do so as she was then known as Mrs Hayland, not Mrs Elder. I'm sure that my dad could have found me if he had really wanted to. My name hadn't changed and I was an adult by the mid 1950s, so there should have been no impediment to him finding me had he chosen to look. Maybe he wasn't interested and didn't bother. I shall never know.

These details that I had uncovered explained why I never had a brother or a sister. If my mum and dad had the kind of relationship that I suspect they had, they weren't going to produce a second child. Being an only child is not something that has bothered me during my life, but I should like to have known what it was like to have had a brother or a sister or even both. And why was I born in Harrow? I've often wondered but I never thought to ask my mother. She and her family lived in Isleworth, not Harrow. Perhaps she had to have her baby away from family and home. So many unanswered questions.

Before the war my dad wrote a book, "Who is Nemo?" under the pseudonym Roy Douglas. It was published by George Harrap in 1937. The central character was a villain, whose name was Tony! *Should I read any significance into that?* I wondered!

34
Life Today

I find it quite hard to believe I'm the age I am. Where did all those years go? And how did they go by so quickly? *This wasn't part of the plan!* It doesn't seem fair somehow. I feel I have a lot of living still to do. Maybe I will! I should love to be around when the grandchildren become teenagers. It would be lovely to see them married and with children of their own, but that's wishful thinking. Having had a spinal thrombosis, I'm lucky to be as well as I am; I often remind myself that there are many folk much worse off.

You find out lots of things about yourself as you get older. Some you could forecast, such as hair turning grey, (at least I still have hair!) but others can come as a surprise. It was Maurice Chevalier who made the apt remark, "Old age is not so bad when you consider the alternative." Of course, what you don't know is whether all the changes you are experiencing as you grow older are also being felt by other people. *Is it just me?* And you can't ask.

Four years ago Donna and I moved from East Grinstead to Horsham. Although we had friends in East Grinstead, the town itself had lost its attraction for us. It seemed very drab and the traffic was a nightmare. Unlike other towns of similar size in the south, East Grinstead has no ring road, no by-pass, so the single-track London Road is clogged with traffic every morning and evening. Donna and I had always liked Horsham on our occasional visits, and both Julie and Robert were now living there or in Julie's case only a couple of miles away. Moving to Horsham, admittedly downsizing a little, we were nearer the grandchildren. As things have turned out, it was just as well that Donna and I were close at hand when little Lucas was so poorly. Now we like Horsham even more! It is such a vibrant town, so much going on, superb restaurants, lots of cafés, an attractive, indoor shopping mall, a large park and streets where traffic flows, and Horsham people are so friendly. So, life today, for us here in Horsham, is good. Further afield however, there are a number of issues that concern me. I guess this is my "soap-box" time!

First, and I know I've mentioned this earlier, is the issue of parenting. Please don't get me wrong: I know that many parents do a superb job, often in difficult circumstances, but certainly not all. In many other countries, it seems, parents take their role far more seriously than many do in England. I don't want to give the impression that I think it is easy or straightforward being a parent: I know it isn't. And today, with more families experiencing levels of poverty, as well as all the "adult" influences affecting children, being a good parent is harder still. There is probably no such thing as the perfect parent, but how many can say they were, or are, "good enough" parents? Producing a child is easy; being a good parent isn't. Yet if you have brought a child into this world you have a responsibility to look after and protect that child, give him or her love and security, and make positive contributions to the health, welfare and education of that child. Some sound moral guidance would be welcome too. Many parents are not providing all those things. As a consequence, not only are those children missing out, society is, too.

The most crucial years for a young child, as far as mental, educational and emotional development are concerned, are from 0 to 3 years old. In fact the influence of the parent, especially the mother, begins before birth. Much research has shown that the conditions an unborn baby experiences will influence its later development. The emotional state of the mother, the pregnant mother's diet, the music and language the unborn baby hears, can, and probably will, have an impact on the child, either positively or negatively. Simply talking to the baby from birth makes a big difference. When the baby hears words, the world is being opened up for him or her. Such a lot of learning goes on in those first 12, 24 and 36 months, which some parents fail to appreciate. As the Start Right report said, "Parents are the child's first educators ... their role is fundamental to successful early learning." (Start Right Report, p. 42)

Many of you reading this will say, "I know all that." But what, as a country, are we doing to improve the quality of parenting? Not an easy or straightforward task, I accept, but in my view it isn't something that should be ignored or left to chance. If we don't grasp that nettle, society, meaning all of us, suffers the consequences. Sure Start schemes have helped but they don't reach all those in need, and the recent government cutbacks have led to many Sure Start centres being closed down. That is a tragedy. Surely as a society there is more that could be done. I don't have answers but those in a position to do something about this issue should take some responsibility and act. The next government could set up a commission to consider and recommend ways in which the quality of parenting in England could be improved. As part of my M.Ed. degree, I wrote a dissertation on this subject in 1994, and as a result of my research locally in Crawley, I came to a number of conclusions and made a number of recommendations. I don't know how widely this work was read, but the issues linked to "less than adequate parenting" still blight schools and wider society.

In 1995, I worked as a group leader for the Open University, which was trialling some materials for a new course, "Parents and Under 8s". I hosted several meetings with a group of parents from Blackwell Junior School, East Grinstead, who had volunteered to take part. Our meetings were always lively and productive. Hopefully, the findings and report were useful to the School of Health and Social Welfare at the Open University. In 1999 I wrote a paper for the Community Education Association on the topic of parenting. Improving the quality of parenting in England would, in my view, have a major influence on the happiness and stability of society and would certainly result in more children doing well in school.

I also feel strongly about the current state of our democracy in Britain. Politicians are held in very low esteem in the UK today, and is it any wonder? Surely for democracy to work, there has to be some honesty. Ordinary members of the public are not going to believe or participate in the system if politicians behave in a dishonest or underhand manner. At election time, each political party, individual politicians and the leaders of those parties, should set out their policies clearly so that Joe Public can make an informed choice. I have no quarrel with voters choosing to vote for a political party with which I disagree; that is their prerogative, and if that party wins a majority of seats and becomes the government of the country, so be it. What I object to, because it annoys me, and because it fundamentally undermines the whole democratic process, is politicians saying before an election that they are in favour of a particular policy and then after the election doing the exact opposite. It is deceitful, lacking in principle, opportunist and treats the voters with contempt. The politicians are not telling us what their policies are, things are said solely for the purpose of obtaining votes. So is it any wonder that the public are turned off and don't bother to vote?

In the last General Election in 2010, both the Conservative and Liberal Democrat party leaders made pre-election statements that they have since totally betrayed. Two examples will suffice: Nick Clegg on the subject of student fees and David Cameron on the National Health Service. They obviously take the voters to be fools. My point is that if we cannot believe what politicians are telling us are their beliefs and policies, then democracy cannot work. When you add expenses scandals and other undignified and, at times, corrupt behaviour by MPs, it is no wonder that the public have so little faith in our politicians. Does this matter? I believe it does. Not only do we have governments that have often been elected by a minority of the population, but it also opens the door to those parties who basically have a single objective, parties such as UKIP and BNP. The leaders of the major political parties need to be more honest if respect and support for our politicians and our political system is to be regained. Don't hold your breath!

I always say to young people who are about to vote for the first time that, yes, they should definitely vote and, secondly, they should be clear in their own minds as to what they believe in, what their personal convictions are, what really matters to them. If they say to themselves, *What matters for me? What do I believe is really important? What kind of a country do I want to grow up in and want my children to grow up in?* they are very likely to realise pretty quickly which political party to vote for, assuming they know what the main political parties stand for or what their history is: another good argument for studying History, in this case, the history of your own country.

As an older person, I can recall the post-war Labour Government of Clement Attlee, which put into effect many of the proposals of the Beveridge Report, drawn up during the war in 1942, such as the greatly improved scheme of National Insurance and the introduction of a National Health Service, largely the creation of Aneurin Bevan. And from my study of History I know that at the beginning of the 20th century, with pressure growing to grant all men and women the right to vote, it was necessary to have a political party that represented the interests of working class men and women. For a long time there was a strong link between the Labour Party and the Trade Union movement. New Labour, led by Tony Blair, had a different agenda, wishing to appeal not only to members of the working classes but also to the middle classes. In making this change, the Labour Party lost some of its original philosophy and beliefs. For all his good intentions and initial achievements, and despite the undoubted success of the Irish peace initiative, Tony Blair lost all credibility by taking the country to war in Iraq, inexplicably following the lead of George Bush. The Labour Party is opposed to essential services, which are vital to the welfare of the country and its citizens, being run by private companies for profit. Such services should be in public ownership, it always argued. These days we see services such as water, gas, electricity and railways not only in the hands of profit making private companies, but often of foreign companies. Today's Labour Party needs to regain some of its basic beliefs and be more open and confident in publicising what it stands for, especially because there are many families in Britain today who are suffering economic and social hardship and who could do with a strong Labour Party to speak for them and fight their corner. As an aside: I loved the cartoon that showed Tony Blair looking down upon Margaret Thatcher's funeral. "Do you think they'll let me lie in state?" he asks. To which his friend replies, "Well, it didn't stop you in office."

Conservatives, on the other hand, have a commitment to tradition, the preservation of traditional institutions and belief in private enterprise and are opposed to nationalisation and the public ownership of essential services. The Party supports and is supported by big business, from which it receives considerable financial backing. Many of the supporters of the Conservative Party are wealthy people with money, with landed or business interests, who naturally want these to be preserved. Because the rich pay the most taxes, (though not enough, according to some), Conservatives are considered to be the party of low taxation. The present coalition government has lowered the rate at which the highest earners, the wealthiest, pay tax. And the Office for National Statistics tells us that just under half of the total wealth in the UK is in the hands of only ten per cent of the population. Conservative policy therefore favours those with money and property – the "haves" rather than the "have nots". Conservative politicians who have grown up in conservative families and households, who went to independent schools, then Oxford or Cambridge, and who are sitting on large fortunes, will naturally want to perpetuate this state of affairs. It's in their interests. But is it in yours?

Historically one associates Liberals with individual freedom and fairness, and for a long time in the 19th century they were the political opponents of the Conservatives. They have at times been radical, for it was a Liberal Government that introduced Old Age Pensions and the first scheme of National Insurance in what was called "the People's Budget" in 1909. Liberals have generally been on the side of "progress", in contrast to Conservatives who would prefer to keep things as they are or indeed to return to what they used to be. With our "first past the post" system of electing members of Parliament, the Liberal party has been squeezed out by the two major political parties. Many European countries have a system of proportional representation, which gives smaller parties more chance of obtaining seats in Parliament, but while it can be said to be more fair, it usually leads to a proliferation of political parties in the Assembly and therefore to coalition governments. The Liberal Democrats (as they now call themselves) would benefit from a PR voting system, but neither of the two major parties is likely to introduce it.

Understanding what the main political parties stand for and traditionally represent should help young people when it comes to deciding who to vote for. Leopards don't change their spots, well Conservative leopards don't! I have never voted Conservative in my life and would never do so, as what they represent is alien to my beliefs. Currently I find it offensive that our country is run by a cabinet made up largely of millionaires, many educated at Eton, who have no understanding of the lives of ordinary people and their problems and needs. The so called "bedroom tax" is pernicious and ineffective and harms the disabled most of all. Who would have thought that Britain, one of the richest countries in the world, would need food banks so that families made hungry by the Government's policies can survive? No wonder Church leaders have condemned the present situation as involving distress for many, a situation of which the Eton educated ministers can have no comprehension. And despite ensuring that the wealthiest become even wealthier, the present government saw fit to prevent nurses from having a 1% rise in their wages, even though this is what had been recommended by the independent review body. And legal aid is being phased out, so seeking justice in the courts will in future be the prerogative of those who can afford it.

This is the government that wanted to sell off our woods and forests when it first came to power, until a huge public outcry put a stop to it. Members of the organisation 38 Degrees argued against the privatisation of child protection services and recently persuaded the government to stop the proposed sale of the Land Registry. But the country's prisons and the probation services are now in the hands of private companies who run them to make a profit.

The same is true of the NHS: partly because of increasing costs but also with other motives, many in the Conservative Party support the privatisation of the NHS. Indeed this is already happening. Are the public aware of this? Consider who would gain and who would lose. A private health service, as in USA, a policy favoured by Margaret Thatcher, would not be a disadvantage to those with money. But if you couldn't afford to pay for treatment or medication, you would suffer. So are we going to allow one of our greatest national institutions, the envy of the world, to be removed from government control and sold off into the hands of private companies?

This is just scaremongering, you may say. Not according to the chairman of the British Medical Association, who recently criticised the Government for its lack of investment in the NHS, while doctors at the BMA conference said that the Government's health changes had created "market lunacy". The leader of the NHS Consultants Association, referring to the promise before the 2010 election that there would be no top down reorganisation of the NHS, said, "they lied to the public and they lied to doctors and nurses ... in reality the Health and Social Care Act of 2012 opened the door for a massive increase in NHS privatisation." Surely it is time for the public to become outraged at this.

Conservative readers may not agree with my analysis or views, but I said this was my soap-box time and these are some of the things I feel strongly about.

It is not only politicians that you cannot trust today. In the past, the public knew they could rely on the police. They would always do a good job of protecting individuals and could be relied upon to hunt down criminals. Individual policemen always upheld the law. This, sadly, is no longer true. What on earth has happened? The worst example of police wrongdoing, because it emanated from the very top, was of course Hillsborough. Fortunately, at long last, that particular wrong is being put right, at least partially, and of course far too late for many families in Liverpool. What a disgraceful piece of collective treachery that was. Recently there have been too many examples of individual members of the police force being corrupt, usually for personal profit. A recent survey showed that one in four people in the UK do not trust the police.

Another example: we all used to trust banks and bankers. They had our best interests at heart. Today, that notion has been totally eroded. Hundreds of examples have come to light of banks advising their customers that a certain course of action, an investment for instance, would be in their best interests, when the reality is that it would be the bank that would benefit. Too bad that the customer lost out: "We're here to make a profit." We all know that it was the action of irresponsible banks and bankers that led us into recession. Serving their customers' interests, rather than their own, is what banks should be doing.

Can we trust all members of the clergy today? Would you be happy leaving your young child in the care of an individual member of this or that church? You will say that there's nothing new in children being abused by churchmen, and you would be correct. But isn't it disgraceful that stories are still surfacing of such incidents? It's good that the facts are being brought out into the open. Paedophile bishops and unsavoury priests have been exposed, but for how long were their activities known about and kept hidden? A conspiracy of silence seems to have prevailed. Not all churchmen are corrupt, obviously, neither are all policemen. But it leaves me wondering: who can you trust?

We now know of abuse being carried out, over many years, in care homes, places that were supposed to be looking after young, vulnerable children, in many parts of the UK: in Wales, Scotland, Rochdale, and many others. In London, the perpetrators, it is alleged, were politicians, with local authorities "turning a blind eye". The agony and suffering that these children have endured is hard for us to imagine and the victims have had to carry the pain, the shame and the anger with them all their lives. An abject apology from some high-ranking cleric doesn't seem sufficient, does it?

It makes me really angry when someone takes advantage of their position to exploit or harm others for their own benefit, be it sexual, financial, racial or whatever. Children are vulnerable, so too are the elderly, yet individuals within these groups in our society are often the ones who are exploited. It is shameful, yet the overwhelming majority of citizens of the UK are decent, honest folk. Some leadership and example from the leaders in politics, the police and the churches would be welcome.

Recently NHS England were considering plans to sell off our individual health records to private companies. After massive opposition from swaths of the public and from the medical profession, this plan was put "on hold". As I write, the latest "plan" is to sell our personal tax details to private companies, details of our income, pensions, the tax we pay, our tax histories. I find this quite appalling, especially when we are being told we should guard our private financial details from hackers etc. One Tory MP described the proposal as "borderline insane". And the latest "threat" is the deal being prepared by the EU and the US, the Transatlantic Trade and Investment Partnership (TTIP), by which the country's judicial independence would be surrendered to multinational corporations. Are people aware of what is going on? Again I ask, what kind of a country will our children and grandchildren be living in?

Something I reflect on is the change that has come about to people's lives, indeed to my life, in the last 60 or 70 years. Many young people, who take today's technology for granted, would find the things I grew up with really strange. My mother had a mangle to wring out the washing and a device, clamped to the kitchen table, with a handle, which turned meat into mincemeat! I enjoyed turning that handle! In my early years we didn't have a car, but travelled everywhere by bus or train. I don't remember my grandparents ever owning a car. My parents and I listened to the radio or an old gramophone: my first experience of watching television on a regular basis was at university in the mid 1950s. The pace of life was much slower at the beginning of the second half of the last century. I know that is common knowledge, but I am reminiscing and it's fun to think back to those days. If a message was urgent and the recipient had no telephone, then a telegram was sent. Letters were posted.

Today communication is virtually instant with electronic mail, fax machines and skype, not to mention Facebook, twitter, mobile and smartphones and iPads. My parents would be amazed that you can not only talk with someone in another country but see them at the same time on your computer. If Dad were to return today and hear about the superfast highway, he would think you were talking about the new road between the M5 and Barnstaple! Goodness knows what he would make of Oysters and BlackBerries!

As for moving with the times, not everyone does so. I asked a friend only a year or two ago, if he could let me have his email address.

"Email?" he said, looking astonished. "I'm just getting used to the telephone!"

Today I find it frustrating that, if I want to write to someone and I don't have their email address, I have to write a letter, address an envelope, find a stamp and walk to the post-box! And wait two or three days for an answer! On the other hand, I do miss the old 78 and 33 records: today it's all CDs, and DVDs have replaced videos. When I wanted to look something up, I used to use a reference book or pop down to the local library. Now I can google. If I am out with Rob, and I have a query about something, he will use his smartphone, which of course operates like a computer. It's as if he is carrying an encyclopaedia around with him. He could probably tell you when it's high tide in Honolulu!

It's not so long ago that I retired and my former colleagues would probably be amazed that their former "boss" is moderately proficient with a computer, as in my last years as a Head, such devices were only beginning to be used and clearly I was a novice. Donna does all kinds of amazing things with her photographs on our computer: I had always thought that "Photoshop" was a photo shop! It's interesting, isn't it, that folk who acquire one new piece of gadgetry nearly always go on to have two or more: one car, then two; ditto with telephones, televisions, computers and suchlike. And is the Kindle going to replace books? I hope not. I understand how convenient a kindle is, when going on holiday and on aeroplanes for example, but it would be a sad day if books and therefore libraries disappeared. As one former student of mine said to me recently, "I've just started reading real books again. I got so far into the novel I'm reading on my Kindle, but realised there's no substitute for physically turning the last page of a book!" When I ask my wife how far she is into her latest book on Kindle, she says, "58%"!

I heard someone say recently that if there's a book you know you want to read, you can do so on a Kindle, but for the books you don't know about, you need a library. Another change from days gone by is today's "shopping online". It is quick and convenient, although as one lady told me, "I like to see what I'm buying." The downside, of course, is the threat to jobs in shops throughout the country. Some businesses and shops have disappeared, Woolworths, Comet, Blockbuster for example, but there will be others – those who fail to adapt.

Our children, Julie and Robert, didn't have a television or a computer in their bedroom as they were growing up. We were fortunate to have a spare room, where we installed a television which they could watch, and where they could bring their friends and socialise. Today's parents of teenagers have difficult decisions to make. Although computers are now virtually essential for students at school, the obvious downside of each child having one in their own bedroom is the danger that can come from uncontrolled access.

I read that a school in Swindon decided to get rid of its ban on mobile phones and instead make use of them in lessons to support learning. *If you can't beat them, get them to join you!* Teachers now plan their lessons with their students' technology in mind and the students enjoy using their smartphones for this purpose. It is quite a revolutionary move, but not only are phones no longer a nuisance and a distraction, it appears that the quality of learning has improved. It is a natural step for the work done in the lesson to be carried on at home since much of it will be centred on the technology of each phone. I understand that pupils without smartphones share with those who have. Learning is genuinely and literally in the hands of the students, as it should be. I'm sure that other schools will follow suit.

The world of athletics has seen many changes too. Today we have synthetic, all-weather tracks, "safe" landing areas for high jumpers and pole vaulters, electronic timing and advanced photo-finish apparatus, heart-rate monitors, physiological testing, and much more. And linking developments I have mentioned, television coverage has brought spectacles such as the Olympic Games to a worldwide audience. Truly the world seems to be growing and shrinking at the same time: billions more people in our global village, all of whom need feeding, plus communication developments that bring us all closer together. And while I digress on the subject of the advancements made in my lifetime, we do well to remember all those in different parts of the world who still live without technology. In their ignorance, their state of not knowing, they may be more content and less fraught than we are.

I wish Bob, my dad, had been around during the last 20 years. He would have enjoyed the success that his favourite football team, Chelsea, have had. He would also have enjoyed the joke about Bill, who always went to watch his favourite football team with his father. Sadly, his dad died, but Bill thought, *I know Dad would have wanted to go to the match*, so he decided to put his father's ashes in a bottle and take them with him to the match. "Sorry," said the guy on the gate, "bottles of pop aren't allowed in the ground."

The London Olympics would have thrilled Dad and kept him glued to his TV. But he would have been horrified at the current economic and political scene. He hated injustice. He would certainly be railing against President Obama, who promised he would close Guantanamo Bay detention centre, but hasn't. I can imagine what Dad would have said about that and about the bankers and a lot else! Perhaps he is better off not knowing.

Me? Well I have enjoyed helping young people achieve their goals, both in the classroom and on the track, trying to persuade them to make the most of their talent. In doing so, I have learned a lot. I am not one of the grumpy, old folk who criticise today's youngsters. Those I have had the good fortune to meet and work with have been smashing kids, the boys and the girls, and always great company. My hope is that my children and grandchildren can live to see a fairer, more prosperous, less fragmented and happier Britain, and a more peaceful, contented world in which they, and indeed all children, can grow and prosper. If all families want this for their children, why can't we put differences aside and all work together to achieve it?

Additional Details I

Athletes Coached

This is a record of the best performances of the athletes I coached (international, county and club runners). A more complete version can be found in the ebook. [Square brackets indicate when the athlete was not being coached by me]. <u>Rankings refer to the athlete's position in their age group that year in UK unless indicated otherwise.</u>

Statistics are as accurate as my records and memory permit. I am very grateful to athletes and statisticians who have provided me with details I didn't have. Back numbers of "*Athletics Weekly*" have been a mine of useful information. Apologies for any errors or omissions.

<u>Highgate Harriers</u> (late 1950s)

Alan Alderson and **Phil Cummings**: keen young runners and good on the sandhills

Brian Denham and **Peter Rogers**: good juniors

Peter Bushnell, Dick Corbett, Robin Shilling and **David Yaffe**: good club runners

Bob Slowe: excellent club runner & Middx representative XC & track [later Marathon]

<u>Watford Harriers</u>

Cliff Redman: *all Cliff's rankings are as a Junior athlete*

1959: 2 miles 9:33.0 *ranked 9th*; 3 miles 14:28.8 *ranked 2nd*

1960: 5th Junior Invite 1500m 3:55.9 (White City) *ranked 6th*; 3 miles 14:14.0 (Alperton) *ranked 1st*; 2 miles 9:11.0 (Paddington) *ranked 1st*; 3rd 1500m SC 4:17.0 (Eton Manor) *ranked 3rd*; 5th Junior Invite Mile 4:15.2 (White City) *ranked 8th*

1961 & 1962: 1st Herts Junior XC ... injuries curtailed his running as a senior athlete

In Essex (I moved to Essex in 1958)

Chelmsford AC

John Archer (KEGS)

1961: 1st Trophy Meeting 880 yds 1:58.5 *ranked 10th Youth*

1962: 1st LAC Schools Mile 4:21.8;2nd 1500m SC 4:39.3 *ranked 5th*; 2nd Southern Youths Mile 4:18.5 *ranked 3rd*; 2nd ESAA IB Mile 4:32.2 (Hull); 1st Leyton Floodlit 880 1:57.0 *ranked 6th Junior*

1963: 1st Essex AAA Junior 880 1:56.3; 2nd ESAA SB 880 1:55.4 (Chelmsford)

[1964 at Loughborough...I was no longer coaching John.

1st Trophy Meeting 880 1:53.3 *ranked 5th Junior*; 1st Essex AAA Jun 880 & 1500m SC; 4th Invitation Junior 880 (in GB v Poland match) 1:53.8]

Bob Chapman (KEGS)

1962-1964: regularly in 1st 3 in Essex Schools and County XC & track races

1965: 3rd LAC Schools 880 1:58.7; 5th ESAA SB Mile 4:10.4 (Watford) *ranked 5th Junior* & 1500m 3:52.4 (Watford)

Andy Davis (USAF)

1963: 1st Essex AAA 880 1:55.7; 2nd USAF Champs Europe 440 Hurdles & 1st USAF 880

Mike Erith

1963: 1st Essex Schools JB 880 2:04.0 (Barking); 5th ESAA JB 880 2:03.0 (Chelmsford)

1964: 1st Essex Sch IB 880 2:01.5 (Southend); 1st Southern Youths 880 2:00.9 (Hurlingham); 5th ESAA IB 880 1:58.6 (Hendon)

1965: 1st Match Mile 4:31.4 (Thurrock); 1st Match Junior 880 1:56.5 (Hornchurch)

1966: 1st Essex Sch 880 1:59.1 (Newham); 7th ESAA SB 880 1:56.5 (heat 1:55.5) (Blackburn)

[much later...1971: 1st London Hosp Ch 400m 52.4; 2nd Essex Senior 800m 1:54.9 (Southend); SCAAA Open Meetings: (Hornsey AC) 2nd 800 1:54.9, 4th 800 1:53.1 (pb), 2nd 1:55.5 (Crystal Palace);

1996-2003 London Marathon: best 1998 2:52, also 1999 Chicago
2:48, 2001 Berlin 2:50

2004: 1st National Vets 800 (Cardiff), 1st World Masters M55 800 2:08.9
ranked 1st World M55 800m & 1st UK M55 800m, 1500m & 3k;
2008: 1st M60 in World Biathle (run-swim-run)]

Bill Farnham (KEGS & Brentwood AC)

1960: 6th Southern Youths XC (PHF); 1st Essex Sch IB XC; 1st Essex Sch
SB Mile 4:34.2 (Harlow)

1961: 1st Essex Youths XC (Romford); 2nd Essex Jun Mile 4:19.7 *ranked
in top 25*

1962: 4th ESAA SB XC (Birkenhead)

Peter Fulcher

1964: 1st Essex Schools IB Mile 4:32.8; 8th ESAA IB Mile 4:32.1
(Hendon)

1965: 25th Inter-Counties XC (Essex team 2nd)

1966: 21st National Youths XC; 22nd Inter-Counties XC; 1st Southern
2000m Jun SC 6:09.6; 3rd AAA 2000m Jun SC 6:05.4 *ranked 14th*;
1st 1500m Jun SC 4:34.1 (Hendon) *ranked 10th*

1967: 13th Southern Jun XC; 22nd National Jun XC; 14th Inter-Counties
Jun XC; 1st Inter-Club 3000m SC 9:27.6 (Southend) *ranked 4th*

1968: 7th Southern Jun XC; 27th National Jun XC (Sutton Coldfield); 17th
Inter-Counties Jun XC

[1969-1976: well placed in Cross-Country Champs; ran many road relay
legs for Chelmsford AC]

Penny Gardner

1962: 1st Southern Inter 880 yds 2:25.7 *ranked 5th*

1963: 1st Inter-Counties 880 (Clacton); 1st Essex Schools IG 880 2:20.2;
2nd ESAA IG 880 2:17.4 (Chelmsford); 2nd Southern Women's 880
2:17.5 (heat 2:16.9); 1st Essex XC League

1964: 4th Southern Inter-County XC (PHF); 3rd National Junior XC
(Richmond); 3rd Leyton Floodlit 800m 2:15.6 (1st A Packer,
2nd M Tagg); 1st Coronation Trophy 440 59.7 & 1st 880 2:21

(Chelmsford); 2ⁿᵈ Southern Mile 5:02.6 (Chiswick) *ranked 2ⁿᵈ*; 2ⁿᵈ
Vauxhall Meeting 880 2:14.8 (Luton) *ranked 18ᵗʰ*; WAAA 880 heat
2:15.9 & 2ⁿᵈ Mile 4:56.9 (White City) *World Best for 18 yo and
ranked 2ⁿᵈ*

1965–1970: always in 1ˢᵗ three in SE Essex XC Lge; 1970: 2ⁿᵈ fastest in
Southend Women's Relay

Peter Hatcher (Brentwood AC)

1961: 18ᵗʰ ESAA SB XC (Peterborough)

1962: 1ˢᵗ Essex Junior Mile 4:20.7 (Grays); 2ⁿᵈ ESAA SB Mile 4:23.6
(Hull); 3ʳᵈ Schools International Mile 4:20.8

Barbara Horton

1964: 1ˢᵗ Essex Sch IG 880 yds 2:27.6; 8ᵗʰ ESAA IG 880 2:30.7
(heat 2:23.1) (Hendon); 1ˢᵗ Match Inter 880 2:22.9 *ranked 6ᵗʰ*
(Southend); 1ˢᵗ Essex Jun XC

1965: 1ˢᵗ Essex Schools IG 880 2:23.6; 3ʳᵈ WAAA Inter 880 2:25.3; 1ˢᵗ
Inter-Club 440 60.3 *ranked 4ᵗʰ*; 1ˢᵗ Leyton Floodlit Meeting 880
2:21.7 *ranked 9ᵗʰ*; 11ᵗʰ Essex Senior XC

Brian Hill-Cottingham

[1956-1960 many excellent performances on XC & Track before I began
coaching Brian, including:

1959: 1ˢᵗ Essex Jun XC and 17ᵗʰ in the winning Essex XC in the Senior
Inter-Counties; 2ⁿᵈ Essex 3 Miles 13:45.4 (Leyton) *ranked 15ᵗʰ*

1960: 10ᵗʰ Inter-Counties XC (Brighton); 6ᵗʰ for England XC (ECCU)
in Belgium; 13ᵗʰ National XC (West Bromwich); 21ˢᵗ International
XC (Glasgow); 4ᵗʰ Invitation 5000m 14:09.2 *ranked 7ᵗʰ* 3 miles
time 13:43.8 (White City); 2ⁿᵈ Walton "10" 50:07; 5ᵗʰ for ECCU
in Lyons; + many road relays including lap record in Chelmsford's
Sidney Taylor Relay]....

I began coaching Brian towards the end of 1960

1961: 1ˢᵗ North of the Thames XC; 2ⁿᵈ to Gordon Pirie AAA 3 Miles
13:39.91(White City) *ranked 11ᵗʰ*;8ᵗʰ Invitation 1500m (during
GB v USA) 3:50.7 *ranked 15ᵗʰ* and 3rd to D Ibbotson & Frank

Salvat 3000m 8:03.8 (White City) *ranked 4th;* 2nd Invitation 3000m 8:08.4 beating S Iharos, M Bullivant & D Ibbotson (White City); 2nd GB "B" v Switzerland 5000m 14:44.2; 2nd Hogs Back 9 miles Road Race 45:56 (1st Martin Hyman 45:54)

1962: 13th Inter-Counties XC; 1st beating Alain Mimoun & Alan Perkins for ECCU (Dunkirk); 3rd Southern XC; 1st Home International Indoor 2 Miles 8:52 (Wembley); 1st Essex AAA Mile 4:10 CBP (Grays); Southern 3 Miles 13:38.8 (Motspur Park) *ranked 17th*; 3rd to Mel Batty & D Ibbotson 2 Miles 8:50.4 (W City) *ranked 11th*

1963: 3rd AAA 2 miles indoor and 1st International 2 miles 8:52.0 (both at Wembley); plus many road relays, some with Buddy Edelen. Brian ran for the club for another 10-12 years mainly on road & XC

Chris Joslin

1963–1965: competed on the country and track for Chelmsford AC as a youth and a junior

Christine McFarlane

1967: 1st Essex Schools Jun 150 yds 18.4; 4th S/F ESAA JG 150 17.3 (Peterborough)

1968: 1st Festival Trophy Inter 220 26.7 (Chelmsford); 1st Trophy Meeting 100 yds 11.5 (Harlow)

1970: 19th ESAA SG XC (Peterborough); 2nd Essex Schools SG 200m 26.3

1971: 3rd ESAA SG 400m 57.5 pb (Crystal Palace); 3rd Essex Lge 200m 25.9 (Southend)

1972: 2nd Essex WAAA 400m 58.0 (Barking)

Jacqui Philp

1966: 2nd Essex WAAA Inter 100 yds 11.6 & 1st 220 26.3; 4th WAAA Inter 80mH 12.0 *ranked 5th*

1967: 2nd WAAA Indoor Inter 60mH 9.5 (Cosford); 1st Winter Track Mtg 330 41.0 (Chelmsford);3rd Southern Inter Pentathlon 3501 pts; 1st Essex Ch 100, 220 & 80mH; 1st Southern Inter 80mH 12.0 and

3rd 220 26.7; 1st Essex Schools IG 80mH 12.0 (Ex Sch Record); 6th Inter-Area Senior Pentathlon 3926 pts (Harlow); 1st Festival Trophy 100 11.7 & 220 26.2 (Chelmsford); 1st ESAA IG 80mH 11.8 (11.5 in s/f ESAA CBP – Peterborough); 1st WAAA Inter 80mH 12.1; 3rd WAAA Inter Pentathlon 3895 pts; 2nd Essex Pentathlon 3946 pts *ranked 3rd Inters and 6th Senior* (inc 80mH 11.7) *End of year ranking 80mH: 11.5 2nd with Susan Scott (Birchfield) 1st 11.3*

1968: 2nd ESAA SG 80mH 11.8 and 1st 4 x 110 SG Relay 48.4 (Portsmouth); 2nd Essex Pent 3936 pts *ranked 20th*; 5th Trophy Mtg 200mH 29.7 (Crawley) *ranked 6th*; 3rd WAAA 80mH heat 11.6, 6th semi 11.7 (White City); 8th WAAA Pent 3812 pts; 1st Inter-Club match 100 11.4 & LJ 17ft 10in

1969: 4th Essex WAAA 200m 25.6; 3rd Southern 100mH 14.5 *ranked 8th*, in heat 14.2w *ranked 5th* (Crystal Palace); 5th Inter-Terr Pent 4057 pts pb *ranked 14th*; 6th Southern Pent 4018 pts (Chelmsford); 3rd ESAA SG 100mH 15.5.. hit hurdle.. (Motspur Park); 6th WAAA 200mH time 28.4; 2nd 200mH 28.8 (C Palace) *ranked 7th*; 1st Southern WAAA 200mH 29.4

1970: now at Dartford College of PE ... so my role as coach was much less. 1st Coronation Trophy 100mH 14.8 (Chelmsford); 6th Southern LJ 5m 49/18ft 0¼in; 3rd Pent 4178 pts pb *ranked 14th* (Edinburgh); WAAA 100mH 15.1 heat/semi; 6th 200mH 28.4 pb (W City) *ranked 10th*; *End of year ranking for 200mH 8th: 28.4, 28.9, 29.0, 29.4, 6th WAAA, 2nd during men's UK v Benelux*

1971: 4th Southern Pent 4065 pts (C Palace) *ranked 12th*; 1st Borough Trophy 100mH 14.6 *ranked 18th* and 2nd LJ 18ft/5:48 (Enfield); 1st Short Trophy LJ 18ft 2½in/5.55 and 1st 100mH 14.8 (Southend)

1972: 1st Essex WAAA LJ 18ft 2in/5.54; 4th Dartford v Bedford v Chelsea 100mH 14.8 *ranked 25th* and 1st 200mH 29.0 *ranked 10th* (C Palace); 1st Essex Pent 3522 *ranked 11th* (new scoring tables)

Continued to compete up to 1980, including:

1974: 5th Southern Pent 3579 pts *ranked 18th*

1975: 2nd Long Jump 19ft 1¼in/5.82 *ranked 27th*

1976: 2nd Joe Louis Trophy 100mH 14.7 *ranked 23rd*; 2nd Essex Pent 3434 pts *ranked 21st*

1977: 5th Southern 100mH 14.6 *ranked 22nd*

NB Jacqui was in UK rankings every year, often in more than one event

Hadleigh Olympiads
Michael Dale (Southend HS)
1968: 2nd Essex Jun 440 51.8 and 1st Jun 220 22.7; 2nd Essex Schools SB
         220 22.8; 4th ESAA SB 220 s/f 22.9 (Portsmouth); 5th Southern
         Jun 220 22.8 (Hendon)

I left Southend HS at the end of summer 1968…

[1969: Michael's last year at school: 1st Essex Jun 400m 51.0; 6th Southern
         Jun 200m 22.5

1971 & 1972: various meetings representing Hadleigh Olympiads]

Len West (Southend HS)
1967: 1st Essex Boys XC; 1968: 1st Essex Schools Inter 1000m SC 2:55.6
1969: 2nd Burn Cup XC 4 miles (Buckhurst Hill); 3rd Essex Schools SB
         XC; 18th ESAA SB XC (Leicester)

[…much later 1974: 1st Southend XC Ch 54:37…also 1977: 3rd and 1979
         1st 53:09]

Southend AC:
Liz Butler
1966: 1st Essex WAAA Jun HJ 4ft 7in; 1st Southern Jun HJ 4ft 7in; Jun
         Pent 3271 pts *ranked 7th*; 6th WAAA Junior Pent 3147 pts (Harlow)
1967: 1st Essex Jun HJ 4ft 7in; ESAA IG 80mH 12.5 in semi
         (Peterborough)
1968: 1st Inter HJ 4ft 9in (Harlow) & 4ft 8in (Chelmsford); 1st Essex
         WAAA Inter 80mH 12.4 and 1st HJ 4ft 9in; 2nd Southern Inter
         HJ 4ft 9in; 1st Trophy Mtg 100 yds 11.8 *ranked 7th*; 1st Essex Inter
         Pent 3863 pts *ranked 7th*; 4th WAAA Inter 80mH 12.1 (heat 12.0)
         and 5th HJ 4ft 11in (Stretford); 2nd Essex Sch v London Sch 80mH
         11.9 and 3rd HJ 4ft 11in
1969: 1st Essex WAAA LJ 18ft 1½in & 2nd HJ 5ft 1in; 7th Southern Pent
         3959 pts (Chelmsford); =2nd ESAA SG HJ 5ft 0¾in (Motspur
         Park); 2nd International Schools SG HJ 5ft 1in; 6th WAAA Pent

4062 pts *ranked 13th* (Birmingham); 1st Essex Pent 3994 pts (Southend)

1970: 2nd Essex WAAA 100mH 14.8 (Chelmsford); 5th Southern 100mH 14.6 (CP) *ranked 17th*; 3rd Atalanta Trophy 100mH 14.5w (Chiswick); 6th in heat ESAA SG 100mH 14.9 (Solihull)

Jackie French

1968 & 1969: ran as a Junior on the track and cross- country and in road relays for Southend AC

1970: 1st Borough Trophy Inter 400 59.9 (Enfield); 3rd Southern Inter 400 61.5 (Enfield)

1971: 1st Holroyd Trophy Inter 200 26.6 (Southend); 2nd Essex WAAA Inter 400 59.8 (Harlow); 6th Southern 400 60.5 (Watford); 5th Inter-County Sch Inter 400 59.2 and 3rd 800 2:21.8; ESAA IG 400m elim in heat 59.0 (Crystal Palace); 3rd Southern Inter I/C 400 60.4

1972: 2nd Essex Schools SG XC (Chingford); ran in ESAA SG XC (Sandown IOW)

Also in Essex

Malcolm Absolom (Leyton HS and Eton Manor AC)...Malcolm's lifetime track PBs in bold:

Malcolm raced a lot so I have been selective and included mainly his best performances...

1962: 5th ESAA JB XC (Birkenhead)

1963: 8th ESAA IB XC (Coventry); 3rd ESAA IB Mile 4:19.7 (Chelmsford)

1964: 3rd Southern Jun Mile 4:14.9 (Hurlingham); 4th ESAA SB Mile 4:16.4 (Hendon); 1st Essex Jun Mile 4:20.6; 2nd Leyton Floodlit Jun Mile 4:17.0; 7th Nos Galan Mile 4:23.8 (1st John Whetton 4:21)

1965: 1st North of the Thames Jun XC; 12th Southern Jun XC; 2nd ESAA SB XC (Colchester) – *ranked 3rd Junior XC*; **2nd 2000m SC 6:02.6 (Barking)**; 1st Essex AAA Jun Mile 4:14.7 CBP; 1st Essex AAA Jun

443

2 Miles 9:06.6 (Barking); 3rd Southern Jun Mile 4:14.5; 3rd ESAA SB Mile 4:10 (Watford) *ranked 3rd*

1966: 3rd Essex AAA XC; 2nd London XC Ch (PHF); 13th Nos Galan Mile 4:24 and 12th 4 Miles 18:52

1967: 3rd Southern Jun XC; 4th National Jun XC; 2nd Junior I/C XC *overall ranked 7th Junior XC*

Ran fast legs in Road Relays at Chingford, Hornsey & Walthamstow where he ran fastest leg in record time taking Eton Manor AC from 16th to 2nd place; 1st Victoria Park "5" road race; 3rd SCAAA v OUAC 2 Miles 8:58.8; 1st Essex AAA 2 Miles 8:51.6; 3rd Essex AAA 3 Miles 14:03.4; 1st Stevenage "11" 55:41; 2nd AAA U21 v Loughborough U21 2 Miles 8:55.6; 2nd Chigwell "10" 50:31 (1st Ron Hill); **21st AAA 3 Miles 13:46.8 (White City 1st Ron Clarke 12:59.6)**; 3rd GLC XC Champs (PHF)

1968: 35th National XC (Sutton Coldfield); 1st Victoria Park "5" road race; ran lots of road relays; 1st Essex AAA 3 Miles 14:02.0 & 2 Miles 9:08.6; 8th Inter-Counties 3 Miles 13:47.8 (White City); 3rd for SCAAA 3000m 8:07.2 (C Palace); 6th Southern Mile 4:06.9; 5th in heat AAA Mile 4:07.0 (W City); 3rd Mile 4:05.6 (Hornchurch); 2nd Inter-Club Match 880 yds 1:54.3 & 1st 5000m 14:34.4; **2nd 880 yds 1:53.9 (Hornsey); 8th Mile 4:04.0 (Motspur Park)**; 1st for Woodford Green AC 1500m 3:52.4 (Stockholm); 3rd Invitation 3000m 8:13.4 (W City); **1st 2 Miles 8:48.2 (Hornchurch)**; 1st GLC Champs 3 Miles 13:57.0 (Hurlingham)

Malcolm was now at Borough Road College ... I occasionally saw Malcolm but was not coaching him
[4th for ECCU XC team (in France); 3rd GLC XC Champs (PHF); fastest time in Chigwell XC relay; 1st National PE Colleges XC Champs (Richmond Park)

1969: 1st Essex XC; 4th AAA Indoor 3000m 8:14.6 (Cosford); 2nd University Colleges XC (PHF); 14th Southern XC; 2nd Invitation 3000m 8:13.0 (Cosford); 1st Victoria Park "5"; fastest leg Hornsey Road Relay; 1st for BRC v SCAAA v OUAC Mile 4:06.4; 1st Hampstead "10" 49:28; 1st Essex AAA 5000m 14:30 (Harlow – Mel Batty 2nd in same time); 1st Essex 3000m 8:26.3; **3rd Southern**

Lge 3000m SC 9:45.6 (Grays); 8th Invitation 3000m 8:12.0 (W City); 1st Erith "6" 31:09; fastest lap in several road relays; 1st Rochester "5"; 3rd Nat PE Colleges XC Ch (Richmond Park); 10th for ECCU XC (Belgium)

1970: 1st for BRC v St Mary's v Soton XC (PHF); 5th Southern 10000m 29:38.6 (C Palace) *ranked 28th*; **1st BRC v AAA 3000m 8:02.6 (Motspur Park)** *ranked 11th*; 9th I/C 5000m 14:09.0 (Leicester); 2nd BRC v Loughborough 1500m 3:50.5 (Mike Tagg 1st) but 1st in 5000m 14:20.6 (Mike Tagg 2nd!); **2nd BRC 1500m 3:49.4 (Isleworth)**; 1st PE Colleges v SCAAA v UAU 1500m 3:51.9 (W London); 1st Southern 3000m 8:16.2 CBP (M Park); 4th 3000m 8:08.6 (Reading); Fire Brigade Mtg 3000m 8:10.4 (W City)

1971: 15th Southern XC (PHF); **6th SCAAA 10000m Ch 29:28.2 (C Palace);** 1st Mile 4:08.0 (Harlow); **5th I/C 5000m 13:53.6 (Leicester)** *ranked 18th*; 7th British Int Games 5000m 14:01.4 (Edinburgh); 1st BRC v RAF 1500m 3:53.9 (Isleworth); 4th Reading Gala 3000m 8:08.2 *ranked 20th*]

From 1973 Malcolm ran for Stoke AC

Christine Brannon (Havering AC)

1967: 16th National Jun XC; 4th Southern I/C 880 yds 2:30.6 – heat 2:29.4 (C Palace)

1968: 16th ESAA IG XC (Rochdale – the 1st ever ESAA XC for Girls); 3rd fastest Essex Inter Road Relay; 3rd Essex WAAA XC

1969: 12th Southern Inter XC; 3rd Essex Schools IG 880 2:25.3; 4th Essex WAAA XC (Gt Wakering)

1970: 2nd fastest Essex Road Relays; 10th London XC (Crawley)

1971: 15th Southern I/C XC (Watford); 15th Southern XC (Brighton); 1st Essex WAAA 800m 2:17.9 and 1st 1500m 4:40.1 (Harlow); 2nd SCAAA Open Mile 5:05.8 (C Palace); WAAA heat 4:39.0 *ranked 28th*; 3rd BMC 3000m 10:03.6 (Hayes) *ranked 7th*; 10th fastest in National Road Relay; 4th Essex WAAA XC

1972: 2nd City Charities 800 2:18.6; 2nd fastest in Essex Road Relays (fastest: Rita!); 4th Essex WAAA XC (Corringham); 9th Nos Galan Mile 5:15....I no longer coached Christine after 1972

[1973-1978: ran XC, road & track for Havering AC inc 1500m in 4:40.5 and 800 in 2:16.3 in 1978]

Iris Lincoln – later Iris Cook (Essex Ladies AC)......Iris' track pbs in bold

[1963: 2nd Essex Sch IG 880 2:26.4; 1st Southern Inter 880 2:20.5

1964: 8th National Jun XC (Richmond); 10th Southern Sen XC (Greenford); 3rd Essex WAAA 880 2:18.8; 6th in heat WAAA 880 2:16.0; 2nd Gibson Trophy 880 2:14.5 (Ilford)]

I began coaching Iris in 1965....

1965: 2nd Essex Sen XC (1st Rita!); 3rd Southern XC; 18th National XC

1966: 5th Southern XC; 1st Trophy Mtg 440 59.8 (Aldershot); 4th WAAA Mile 5:01.2 & 880 heat 2:12.0; 2nd Southern I/C 880 2:11.7 (Chelmsford); 2nd British Games 800m 2:07.8 (W City) *ranked 5th*; 2nd Southern 880 2:13.2; 2nd Mile 4:53.1 (Dublin) *ranked 3rd*; 1st WAAA 3x880 for Essex Ladies AC 6:36.8 (*UK/C'wealth Record*) Iris ran 2:08.9 (with Rita & Jean Dicker)

1967: 6th National XC; 10th International XC (Barry); 1st Crawley Invitation Mile 4:58.2 *ranked 6th*; 1st Essex WAAA 880 & Mile; WAAA elim in heat 2:10.5; 2nd in special 880 2:09.2; 2nd for GB in international 800m 2:06.3 (Cologne) *ranked 4th*; 4th Nos Galan Mile

1968: 1st 400m 58.6 (East London); 1st BMC ¾ Mile 3:30.7 (C Palace); 1st Essex WAAA 440 58.4 and 2nd 880 2:11.5; **5th Southern 400m 58.0**; ran 880s 2:09.8 (Brighton), 2:08.1 (SCWAAA 3x880), 2:08.6 (Crawley); **1st BMC Mile 4:45.7 (Leamington)** *ranked 1st*; 2nd BMC Mile 4:47.3 (Welwyn); **7th WAAA 800m 2:05.8** *ranked 5th*; 4th Welsh Games 880 2:08.7 (Cardiff) – Iris not selected for Mexico Games; 2nd Essex WAAA XC; 1st Nos Galan Mile

1969: 2nd Southern I/C XC; 4th National XC (Aldershot)

Iris married Tony Cook, went to Australia ... I was no longer coaching her

[1970: 2nd Australian Ch 1500m 4:31.6 (Melbourne); 2nd Ex WAAA 800 2:14.0; 3rd Ex XC (Chingford)

1971: 7th Southern I/C (Watford)

1979–1984 ran Marathons in Australia and London and 1985 2:48.46 (Osaka, Japan 1st Joyce Smith)]

Rita Lincoln – later Ridley (Essex Ladies AC)

Won Essex Women's XC title 10 times between 1963 and 1974

Southern Women's XC : 1966: 1st; 1967 1st; 1968 6th; 1969 1st; 1970 didn't run; 1971 1st; 1972 4th

Southern Women's Inter-Counties XC: 1963-1975 1st 6 times 2nd once and 3rd once

English National XC: 1965: 2nd (Blackburn); 1966: 8th (Oxhey, Watford); 1967: 4th (Blackburn); 1968: didn't run; 1969: 1st (Aldershot); 1970: 1st (Blackburn); 1971: 1st (Wolverhampton); 1972: 1st (High Wycombe); 1973: 2nd (Rawtenstall Nr Bury); 1974: 1st (Leicester)

International XC : 1967: 2nd to Doris Brown USA (Barry); 1968 & 1969 didn't take part; 1970: 2nd to Doris Brown (Frederick, Maryland); 1971: 10th (San Sebastian); 1972: 3rd when Joyce Smith won (Cambridge); 1973: 4th (Waregem, Belgium); 1974: 3rd (Monza, Italy)

Cinque Mulini (San Vittore Olona Italy): 1st in 1971, 1972 & 1974

Nos Galan Women's Mile : 1965 2nd; 1966, 1967, 1969 1st; 1970 3rd; 1972 2nd; other years didn't run

Fastest lap in National Road Relay 1966 & 1967 ... in Southern Women's Road Relay 1968 ... and in the Essex Ladies AC Road Relay every year 1969 to 1973

Track

Essex WAAA 1965: 1st 880 2:15.8 & 1st Mile 5:04.8 both CBPs; 1966: 1st 880 & Mile, 2nd 440 59.4

1968: 1st 880 2:11.2 & 1st Mile 4:58.2, 3rd 440 58.6; 1970: 1st 800m 2:12.1 & 3rd 400m 58.8; 1972: 1st 800 2:12.3

Southern WAAA 1965: 2nd Mile 4:54.8 *ranked 4th* (best ever by 18yo) (Chiswick)

1966: 3rd Mile 5:02.4; 1968: 1st 800m 2:10.0; 1969: 1st 1500m 4:24.3 (Crystal Palace)

1970: 1st 1500 4:20.1 (C Palace); 1972: 1st 800m 2:08.4 (C Palace); 1973: 2nd 1500m 4:20.4 (C Palace);

WAAA: 1964: 5th Mile 5:05.8 (White City); 1965 2nd Mile 4:56.9; 1966 1st Mile 4:47.9 CBP *ranked 2nd* (best ever by 19yo); 1967 1st Mile 4:46.0 *ranked 2nd*;

1968: 1ˢᵗ 1500m 4:25.3 *ranked no 1 in UK and 5ᵗʰ in the World*;

1969 2ⁿᵈ 1500m 4:15.9 *ranked no 1 in UK, 7ᵗʰ in Europe & 8ᵗʰ in the World*;

1970 1ˢᵗ 1500m 4:15.4 CBP *UK Nat & A/C Record* (C Palace);

1971 1ˢᵗ 1500m 4:14.3 CBP *Commonwealth, UK Nat & A/C Record* (C Palace);

1971 Invitation 800m (Leicester) 3rd 2:05.5 *ranked 6th*

1972 (after back injury & illness) 9ᵗʰ 1500m 4:19.3*; 1973: 3ʳᵈ 1500m 4:19.8 (still had back trouble).

*A special 1500m race was held to finalise selection for the GB team for the Munich Olympic Games. Rita came 3ʳᵈ 4:18.6 so was not selected – see text Chapter 25.

International track races (all at 1500m except where shown)

1969 July: GB v Czechoslovakia (Brno) 2ⁿᵈ 4:21.0

Aug: European Championships (Athens) 7ᵗʰ 4:15.9 (*British Record*)

1970 June : GB v Netherlands (The Hague) 1ˢᵗ 4:22.3

July : for England in the Commonwealth Games (Edinburgh) 1ˢᵗ 4:18.8

Aug : GB: European Cup (Qual) (East Berlin) 2ⁿᵈ 4:17.3

Aug : GB: European Cup Final (Budapest) 4ᵗʰ 4:19.8

Sept: GB v Poland (Warsaw) 1ˢᵗ 4:17.8

Sept: GB v Rumania v Hungary (Bucharest) 2ⁿᵈ 4:22.1 and 6ᵗʰ 800m 2:08.7

1971 May: GB team (Warsaw) 1st 4:18.6 and GB team (Rome) 5ᵗʰ 800m 2:06.6

June: International Games (Edinburgh) 2ⁿᵈ 4:15.6

July: BMC (Edinburgh) Mile 1ˢᵗ 4:37.4 (*Scottish A/C Rec...only .6 off World Record*)

Aug: European Champs (Helsinki) 4ᵗʰ 4:12.7 (*C'wealth, UK A/C & UK Nat Rec*) Aug: GB v West Germany (Crystal Palace) 3ʳᵈ 4:16.3

Sept: Invitation (Munich) 5ᵗʰ 4:15.5

Sept: Welsh Games (Cardiff) 1ˢᵗ Mile 4:39.5 (*Welsh A/C Record*)

Dec. Invitation (Erpel West Germany) 4ᵗʰ 1000m 2:38.4

1972 June: Invitation (Zagreb) 3ʳᵈ 800m 2:06.5

1973 **May: Invite (Formia Italy) 3ʳᵈ 3000m 9:13.6** *ranked 2ⁿᵈ*

June: International Games (Edinburgh) 5th 4:19.1

June: GB v Netherlands v Czechoslovakia (Drachten Netherlands) 4th 4:24.5

Aug: Highland Games (Edinburgh) 3rd 4:24.4

Aug: Invitation in UK v Hungary match 5th 800m 2:09.1

1500m British Records set: 4:15.9 (1969 European Champs Athens); 4:15.4 (1970 WAAA); 4:14.3 (1971 WAAA); 4:12.7 (1972 European Champs Helsinki)

Rita's track PBs: **800m 2:05.5; 1500m 4:12.7; Mile 4:37.4; 3000m 9:13.6**

Tony Maxwell (Woodford Green AC) Tony's PBs in bold:

[1960: 2nd AAA Jun 1500m SC 4:20.1 *ranked 7th* (Hurlingham)

1962: 2nd (to John Cooper) UAU v Midland Counties 440 Hurdles 57.1 (Loughborough)

1963: 12th UAU XC (Brentwood); 1st CUAC Trials Mile 4:12.6; 2nd CUAC v AAA Mile 4:12.2; 2nd CUAC v OUAC Mile 4:14.2 (White City); 3rd CUAC v Loughborough 880 1:57.9; 3rd CUAC v OUAC v Birchfield 880 1:54.9 and 3rd 3K SC 9:37.0 (Iffley Road); 3rd CUAC & OUAC v Harvard & Yale Mile 4:13.3 (W City); 2nd Mile 4:11.2 Sward Trophy and **3K SC 9:35.2 (Chiswick)**;

1964: 6th 1500m 3:53.6 (Leyton); 1st UAU v SCAAA Mile 4:13.4 (Twickenham); 6th Southern Mile 4:09.2 (W City)]

I began to coach Tony about this time...

1965: 5th Kinnaird Mile 4:09.0 (Chiswick)

1966: 3rd fastest leg Chingford Road Relay; 1st Leyton Floodlit 1500 3:50.7; **1st WGAC v Army v CUAC 880 1:52.4**; 1st Essex AAA 880 1:55.1 (Thurrock); 1st Kinnaird Mile 4:07.5 (Chiswick); 3rd AAA v SCAAA Mile 4:08.1 (Bedford); **2nd WGAC Club Ch 440 50.3**; WGAC 3rd AAA Medley Relay 880 1:54.4; 1st Trophy Mtg 2 Miles 9:21.2; 1st GLC Mile 4:13.6; **2nd BAAB 1500m 3:49.3 *ranked 18th*(Rouen)**; 3rd Metropolitan XC Lge (Hainault)

1967: 2nd fastest leg Chingford Road Relay; **1st SCAAA v OUAC Mile 4:07.2**; 1st Vancouver Tr 1500 3:55.5; **1st Coronation Trophy 3 Miles 14:16.8 (Chelmsford – beat George Knight)**; 2nd Essex Ch

2 Miles 8:55.4 (Hornchurch); 10th Inter-Counties Mile 4:12.2 (heat 4:07.5)

1968: 3rd Victoria Park "5"; retired with persistent Achilles injury

[1972 & 1973: XC for WGAC; 1974: Road Relays and Harlow Marathon 2:40:17]

Jill Pettitt (Ilford AC)

[1965: 1st Essex Schools JG 150 17.8; 1966: 3rd Essex WAAA Inter 220 26.9

1967: 3rd Southern I/C Inter 220 26.5;]

I began to coach Jill…

1968: 2nd Essex WAAA Sen 220 26.1; 1st Essex Schools SG 220 26.1; ESAA s/f SG 220 25.9 (Portsmouth); WAAA Ch 400m 57.9 (heat) 58.6 (s/f) (White City)

1969: 2nd Essex WAAA 200m 25.3 (Newham); 1st Essex Schools SG 200m 25.8 (Record); 4th ESAA SG 200m 25.5 & 3rd 4 x 100 Relay 48.7 (Motspur Park)

1971: 3rd Essex WAAA 200 25.5 & 3rd 400 58.3 (Harlow); WAAA 400 6th in heat 56.9 (C Palace)

1972: 1st Essex WAAA 400 57.9 (Barking); 7th Southern 400 57.7 (CP)

1973: 2nd Essex WAAA 400 59.1 (Newham); 8th Southern 400 58.3 (57.3 in heat) (CP); WAAA 4th in heat 57.4 (CP); 2nd SCAAA Open Mtg 400 56.6 PB *ranked 29th*

Clive Ridley (Walthamstow AC) Clive's PBs in bold:

[1962: 6th Leyton Junior Floodlit Mtg 880 1:56.6 (Eton Manor)

1966: 1st Chingford Lge 880 1:56.6; 6th Nos Galan Mile 4:18.0;]

I began coaching Clive…

1967: **2nd Essex AAA Mile 4:08.5 PB** (1st Roy Young); 6th Southern Mile 4:16.1 (Motspur Park)

1968: 2nd Open Mtg Mile 4:13.6 (Cambridge); 1st Hackney Borough Trophy 880 1:55.5

1969: 2nd Essex AAA 1500 3:55.0; Southern 800m 1:56.4

1970: Southern Lge Div 4 800 1:55.1 (North London); 2nd S Lge Div 4 800 1:56.4

1971: 1st Essex AAA 1500 3:57.1; 7th Reading Mile 4:13.6; 1st Victory Trophy 1500 3:54.0 (Southend); 4th Brigg Mile 4:14.5 (Southgate); **7th SCAAA Open 800 1:53.6 (C Palace)**

1972: 6th Chingford & D XC (PHF) & Road (Walthamstow); **6th SCAAA Open 1500 3:51.3 (CP)**

I had moved away...

1973–1979 Clive continued to run for Walthamstow AC on track, in road and XC including 1977 1st Ilford 10 Miles XC 53:25

<u>In Bedfordshire</u>: (I moved to Bedfordshire in 1973)

Margaret Ashcroft (Wallasey then Luton AC)

[1972: 2nd Cheshire XC; 2nd Cosford Indoor 3000 10:08 *ranked 5th indoors*

1973: 6th W I/C XC (Leicester); 20th National XC (Rawtenstall); 2nd fastest Northern Road Relays (Derby); 8th fastest National Road Relays; 2nd Cosford 1500; 1st Cheshire XC; 3rd Nos Galan Mile

1974: 1st Cosford 1500 4:38.2; 9th I/C XC (Romford); 5th Northern XC (Blackburn); 2nd Cosford MCAAA 3000 10:09.0; 1st Cheshire XC]

I began coaching Margaret...

1975: 3rd National 4K XC (Kinver); 3rd Nat Indoor 3000 10:07.8; 1st Ampthill XC; 1st Cheshire XC

1976: 2nd Midland Indoor 1500 4:49.9; 2nd fastest time Ilford Road Relays; 3rd WAAA Indoor 3000 9:51.6; 6th WAAA 3000m 9:52.6 *ranked 23rd* ; 1st Cheshire XC; 14th Southern XC (Ipswich)

1977: 12th WAAA 3000 9:48.0 *ranked 29th* (C P); 1st Cheshire XC (Crewe)

[1978: now Margaret Lockley and "*advised by Harry Wilson*" 18th National XC (High Wycombe); 1st WAAA Marathon 2:55:08 (Isle of Wight); 1st Milton Keynes Marathon 2:51:09; 6th New York M'thon 2:50:58; 1st Cheshire XC (Winsford) *Margaret won Cheshire Women's XC title 6 times '73-78*; 1979: 6th WAAA Marathon 2:54:50 (Sandbach)]

Debbie Buckley (Luton AC)

1975: 80th ESAA JG XC (Guildford); 9th ESAA JG 1500 5:04.0 (4:52.5 heat) (Durham); 8th WAAA Jun 1500 4:53.3 (4:50.8 heat) (West London); 2nd Beds Jun XC

1976: 33rd National Jun XC (Blackburn); 27th ESAA IG XC (Leicester); 4th WAAA Indoor Inter 1500 5:02.2 (4:54 heat) (Cosford); 2nd Feltham AC Easter Monday 2½ miles road race; 1st YA Lge 1500 4:57 (Twickenham); 1st 1500 4:51.7 (Chelmsford); 6th ESAA IG 1500 4:45.9 *ranked 26th* (Cannock); 7th Southern XC Lge (Brighton); 1st Beds Inter XC (Stopsley); 29th Inter/Lge XC (Bolton)

1977: 16th Southern Inter I/C XC (Camberley); 1st Icknield Lge XC ; 7th WAAA Indoor Inter 1500 4:54.0 (4:47.6 heat) (Cosford); 30th ESAA IG XC (Redditch); 1st SW Lge 1500 4:42.2 *ranked 22nd* (Woodford); 1st SW Lge 3000 10:18.6 *ranked 11th* (Oxford)

Erwin Hartell (1970: Hadleigh Olympiads...later Bristol & West AC)
Erwin's PBs in bold:

[1969 3rd ESAA SB 800 1:51.9 (Motspur Park) *ranked 5th Junior*; 5th GB Juniors v French Juniors 800 1:54.8 (Dole)]

1970: 1st Southern Open Meeting 800 1:51.0 (Crystal Palace) *ranked 1st Junior*; 4th Southern Champs 800 1:51.5 (Motspur Park); Erwin went to USA – see text chapter 18

[1975 Western Kentucky/Bristol team 4x1 Mile 4:07.5; 4x880yds 1:52.3; Mile 4:06.0 (all in USA);1st British Lge Div 3 for Bristol AC 800 1:52.3 (Bristol); 3rd Southern Champs 1500 3:43.8 (C Palace); 2nd City Invitation Mile 4:01.3 (West London); **3rd Welsh Games 800 1:49.3 (Cardiff)** *ranked 9th* ; 1st Brit Lge Div 3 800 1:49.7 and 1st 400(B) 50.3 (Stretford); **3rd AAA Champs 1500 3:40.6 PB (CP)** *ranked 8th*; Bristol/WKU Inter-club 4x1500 relay 2nd leg 3:48.3 1st team 15:12.6 - *UK A/C & Brit Club Record* (Cwmbran); 1st Pye Gold Cup 800 1:51.5 (Cwmbran); 3rd Pye Gold Cup 800 1:49.6 & 1st 1500 3:49.2 (C Palace); 3rd UK v Sweden 800 1:49.5 (Meadowbank); *UK Merit Rankings 1975: 7th in 800m (4 times under 1:50) and 6th in 1500/Mile]*

1976   3rd Open Meeting 800 1:51.4 (Wolverhampton); 6th GB v USSR
1500 3:43.3 (Kiev) *ranked 17th*; **3rd in heat Kraft Games 800
1:49.3 *ranked 14th***, 7th in final 1:50.4 (C Palace) *UK NUTS Merit
Ranking 1976: 11th in 800m*

1977   in USA: Mile 4:07.3; 1000 yds 2:09.0 (Bloomington); 4th 800
1:50.2 (Gainsville) & 3rd 1500 3:43.4; 1st 1500 3:47.1, 4th 1500
3:44.0 (Knoxville); 4th 1500 3:43.0 (Cerritos);

1978: 3rd Invitation 2000m 5:08.1 (C Palace); 4th Invitation Mile 4:03.2
(Birmingham); 1st Brit Lge Div 2 800 1:53.2 (Southampton); **7th
Emsley Carr Mile 4:00.0 PB** (behind Robson 3:55.8, Williamson
3:56.4, Foster, Cram both 3:57.4, Hutchings 3:57.8 & Masback
USA 3:58)

In Sussex
East Grinstead AC:

Peter Benton, Val Evans, Ben Ivorson, Jonathan Stayton: all keen young
runners

Georgina Hayward: talented high jumper PB U17 1:60 1999 (Crystal
Palace)

Tony Read
1996   1st Sussex AAA JB 1500, ran in ESAA JB 1500 (Sheffield); 1997
AAA U17 1500m 4:12.81 heat
1998   ESAA IB XC (Cheltenham); 1st IB Sussex AAA 800m, 1st Sx Sch
1500, ESAA Ch IB 1500 4:08.17 heat (Exeter), High jump 1:80
(Horsham)

Craig Ivemy (Hailsham Harriers) Craig's PBs in bold:
[2000: 1st Sussex Schools JB XC; 1st Sussex AAA U15 XC; 5th Schools I/C
XC (Chelmsford); 11th ESAA JB XC (PHF); 1st Sx AAA Jun 1500;
1st Sx Sch 1500 4:22.2;]
I began to coach Craig...
2001: 1st Sx AAA XC (Lancing); 5th Southern U15 XC (PHF); 1st Sx Sch

IB XC (Crawley); 8th Inter I/C (Nottingham); 2nd SX AAA Inter 1500 4:10.5; BMC 3000 9:02.7 (Watford); 1st Sx Sch 3000 9:03.7 (Crawley); 1st Sx AAA 3000 9:02.0 (Lewes); 7th ESAA IB 3000 8:55.9 heat 8:51.5 (Exeter); 4th AAA Inter 3000 8:50.87 *ranked 12th* (Sheffield); 2nd & 1st Sx Lge XC (Goodwood & Lancing); 1st Phoenix 3.8K Road Race 12:08 (Brighton); 13th Margate U17 4K XC 12:47

2002: 1st Sx AAA XC (Brighton); 1st Sx Sch IB XC (Crawley); 6th I/C U17 XC (Nottingham); 6th National Jun XC (Bristol); 5th ESAA IB XC (Chelmsford); 5th Home Schools International (Derby); 3rd BMC 1500 4:02.92 (Millfield); **1st Sx AAA U17 800 1:59.79** and 1st 1500 4:06.17 (Crawley); 4th Southern Jun 1500 4:02.3 (Watford); **2nd 400 55.5 (Horsham)**; 1st Sx Sch IB 3000 8:42.9 (Crawley); 1st I/C Sch 1500 4:07.4 and 3rd 400 55.9 (Basingstoke); **time trial 2000 5:33.8 (Horsham)**; 1st ESAA IB 3000 8:43.84 (Nottingham); 1st Sx AAA U17 3000 9:06.0 (Horsham); 2nd Schools International 3000 8:38.61 (Glasgow); 1st I/C Sch 1500 4:04.07 (Kingston); 1st AAA U17 3000 8:38.43 *ranked 3rd* (Birmingham); 5th BMC 1500 4:01.65 *ranked 20th* (Watford); 1st Sx Lge XC (Lancing)

2003: 1st Sx AAA U17 XC (Bexhill); 1st Sx Sch SB XC (Brighton); 3rd I/C U17 XC (Nottingham); 4th National XC (PHF); 10th ESAA SB XC (Brighton); 4th BMC 1500 4:00.46 (Millfield); 6th South'n 1500 4:00.63 (Watford); 2nd BMC U20 3000 8:31.03 *ranked 12th* (Withenshaw); 1st Sx Sch SB 3000 9:02.00 (Crawley); 10th ESAA SB 3000 8:43.59 (Sheffield); 5th European Youth Olympic Festival GB U18 3000 8:34.77 (Paris); 7th BMC 800 2:00.7 (Brighton); 4th Open 1500 3:59.45 (Watford); 1st Sx Lge XC *U20 & Sen course rec* (Goodwood); 1st Phoenix 7.3K Road Race 22:29 (Brighton); 10th Reebok XC & Euro Trials (Liverpool); 5th Lotto XC running for England (Belgium)

2004: 3rd BMC U20 3000 8:27.77 (Millfield); **(2nd U20) 50th anniversary 4 min mile 4:18.53 (Oxford);** 1st Sx AAA 5000 15:15.74 (Crawley); **13th BMC Grand Prix 5000 14:41.33 (Solihull)**; 1st Sx Sch SB 3000 8:31.4 CBP (Crawley); 2nd AAA

U20 5000 14:49.25 (Bedford); 3rd International Match for GB 3000 8:28.13 (Manchester); 2nd ESAA SB 3000 8:30.78 (Gateshead); **4th Invitation 3000 8:24.61 (C Palace)**; **3rd BMC 1500 3:58.8 (Eltham)**; 4th BMC 800 1:59.8 (Brighton); 1st Inter-Area 3000 8:38.72; 1st Sx AAA U20 3000 8:48.8 (Crawley); 5th Commonwealth Youth Games 3000 8:50.16 (Bendigo Australia); At Loughborough Autumn 2004.....Injuries ended his career prematurely

Emma Satterly (Phoenix AC): represented Sussex at XC and Track

Kent:
Gemma Viney (Blackheath H): 1999: 3rd ESAA IG 3K (Bury St Edmunds) also XC and road relays

Oxfordshire
Iona Robertson (Headington Road Runners): good XC & Track runner

Additional Details II

Courses I attended as a coach at Lilleshall & Loughborough

<u>AAA Loughborough Summer School – late 1950s & early 1960s</u>
I attended as a novice AAA Honorary Coach learning from Geoff Dyson (Chief Coach), Jim Alford (Middle Distance coach), John Le Masurier (South), Denis Watts (North) and others

<u>WAAA Lilleshall 1963</u>
Among the athletes invited to attend: Penny Gardner, Francis Slaap
Administrators : Maria Hartman, Ken Oakley, George Stratford
Coaches: Denis Watts (Chief), Joe Goscomb, Fred Housden,& Graham Tanner

<u>WAAA Bovril Course Lilleshall 1964</u>
In my Middle Distance group: Mary Hodson, Margaret Moir, Anita Webb, and others   .....
Coaches: as above

<u>WAAA Bovril Course Lilleshall 1965</u>
My Middle Distance group included Sheila Taylor
Coaches: as above

<u>Loughborough Summer School AAA "A" Course 16–20 August 1965</u>
I took the Middle Distance group of intending coaches & those working towards Senior Coach award

<u>Loughborough Summer School 1966/67/68</u>
I was working on courses for existing Middle Distance coaches and on research projects (High Jump)

<u>WAAA Potential Olympic Athletes Course (Bovril) Lilleshall 4–8 April 1966</u>

My Middle Distance group: Mel Didham, Mary Hodson, Iris & Rita Lincoln, Margaret Moir, Jane Perry, Rosemary Stirling, Sheila Taylor
Coaches included: Dorothy Hyman (Sprints), Derek Hayward (LJ), Fred Housden (Hurdles),
+ Robbie & Ann Brightwell, Brenda Bedford, Mary Peters

WAAA Potential Olympic Athletes Course (Bovril) Crystal Palace 2–7 April 1967
My MD Group: Mel Didham, Iris & Rita Lincoln, Margaret Moir, Rosemary Stirling, Sheila Taylor
Coaches included Fred Housden (Hurdles), John Le Masurier (Nat Coach),
+ Ann Brightwell and Mary Rand (Gold Medallists Tokyo)

WAAA National Coaching Course (Bovril) Lilleshall 8–13 April 1968
My MD group: Marie Herron, Iris and Rita Lincoln, Phyllis Lowis, Joan Page, & Sheila Taylor,
In other groups: Jacqui Philp (High Jump), Ann Wilson (LJ) both from Essex
Chief Coach: AAA National Coach Denis Watts

WAAA Summer School Lilleshall 24–30 Aug 1968
I tested aspiring senior coaches on High Jump

WAAA National Scholarship Course (Birds Eye Foods) Crystal Palace 22–27 March 1970
My MD group: Elizabeth Barnes, Susan Barnes, Angela Lovell, Linda Motton, Pauline Moult, Gloria O'Leary, Elizabeth Parncutt, Paula Yeoman
Jacqui Philp in Hurdles group
Chief Coach Fred Housden (Hurdles) + Dorothy Shirley (High Jump),
Visiting lecturer David Hemery (Gold medallist Mexico)

Additional Details III

British Milers' Club YA Residential educational & training Courses that I attended as a coach
Coaches and notable athletes attending

Lectures were regularly given by Frank Horwill, David Lowes and myself. Other lecturers included David Arnold, Liam Cain, John Cooper, George Gandy, Rod Lock & Peter Thompson who all coached groups of athletes on the courses they attended

Oct 1996: (training day) Bedford
Phil Banning: Atlanta Olympics slide show.
Coaches inc: Bud Baldaro, Mike Down & Norman Poole who interviewed GB runner John Mayock

April 1997: Ardingly College
Athletes inc: Neil Speight, Rachel Ogden, Julia Bleasdale, & Emma Pidgeon,
GB International Mark Rowland, 3000m SC UK record holder & coach, interviewed by TE

Oct 1997: Aldershot – Army School of Physical Training – Theme: "Are you fit to race?"
Practical testing...by Frank, Peter Thompson, Glen Grant & Joe Dunbar (physiologist - St Mary's)
Athletes inc: Mark Glennie, Steve Vernon, Ed Jackson, Sam Houghian, Chris Thompson, Louise Damen, Jo Fenn, Charlotte Moore

March 1998: Uxbridge
Coaches inc: Sean Kyle, Ridley Griffith & Roger Williams
Athletes included James McIlroy, Andrew Robinson, Steve Vernon, Angus Maclean, Ed Jackson
GB international Peter Elliot was interviewed by Norman Poole

April 1999: Ardingly
Other coaches: Sean Kyle, Liam Cain, James McIlroy, Roger Williams, Bill Anderson
Athletes included: Angus Maclean, Liz Braithwaite, Lee Merrien, Maria Lynch, Faye Fullerton

Oct 1999: Ogmore
Other coaches: Phil Banning, Brendan Hackett, Maria Lynch
Athletes inc: Ed Prickett, Richard Ward, Steve Ablitt, Angus Maclean, Mark Glennie, Peter Bridger,
Ricky Soos (pbs then 1:59 & 4:10), Chris Reynolds
Angus Maclean and Emma Davies were interviewed by Peter Thompson

April 2000: Ardingly
Other coaches: William Anderson, Chris Wooldridge
Athletes in my group included: Angus Maclean, Richard Ward, Ed Prickett, Ed Jackson, Rob Whittle
Also on the course: Charlotte Moore, Liz Braithwaite, Hannah England (pb then 800:2:28!)
Chris Wooldridge was interviewed by TE

Oct 2000: Ogmore
Other coaches: Ridley Griffith, David Leach, Steve Mosley
Athletes inc: Steve Ablett, Chris Reynolds, Colin McCourt, Mark Glennie, Tommy Davies, Tom Penfold

April 2001: Ardingly
Coaches: William Anderson & Ollie Wright
International athlete and coach Christina Boxer was interviewed by TE

Sept 2001: Ogmore
Other coaches: Ridley Griffiths & Chris Wooldridge
Athletes (70+ attended) inc: Steve Ablett, Chris Reynolds, Tom Penfold, Craig Ivemy, Sally Oldfield, Iona Robertson

<u>March 2002: Oxford</u>   [BMC/OAA]
Organised locally by Iona Robertson for local athletes – seniors & juniors

<u>April 2002: Ardingly</u>
Athletes had fitness tests on: VO2 Max, basic sprint speed, strength & flexibility

<u>Oct 2002: Ogmore</u> (130 on the course)
TE conducted an athletes' seminar.......Coach John Anderson was interviewed by Peter Thompson

<u>Oct 2002: Birmingham</u>   BMC/UKA Coaches' Symposium
Ian Harris: "Coaching Mbulaeni Mulaudzi – 800m Commonwealth Gold/ World Bronze"
Coaches present (inc TE): George Gandy, Frank Horwill, Norman Poole, Mark Rowland, Alan Storey, NevilleTaylor & Bruce Tulloh
Mark Rowland was interviewed by Dave Sunderland and Norman Poole

<u>March 2003: Ardingly</u>   (BMC 40th anniversary 1963–2003)
Lectures were given by Frank "Thoughts on the 800 metres"
By David Lowes "The Key to 1500 metres success" and "The need for a good 400m capability for 800 & 1500 success" and by TE "Strategy and Tactics"
Athletes inc: Phil Winfield, Paul Erwood, Craig Ivemy, Todd Leckie, Hannah Bates, Julia Orr
Former GB 800m international Chris McGeorge was interviewed by TE

<u>Sept 2003: Ogmore</u>
Coaches inc: Tom King, Les Pittwood, Ridley Griffiths, Gordon Cooper, Alan Carver (physio)
Athletes inc: Paul Erwood, Craig Ivemy, Tommy Davies, Tom Penfold, Kieran Flannery,
Daniel Stepney, Julia Bleasdale, Emma Satterly, Hannah Bates, Julia Orr.

March 2004: Ardingly
Other coaches inc: Jim Bennett, Stella Bandu
Athletes inc: Eleanor Baker, Hannah England (pb then 1500 4:28), Paul Erwood, Kieran Flannery, Craig Ivemy, Julia Orr, Carolyn Plateau (pb then 1500 4:29), Daniel Stepney
UK International and Olympic athlete, Andrew Graffin, was interviewed by TE

Oct 2004: Ogmore
John Cooper: profile of Ricky Soos
Paula Fryer and James Thie were interviewed

April 2005: Ardingly   (130+ on the course)
Other coaches inc: Dave Arnold, Jim Bennett, Stella Bandu, David Leach
Athletes inc: Craig Ivemy, Lucy McLoughlin, Ross Millington

Sept 2005: Ogmore
Other coaches inc: Dave Arnold, John Cooper, Mike Erith, Ridley Griffith, David Leach, Bob McGaffin, Les Pittwood, Alan Souch
Athletes inc: Darrell Bellinger, Kieran Flannery, Blue Haywood, Lucy McLoughlin, Matt Wood
3 National Champions: Kieran Flannery (U20), Matt Wood (U18) and Lucy McLoughlin (U15) were interviewed by TE

I was unable to attend BMC Courses after Sept 05 as a result of my spinal thrombosis (Nov 05)

Additional Details IV

Books and articles I have used or referred to:

Concerning athletes and athletics
GHG Dyson, *"The Mechanics of Athletics"* (1962)
Ed GFP Pearson, *"Athletics"* (1963)
Bruce C Ogilvie & Thomas A Tutko, *"Problem Athletes and How to Handle Them"* (1966)
"Athletics Weekly" (1960s and 1970s)
Frank Horwill, *"Obsession for Running"* (1991)
David Young, *"The History of the English Schools' Athletic Association 1925–1995"* (1995)
Brendan Hackett, *"Success From Within"* (1998)
Toby Tanser, *"Train Hard, Win Easy – The Kenyan Way"* (2001)
David Lowes, *"Where to Run – part 2"* BMC News Vol 6 Issue 1 (Spring 2009 edition)

Not concerning athletes or athletics:
Rudolf Steiner, *"Education for Adolescence"* (lectures in German 1921 – pub. in English 1980)
Roy Douglas, *"Who is Nemo?"* (1937)
John Betjeman, *"Summoned by Bells"* (1960)
Lady Plowden, *"The Plowden Report: Children & their Primary Schools"* (1967)
Ronald Hyam, *"History of Isleworth Grammar School"* (1969)
Paulo Friere, *"Pedagogy of the Oppressed"* (1972)
Ronald Davie, Neville Butler, Harvey Goldstein – Report of the National Child Development Study, *"From Birth to Seven"* (1972)
Pat Daunt, *"Comprehensive Values"* (1975)
Robert James Waller, *"The Bridges of Madison County"* (1992)
Christopher Ball, *"Start Right: The Importance of Early Learning"* Royal Society of Arts (1994)

Tony Elder, *"The role of parents in the educational development of their pre-school age children and the perception that parents have of that role."* (MEd dissertation 1994)

John Abbott, *"The Child is Father of the Man"* (1999)

Sarah Waters, *"The Night Watch"* (2006)

Specifically Historical:

Alan Bullock, *"Hitler – a study in tyranny"* (1952)

Alan Bullock, *"The Life and Times of Ernest Bevin"* (1960)

Robert Fisk, *"The Great War for Civilisation – The Conquest of the Middle East"* (2005)

Adam Tooze, *"The Wages of Destruction"* (2006)

Edward Acton & Tom Stableford, *"The Soviet Union – a documentary history"* Volume 1 1917–1940 (2005) Volume 2 1939–1991 (2007)